Handbook of
Theory and Research
for the
Sociology of Education

Handbook of Theory and Research for the Sociology of Education

EDITED BY JOHN G. RICHARDSON

GREENWOOD PRESS

New York • Westport, Connecticut • London

Library of Congress Cataloging in Publication Data

Main entry under title:

Handbook of theory and research for the sociology
  of education.

  Bibliography: p.
  Includes index.
  1. Educational sociology—Addresses, essays, lectures.
2. Educational sociology—United States—Addresses,
essays, lectures.   3. Educational sociology—Great
Britain—Addresses, essays, lectures.   4. Educational
sociology—Addresses, essays, lectures.   I. Richardson,
John G.
LC191.2.H36   1986   370.19   85–931
ISBN 0–313–23529–5 (lib. bdg.: alk. paper)

Library of Congress Catalog Card Number: 85–931
ISBN: 0–313–23529–5

First published in 1986

Greenwood Press, Inc.
88 Post Road West, Westport, Connecticut 06881

The paper used in this book complies with the
Permanent Paper Standard issued by the National
Information Standards Organization (Z39.48-1984).

Printed in the United States of America

10 9 8 7 6 5 4 3 2 1

Contents

Part III   Educational Transmission and Reproduction

Part IV   Methodological and Theoretical Issues in the Sociology of Education

Tables and Figures

Introduction

A volume designated as a *Handbook* must presume at least two achievements about a substantive field. The first is a sufficient body of empirical work which is a base for theoretical development. The second is that the potential for theoretical growth has been exploited, and some measure of disciplinary advance is evident. This *Handbook* is undertaken in the recognition that the sociology of education meets these two criteria.

The present volume presumes a third achievement. The sociology of education, unlike most other substantive fields, is grounded in a number of writings of the classical European tradition. The achievement which lends additional strength to empirical work and theoretical growth is how both are heir to that tradition and yet are innovative in their own terms.

The contributions to this *Handbook* are from British, French, and American sociologists. The sociology of education traverses these three societies. Nonetheless, it is predominantly from these societies that the significant empirical work and theoretical growth which has shaped the sociology of education over the past several decades has come. An objective of this volume is to join these contributions and make visible their parallels and points of convergence, and continuities from the classical tradition.

To prelude the organization of the volume, a summary of the significant classical works is given, followed by a descriptive account of the developmental passage from *educational sociology* to the sociology of education.

EDUCATION AND THE CLASSICAL TRADITION

The study of education as both process and institution is without dispute a prominent part of the classical European tradition. Yet this fact is often overshadowed by the tendency to associate the origins of sociology with themes of large-scale economic and political transformation. It is true that seminal works in sociology concentrated on broad alterations in the *division of labor* or *patterns of domination* as older, traditional communities gave way to a more expansive, contractual social order. It is equally true, however, that the subject of education was understood by many as *key* to these major changes. As such, the sociology of education enjoys a heritage of specific classical works, and the depth of much contemporary theory and research is in ways owed to this classical tradition.

We need only consider the names of Herbert Spencer, Emile Durkheim, and Max Weber. In *Education: Intellectual, Moral, and Physical* (1912), originally published in 1860 as four review articles, Spencer outlined a natural method of education, arguing that education was the means to secure effective control over one's life. It was a natural method insofar as the conduct of instruction was voluntary and pleasurable and became "useful" and resourceful knowledge extending into adulthood. Here Spencer's sociology of education reflects the late nineteenth-century debates over the instrumentality of knowledge or, in Spencer's own terms, the "comparative worths" of knowledge. While Spencer was no advocate of state interventions, any rereading of *Education* reminds that questions of pedagogy are closely linked to the competitive discourse over the jurisdiction of state authority. In *Sociology and Education* (1924/1956), Durkheim presents a strikingly modern analysis of the "tension" between the broad functions of a popular instruction and the narrower, differentiating interests of a secondary education. In *Moral Education* (1925/1961), a subtle and far-reaching discussion of the social antecedents to childhood socialization is outlined. Yet it may be that *The Evolution of Educational Thought* (1925/1977) represents Durkheim's real contribution to a sociology of education. Here he claims a centrality for education, in pointed critique of the "old French prejudice which looks with a kind of contempt on the whole business of educational theory" (p. 4). In these lectures, Durkheim interweaves a commanding historical analysis of the evolution of pedagogy and a sociological analysis of the ways in which earlier ideas about education later become embedded in particular organizational forms. And finally, from the multifaceted work of Max Weber, we are led to education by way of comparative studies which sought the affinity between types of social order and their sustaining ideals of elite socialization. From work as diverse as the classic essay on the Chinese literati to the origins of the Occidental city, we are given theoretical strategies which are transposable to a variety of contemporary topics, be they the forming of the British gentleman or the comparative distribution of popular, elite, or bureaucratic education.

The depth of these classical roots gave to the sociology of education an early momentum which contributed to its maturation as a substantive field. The topic of education gained early prominence because it could easily be integrated with the prevailing issues of economic and political transformation. The advantages of these classical beginnings derives from how writings identified the problems of education, the puzzling relation between a resiliency of early socialization and later, intractable social consequences. Early sociological writings defined a way of seeing education, and whether intentionally or not, they gave to it a central place as a rightful topic of sociological theory. *Ways* of seeing education is more accurate, for while Spencer's natural method of instruction encouraged independent and "pleasurable" learning free from state intervention, Durkheim saw nothing "so false and deceptive as the Epicurean conception of education," toward which the state cannot remain indifferent. The contrast between these two thinkers tells of the centrality of education, and, not by accident, the writings of each were often taken as theoretical foundations to architects of national educational systems.

FROM EDUCATIONAL SOCIOLOGY TO THE SOCIOLOGY OF EDUCATION

From the early momentum of the classical tradition, the field of educational sociology arose after the turn of the century as the academic expression and practical application of the principles of sociology. The era of educational sociology marks a reduction in the scale of what was asked and what was studied. The grand visions of the classical tradition gave way to more modest questions, most tied to local contexts and committed to pragmatic answers. Such a shift parallels the expansion and institutionalization of educational systems in both the United States and Europe. In England, educational sociology was the stepchild of psychology, remaining under the shadow of the *British Journal of Educational Psychology*, founded in 1931, and until the 1950s had virtually no competition from sociology (Taylor 1973, p. 13), whereas critical scholarship documents a substantial legacy of sociological forerunners from 1900 to the takeoff of sociology of education in 1954 (see Szreter 1984). In the United States, the growth of educational sociology was confined largely to the organizational arena, seeing the formation of a National Society for the Study of Educational Sociology and the establishment of the *Journal of Educational Sociology* in 1926. Although the National Society attracted a professionally diverse membership, this organizational growth was not accompanied by a corresponding advance in either theory or empirical research. The failure to advance conceptually could be attributed to the very modesty of focus, for, as Orville Brim reviewed (1958, p. 10), research on education was concerned with "limited operating problems" where "little effort was made to formulate these problems in the theoretical terms of sociology." In the United States, educational sociology remained an unattractive and underdeveloped area well up to the mid-1950s (see Conrad 1952). It was not until 1967 that the *Journal of Educational Sociology* was brought under the auspices of the American Sociological Association and retitled *Sociology of Education*. This change in title is some measure of standing in the discipline, and it signified an independence from the early, practical ties to education. For England, this independence came only recently with the founding of the *British Journal of Sociology of Education* in 1980.

The signs of change foreshadowing the shift to a sociology of education were discernible by the 1950s. Importantly, the shift was prompted by trends outside the discipline: the return to education of its centrality to a major theme of the latter half of this century, individual opportunity versus social inequality.

The initial, significant trend which stimulated the redefinition of educational sociology was the expansion of secondary education. As Martin Trow showed in his seminal article on the transformation of American education (1961), by 1945, American secondary education had begun "the painful transition on its way to becoming a mass preparatory system" (p. 154). The sociological implications of this transition were considerable, for the change accentuated the diffuse concerns over school achievement and occupational mobility. The transition made sharp social divisions widely visible by "changing the character of the students who do not go on to college when increasing majorities of students do so" (p. 162). Such problems of educational mobility were not something particular to the United States but had been anticipated in Europe as well. In England especially, the publication of *Education and Social Change* by Sir Fred Clarke in 1940 capped a movement of some twenty years which had vigorously pressed for a wider access to secondary education. Ten years earlier in the United States, the *National Survey of Secondary Education* published the most comprehensive study of secondary education for its time (and beyond), anticipating the "painful transition" to a mass, preparatory system. The timing of this common focus did not reflect a coincidence of intellectual concerns alone, but it reflected as well the renewed strategic place which secondary education had assumed in Europe and the United States.

Secondary education had become the critical institutional link to higher education and to those expanding occupational levels accessible only through university attainment. As such, secondary education had become the focal point of a political and academic discourse, for it was at this level that the life chances of so many were in critical ways defined. Yet the aims and tenor of this discourse were different for the United States and Europe—in part, because the strategic place of secondary education had been so historically different for each.

As England exemplifies, a major focus of political debate was to integrate the elementary and secondary levels, to replace them with a more uniform, two-stage sequence. For France, parallel secondary ladders, the *lycée* and the *collège* systems, have led to alternative destinies, the former ending with the *baccalauréat*, while the latter is not typically a route to a university education. For the United States, a uniform and hierarchical ladder was an early feature of common schooling, where the expansion of secondary schools most often arose once a sufficient base of elementary common schools was in place. While the substance of European discourse revolved around the social and political implications of separate, parallel systems, each historically rooted in sharp class divisions, American discourse has been tempered by the early legislation of state-supported, public systems of education and yet complicated by the inescapable dilemmas of pluralism.[1]

By the 1950s, the expansion of secondary education gained in political meaning as advanced societies confronted the sectoral shift to white-collar, managerial, and professional occupations. Education became increasingly aligned with the economy, and while the former may assume different shapes in different societies, economic changes were read as superceding those differences. Across political differences and cultural traditions, the dictates of a *technological* economy were seen as impinging upon educational systems in common ways. As Halsey, Floud, and Anderson remarked in their introduction to *Education, Economy, and Society* (1964, p. 2): "Education attains unprecedented economic importance as a source of technological innovation, and the educational system is bent increasingly to the service of the labor force, acting as a vast apparatus of occupational recruitment and training." The technological society now meant that education was a productive investment, a form of "human capital," and inequalities in educational access became the primary source of social inequalities.

The assumption that economic development must increasingly rely upon efficient educational investment raised the political worth and practical utility of sociological research. For American society, the problems of a mass, preparatory secondary system were magnified by political mandates to undo racial and cultural barriers to equality of educational opportunity. For England and France, sociological research focused on processes of "selection" for secondary schooling within the context of a Welfare State. The upsurge of empirical research in the 1950s and 1960s moved topics of "ability," "talent," "family social background," and "achievement" into center place. The outcome of this cumulative research, conducted in different arenas, converged on two conclusions. From the European arena came the conclusion that, in actuality, "schools and universities function badly as selectors and promoters of talent" (Halsey et al. 1964, p. 5). From American research on educational opportunity came a conclusion that schools could not be held responsible for as much income and occupational inequality as previously believed and the reluctant judgment that family and cognitive factors were primary determinants of educational attainment.

Apart from the substantive truth of these conclusions, the way in which the structure of national systems of education may condition sociological inquiry remains relevant to the subsequent development of theory. It is with some irony that these empirical conclusions gave way to subtle, yet important, differences in theoretical focus between American and European sociology.

Within the United States, a predominant approach was to measure educational attainment from individual variations in cognitive and social background factors. Against the backdrop of a relatively uniform and broadly accessible educational system, it is reasonable and defensible to take the individual as the central actor. The uniform sequence of educational mobility allows for points of flexibility along the course of formal schooling. The predominance of the *status attainment theory* in American sociology attests to this, for models of attainment accurately visualize a series of linked pathways that may be inconsistently, as well as consistently, connected. Family background variables initiate the course of attainment, and yet they may be deterred by the social composition of an individual school or school district. The attention in American sociology given to the independent influence of peer subcultures would often cite them as at odds with the learning imperatives of a technological society.

Research on equality of educational opportunity also reflects the institutional shape of American schooling. While the influential report on *Equality of Educational Opportunity* (Coleman et al. 1966) confirmed the degree to which children were segregated by race, differences between schools in facilities and resources did not explain much of the variation in student educational achievement. In the subsequent study *Inequality*, by Jencks and associates (1972), the school one attended was again not found to explain much of the variation in occupational status or income. The failure of between-school differences to explain much of the variation in educational attainment largely affirmed that one school was much like another. Here a fit between this acknowledgment and the organization of American schooling is noteworthy, and attention turned to the theoretical relevance of an educational system marked by successive levels nested within others.

One consequence of acknowledging the absence of significant differences between schools was a turn away from the survey of resource differences between schools to a focus on processes *within* schools, to the analysis of status interactions, and to modes of resource utilization within classrooms which may account for the continuation of unequal educational outcomes. Status hierarchies that are institutionalized in the wider society become integral parts of classroom organization and can often be unintentionally enacted by teachers and peers. The influence of various levels of schooling are seen as exerting "contextual" effects, where the micro realm of the classroom cannot be taken as isolated from the broader patterns of social stratification. Selection processes within schools, from homogeneous groupings to high school tracking, are micro arenas which can structure larger inequalities beyond schools.

From empirical work conducted within an era dominated by issues of educational opportunity and school selection, American sociology reached its own point of theoretical settlement where, to reinvoke Brim's caution, empirical findings renewed efforts to formulate research problems in the theoretical terms of sociology. What these terms were to be evinced a dissatisfaction with the premise that a technological society bent education to the service of the labor force. Functional views of education could be reversed in ways that saw schooling as an arena of status conflict, and the educational credential becomes as much a symbolic marker of cultural membership as a mark of training and skill level. In other ways, the labor force is bent to the service of education, as jobs and job titles are created by academic credentialing. Education is critical to the state, for schooling is useful to citizen-making purposes of nation building. The precepts of educational systems become an economical means whereby modern ways of seeing and explaining complex events are given a superior legitimation over traditional ways. These precepts become more and more global in scope and meaning. Thus a master theme of contemporary theoretical terms reverses the earlier premise of a technological society: What is stressed is the *independence* of education as a central institution toward which, as Durkheim argued, few can remain indifferent.

For European systems, the absence of a uniform sequence demanded a different, initial vision, one which could not be so easily disaggregated into nested levels of ascending order. In educational systems with multiple and independent ladders which have long been tightly linked to opposing social class and cultural origins, the central actors are groups. Here individual motivation is defined early on by one's place within the matrix of educational streams, although mobility can be enhanced through "sponsored" mechanisms designed to loosen excessive monopolies over educational access. The many empirical studies on selection for secondary schooling consistently demonstrated the decisive influence of social origin and the apparent weakness of policy changes to disentangle the two. The intricate ties between social origin and educational mobility became particularly visible in the eruption of French university students in 1968. In their epilogue to the original publication of *The Inheritors*, Bourdieu and Passeron succinctly concluded: "In other words, it is a fallacy to suppose that one can directly and exclusively identify even the cross-influence of factors such as social origins or sex, in synchronic relations which, in the case of a population defined by a certain past, take on their full significance only in the context of the educational *trajectory*" (1979, p. 143, my emphasis).

The absence of a single educational trajectory forms a different backdrop for sociological research on educational opportunity. The depth of European experience with divergent and unequal educational ladders accounts for a preponderance of explanations anchored in structural causes, particularly social class. Status is not so much attained as it is predicted by the closer links between family origin, residential neighborhood, and educational sequence. The sharpness of class differences is acutely evident in linguistic styles, which can shape different cognitive orientations. Documentation of how these differences became causes and rationales for school selection represents a significant contribution of European sociology of education.

Yet alongside this tradition of empirical research is a theoretical sophistication that is aware of the dangers of overemphasizing social origins. Differences in class values and orientation cannot be taken as initial determinants of a course of educational attainment, for such value orientations, as Boudon succinctly put it, "should be explained in terms of *decision fields* that are a function of social position" (1974, p. 197, my emphasis). And where much American research sought to measure the effects of schools from cross-sectional surveys, the European experience is evident here too, pointing to an "illusion" of this method— its tendency to "overdramatize" the cognitive effects of social background and yet be unable to explain the attenuation of social origin over time (Boudon 1974, pp. 111, 195).

From empirical work directed to issues of school selection and educational mobility, European sociology of education reached its own settlement favorable to theoretical growth. This is most conspicuous in the burst of conceptual innovation known as the "new" sociology of education which originated in France and England and gained currency in the 1970s and early 1980s (see Karabel and Halsey 1977, pp. 44, 77). The central concepts of this theoretical innovation coincide with American theoretical terms and reflect the assumption that educational systems now enjoy a "relative autonomy" from the traditional constraints of social origin and from the intrusions of occupational and productive changes outside of education. The concepts of this European contribution project an active voice and attempt to capture what the earlier empiricism failed to grasp, namely, the frequent lack of correspondence between educational systems and the economy. It is the "play" between the educational system and the allocation of jobs and the student as "rational" actor set amidst these two that are among the premises underlying the theoretical developments of European sociology of education.

By the end of the 1970s, the sociology of education was now quite unlike its predecessor, educational sociology. The parallel social and economic changes which were at the base of much empirical research within European and American sociology contributed to similarities in educational issues and problems. In turn the sociology of education experienced a revitalization of theory which placed the field at the forefront of sociology itself. The cumulative impact which empirical research has upon theoretical growth forms the outline of the contents of this volume.

ORGANIZATION OF THE VOLUME

The Genealogy of Concepts and the Bearing of Empirical Research

The maturity of the sociology of education is only superficially reflected in its own chronology of events. The measure of conceptual and theoretical advance implies more than a static inventory taken at successive points in time. Seen over the long term, the ties which link established concepts disclose an orderliness of change, what Stephen Toulmin (1972, pp. 200–60) calls the moving picture of genealogies between earlier and contemporary concepts. The forces behind this moving picture are the cumulative judgments which determine the viability of a concept (or a family of concepts) and its claim to some perpetuation. These judgments are guided most specifically by standards of evidence, of what Robert Merton terms "the bearing of empirical research on sociological theory" (1957, pp. 102–17).

Merton identifies four criteria. Two of these—the *serendipity pattern* of confronting unanticipated empirical findings and the *recasting of theory* from repeated observations of neglected facts—are the more indirect sources of advances in theory, whereas the *refocusing of theory* by new research methods and the *clarification* of concepts, both verbally and empirically, are more direct and intentional sources. These four criteria are not independent sources of conceptual

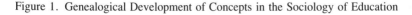

Figure 1. Genealogical Development of Concepts in the Sociology of Education

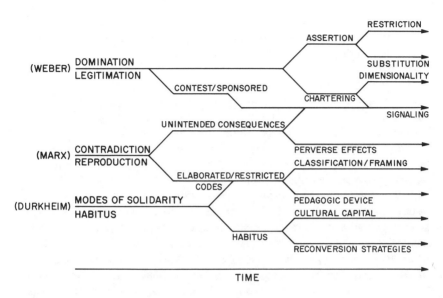

and theoretical change, but overlap. Confronting unanticipated, anomalous findings can stimulate new research methods, and the clarification of concepts can resolve problems of evidence and complement the recasting of theory.

The view offered here, seeing developments in the sociology of education as a *genealogy of concepts*, overarches the collection of chapters in this volume. This genealogical evolution is portrayed in Figure 1, which depicts a "representative set" of central concepts which have had a significant influence on the development of theory and research since the classical era. The contributions to theory and research on both sides of the Atlantic are not frequently set alongside one another, and as a result, the parallels which give overall shape to these genealogies can remain obscure. Yet this can be abridged, and a specific objective of this *Handbook* is to draw out the parallels and convergences across otherwise disparate research arenas. The criteria outlining the bearing of empirical research make conspicuously evident examples of parallel research topics and convergences in the recasting of theory.

The chapters of Part I, "History and the Social Origins of Education," exemplify the recasting or elaboration of theory from the inclusion of neglected facts. The cumulative evidence that educational systems arose often in *advance* of industrial changes, and cannot be explained simply as dependent institutions, is one of the most neglected of historical facts and forms a central premise integrating these chapters. Margaret Archer elaborates a theory of the origins of educational systems which is rooted in Weber's treatment of domination yet is recast to interpret alternative paths in the formation of national educational systems. The bearing of historical evidence generates innovative concepts which denote these paths, the rise of educational systems from *substitution* or from *restrictive* origins. From these different originating conditions, Archer proposes a number of institutional consequences which are expected to follow from these conditions and persist for some time.

The neglect of U.S. regions in which many states originated educational systems well in advance of industrial expansion is a central fact addressed in John Richardson's interpretation of the origins of common schooling in the American states. The concept of *anticipatory settlement* is adapted to the neglected facts surrounding the western regions and suggests a redirection of theoretical inquiry on the origins of public education.

Finally, John Boli and Francisco Ramirez present a most comprehensive theoretical perspective which directs attention away from the nation-state as the basic unit of analysis and to the transnational context as an independent influence upon the rise of mass education. Part of this "world cultural" context was the diffusion of an ontology which diminished the role of intermediary groups standing between the individual as citizen and the legitimate authority of the state. The construction of national systems of mass education was an instrumental means for movements to build the nation-state itself. Their focus on this competition among states leads to a reversal of common arguments about the rise of mass education and succinctly explains why industrial leaders were often late in their construction of national educational systems.

The points of theoretical convergence discernible across these chapters arise precisely because each seeks to incorporate evidence not previously well explained. A result is "improved theory on the basis of suggestive empirical data."

In Part II, "Socialization Processes and Educational Outcomes," the linkages between families, peers, and schools and the implications of educational stratification are addressed in four chapters. In the initial chapter, by Alan Kerckhoff, the triangle of socialization influences is critically examined and the tone is set for subsequent chapters by a *clarification* of how these influences must be conceptualized. At the core of this conceptualization is Kerckhoff's admonishment that effects of families and schools be viewed over time as a "life course trajectory" encompassing the sequence of events linking family origins to subsequent adult statuses. The life course perspective holds promise as a theoretical bridge to enable comparative research on societies which have significantly different sequences of events. The contrast between the relatively uniform educational experience in the United States and the more unequal educational ladders of France and England is again a relevant point yet may be overcome precisely by means of this perspective.

New theoretical directions may be initiated from a concerted attention to neglected facts. In Chapters 5 and 6, the common research topic of academic "ability" is addressed by Carl Simpson and Susan Rosenholtz and by James

Rosenbaum. Both chapters are similarly entitled, yet each advances a theoretical interpretation adapted to different points in the educational sequence. The theory of *ability formation* elaborated by Simpson and Rosenholtz is grounded in empirical research conducted in the early grades. The theory centers on the concept of *dimensionality*, defining how classroom structure shapes the range of tasks and the quality of teacher and peer interactions and in so doing affects the formation of a student's conception of his or her academic ability. Because students are implicated in a given classroom organization for a prolonged period, they will soon adopt a conception of their relative ability consistent with that structure. Although the ability formation theory is contemporaneous to such a "reality construction" perspective, the authors acknowledge a much greater conceptual inheritance, noting that the strength of a reality construction theory lies in the irony of how structures we create often become ones we neither intended nor approved. Beliefs about structures, even when they are local classroom structures, become broadly institutionalized, for indeed beliefs and structures evolve together. It is this point which extends the theoretical inheritance of ability to the classical tradition generally and reveals its genealogical tie to the Weberian notion of legitimation specifically.

With similar theoretical leanings, James Rosenbaum extends the assumption that ability is socially constructed by proposing a tournament model of social mobility. Adapted to the later educational years, Rosenbaum builds upon Turner's (1960) classic distinction between contest and sponsored mobility by adapting a theory of *signaling* to the carry-over of school stratification to occupational careers. This theory for how attributions of potential or diminishing ability are structurally conditioned, likened to one's progress through a tournament, is akin to Simpson and Rosenholtz's contention that beliefs and structures cannot be analyzed apart from each other. Rosenbaum's joining of the signaling theory to a tournament conception of ability not only has the merit of explaining unexpected ("unintended") outcomes of successful or unsuccessful mobility, but also offers an explanation of the intensity with which ability conceptions are internalized and their institutional structures legitimized.

The convergence between these two chapters reveals a continuity of theoretical focus which has sought to resolve what John Meyer (1977, p. 60) identified as "the most puzzling general research paradox in the sociology of American education," namely, that while the level of schooling has considerable effects on individuals, there is little outcome variation between schools. It is indeed a paradox for American education but not so for European education. The differences between the structure of educational ladders, again historically shaped, required a rethinking of educational effects. Not deriving from personal attributes or from resource differences, effects derive from the accommodation students make to the perceived social standing of a school. Neglected facts (or, in Meyer's terms, "evidentiary embarrassments") become resolved by the concept of *chartering*, advancing that school effects can derive from a foreknowledge about the standing of a school yet to be attended. School charters, academic credentials of unequal value, are indeed potent "signals," not only to students, but to employers as well.[2] There is here a noteworthy affinity between the concepts of chartering, dimensionality, and signaling. All have emphasized that structural differences between schools are part of a larger context of legitimation and symbolic climate that is learned in early school grades and continued well beyond formal schooling. In Figure 1 these mutual affinities are indicated, as well as their common heritage to Weber's meaning of "legitimation."

The final chapter, by Carl Milofsky, addresses the important organizational place which special education has assumed in the past several decades. Often an "embarrassing" topic to sociologists of education because it is not typically seen as part of formal, regular instruction, special education nonetheless becomes a convenient datum for social control theories of schooling. Working within the ethnographic tradition of the sociology of education, Milofsky brings data on the daily interactions of schools to bear on such conventional interpretations and joins this research tradition to the large-scale structural trends which have altered the size and composition of school units. In so doing, Milofsky demonstrates how ethnographic research on special education yields theoretically important facts, yet facts which are often neglected precisely because of the status of special education. Milofsky's synthesis of these neglected facts leads to a recasting of conventional interpretations on both special and regular education.

In Part III, "Educational Transmission and Reproduction," the chapters by Basil Bernstein and Pierre Bourdieu exemplify the clarification of concepts which have been central to the work of each author. The works of both Bernstein and Bourdieu account for much the "new" sociology of education, and yet the genealogical ties to the classical tradition are well recognized for both. Nonetheless, their conceptual reformulations have been adapted to contemporary changes and have penetrated well beyond national peculiarities.

Basil Bernstein's early formulations of "elaborated and restricted (linguistic) codes" and the distinction between "classification" and "framing" are concepts rooted in Durkheim's alternative modes of solidarity. Bernstein's more recent elaborations of "pedagogic discourse" are informed by Durkheim's *Moral Education* and *The Evolution of Educational Thought*. In his chapter, he elaborates the concept of *pedagogic device*, linking it closely to classification and framing and to forms of educational codes. The pedagogic device is the mediator of claims for types of knowledge which are exerted upon educational systems, stemming from changes in economic production and hierarchies of power. The pedagogic device attempts to clarify the processes which account for the successful translation (transformation) of various knowledge claims, processes which entail multiple actors outside of educational systems as well as processes internal to schools. The theoretical problem addressed by Bernstein mirrors, in some ways, the ideological topic pressed by Spencer in his *Education*. In contrast to Spencer, however, the "comparative worths" of knowledge would be problematic to Bernstein, for what successfully enters as educational curricula, becoming the pedagogic discourse of schools, is a social struggle centered in the pedagogic device. In this light, Spencer's own claim for a scientific knowledge reflected the interests of a rising middle class in "useful" knowledge and explains, as well, the formation of an independent secondary ladder of new public schools tailored to these interests. Bernstein's clarification of the pedagogic device offers a means to interpret these social struggles and their institutional outcomes. His clarification also attempts to render earlier concepts of classification and framing more dynamic and more suitable to the comparative diversity (or similarity) in types of knowledge promoted in educational systems.

Bourdieu's influential concept of *cultural capital* is an ingenious relocation of Marx's use of economic capital. The more elastic concepts of *habitus* and *reconversion strategies* are theoretical continuities from Durkheim. The concept of habitus first appears in Durkheim's *The Evolution of Educational Thought* (p. 29), wherein he speaks of it as explaining "the emergence of an idea which was totally unknown in the ancient world and which by contrast played a substantial role in Christianity: the idea of conversion." With similar reasoning adapted to the place of contemporary education, Bourdieu takes the power inherent in the notion of conversion to analyses of strategies made available to and adopted by social groups as their structural positions are objectively changed. In his chapter, Bourdieu differentiates between the forms of capital, distinguishing now social and cultural capital. The particular focus of the chapter, however, is on the processes of conversion, clarifying how these processes are the core of strategies adopted by individuals and social groups.

The final section on "Methodological and Theoretical Issues in the Sociology of Education" comes at the end of the volume, designed with conscious intent, for both typically come *after* the conduct of empirical research. Two of these chapters, the one by Raymond Boudon on "Education, Social Mobility, and Sociological Theory" and that by Richard Rubinson and John Ralph on "Methodological Issues in the Study of Educational Change," are strikingly complementary. Both exemplify how serendipitous findings can stimulate new research methods and a refocusing of theoretical interests.

Raymond Boudon commences with a recognition of the unanticipated finding which consistently shows that an increase in educational equality has had little effect on income or occupational inequality. This finding can be traced from the influential Coleman report on *Equality of Educational Opportunity* to the near simultaneous publication of *Inequality* (Jencks et al.) in 1972 and Boudon's own work in *Education, Opportunity and Social Inequality* in 1974. These "puzzling" findings are addressed by Boudon, who shows how this example of serendipity ought profitably to be taken as a "normal fact," and from that he builds general theoretical models that can explain the dynamics of social mobility across societies which may vary considerably in their forms of stratification. Boudon's own theoretical interpretations exhibit genealogical ties to the classical tradition, particularly to Marx and Durkheim. The notions employed by Marx of *reproduction* and *contradiction* are discernible in Boudon's theoretical interpretations. While often identified with "socialist theories of schooling," with no such affinity Boudon reactivates the meaning of each as generating emergent, "unintended consequences."[3] Boudon's concept of *perverse effects* is designed to capture the contemporary unintended outcome in which the rational behavior of individuals seeking to increase their education has the effect of raising the amount of schooling needed for effective income or occupational returns. While there are returns for individuals, the collective effect is a certain depreciation, evident by a lack of change in the structure of income inequality. The theory of the concept of perverse effects is rooted in the Durkheimian notion of *methodological individualism*. Yet its empirical base is the contemporary circumstance which both enforces and legitimates educational attendance *without any real regard for the collective consequences*.

The world-level expansion and institutional autonomy of educational systems are contemporary changes which significantly strengthen the interpretation of schooling as an emergent dynamic. In their chapter on methodological issues in the analysis of educational change, Richard Rubinson and John Ralph move from a substantive critique of empirical evidence on educational expansion to converge with Boudon by their formulation of quantitative methods which can incorporate the self-generating processes of schooling. Many of the anomalous findings reviewed by Rubinson and Ralph come from comparative studies. As they note, one response has often been to resist a refocusing of theory and to return to the haven of one's own discipline. In contrast to such retreats, to Rubinson and Ralph these inconsistencies become sources of data for cross-national comparisons. Their refocusing of theory converges with the global context advocated by Boli and Ramirez, and we see that both chapters suggest a research agenda for a historical and comparative sociology of education.

The final chapters, by Barbara Heyns and John Meyer, address quite different issues, yet in their own way they convey parallel assessments on both conceptual and measurement issues. Both chapters exemplify a clarification of sociological research on education. In her review of one of the most enveloping of research topics, Barbara Heyns examines a range of literature which has sought, over the past twenty years, to detect the sources of "school effects." In a similar vein, John Meyer scrutinizes "types of explanation" typically assumed and followed in the sociology of education. For both, there is a point of convergence which emerges from their mutual assessment that much research typically fails to conceptualize and measure educational effects adequately. Their independent explanations for why this is so is an uncommon statement in the sociology of education: expressed most sharply by Meyer, the sociology of education is intimately, and in ways unreflectively, committed to the very goals and rationales that are embedded in modern educational systems. The persistence of null findings or of unexpected reversals can be predictable outcomes precisely because sociological research often proceeds with the implicit acceptance that schools and schooling must have certain effects. As Heyns notes, current research on effective schools is fueled, in part, by the cultural resonance this topic possesses, and many of the research questions that are posed cannot be easily formulated detached from the pragmatic needs and interests of educational personnel. More pointedly, Meyer's dissection of the various types of explanation suggests the need for an additional imagery of education, one likened to religious institutions which, save for the family, possess a similar depth of historical and authoritative legitimation.

NOTES

1. The differences between European and American educational systems generally and the place of secondary education especially are more than just separate versus uniform ladders. They lie also in the *timing* of the historical emergence of secondary education relative to other levels. Durkheim (1925/77, pp. 17–18) was keenly aware of this with regard to France: "However, as a result of something peculiar to France, it happens that throughout the major part of our history secondary education has provided the focus for the whole of our academic life. Higher education, after having given birth to secondary education, very soon became extinct and was only reborn in the aftermath of the 1870 war. Primary education appears only very late in our history and only really got off the ground after the Revolution. Thus, throughout a large period of our national existence the entire educational scene is dominated by secondary education."

2. In an empirical analysis of two quite different educational systems, Hope (1983) joins the meaning of the concept of *chartering* to an empirical measure which is sensitive to the proposed autonomous effects of schools. Such empirical work following the clarification of a concept is a vivid example of Merton's fourth criterion.

3. Boudon's use of the concepts of *reproduction* and *contradiction* to describe emergent effects is a divergence from their more common use in radical critiques of schooling (see Giroux 1983). As Boudon retells (1982, p. 3), the lineage of the former use underwent a period of obscurity after Marx, only to be reintroduced in 1936 by Merton in his celebrated article on "unanticipated consequences." This meaning was to lay fallow again until its reactivation in sociology of education, principally by Boudon.

REFERENCES

Boudon, Raymond. *Education, Opportunity and Social Inequality: Changing Prospects in Western Society*. New York: John Wiley & Sons, 1974.
———. *The Unintended Consequences of Social Action*. New York: St. Martin's Press, 1982.
Bourdieu, Pierre, and Jean-Claude Passeron. *The Inheritors*. Chicago: University of Chicago Press, 1979.
Brim, Orville G., Jr. *Sociology and the Field of Education*. New York: Russell Sage Foundation, 1958.
Coleman, J. S., et al. *Equality of Educational Opportunity*. Washington, DC: U.S. Government Printing Office, 1966.
Conrad, Richard. "A Systematic Analysis of Current Researches in the Sociology of Education." *American Sociological Review* 17 (1952): 350–55.
Durkheim, Emile. *Sociology and Education*. New York: The Free Press, 1956 (originally published in French in 1924).
———. *Moral Education: A Study in the Theory and Application of the Sociology of*

Education. New York: The Free Press, 1961 (originally published in French in 1925).

————. *The Evolution of Educational Thought: Lectures on the Formation and Development of Secondary Education in France*. London: Routledge & Kegan Paul, 1977 (originally published in French in 1925).

Giroux, Henry A. "Theories of Reproduction and Resistance in the New Sociology of Education: A Critical Analysis." *Harvard Educational Review* 53 (1983): 257–93.

Halsey, A. H., Jean Floud, and C. Arnold Anderson. *Education, Economy and Society*. New York: The Free Press, 1964.

Hope, Keith. "Are High Schools Really Heteronomous?" *Sociology of Education* 56 (1983): 111–25.

Jencks, C., et al. *Inequality: A Reassessment of the Effect of Family and Schooling in America*. New York: Basic Books, 1972.

Karabel, Jerome, and A. H. Halsey. *Power and Ideology in Education*. New York: Oxford University Press, 1977.

Merton, Robert K. *Social Theory and Social Structure*. New York: The Free Press, 1957.

————. "The Unanticipated Consequences of Purposive Social Action." *American Sociological Review* 1 (1936): 894–904.

Meyer, John W. "The Effects of Education as an Institution." *American Journal of Education* 83 (1977): 55–77.

Spencer, Herbert. *Education, Intellectual, Moral, and Physical*. New York: D. Appleton, 1912.

Szreter, Richard. "Some Forerunners of Sociology of Education in Britain: An Account of the Literature and Influences c. 1900–1950." *Westminster Studies in Education* 7 (1984): 13–43.

Taylor, William. "The Organization of Educational Research in the United Kingdom." In *Research Perspectives in Education*, edited by William Taylor. New York: APS Publications, 1973.

Toulmin, Stephen. *Human Understanding*. Princeton, N.J.: Princeton University Press, 1972.

Trow, Martin. "The Second Transformation of American Secondary Education." *International Journal of Comparative Sociology* 2 (1961): 144–66.

Turner, Ralph. "Sponsored and Contest Mobility and the School System." *American Sociological Review* 25 (1960): 855–67.

PART I

History and the Social Origins of Education

1

MARGARET S. ARCHER

Social Origins of Educational Systems

INTRODUCTION

Since the term *educational system* has generally been used indiscriminately, referring to anything from primitive initiation rites onwards, to define it clearly serves three distinct purposes: identifying what is to be explained, dating when each nation acquired a system, and locating the time from which analysis must back-track in search of explanation. The definition adopted is one which follows the everyday meaning of the words *state educational system*, and it should be stressed that very dissimilar types of education can conform to it. Hence *a state educational system is considered to be a nationwide and differentiated collection of institutions devoted to formal education, whose overall control and supervision is at least partly governmental and whose component parts and processes are related to one another.* Both the political and the systemic aspects are stressed in this definition which insists that they must be present together before education can be deemed to constitute a system, for the appearance of either characteristic alone is not uncommon. Many European courts controlled elitist or military academies without having any further involvement in the education of the nation; the Catholic church in Europe operated educational networks, leading from catechization to ordination, yet quite independent of the political center.

Particular attention is given to England and France as case studies, partly because they are both countries whose educational systems emerged autonomously and partly because of two major differences between them. On the one hand, it is generally agreed that their present systems of education are very different and that they have undergone dissimilar forms of historical development. On the other hand, even more indubitable is the diversity of their political,

Reprinted in slightly revised form from the University Edition, *Social Origins of Educational Systems*, Beverly Hills and London: Sage, 1983, chapters 2 and 3. (The original study was a comparative analysis of England, France, Russia, and Denmark, two decentralized and two centralized educational systems.)

economic, and cultural histories. Thus the range of variation which the theory advanced here confronts is deliberately maximized.

Private Ownership, Mono-Integration, and Subordination

When educational control was rooted in private ownership, prior to the emergence of state systems, this resulted in the same generic relationship between education and the rest of society. The fact that one particular group virtually monopolized formal instruction meant that education was firmly linked to only a single part of the total social structure, namely, that institution with which the dominant group was associated (in whose role structure they held positions as ordained clergymen or priests, with whose operations they were occupied, and whose goals they sought to attain). The link consisted of the flow of physical, human, and financial resources from the ownership sphere to education and the counter-flow of educational services, appropriate to the dominating sector. Where churches constituted the ownership groups, these services consisted in religious socialization and a supply of ecclesiastical recruits. Such interdependence between two social institutions did not imply that it was equally advantageous to both, nor that their "interchange" was freely determined, nor that it contributed to the persistence of the two parts concerned or to that of the wider social system.

The term *mono-integration* is used to denote this common structural characteristic. It thus refers to one of the possible relationships which could be maintained between education and all other parts of society at a particular stage of institutional differentiation. Logically, education could be interdependent with all others, with some, or with none at all: mono-integration is used when it is related to only one. It is not, therefore, a property of any institution as such, but of relations *between* institutions: it constitutes an emergent property which conditions subsequent processes of educational interaction and change. For when education is mono-integrated, two major implications follow—one for education itself and the other for the rest of society (with the exception of the lone institution to which it is linked through ownership).

Domination

When education is a mono-integrated and subordinate institution, its control and the power to define instruction rests in the hands of its owners, who are termed the *educationally dominant group*. This is chosen as a neutral concept to designate the educational powers once enjoyed by a particular social group, which differentiated it from all other members of that society. *Domination*, following Max Weber, is defined as the opportunity to have a command concerning education obeyed by a given group of persons. As such, it may be quite distinct from other forms of social dominance: those with educational control may or may not be the ruling class, the political elite, or the most wealthy group in society. When compared cross-culturally, dominant groups can be very dissimilar and may originate from different parts of their respective social structures.

Prolonged educational stability corresponds to the lasting domination of a particular group. This stability may endure either because the dominant group remains unchallenged or because it successfully overcomes threats to its control. Such challenges are called *assertion* and defined as the sum of efforts made by another group(s), which does not have the opportunity to issue educational commands, to overthrow the existing form of domination.

For the dominant group to retain its position of exclusive control it must continue to be the only supplier of the resources upon which educational operations depend (i.e., school buildings and paid teachers). Yet, since it is impossible for any one group fully to monopolize these resources itself (if only because of the human component), the dominant group has to preserve its *monopoly* of supplying educational resources by preventing others from converting financial and human assets into schools and teachers. On the one hand, an *ideology* legitimating this monopoly can be used by the dominant group to defend the exclusivity of its control by convincing others that they lack the right, the ability, or the experience to engage in educational activities or that the type of instruction already provided is the best, the proper, or the only form possible. On the other hand, a series of *constraints* can be employed to prevent alternative groups from supplying the facilities for imparting instruction. These may vary from the symbolic to the coercive, depending largely upon the nature of the dominant group itself. Use of either is conditional on members of the dominant group wishing to maintain control and the structural relations on which it is based. It is not necessary to assume that this desire is universal when seeking to specify the conditions for the maintenance of domination, for without it the prerequisites simply will not be developed.

All three factors—monopolization of educational facilities, protective constraints, and legitimatory ideology—are together considered to represent the necessary, but not the sufficient, conditions for maintenance of domination. Without constraints, the monopoly is vulnerable; without an ideology recruiting positive support rather than enforced compliance, it is even more so. However, neither may develop until monopoly ownership is challenged, but at that point it is best buttressed if the three elements are mutually reinforcing.

In both France and England, the dominant groups were concerned to defend their control of instruction but showed varying degrees of success in developing the three prerequisites for its maintenance. In France, the Catholic church and its multiplicity of teaching orders early acquired a monopoly of educational facilities, for the Reformation served to underline that religious orthodoxy must be taught, not assumed. In the following two centuries, a patchy but countrywide network of confessional schools developed. Ownership was ecclesiastical: either religious orders opened schools or local priests held classes on church premises. Teaching was closely controlled by the church and was generally undertaken by the clergy or by a Catholic lay teacher certified by the regional bishop. Postelementary education was the preserve of the religious orders and various types of *collèges* were owned, operated, and staffed by Jesuits, Barnabites, Doctrinarians, Oratorians, etc., although the scholastic Jesuit model prevailed there, as in the universities. Instruction was "characterized by a concentration on Catholic doctrine and literary classicism; the former led to religious conformity, the latter to the intellectual homogeneity of the ruling elite."[1]

This substantial monopoly was reinforced by an ideology based on traditional legitimation. Appeal was made to the supreme moral authority of the apostolic church, whose priests had the exclusive right to pronounce on ethical matters. Since every academic subject and issue was held to have moral implications, the clergy was presented as the only body which could properly teach. Thus the educational ideology was fundamentally religious but included strong elements of social elitism and political conservatism, which broadened its appeal beyond the strictly theological. Symbolic constraints were also available within the church, which did not restrict itself to the use of the pulpit for disseminating its ideology. Religious sanctions were imposed on parents to ensure the catechization of children, on pupils in the boarding-schools to induce doctrinal orthodoxy, and on recalcitrant communities harboring schismatics who might be tempted to enter the educational market to perpetuate heresies. Thus the strong monopoly was protected by the use of religious constraints originating within the controlling group, along with those deriving from education itself, i.e., discrimination and exclusion of potential critics from instruction, promotion of potential supporters through giving privileged educational access, and the use of tuition for spreading supportive values—devices generally employed by every dominant group.

In England, at the end of the eighteenth century, the security of Anglican domination was much more the product of lack of threat or opposition. The majority of facilities was owned by the church, but at elementary level, it represented only a thin network of parish and charity schools. Since Brougham's Royal Commission of 1820 branded England as the worst educated country in Europe, the Anglican monopoly was clearly not extensive. It depended on the absence of organized opposition: a competing network of Dissenting establishments had yet to be consolidated, while the individual dame-schools plugged the gaps without constituting any concerted threat.

Anglican control of secondary and higher education was more firmly based. Not only were many of the endowed schools religious foundations, but also the clergy enjoyed a complete monopoly of educational personnel. It supplied the vast majority of staff and controlled the profession as a whole, since an ecclesiastical licence was needed to become a teacher. The classical curricula of public and endowed schools, reflecting the state of knowledge at their foundation, were definitions of instruction upheld by the church because of their relevance to ordination. The same was true of the universities, where an entirely Anglican teaching and student body meant that higher education was permeated with religious orthodoxy and largely geared to reproducing the Anglican oligarchy over time—between 1800 and 1850 nearly half of those matriculating at Oxford were subsequently ordained. The governing elite provided supportive legal constraints, the most important being the Test acts, limiting university graduation to Anglicans alone and the judicial upholding of the statutes pertaining to endowed foundations which served to protect the church's definition of instruction. In England, a defensive ideology was not properly elaborated until Anglican domination came under attack.

The Effects of Domination on Other Parts of the Social Structure. The nature of the dominant group's definition of instruction gave rise to specific kinds of educational outputs which could be either a help or a hindrance to contemporaneous operations taking place in other parts of society. These must be investigated to learn what supportive pressures the dominant group's activities in the educational field generated from other sectors of society and where they met with the greatest opposition. This is not simply a matter of correlation, but a structural influence on group interaction, which in turn is modified or reinforced by other influences. If this is the case, then *the fact that the distribution of adventitious benefits and obstructions was very different in the countries concerned is of corresponding importance for understanding the educational conflict which took place.*

Because of their supreme control over education, the dominant groups in both England and France were able to design the form of learning which best served their purposes, with almost complete disregard for the requirements of others. It is not surprising, then, that in each case the narrowness of instruction and the homogeneity of its outputs obstructed more activities than those which it accidentally aided. (A broader, more differentiated education would have produced more adventitious beneficiaries, each of whom would have gained something from different parts of instruction.) However, it is not the number of parties who were obstructed or aided which is crucial, but rather qualitative characteristics of groups of people in these categories—who they were, what resources they had at their disposal, and how willing they were to engage in support of, or opposition to, the dominant group.

In France, Catholic domination sponsored a tradition of scholastic classicism which served its own purposes but increasingly meant that "a gap widened between it and society." To Diderot, it was useful only to the most useless of occupations—the priesthood and the professoriat. Similarly, in the mid-eighteenth century, Rolland stressed its incompatibility with public administration and went on to underline its disservice to military and commercial activities: "Are public schools destined only to produce clergymen, judges, physicians and men of letters? Are soldiers, tradesmen and artists unworthy?"

Even the *ancien régime* monarchy was not a clear-cut beneficiary. Certainly the Catholic definition of instruction which hindered social mobility, confirmed social privilege, and stressed duties associated with station in life served to reinforce the stratificational system upon which absolutism rested. But, on the other hand, Jesuit ultramontanism was antithetic to the monarchy's Gallican policy in religious matters, and its scholasticism was decreasingly useful to government service. It was only with the expulsion of Jesuits and their replacement by the more modernistic Oratorians as the leading teaching order, that the monarchy eventually became an unambiguous adventitious beneficiary and the sole one at that.

In England, the developing capitalist economy was seriously impeded by the Anglican definition of instruction and the values it embodied. This taught deference to squire and clergy but not to entrepreneur and merchant; it defended hereditary privilege but not newly acquired property; it preached catechism and constitution but not industrial skills and the spirit of capitalism; it taught classics and pure mathematics but not accountancy and applied science. Equally, it penalized other religious organizations since the constraints which prevented Dissenters from attending many endowed schools, from participating in university graduation, and from entering the teaching profession hindered a range of denominational operations.

On the other hand, the Anglican dominant group had a clear adventitious beneficiary in the political elite. Increasing working-class unrest in the early nineteenth century made the contribution of religious instruction to social quietism proportionately valuable. Equally complementary with the goals of both political parties was the social exclusivity of Anglican secondary and higher education—for the status characteristics which were confirmed through education were the same as those employed by the governing elite when making ascriptive poltical appointments. The production of churchmen was in no way incompatible with the production of statesmen.

Support for the Dominant Group. Adventitious beneficiaries do not convert directly into supportive groups. Indeed, they may not move in this direction at all since other factors can neutralize or counteract the structural predisposition toward their becoming loci of support. To recap, those receiving rewards must be aware of it and must not have social ties, values, or any other source of allegiance which militates against solidarity with and defense of the dominant group. In neither England nor France did such factors nullify the influence of educational relations on the formulation of alliances for the maintenance of domination.

On the contrary, in France, conditional influences originating from other social relationships reinforced the educational predisposition for an alliance between clergy and nobility. As enlightened thought simultaneously became more secular and more radical, the nobility was not slow to recognize the rewards it received from clerical instruction. Furthermore, the clergy and the nobility constituted the two privileged Estates—they were united by social ties and similar vested social interests in the retention of privilege—a link which went far beyond their educational relations. Once the Jesuits had been expelled in 1762 and the Oratorian order, with its Gallican outlook and more modern curriculum, had stepped into the gap, then social, religious, political, and educational factors encouraged the nobility to act in a supportive capacity.

In England, too, the education alliance between Anglican church and political elite was cemented by other factors, although complicated by party politics. By the early nineteenth century, Tories and Whigs alike acknowledged the services of the church to social control and to legitimating elitist government: both supported the National Society for Promoting the Education of the Poor in the Principles of the Established Church. Social ties of family and class linked Anglican leaders to members of both political parties. Nevertheless, the traditional "church and king" outlook was more prominent among Tories than in the Whig Party, which increasingly received the Dissenting vote after 1832. Thus, while Whigs remained consistent in their support of religious instruction, it was the Tories who finally emerged as strong allies of Anglican education.

Assertion

Only the necessary conditions for successful assertion are outlined, and these consist of the factors required to overcome domination—to evade its constraints, to reject its ideology, and to damage its monopoly. Without them there will not be far-reaching changes, but conflict may be resolved in favor of existing domination, for this depends on the outcome of interaction itself. What is being specified, then, are only those factors without which latent opposition cannot be transformed into assertion and an assertive group cannot overcome the dominant group.

First, opposition must acquire bargaining power, i.e., sufficient numerical support and organizational strength to challenge domination. Both involve a desire for concerted action to transform educational control which overrides social ties with the dominant group and any conviction that its legitimatory ideology may have carried. In other words, diffuse discontent must be consolidated into organized assertion if constraints are to be subverted. To this end, a counter-ideology is required, partly to inform the movement of its goals, to recruit participants from the obstructed institution(s) as well as support from a wider audience, and, ultimately, to justify using the bargaining power at its disposal. But, above all, the ideology of the dominant group has to be challenged and negated by a separate philosophy which legitimates the goals and activities of the assertive group and specifies its new definition of instruction. Finally, the assertive group must successfully engage in activities which are instrumental in devaluing the dominant group's monopoly.

Instrumental activities can take two different forms—substitution or restriction. Substitution consists in replacing the supply of educational facilities, which the dominant group had monopolized, by new ones. In practice, this means devaluing its monopoly by building and maintaining new schools and recruiting, training, and paying new teachers to staff them. Here domination is challenged by competition on the educational market—the aim of the assertive group being to price the dominant party out of it or to relegate it to a small corner of the market. In either case, a transfer of control takes place and macroscopic changes are introduced. Restriction, on the other hand, consists of removing some of the facilities owned by the dominant group or preventing it from supplying these resources to the educational sphere. Thus the monopoly is devalued coercively; buildings may be appropriated, educational funds confiscated, or personnel excluded from teaching and administration. Here domination is challenged, not by market competition, but by coercive power—the aim being the forcible transfer of educational control.

The nature and timing of confrontation between domination and assertion depends upon the balance of factors present on the two sides. There are two limiting cases: unchallenged domination, when no group has acquired any of the factors necessary for assertion (which corresponds to institutional stability), and, on the other hand, a situation where the prerequisites of domination are matched by the preconditions of assertion (which corresponds to overt institutional conflict). The three components of assertion may be developed simultaneously or over a period of time, but for analytical purposes, they will be examined sequentially for the two countries.

The Consolidation of Bargaining Power. Bargaining power is essentially a matter of numbers and organization; it can obviously vary in strength and plays an important part in determining the relative success of different assertive groups. Several elements jointly contribute to influencing the bargaining power acquired. These can be classified as factors which restrain the development of a large and committed assertive group versus those which further its actualization. When the obstructions stemming from the prevailing definition of instruction all focus upon the same social group, a higher proportion of its members are likely to be active in the pursuit of educational change. Equally, if frustrations are experienced by different social groups which are nevertheless closely linked by other kinds of social ties, their alliance increases overall bargaining power. Both of these represent a particular type of mobilization, where a single assertive group develops with a large number of potential activists. Here there will be a polarization of conflict between domination and assertion. On the other hand, if frustrations are diffused among a number of different social groups which are not linked to one another, pluralistic assertion is more likely and each group will have a more limited pool of potential participants. Because each will have greater difficulties in acquiring strong bargaining power, educational conflict will be complex and protracted.

Other factors can operate in a cross-cutting or reinforcing fashion. Strong links, on grounds other than educational, with the dominant group or its supporters can reduce the number of those actively opposing it. Similarly, the existence of social antagonism between the assertive group and other sections of society reduces the probability of recruiting allies and thus fulfills a similar restraining function. Bargaining power will then be stronger the greater the independence of the obstructed group from the dominant group and the greater its links with other parts of society, especially if these in turn are ill-disposed toward the dominant group on other grounds.

France provides a striking example of a country where the polarization of educational conflict was not restrained by other social ties or allegiances and the consolidation of bargaining power by the assertive group was correspondingly easy. Most important here was the fact that obstructed operations gave rise to frustrations which were experienced cumulatively in one group: the bourgeoisie. Not only was Catholic education irrelevant to its activities in commerce and finance, but school enrollment and graduation placed it in an anomic position when its members could not gain appointments commensurate with their qualifications. "Each year instructed, ambitious and intelligent young men graduated ... but their legitimate ambition came up against unscalable obstacles, money, titles. . . . The Army, high positions in the Church, judicial offices were all the prerogatives of rich and noble families.''[2] These multiple grievances led to the recruitment of activists from all sections of the bourgeoisie committed to educational change.

On the other hand, there were few links between the bourgeoisie and the privileged Estates to restrain participation in assertive activities. On the contrary, social, economic, and political factors conditioned opposition to privilege itself, that is, to the First and Second Estates, the dominant group, and its noble supporters. Simultaneously, the bourgeoisie could recruit allies from among the people, given that the latter were subject to indoctrination by clergy, repression by nobility, and financial exploitation by the state.

Thus predispositions toward educational assertion were superimposed on further sources of social division and political opposition. Far from participation in educational conflict being restrained by other social ties, it was encouraged by them, and assertive bargaining power was augmented proportionately. Educational conflict thus harnessed itself to social conflict structured by legal privilege.

By contrast, the factors influencing the formation of educational opposition in England were complex and cross-cutting, eventually resulting in the emergence of two distinct assertive groups. Initially, it seemed that middle-class assertion would not experience great difficulties in generating bargaining power since two of the major operations impeded by Anglican instruction—the development of the capitalist economy and the progress of Dissenting denominations—affected many of the same people. The entrepreneurial and Dissenting groups were not perfectly superimposed, but there was a large overlapping sector where frustrations were doubled—where fathers were compelled to become self-taught industrialists and their children were debarred from a polite education by religious affiliation and trade connections. At the same time, educational activism was tempered by the significant percentage of the middle class which remained committed Anglicans and by the high proportion of factory owners afraid to lose child labor.

Nevertheless, during the first decades of the nineteenth century it appeared that alliance with the working class would considerably augment bargaining power. Shared opposition to the church as the educationally dominant group and to its supporter, the political elite as the ruling class, promoted joint action.

However, the nonenfranchisement of the working class in 1832 accentuated the divergent political interests of industrial workers and entrepreneurs. In turn, this signaled the emergence of independent educational assertion on the part of labor. Consequently, the consolidation of bargaining power became more difficult for both forms of assertion since they had to recruit participants to oppose the dominant group and the other assertive party. Unlike France, political alignments in England fragmented educational alliances rather than cementing them, and this partly accounts for educational conflict being much more protracted in England.

The Elaboration of Ideology. The possession of an ideology performs three vital functions for an assertive group. *Ideology is a central factor in challenging domination since the legitimation of educational control must be negated by unmasking the interests served, thus reducing support for the prevailing definition of instruction. Secondly, it is crucial in legitimating assertion itself and is thus related to the consolidation of bargaining power. Finally, it is vital for the specification of an alternative definition of instruction, the blueprint which will be implemented in schools if the assertive group is successful.* The elaboration of assertive ideologies can be facilitated or hindered by cultural factors and the distribution of social values in a given country.

The analysis of educational ideologies is important for two reasons. On the one hand, ideological factors exert an independent influence upon educational interaction. As Weber argued, struggle in the realm of ideas parallels rather than reflects group conflict and, although related to the structured interests of participants, contributes something of its own to determining the outcome between them. Here we see that educational ideologies played an important role in the recruitment of support and formation of assertive alliances—sometimes overriding differences of interests, sometimes introducing cleavage within an interest group. On the other hand, educational ideologies are vital to the understanding of educational change. The precise definition of instruction advocated by a group cannot be derived directly from its interests. These interests do not dictate the content of the ideology adopted (for more than one educational philosophy may be compatible with them) or within it the exact nature of the blueprint adopted (for more than one specific curriculum, type of school, etc. may serve group interests and contribute to the attainment of group goals). Thus, to account for the aims pursued in assertion and the changes introduced if successful, the ideological source of the new definition of instruction must be examined.

In France, educational values encouraged polarization between domination and assertion and buttressed the alliance against the Catholic church. Initially restricting themselves to anticlericalism, rather than anti-Catholicism, the bourgeois assertive group appealed to French enlightened thought and especially to the educational philosophy of Diderot. His stress upon utilitarianism, nationalism, and meritocracy captured their aims perfectly, specifying the type of education desired and negating the Catholic definition of instruction so successfully that even the monarchy supported the expulsion of the Jesuit order. This particular strand of thought was, however, too explicitly elitist (though on meritocratic, not traditional, grounds) to recruit popular support, which the bourgeoisie needed in the educational struggle as in political conflict. To gain it involved papering over the divisions which threatened the unity of the Third Estate by legitimating educational assertion to the people as an inextricable part of their battle for political rights. The thought of Condorcet and Sieyès contributed much to legitimating assertion on a wide social basis by relating the political attack on the nobility to the educational assault on the clergy and blending the two into a single challenge to privilege itself—whose abolition could be achieved only by the united action of the Third Estate.

In England, on the other hand, cultural and ideological influences complicated alliances and prevented the clear-cut polarization of educational conflict. The existence of Dissent was initially helpful in crystallizing opposition to Anglicanism, for it represented pluralism in religious values. Almost immediately, however, strong denominational commitment reduced unity within the embryonic assertive group because it clashed with the secular utilitarian element. This strain was apparent during the early years of the British and Foreign School Society, where schism developed between the secular and Quaker elements, which eventually left the society in Dissenting hands.

However, the victory of Dissent (which became more pronounced when working-class unrest cast doubts on the restraining power of classical economics and secular ethics and thus revalued religion for popular control) had a serious backlash. Effectively, it alienated the working-class leadership to whom secularism had strongly appealed, because it harmonized with the intellectual traditions most influential in popular educational thought—the secular rationalism of the French Revolution and early English anarchism. Ideologically, the working classes were as tenacious in their adhesion to secularism as was Dissent in its defense of denominationalism. It took other factors to precipitate the final breakaway in the early 1830s, but secular socialist values then played a major role in the crystallization of an independent, popular assertive group in the corresponding reduction of middle-class bargaining power.

The Development of Instrumental Activities. Use of either a restrictive or a substitutive strategy to devalue the monopoly of the dominant group *is conditioned by the social distribution of resources. Thus few assertive groups have free choice between the alternative kinds of instrumental activities.*

For a group to begin assertion by means of a restrictive policy, it needs some degree of access to the national legislative machinery. The social distribution of political power, therefore, structures the availability of restrictive strategies to different assertive groups associated with various institutions. However, the fact that legislative influence is essential does not imply that any group initiating a restrictive strategy is synonymous with the political elite itself or possesses extensive political power, especially if the economic distribution is such that the adoption of a substitutive strategy is precluded. However, in such cases the use of restriction to damage the dominant group's monopoly is dependent on a concordance of goals between the assertive group and the political elite. This

unanimity need not be present at the start but may be generated in the course
of assertion. The support of governing elites can be won by convincing them
that existing educational control is politically undesirable and by specifying an
alternative definition of instruction which is more conducive to their aims. However, unless the political elite can be recruited as a strenuous ally, then only a
substantial shift in the societal distribution of power to the advantage of the
assertive group gives it any chance of executing a restrictive strategy. Ultimately,
it is only when the assertive group is very closely allied to, or in fact coterminous
with, the political elite that restrictive strategies can be successful and engender
macroscopic educational change.

For a group to begin its assertive activities by employing a strategy of substitution, it needs access to some degree of economic surplus which can be
directed to devaluing the existing monopoly of educational facilities. Although the economic distribution conditions the differential availability of this
strategy to various assertive groups, once again it does not determine the outcome of assertion. First, the crucial factor in developing this kind of instrumental activity is not the absolute amount of wealth at a group's disposal, but
the proportion of it which can be mobilized for educational purposes (thus relative bargaining power is significant here). Secondly, if the assertive ideology
legitimates opposition among a wider audience of potential supporters, the resources made available to this end are increased. Thirdly, while the provision
of alternative physical facilities in education is capital intensive, considerable
progress can be made through concentrating on competition in the field of human resources (which is why so many assertive groups have made use of the
Lancasterian method, grossly deficient as a means of instruction but strategi-
cally ideal in yielding maximum educational encroachment for minimum
investment).

*Thus it can be seen that the economic distribution exerts an influence on the
selection and development of substitutive strategies which exactly parallels that
exerted by the power distribution on restrictive strategies.* In both cases the
initial adoption of a strategy is influenced by the original resource distribution,
but the outcome cannot be predicted from it. However, in substitution, as in
restriction, if the policy is to succeed, resources must be accumulated in the
course of interaction. This has the further implication that *just as the political
elite was considered to be the type of assertive group most likely to succeed in
restriction, so the economic elite is best placed to carry through substitution.*
Indeed, the assertive groups which have the greatest probability of failing to
develop either kind of instrumental activity are those which occupy the lowest
position on both the wealth and power dimensions simultaneously. These in
fact are usually the only groups which can be said to have a free choice between the two strategies—though progress with either is difficult but not
impossible.

In France, we have seen that a variety of factors helped to structure a single
assertive alliance, and here the distribution of resources encouraged the pre-

revolutionary bourgeoisie to follow a restrictive strategy. As a predominantly professional-commercial group, rather than an industrial middle class, it was not poor but was far from being in an economic position to compete with the resources of the Catholic church—and it is financial relativities which are crucial in substitution. Furthermore, the assertive alliance with the popular section of the Third Estate was not one which substantially added to the financial resources of opposition. On the political dimension, however, the bourgeoisie had influence only in the provincial parliaments which were consultative, rather than decision-making, bodies. Nevertheless, these could be employed as platforms, for the expression of bourgeois views and the success of certain presidents (especially Rolland and La Chalotais) in initiating the expulsion of the Jesuits confirmed the adoption of a restrictive strategy against the church. It encouraged the search for allies and the attempt to unite the Third Estate in order to strengthen bargaining power and exert greater political pressure, for in France, political power would have to be augmented during educational interaction if assertion was to succeed.

The English case presents a complete contrast, for the middle-class alliance of entrepreneurs and Dissenters represented a group whose respective economic and political positions clearly favored the adoption of a substitutive strategy. In terms of financial surplus, they were, as their economists never failed to underline, the group making the greatest contribution to national wealth. However, despite having largely taken over from the landed interest as the economic elite, their political participation was minimal before large-scale enfranchisement in 1832: after it, parliamentary representation and cabinet influence still remained small for several subsequent decades. It is not surprising, then, that in the first half of the nineteenth century, this group concentrated on devaluing the Anglican monopoly by substituting new establishments at all levels, either on a proprietary basis or through voluntary subscription.

On the other hand, working-class assertion came from a group which had neither political influence nor economic surplus and thus lacked the factors predisposing toward selection of either strategy. Indeed, the tactical debate about whether to engage in educational substitution as a basis for subsequent political change or whether to seek franchise reform first as a means for obtaining educational change later on, was to divide the Chartist movement. Nevertheless, it was the substitutive strategy which was adopted immediately after and largely because of political disappointment in 1832. The chance of being in a position to manipulate legislative machinery for educational reform then appeared remote; substitution could be immediate, and the argument of Lovett that an instructed class had better chance of enfranchisement was influential. Relative to working-class resources, the sums mobilized for substitution of elementary schools, halls of science, and mechanics' institutes were impressive—but more as an index of class commitment to educational change than as a serious threat to the dominant group or the growing network of institutions founded by the assertive section of the middle class.

Educational Conflict

France is a clear-cut case where an assertive group succeeded in devaluing the monopoly of the dominant group and gained educational control on the basis of a restrictive strategy. As such, it illustrates the important fact that possession of political power alone does not confer the ability to define instruction, although control of the legislative machinery is a necessary condition for restricting others and preventing them from doing so. For on the basis of this kind of strategy, there are two stages involved in attaining educational control—one negative, the other positive.

The first is *restriction* itself which is essentially a destructive phase comprising the closure of schools, proscription of teachers, and dismantling of the previous apparatus for educational administration. It is not synonymous with educational control (although it is a precondition of it) precisely because it is negative and may merely destroy the functioning of education altogether for a time. The second stage, where control is attained and a new definition of instruction is imposed, involves the *replacement* of new educational facilities. For this to occur not only requires access to legislative machinery, but also the political capacity to mobilize sufficient resources.

In France, the Revolution in itself gave the Third Estate legislative control through which to devalue the dominant group's monopoly, but it did not enable them to proceed with replacement. The bourgeoisie was now politically powerful but still dependent on the support of the people in education, as in politics, and this severely constrained replacement. Not only did it invoke the problem of defining a common denominator of reform, acceptable to all sections of the Third Estate, which none of the three revolutionary assemblies succeeded in producing; the more serious constraint consisted in the fact that popular support was incompatible with the high levels of taxation which successful replacement implied. A revolution which had been waged against the tax burden could not risk imposing new levies as one of the earliest actions of government.

The case of England is very different, for pluralistic assertive groups working on a substitutive basis led to the development of separate and alternative educational networks outside the control of the dominant group. Middle-class substitution had begun early in the nineteenth century. Its immediate effect was to stimulate Anglican efforts to retain control, and the National Society was the organization designed for this defense. The assertive group counter-attacked with the foundation of a parallel organization, the British and Foreign School Society, geared to undenominational instruction. A combination of factors reinforced this partitioning of the elementary field among the competing parties. Distrust of state intervention on the part of Anglicans and Dissenters alike, coupled with Tory unwillingness to employ it and Whig commitment to educational expansion, represented a parallelogram of forces whose outcome was the voluntary system— where schools were financed through the two rival societies. In effect, control of the elementary level was left (and this was itself a product of substitutive conflict) to be determined by competition on the educational market. The factors which had produced the voluntary system (and the religious difficulty was only partly responsible) ultimately had the effect of entrenching it. The wealth of the middle class allowed it to make considerable progress in founding schools and recruiting teachers, though greater damage would have been inflicted on the Anglicans had the iron-masters been less concerned to retain profits from child labor and had the working class not been deflected to found its own network. Simultaneously, Anglican appeals enabled the church to increase its educational resources. Thus strong, differentiated, and autonomous networks of elementary schools continued to develop in parallel. The same was true at secondary level and again in higher education, where the foundation of University College, as a product of middle-class assertion, was matched by the establishment of King's College and Durham University, as Anglican institutions.

Correspondingly, educational conflict did not result in a clear-cut transfer of control to the assertive alliance, as occurred in France. Instead, deadlock developed between the parties involved. The dominant group was threatened but not eliminated: the assertive alliance evaded constraints and entered the educational market but could not monopolize it. Competition was fierce, but since neither party could fatally injure the other, their respective educational networks continued to develop in parallel.

STRUCTURAL ELABORATION: THE EMERGENCE OF STATE EDUCATIONAL SYSTEMS

The educational changes resulting from the social interaction just discussed condition future interaction and further educational change. The aim here is to link a specific mechanism of change (the interaction of educationally dominant and assertive groups) with its effects on the structure of education and the relations between education and society.

These links can be summarized in two propositions, which are held to be universal for nations whose educational systems developed autonomously.

(i) Competitive conflict transforms the structural relations between education and society by inducing the emergence of state educational systems which are integrated with a plurality of other social institutions.

(ii) Simultaneously, this process of interaction introduces an internal restructuring of education itself through the development of four new emergent properties: "unification," "systematization," "differentiation," and "specialization."

UNIVERSAL CHARACTERISTICS OF STRUCTURAL ELABORATION: MULTIPLE INTEGRATION AND STATE SYSTEMS

The competitive conflict responsible for education losing its mono-integrated status also accounts for linking instruction to the central decision-making agency

of a society and to other parts of the social structure. Although both changes
are the universal products of a competitive process of interaction, this does not
mean that they follow from a uniform sequence of events. Instead, their development varies according to which of the strategies—restrictive or substitutive—
was pursued to challenge the monopoly of the educational ownership group in
any given country.

From Restrictive Strategies. We have seen that successful restrictive strategies
are two-stage affairs involving the destruction of private ownership and the
subsequent reintegration of education with other parts of society. Failure to move
from the destructive phase of restriction to the constructive stage of replacement
simply annihilates existing educational provisions. *It is in this need to replace
as well as to restrict, if a new group is to accede to educational control, that
the mechanism is found which accounts for the emergence of state educational
systems.*

To imply that replacement is a difficult task derives from the reasons which
led an assertive group to employ a restrictive strategy in the first place, namely,
that it did not have financial resources commensurate with its political power.
Thus, in France, economic wealth was concentrated outside the assertive group—
in the hands of the landed aristocracy, not the Third Estate, and the significance
of this negative predisposition toward restriction does not stop there. Because
of it, an assertive group which had waged a successful policy of restriction was
then completely unable to replace educational facilities from its own resources.

However, when the assertive group and the political elite are coterminous,
the lack of resources does not preclude replacement. For the advantage such an
assertive group possesses over any other is that it can use the central legal
machinery to organize public educational financing rather than having to provide
such facilities itself. To do this is not an easy or automatic procedure, if only
because it is an innovatory one which involves withdrawing central resources
from existing priorities and/or increasing the fiscal burden on the public. It is
one, however, that presents the trebly irresistible attraction of allowing the
assertive group to control educational output in conformity with its goals, to do
so at national level and at public expense.

However, what takes place in this situation is not merely the integration of
education to the polity, but the emergence of national state education. The
assertive group does not simply replace the old dominant group, for it cannot
subordinate education by making it dependent on resources it owns and supplies.
These are public resources, and with their mobilization for purposes of instruction, educational ownership and educational control become separated for the
first time. There was never any question of the assertive political elite being able
to appropriate public funds and thus to constitute itself as an ownership group,
for such wealth was not even centrally located. The amount which could be
diverted from the national budget was totally inadequate to the task of replacement, whose completion involved supplementing central funding by the political
mobilization of local resources.

The budget of the Napoleonic Imperial University gives the clearest picture of the importance of central mobilization compared with direct central financing. By 1811 the municipalities were charged with the upkeep of the *faculté*, *lycée*, and *collège* buildings, and the principal communes were compelled to create grants for secondary school pupils or pay a contribution into the treasury which was earmarked for this purpose. In sum, the elementary schools, *lycées*, and some *facultés* were made self-supporting, and the university treasury had only to maintain in full the central educational administration.

Thus the assertive group succeeds in bringing about replacement, not through the supplies it provides itself, but by use of its political authority to mobilize the necessary resources. It has gained educational control, not on the old basis of monopoly ownership of facilities, but by virtue of its legislative power. Control ceases to be entrepreneurial and becomes managerial, for although education remains subordinate, it is dependent upon resources owned and supplied by the state, not by a dominant group. The capacity to define instruction becomes firmly linked to political position and, what is completely novel, can be lost with the declining political fortunes of a group. Thus the emergence of national state education is the result of a group attempting to complete a restrictive strategy, but the control it gains over it is of a different and weaker kind than that previously enjoyed by dominant ownership groups.

The assertive group is now in a difficult position, for it cannot gain control (by completing replacement) without support, yet support is conditional upon a diversification of educational outputs beyond the goals designated by the polity. This is one of the two sources of multiple integration, and it is as important for authoritarian regimes as for those based on democracy. *It is, however, an unintended consequence, for the diversification of educational outputs in order to service a multiplicity of operations is the price the assertive group pays for the mobilization of resources. It is the cost of control without ownership.*

In addition, however, some of the new structural relations which develop between education and other social institutions are intended ones and stem from the assertive group itself, for by definition all political elites have a plurality of aims which impinge upon the operations of various institutional spheres. Specific changes in educational outputs will help in their attainment. Since no political elite is truly monolithic, subgroups like the military may want educational outputs rather different from those sought, for example, by heads of civil administration—and demand them at the point when replacement becomes a practical reality. Problems of elite cohesion are solved by concessions which intensify multiple integration.

Ideally, the assertive group would like to establish interdependence imperatively between education and those operations designated in its original blueprint; in practice, this is modified because of the need for support from sectional interests within the elite and for public support outside it. Thus the two sources of multiple integration, the intended and the unintended, intermingle and determine the exact nature of the structural relations which emerge.

The replacement phase in France (1805–33) gave steady priority to developing those forms of instruction from which political elites would gain most, while making shifting concessions to such sections of society whose support was needed. Given strong government but limited funds, initial replacement catered to the civil and military requirements of Napoleon's empire. For him, "to instruct is secondary, the main thing is to train and to do so according to the pattern which suits the State."[3] Resources were concentrated at the top, founding a national network of *lycées* whose *baccalauréat* gave direct entry to state employment or to *grandes écoles* retailored to meet etatist requirements: St. Cyr supplied army officers, Polytechnique furnished numerate civil servants, and École Normale stocked the highest reaches of the teaching profession. Thus ability was harnessed to state service, and a diploma elite was created among the professional bourgeoisie, giving it vested interests in educational maintenance.

Although the individual had no right to instruction if the state had no need of it, the wish, as Napoleon stated, "to use the masses for manual labour and above all . . . to obey and to die beneath the flag"[4] required a political socialization which would cost money. To provide this at state expense would have subtracted from secondary and higher provisions, but to concede to Catholic pressures for readmission to the educational field had the double advantage of securing church support for the new system while passing it the bill for elementary instruction. Thus the forms of multiple integration developed under the empire linked post-elementary outputs as closely as possible to the military, bureaucratic, and political operations of state, while the traditional interdependence between the church and elementary schooling remained basically undisturbed.

However, Catholic support proved nominal, and despite stringent state controls, the church persistently exceeded its brief and pursued autonomous religious aims: "The main goal of primary instruction was as before to instruct people in the Catholic religion."[5] Given that the church increasingly used its position to contest rather than buttress the state system, the new bourgeois government of the July Monarchy replaced this support base by one which Napoleon had completely neglected: the economic elite. The establishment of vocational schools (*primaires supérieures*), in 1833, provided the skills now sought in commerce, industry, and business administration, thus rupturing the previous integration between religion and elementary education and replacing it with a new structural relationship with the economy. And this occurred without disturbing the connections previously established between higher levels of instruction and the state, which were simply too advantageous for subsequent political elites to dispense with—there Napoleon had rightly forecast that "public education is the future and the duration of my work after me."

From Substitutive Strategies. Here the integration of education to the polity is an indirect and unintended consequence of interaction: those embarking on substitution aim to assume the position of the dominant group and to alter the part of society which education serves. Instead, the immediate effect of this type of assertion is to introduce a rudimentary form of multiple integration, while the ultimate result is the emergence of a state system, thus reversing the order in which these two features appear, compared with systems originating from restriction.

The immediate effect is produced because no assertive group enters market competition unless it seeks a very different kind of instruction from that provided by the dominant group. Consequently, the output from assertive schools is designed to serve institutional operations previously obstructed by the only form of education available. Furthermore, since there is no reason to suppose that the dominant definition of instruction will only prove a hindrance in one quarter, or that the leading assertive group can contain or accommodate all other educational grievances, there is nothing to prevent the mobilization of other assertive groups. If operational exigencies lead those from different social institutions to contemplate substitution on their own behalf, nothing but their own limited resources can stop them. But any new group engaging in market competition only does so because it is profoundly dissatisfied with the two definitions of instruction now in existence, and what it provides is something different again. Thus the Mechanics' Institutes and Halls of Science of the English working class developed a nonvocational definition of instruction, geared to popular enlightenment and serving the political advancement of a group which both Anglican and entrepreneurial schooling repudiated or repressed.

This form of multiple integration is rudimentary because, although "education" as a whole now services a plurality of social institutions for the first time, the various independent networks of establishments are completely separate from one another. There is in fact no "education as a whole" except in the sense of it being the sum of these various parts, owned by different groups, serving diverse institutional operations, and operating in isolation from one another. The networks are totally segregated in terms of roles, personnel, administration, financing, intake, examination, and, above all, definition of instruction.

Moreover, all the networks tend to grow in strength, for the crucial thing about substitutive strategies is that they are incapable of forcing the old dominant group out of the educational market however successful and attractive the new provisions prove. Competition cannot ultimately exclude the dominant group, for it cannot be deprived of the facilities it owns or the right to keep on supplying them. Here the factors originally predisposing toward adoption of a substitutive strategy have further implications. This course of action was followed by groups whose economic surplus outweighed their political influence and who generally lacked any access to the central legislative machinery (necessary for successful restriction). Such being the case, and no major redistribution of political power having occurred, the assertive group lacks the legal constraints to eliminate the dominant group entirely or to prevent others from entering the market and complicating competition.

However, the origins of multiple integration proper are found in these vigorous independent networks, each one embodying a different definition of instruction. Basically, this comes about through a process of incorporation as these segregated networks become connected together to form a system. This is not a simple additive process: the type of national education which emerges is not just the sum of these various sets of establishments. It is the product of negotiation, conciliation, concession, and coercion, all of which result in modifying the original networks—accentuating some, altering others, and partially suppressing certain institutions. Nevertheless, diversity in the emergent system stems from the incorporated networks retaining much of their early distinctiveness and continuing to supply many of the services for which they were originally established. Once again, the mechanism which produces both universal changes is nothing other than the consistent pursuit of their educational goals by the conflicting parties. To trace the emergence of change from interaction is to focus on what competition does to the groups involved and to their prospects of attaining educational control.

The situation in mid-nineteenth-century England was typical—rivalry "did not produce a surplus of schools and cheap education, as some educational 'free-traders' expected, but tended to paralyse the activities of all parties, so that schools were built that could not be maintained and children were taught for such short periods that they could benefit very little from the instruction given."[6] Increasingly, then, the independent networks were locked in conflict, and prospects of retaining or attaining educational control through further market efforts diminished accordingly.

From this situation of stalemate, pressures develop which culminate in the integration of education to the state. Each of the competitive parties seeks to break out of the deadlock and this can be done in only one of two ways: by obtaining considerable new resources or by acquiring legal constraints to use against competitors. It is obvious that the central government is the only source of the latter but less self-evident perhaps that it is also the greatest untapped supply of wealth for educational purposes.

It matters little who makes the first move toward state intervention, although the competing group with the closest link to the political elite is usually the earliest to hope for legal protection (like the Anglican church turning to its old adventitious beneficiary, the Tory Party, and receiving backing, for the voluntary system undoubtedly worked in the Anglicans' favor). Education is irresistibly dragged into the political arena, for all competing groups are threatened if one alone makes headway with central government. Thus profound educational conflict produces a strain toward state intervention as a means to advance or to protect the various networks. *The development of a state educational system does not originate from the goals of either dominant or assertive groups. It is the eventual and unintended product of all of them seeking state intervention for their own ends simultaneously.*

Because all competing groups do this simultaneously, the conflicting parties in education have to accommodate themselves to the structure of political conflict. Unless they can insert their aims prominently in the program of an influential political grouping, they have little chance of extracting governmental support and recognition. Hence a period of alliance formation follows in which political opposition (organized in parties in the case of England) meets educational competition (the independent ownership groups). Thus the Educational League was formed after the liberal majority in 1868 to "make the government go faster" and dismantle the voluntary system, still favoring the Anglican church. It was an alliance of Nonconformists, radicals, and entrepreneurs, together with the Trades Union Congress in pursuit of national unsectarian education maintained from local rates. The counterpart of the league was the defensive National Educational Union through which the established church, sponsored by the Tory Party, sought to consolidate its position by "judiciously supplementing the present denominational system of national instruction."

The alliances formed may vary in the strength of their political sponsorship, through the two-way accommodation involved. On the one hand, several educational groups might have to work through a single political party, one doing so through elective affinity, another perhaps through lack of alternative: the price of putting effective pressure on Parliament by working via the league, through the Liberal Party, was a dilution of goals for both the Nonconformists and the working class, which had to abandon their denominational and socialist definitions of instruction, respectively. On the other hand, the parties may differ in the strength of their solidarity with the educational pressure groups: the Anglican Union gained clear-cut support from the Tory Party, without substantial dilution of its educational goals, while the league was merely a pressure group within liberal politics whose effectiveness was muted by other party considerations.

These alliances transmit educational conflict from the market-place to the center of the political arena. However, political struggles over education take place in the context of establishment market positions—of flourishing and functioning networks, for which their political allies seek central financial support and legal recognition.

Political conflict itself, then, has the effect of preserving the networks, sometimes through successive parties giving financial aid and legal backing when in government to different ownership groups (thus positively strengthening them), sometimes through opposition preventing government from undermining a network through financial or legal sanctions (thus defending them negatively), and, ultimately, through the compact they thrash out on the educational question.

The settlement of 1870 reflected the balance of power between the two coalitions. It established the "dual system": rate-aided school boards could be elected where the Education Department was satisfied that a shortage existed (a major advance for assertion); voluntary denominational schools were to continue receiving government grants but not to gain rate-aid (a continuing recognition of the Anglican church, which remained the largest proprietor). The liberal cabinet had steered a course between conciliating the forty members of Parliament affiliated to the league and not alienating its Anglican members by depriving the church of the right to control what it owned. Non–decision making was of paramount significance, for the party political defense of vested interests had militated against the introduction of a single national system of education.

However, through this political process of concession, compromise, and compact the independent networks do become increasingly public: they receive public funding and in return have to yield some autonomy to accountability; they gain legal recognition but have to cede some independence to incorporation. Central agencies are developed by government to control the public financing of instruction and to ensure adherence to the rules concerning legal recognition, with the national educational system emerging as the end-product.

How this works and who it benefits reflects the balance of power between the parties. The last third of the century was dominated by conservative rule. The 1870 liberal settlement proved a formula favoring the assertive alliance: after 1875 the Anglicans complained constantly of falling subscriptions, rising costs, and competition from the school boards and succeeded in activating Tory support for their cause. By a series of legal and administrative steps utilizing the new instruments of central control—auditing of school expenditure and intensified use of the code of instruction—the unseen grip of the Treasury tightened differentially on the networks. Henceforth, conservative efforts were devoted to defending the established rights of the church at elementary level (still enrolling 64 percent in the late 1880s), by pressing the rate-aid, and to protecting Anglican entrenchment at the secondary level, by seeking to dismantle the higher grade schools.

Despite considerable opposition from the liberals, the labor movement, and the Free Churches, these were the major components of the Tory Act passed in 1902 which created a single central authority for English education and linked the networks together for the first time to form a national system. Thus the types of interaction which link education to the polity are quite different from those which characterize systems with restrictive origins. There a political elite sought financial support to develop national education; here educational entrepreneurs seek political support to consolidate their control. There educational systems developed centrifugally, by governmental initiative spreading outward; here they emerge centripetally, from peripheric innovations which converge on government. In the former, *a powerful elite founds a national educational system in order to serve its various goals; in the latter, educational networks already serving different goals become incorporated to form a national educational system*. Systems with substitutive origins are then bred out of the private competitive networks by institutionalized political conflict, their final form being shaped by the interplay between government and opposition.

Structural Elaboration within Educational Systems. There appear to be four types of internal change which are universally related to the emergence of educational systems, whichever their social origins: unification, systematization, differentiation, and specialization. The first pair are associated with the attachment of national education to the state and the second pair with its multiple integration to different social institutions.

UNIFICATION

The first universal characteristic of state systems refers to the scope and nature of educational administration. *Unification involves the incorporation or development of diverse establishments, activities, and personnel under a central, national, and specifically educational framework of administration.* In turn, this results in certain uniform controls emanating from the center and the standardization of certain educational inputs, processes, and outputs on a nationwide basis. Such unification may be partial, as some kinds of educational institutions, some forms of instruction, and some types of teachers may remain outside the central administrative framework. However, the degree of unification is not simply a function of the size of the free or private sector in education. Unification varies both in extensiveness and in the intensity of administrative control.

Not every aspect of unification mentioned in the definition has its origins in the advent of state systems: both the French Catholics and the English Anglicans could perhaps claim to have administered a national educational network, but their administrative agencies were neither linked to the political center nor were they specifically educational in character. Thus the significance of state systems for this type of internal change is that only with them are all aspects of unification found in conjunction.

As the definition makes clear, unification is equally characteristic of systems with substitutive origins, which emerge through incorporation, and of systems with restrictive roots, which develop through replacement. In the former, the development of a central authority for education is a slow and cumulative process which is not completed until incorporation has taken place. The administrative framework is gradually elaborated and dissociated from other bodies (Charity Commission, the church, Poor Law agencies, etc.) as a direct product of the networks seeking public finance and legal recognition. When systems have restrictive origins, unification is generally quicker and more dramatic. Once the restrictive phase has been accomplished, replacement immediately takes a unified form—it is centrally directed, national in scope, and controlled and orchestrated by specialized administrative agencies, which are often (as in France) new organs designed for the purpose.

Unification is not synonymous with the centralization of education, although the former is clearly a precondition of the latter. The concept of centralization denotes specific relations between the unified parts. "A centralized system is one in which one element or sub-system plays a major or dominant role in the operation of the system. We may call this the leading-part, or say that the system is centered around this part. A small change in the leading-part will then be reflected throughout the system, causing considerable change."[7] A centralized system is thus a special type of unified system, but not all unified systems are centralized; to argue otherwise is to assume that in all forms of state education the largest educational changes follow from the smallest initiatives of the political elite. On this point one can fully concur with Percy Cohen that it is simply not the case that state institutions always influence others more than the state is influenced by them. The existence of a central administrative framework does not automatically make it the leading part. Centralization is thus regarded as a variable elaborative characteristic, whereas unification is a change which is universal upon the emergence of state systems.

SYSTEMATIZATION

Accompanying unification, through which new educational boundaries are defined, are further internal changes which represent a transition from summativity to wholeness as the new systems become consolidated. Instead of national education being the sum of disparate and unrelated sets of establishments or independent networks, it now refers to a series of interconnected elements within the unified whole. *Systematization consists of the "strengthening of pre-existing relations among the parts, the development of relations among parts previously unrelated, the gradual addition of parts and relations to a system, or some combination of these changes."*[8] Two other aspects of systematization may be gradually refined in the decades following the emergence of the state system: first, a series of national examinations (or ones whose validity is nationwide) corresponding to the boundaries delineated by the administrative framework and graded in relation to the various levels; second, regular forms of teacher recruitment, training, and certification valid throughout the system and appropriate to the various levels. This progressive systematization is analytically distinct from unification, since the latter is equally compatible with summativity. Empirically, however, these two changes go hand in hand, for both appear to be universal upon the emergence of state systems.

One of the most important aspects of this change is the development of hierarchical organization, i.e., the gradual articulation of the different educational levels which may previously have been unrelated, controlled by different ownership groups, and completely uncoordinated. Hierarchical organization develops because educational goals, even if focused intently on a given level of instruction, are hampered by a lack of complementarity with inputs, processes, and outputs at other levels. The impetus toward this form of change is not provided by some abstract "strain toward efficiency," but reflects the increased coordination required if a multiplicity of educational goals are to be attained and the pressure exerted by their advocates to see that they are met.

DIFFERENTIATION

In the antecedent period, one consequence of ownership was a relatively low degree of differentiation between education and the institution whose elite subordinated it—low in terms of the definition of instruction itself (usually confounded with the operations of the subordinator, education, for example, being considered as the formation of the Christian); in terms of the educational role structure (often completely overlapping that of its subordinator and illustrated most clearly by the religious teaching orders); and, finally, of course, in terms of its administrative framework. *Multiple integration*, on the other hand, *is associated with the development of a specialized educational collectivity, occupying a distinctively educational role structure and transmitting definitions of instruction which are not coterminous with the knowledge or beliefs of any single social institution.*

For the pursuit of diverse educational goals and the effective pressure of a plurality of groups together prevent the new educational system from being organized at the same low level of differentiation. Quite simply, a form of education which remained confounded with, for example, religious practices and personnel would hardly satisfy military or civil training requirements. If education is to service several operations simultaneously, it can do so only if it stands somewhat apart from all, for proximity to one will be prejudicial to the others.

Where restriction is concerned, the very plurality of political goals vis-à-vis education is itself a reason for educational differentiation, for these preclude the uniform and unifunctional type of education which is associated with a dominant ownership group. Certainly there may be sections of the elite which preferred a low level of differentiation, with an intermingling of political and educational roles and activities, such that trained teachers represented loyal cadres and political ideology dictated the definition of instruction. However, the multiplicity of services sought from education by the various sections of society meant that the pressures they exerted did engender and sustain a higher overall degree of differentiation than was the case in the antecedent period.

The same factors are responsible in systems with substitutive origins, although they operate in a very different way. The political negotiations surrounding the incorporation of the independent networks fundamentally preclude a low differentiation of education. Since each assertive group works through its political alliance to defend the distinctiveness of its network while gaining state support, their interaction necessarily has the effect of opposing a tight relationship between education and one institution alone. Indeed, incorporation could not be negotiated were this the case, for all networks but one would have everything to lose and nothing to gain. Instead, the terms negotiated are essentially ones which deny any assertive group exclusive powers to define instruction, supply its personnel, or control administration. Thereafter, the conjunction of these different interests means that each acts as a watchdog to prevent the reestablishment of exclusive links between education and another party.

SPECIALIZATION

The concept of specialization refers to a range of internal changes rather to any single one. To serve a particular demand may involve the development of new types of establishments or the pursuit of new activities in existing ones; the delineation of new roles, forms of recruitment, and training; the increased complexity of intake policies and the development of branching paths of pupil allocation, within or between levels and types of establishment; additional variety in curricula, examinations, and qualifications throughout the educational system; the development of special facilities, teaching materials, and equipment. These are further effects of multiple integration where specialization in intake, processes, and outputs develop to meet demands whose diversity is incompatible with unitary procedures.

In systems with restrictive origins, we have already seen that some diversification of educational services is the price of elite cohesion and public support. Where substitution is concerned, specialization is transmitted to the new system through incorporation of the independent networks, and the more they were incorporated intact, the greater the initial specialization of the educational system. In both cases *it is the possession of power that determines the demands which are given most specialized attention in the new system.*

These four changes take place within the same system; they may occur simultaneously or sequentially and are forms of growth which can go on indefinitely. Since each aspect of this internal elaboration derives from social interaction, the specific changes which result are not necessarily complementary. They are not synonymous with a better adaptation of the educational system to its environment or with an optimal arrangement of activities for giving maximum services to a variety of social groups. Therefore, no assumption can be made that they constitute a trend toward systemic integration—structural contradiction and social conflict do not necessarily diminish.

STRUCTURAL ELABORATION: VARIABLE CHARACTERISTICS

It appears that variations in the elaborated characteristics are closely related to the way in which the educational systems developed—by incorporation or replacement. In particular, these different social origins produce differences in the strength of the two pairs of characteristics (unification/systematization and differentiation/specialization) relative to one another. This in turn influences the relationships between these pairs and the problems of integration experienced within new educational systems.

From Restrictive Origins. Unification and systematization are the pair of characteristics to emerge first and are inextricably bound together, for there is no intervening period in which a gradual transition is made from summativity to wholeness. Once restriction is completed and replacement begins, the political elite seeks to institutionalize a new definition of instruction which is highly compatible with its requirements. Yet if it is to ensure that the new establishments and personnel provide the services needed, then it must control them closely. Hence one of the first innovations made during the replacement phase is the development of an administrative structure tailored to this task. This must simultaneously guarantee the responsiveness of educational institutions to the directions of the political elite and seek to eliminate countervailing or disruptive tendencies.

In founding the Imperial University (the name given to the new system as a whole), Napoleon could not have been more explicit than he was creating an instrument of government: "Schools should be state establishments and not establishments in the state. They depend on the state and have no resort but it; they exist by it and for it. They hold their right to exist and their very substance from it; they ought to receive from it their task and their rule." *In other words, if the aims of the political elite are to be satisfied, unification must be intense and extensive.* What is significant about such systems is that this group is in a position to design the unified administrative framework in accordance with its goals.

The central administrative agencies formed have a strong, hierarchical distribution of authority in which each lower administrative level is subject to a higher one and ultimate control is exercised at the apex by a political officer. In turn, this means a very low degree of autonomy of decision making in the various regions or in individual schools. It is not uncommon for every decision concerning expenditure, appointments, examinations, curriculum, and recruitment to be referred to a higher authority. Similarly, the autonomy of educational personnel is not great, and it is common in such systems to find that teachers are civil servants and thus subject to more limiting legal statutes than other professions.

This intensive unification is exemplified in the decree of 1808 creating the framework of the Imperial University. To ensure central control, a perfect administrative pyramid was erected which subordinated regional *académies* to the authority of a *grand-maître* who in turn was directly responsible to the head of state, the emperor himself. This legislation proclaimed uniformity in instruction throughout the country and the government's right to enforce it. In consequence, all schools at the same level were to impart identical instruction, and a specific type of school organization corresponded to each level, making each qualification (*Baccalauréat, license, doctorat*) a national one. This is the origin, more than half a century later, of the remark made by the legendary minister of the Second Empire that "*à cette heure, dans telle classe, tous les élèves de l'Empire explique telle page de Virgile.*" Central controls also reached out to enmesh the teaching profession as civil servants and to ally them to the state by more than statutory bonds. To Napoleon, "*il n'y aura pas d'état politique fixe, s'il n'y a pas un corps enseignant avec des principes fixe . . . Mon but principal dans l'établissement d'un corps enseignant est d'avoir un moyen de diriger les opinions politiques et morales.*" The loyalty of the teaching profession, modeled jointly on the Jesuit corporation and the military hierarchy, was to be ensured by a judicious mixture of training, incentives, and surveillance.

Equally important is the fact that unification is very extensive. Thus the decree creating the Imperial University also attempted to give the state educational system an absolute monopoly over all instruction. State controls over private education elaborated and reinforced in 1811, thus greatly increasing the extensiveness of unification. The most important restrictions, which virtually made these establishments part of the public system, included governmental authorization before any school could be opened, subordination to *université* regulations and inability to confer their own diplomas. In addition, to prevent competition with public education, private schools were weakened financially by a per capita contribution to the *Université* paid on each pupil and academically by a requirement that all private pupils entering for the *Baccalauréat* had to present a *certificat d'études* attesting that their last two years of study had been in a public *lycée* or *collège*. Fearing above all resurgence of the Catholic church, their schools were limited to one per *Département* and prohibited altogether in towns where *lycées* existed. Initially, at elementary level, the religious orders were allowed to continue teaching but as part of a dual policy to control the church in the state and the people in society.

However, the boundaries of the state system did not, in fact, become coterminous with those of national education. Private confessional schools lost only about half their pupils after the stringent legislation of 1811 which sought to establish a state monopoly. Indeed, the old dominant group continued to demand freedom of instruction and independent status for its own establishments. Nevertheless, even if these demands met with some success—as, for example, in France after the loi Falloux in the 1850s—the private sector does not achieve much independence, as it cannot escape from the controls and common practices imposed by the unified framework. What to the state had been a partial failure in its policy for monopolizing public instruction, was a continuous and crushing blow to the autonomy of private education.

For instance, the existence of a single series of state-organized examinations limits the definitions of instruction which can be pursued within the private sector. Because of these factors, unification is more marked in systems with restrictive origins, and the private sector is less able to create exigencies for the public sector because it is more closely controlled. Quite simply it is less problematic because it is less different. At the same time, however, the fact that the private sector is unified also prevents it from functioning as a shock absorber for the state system by serving unsatisfied demands and thus channeling a potential source of conflict away from public instruction.

From the start, systematization is equally pronounced, for it develops in tandem with strong unification. Because restrictive strategies, unlike substitutive ones, present the opportunity for beginning largely from scratch, any successful political elite will avoid internal bottlenecks, contradictions, and inconsistencies by dovetailing inputs, processes, and outputs in its own interests. At first, such systematization will involve only those parts and levels to which the political elite has given priority in its replacement policy, although others are added later. Nevertheless, the principles guiding coordination are the operational requirements of the political elite.

Pressures toward further specialization and differentiation arise, as has been seen from multiple integration, which is an unavoidable consequence of the quest for resources and support during the replacement phase. Ideally, the political elite would like to construct a tightly controlled educational system with just that degree and kind of specialization needed to meet the various etatist goals. Instead, realistically, it seeks the maximum contribution and support from other parts of society in return for conceding the minimum amount of diversification.

In France, this aim was achieved by confining to the primary level those forms of specialization which were of little interest to the state. Thus, because demands for increased diversity were minimized and modified by the political elite, the concessions made to them did not reduce the high level of systematization or detract from the streamlined structure of the resulting system. Because they were introduced by government, the new specialized institutions did not escape central administsrative control and thus lower the high degree of unification. *In other words, systematization and unification remained the predominant pair of characteristics as specialization and differentiation were accommodated to them.*

Such systems may properly be termed *centralized.* They have a distinct leading part in their respective administrative frameworks, and small changes initated through them have ramifications for all the other component parts of education. Since changes in the various elements are carefully monitored by the center, their reciprocal influence is not of equivalent strength.

B. *From Substitutive Origins.* The crucial point about substitutive systems is that *unification and systematization are superimposed on the networks which are already specialized and differentiated.* What this means in practical terms is that the degree of unification brought about over the whole range of educational establishments is relatively low. In the same way, systematization is imperfect, and various discontinuities in inputs, processes, and outputs between different parts and levels witness to its incompleteness. The weakness of these two characteristics is a direct product of the interaction which leads to incorporation. It arises from defense of the independent networks in which specialization and differentiation are already entrenched.

As far as unification is concerned, each assertive group has a vested interest in retaining managerial autonomy over its network, since this alone guarantees the continued flow of those services for which the network was founded in the first place. Ultimately, pressures stemming from the assertive groups combine to ensure that unification will not be intense or extensive. The conditions under which a high degree of central administrative control could be introduced would involve the dispossession of the assertive groups and nationalization of the networks. The political balance of power prevents this as each party sponsor protects educational property rights, as first the voluntary system and then the 1870 settlement in England illustrate. The role of the state was still principally that of central paymaster, and the next quarter of a century did not fundamentally strengthen unification.

By the mid-1890s a complex administrative picture had developed from the conflict between the political sponsors. Some reduction in autonomy had been the price of state aid and recognition but not strong, rationalized administration. A patchwork of statutory instruments, financial regulations, and a chaotic array of agencies made up the central machinery for educational control. The main authority for secondary education, insofar as one existed, remained the Charity Commission, which had survived the Taunton attempt at organizational rationalization and represented an organ unresponsive to government. Then the Science and Art Department, originally merely intended to encourage study of subjects neglected by traditional curricula, invaded both technical schools and board schools in the course of awarding its grants, an intrusion resented by both. Finally, the Education Department, supposedly concerned with the allocation of payments to elementary schools, also overlapped with administration of the higher grade level and the training colleges.

What is even more important as incorporation advances is that political action continues to repulse the emergence of a strong central authority with extensive powers. This is largely an effect of the politico-educational alliances themselves. To a significant degree, party hands are tied. However much a strengthened form of central educational administration might make political good sense, there is the support of the educational interest groups to consider. The latter, as highly organized bodies for exerting party influence, constantly use it to minimize such tendencies. The crucial point here is that such pressures are being put on both or all parties simultaneously. In sum then, forceful political initiatives in favor of a strongly unified system are lacking in such countries.

Thus even the Bryce Commission (1895), which represented a liberal attempt at administrative rationalization, underlined that this was not synonymous with making "secondary education purely a matter of state concern." It accepted the existence of a large private sector which would not be highly controlled. It did not propose certification of teachers, only the keeping of a central register; it did not advocate central examination, merely the regulation and coordination of those held by the differing examining bodies already at work. Its careful insistence on guidance, not control, and on coordination, rather than nationalization, indicates the low degree of unification the liberals thought politically feasible. Yet it was to be an even lower degree which was introduced by the Tories in the next seven years. This situation simply bears no comparison with the total commitment of political elites to central unified control in systems with restrictive origins.

The 1899 Act, instituting the Board of Education, represented the weakest form of unification, since it simply brought together the Education Department, the Science and Art Department, and the Charity Commission, while guaranteeing that there would be a separate organizational method for dealing with secondary education. It was so weak that it was virtually unopposed: "A phenomenon that might legitimately, if uncharitably, be ascribed to the fact that the Bill was agreeably innocuous. It afforded such benefits as might be derived from association with a Department of State, without their being obliged to surrender any fundamental liberties they enjoyed.[9] It was unopposed precisely because it was, in the words of the chairman of the London School Board, nothing but a "miserable little piece of Departmental machinery." Nevertheless, for the first time "the existence of the central authority implied that the administration of all public instruction was essentially a unity." However, when compared with countries of restrictive origins, there is no denying that "the rise of a central authority for English education had been a slow, tortuous, makeshift, muddled, unplanned, disjointed and ignoble process."

Furthermore, the unification is not fully extensive, for important parts remain substantially outside the central administrative framework. Certain potential participants in state education simply withdraw, retaining their private status if it appears to them that their position in the unified system would be disadvantageous and if they have the resources to stay independent. This had been the strategy of the Headmasters' Conference from 1869 onward: to ensure that the public schools "should be free from any form of external guidance or control." The private sector in education develops from such cases. However, it is not the existence of a private sector per se which is the peculiar characteristic of systems with substitutive origins. It is the conjunction between incomplete and weak unification which is significant here. For it gives rise to a private sector which is the most independent in the world.

Turning to systematization, here again attempts to preserve the autonomy of the networks limited the extent to which it could develop, just as they had reduced the degree of unification which could take place. The two issues, of course, are closely related, for without strong unification it is unlikely that a high level of systematization can be maintained, and in addition, the defense of specialist activities means repulsing intrusive central control. Again (in exact parallel to the argument about unification), if prominence of individual parts is the political concern of all, then a rational relationship between them is the political concern of none.

Directly reflecting this, the degree of systematization achieved by the English 1902 Act was the lowest possible, for it said nothing about the relations between secondary education and elementary schooling. In practice, the various institutions operating at these two levels showed the greatest discontinuities between one another: they were not dovetailed in terms of pupils' ages, their curricula, or their examinations, but overlapped and contradicted each other at every point. This situation had arisen because the two major political sponsors had consistently pursued incompatible principles of hierarchical organization: the Tory Party advocating the negative principle and the Liberal Party the positive one. Neither of the political antagonists struggled for a rational relationship between all current types of institutions; their aim was to suppress, limit, or transfer their opponents' institutions and then to systematize relations between the remaining parts. It was precisely because neither party was fully successful in the preliminary ground-clearing operation that systematization could not be far-reaching. Thus the Act of 1902 was not able to adjudicate between the two principles of systematization.

Oppositional pressures had forced the inclusion of clauses making it obligatory for the Local Education Authoritys to promote postelementary education in relation to the needs of their areas. The Tory government had only managed to leave the relations between the two levels vague, not to impose its principle of complete separation. When the Liberals finally returned to office in 1905, all they could accomplish was the introduction of 25 percent of free places in secondary schools, so linking the two levels by competitive scholarships. Thus all they could do was partially to impose their principle of hierarchical organization on their opponents' institutions.

At the secondary level itself, less was eliminated and (therefore) even less was coordinated. The middle-class technical schools and extension colleges survived; they remained linked together but uncoordinated with their opposite numbers, the public schools and older universities. Hence the English system entered the twentieth century characterized by overall organizational discontinuity—with occasional links between pairs of institutions (witnessing to the partial success of their sponsors) but without any of the dovetailing devices, such as a uniform teaching body or national curricula and examinations (testifying to the intransigence of their founders).

In other words, educational systems originating from substitution retain specialization of differentiation as their dominant pair of characteristics, and these constantly create strains and problems which, in the future, are barely contained by simultaneous but weaker pressures toward unification and systematization. Such systems are frequently and properly referred to as decentralized—they indeed have no leading part.

NOTES

1. Michalina Vaughan and Margaret S. Archer, *Social Conflict and Educational Change in England and France, 1789–1848*, Cambridge, 1971, p. 134. See also F. Vial, *Trois Siècles de l'Enseignement Secondarie*, Paris, 1936, pp. 48ff.

2. F. Ponteil, *Histoire de l'Enseignement, 1780–1964*, Paris, 1966, p. 46.

3. Quoted in L. Liard, *L'Enseignement Supérieur en France, 1789–1889*, 2 vols., Paris, 1888, p. 69.

4. Napoleon quoted by J. Simon, *Réforme de l'Enseignement Populaire*, Paris, 1874.

5. A. Aulard, *Napoléon Ier et le Monopole Universitaire*, Paris, 1911, p. 242.

6. Eric E. Rich, *The Education Act, 1870*, London, 1970, p. 63.

7. A. D. Hall and R. E. Hagen, "Definition of a System," in Joseph A. Litterer (ed.), *Organizations: Systems, Control, and Adaptation*, vol. II, New York, 1969, p. 36.

8. Ibid., p. 36.

9. A. S. Bishop, *The Rise of a Central Authority for English Education*, Cambridge, 1971, p. 262.

2

_____ JOHN G. RICHARDSON

Historical Sequences and the Origins of Common Schooling in the American States

INTRODUCTION

The sociological study of educational systems encounters two modal types: single, national systems and decentralized, multiple-unit systems. The former encompasses the various national educational systems of many European societies, where a diffuse and state-controlled system subordinates local-level schooling. The latter is most clearly typified by the American states, where the balance between state and national control has historically tipped in favor of individual states and local communities. While European systems might be studied by comparing county or department levels, research largely proceeds from an acceptance of the national character of each system. In contrast, analysis of the American educational system requires explicit attention to differences across states in both the structure and the content of schooling.

The distinction just drawn does not imply the absence of decentralized educational systems among the European states. Archer (1979) contrasts the educational systems of England and Denmark as decentralized to those of France and Russia as centralized. The former originated from a strategy of *substitution* or "devaluing the dominant group's monopoly (of education) by providing a competitive supply of educational facilities" (p. 147). The resultant decentralization maintains a loose integration of the group networks that held some control over instruction prior to the assumption of state authority. The persistence of this loose integration is felt in a set of strains between education and society, because the various groups continue to evade the national authority and to interpret strains as deficiencies in the educational provisions as nationally defined (pp. 246–47). Centralized educational systems, in contrast, had their origins in *restrictive* strategies whereby the national educational structure was fashioned from coercive challenges against a political elite unable to protect its own educational monopoly. The two types of national educational systems, while structurally distinct and dissimilar in historical origins, nonetheless differ from public education in the American states. When we speak of the rise of public education in the United States, we can find strategies of substitution and restriction and the persistence of loose integration, yet we find unified national controls. The American educational system differs from European systems because it arises from a federation of independent states, a fact which forever must qualify the tendency to speak of a homogeneous national educational system.

This qualification makes it almost certain that the history of American education cannot be adequately understood by seeking its origins and development at either a national or local level. Yet much of the literature in educational history has been confined to one or the other level. Thus we have a number of excellent accounts of American education which portray its development as the reflection of a national experience (Cremin 1970), the transmission of national culture (Bailyn 1972), or the triumph of a definitive model of educational organization (Katz 1975; Tyack 1974). Alongside these studies are more historically specific accounts of individual states (Kaestle 1973; Kaestle and Vinovskis 1980; Katz 1968; Lazerson 1971; Schultz 1973) or local city school systems (Troen 1975). Whether a work is an interpretative account or a more detailed case study, within each we can detect attempts to unite the general and the specific. This must be so because the national experience is some amalgam of the histories of the American states, and yet each state is infused in some way with the course of national development.

The task of integrating the detail of individual states with the more general concepts of national development is the focus of this chapter. We do not suggest that literature which explores a national experience or details an individual state or locality is somehow wanting. We do claim, however, that such an approach reaches limits in what it can adequately explain, and some dilemmas of evidence and interpretation are not easily resolved by an alternative perspective on the national experience or by the addition of more case studies. The argument advanced here is that a change in what is traditionally taken as the *unit of analysis* is required. We need to think in terms of an intermediate level capturing both the course of national movement and the specificity of individual states. We propose that the significant unit for analysis of the historical origins of common schooling in the United States is the geographic region, for regions embraced the territorial and economic influences which were so crucial to the development of educational systems in the American states.

The merit of a regional analysis lies in its capacity to identify lines of convergence across states without losing the significance of regional diversity and dissimilarity. During those decades wherein state school systems were formalized, the paramount forces shaping the nation were not wielded so much by states as by the *section* and the *frontier*. In Turner's classic definitions (1932, p. 183), the former was "the outcome of the deeper-seated geographic conditions interacting with the stock which settled the region," whereas the latter represented "a moving section, a form of society determined by the reactions between the wilderness and the edge of expanding settlement." As Turner argued, sections were more important than states in shaping the underlying forces in American history. Our proposed model interprets the significance of one state upon the development of public education nationally by its membership in a group of states exerting an impact disproportionate to their number. The ability of some states to communicate their institutional forms to others is, again, traceable to a regional strength. Viewing the Northeast as a section can explain its disproportionate influence on the spread of common schooling, while viewing western states as moving sections may better explain their convergence with models of schooling communicated by northeastern reformers. In the historical study of education, a focus on regional dynamics can enhance explanation, because many of the problems of evidence can be explained as properties of regions, and many dilemmas of interpretation can be resolved at that level.

The constraint of relating the various states to the national experience was indeed one stimulus to the vigorous reawakening of American educational historiography. This scholarly renewal commenced in earnest with the assertion of "revisionist" interpretations of American common schooling. This began with an initial restatement of the origins of secondary schooling (Katz 1968) and soon broadened to encompass the social bases of educational reform (Field 1976; 1979) and the origins of public education generally (see esp. Bowles and Gintis 1976). A major insistence of revisionist scholarship was that the study of common schooling in the United States be placed within the determining context of industrial capitalism. The correlation between the spread of mass schooling and the sectoral shift from agriculture to trade and manufacturing during the late nineteenth century was seen by these scholars as the core fact to be addressed. Some revisionist work was felt to be a Kuhnian paradigm, for it defined the areas and essential objects of study and predicted the outcomes of such studies.

As in the Kuhnian outline, anomalies that conflict with a dominant paradigm may become so unavoidable that they force alternative interpretations. In sharp contrast to an industrial capitalism–common schooling thesis is the evidence that school enrollment levels at mid-nineteenth century were often higher in predominantly rural states than in urban, industrial ones (Fishlow 1966a, p. 427; Solmon 1970, p. 68; Soltow and Stevens 1977, pp. 232–34; Richardson 1980). In the absence of constraints imposed by an industrial economy or by state compulsion, voluntary attendance at common schools was an established feature of nineteenth-century rural communities.

In addition, reading national as well as state-level literature reveals a convergence in the model of school organization emerging during the decades of the late nineteenth century. Despite differences among specific studies and between theoretical perspectives, there is a consensus that a model of school organization that was national in scope and bureaucratic in form was in place by 1880. In conflict with this is evidence of regional differences in school governance, revealing three distinct models in the pattern of election or appointment of school officers (Richardson 1984a). The model of state-level appointment and local-level election characterized northeastern states and is reasonably defined as bureaucratic. Yet the southern model was the reverse, with state officers elected and local levels appointed. Both levels were elective across midwestern states. The divergence of southern and midwestern states from the bureaucratic model of the Northeast sufficiently jeopardizes the claim that there was a single, national model of school governance.

It is pertinent to our argument that much of the evidence that weakens the capitalism–mass education thesis, as well as any claim of a single, national model of school governance, is taken from regions outside the Northeast. Nonetheless, the determinants of school systems within these regions have either been assumed to mirror those shaping the East or have not been independently explored to any depth. Much of the force behind revisionist accounts of school organization can be explained by the observation that supporting evidence is largely drawn from dominant northeastern states that experienced immigrant and native-born conflicts within industrializing urban centers. Although southern states are often distinguished as recognizably different, the Midwest and the Farwest are more often presumed to be homogeneous with the Northwest with regard to the determinants of schooling and school systems.

In what follows, we distinguish between schooling and school systems, and the relation between the two remains a central point which guides the subsequent discussion. The two are distinguished with purpose. Schooling represents the antecedents or alternatives to the systematization of instruction. These antecedents are linked historically to entrepreneurial activities or private controls. School systems represent the systematization of schooling, marked by the removal or decline of entrepreneurial or private controls. A noticeable tendency in histories of education is to confound the two, to speak of schooling when the variables are institutional or strictly political, or to speak of school systems when the focus is voluntary attendance or private instruction. By distinguishing the two we distinguish the historical evidence and explicate the patterns of difference and similarity across regions. We then use the relation of schooling to school systems to identify a historical sequence in the transitions of schooling, discernible as a national course of direction. Once the sequence of schooling is identified for the national level, we then examine how regions conform to or diverge from that sequence. While similar strategies have posed models of schooling which were competitive for national dominance at the close of the nineteenth century (e.g., Katz 1971), our approach departs from them by explicitly analyzing how this sequence of transitions was interwoven into and forged by regional contexts.

Rural America, Protestant Denominationalism, and Voluntary Schooling

Distinguished from formally organized and state-financed education, schooling encompasses the mode of instruction or cultural transmission and, more narrowly, the level of voluntary attendance at schools. The achievement of relatively high levels of school attendance, beginning with colonial settlement, has been a marker of American exceptionalism, the reshaping of European traditions by the constraints of emigration.

Cremin (1970, p. 16) defines early American schooling as "a kind of Christian paideia" which provided colonists with as much instrumental as moral knowledge critical to successful colonization. This Christian paideia was not simply Puritan culture transplanted to New World soil, but an educational ideal and community practice elaborated through the adaptations of successive generations of immigrants. It was a paideia "institutionalized in Massachusetts," not as formal expectation or political mandate, but as embodiment of community life and transmission of a unified culture. This transmission of culture is most succinctly articulated by Bailyn (1972) as the enterprise of community indoctrination and persuasion. As such, it was a community property implying an unproblematic vision of group continuity, a continuity founded on the capacity of families to teach a formal curriculum. Thus the history of education yields a powerful insight into the transformation of American culture itself. The gradual systematization of schooling portrays the historical weakening of family, church, and community holds over cultural transmission. It marks the independence of education from such moorings, and it recognized education as a deliberate and "willed" enterprise.

These cogent and detailed arguments go well beyond narrative history. They provide wellsprings for more sociological models of educational change and the origins of school systems. The Cremin-Bailyn thesis on early American education extends to the nineteenth century and is at the root of much subsequent literature addressing the evidence on levels of school attendance.

A parallel between nineteenth-century Protestantism and this early Puritan paideia is best formulated by Smith (1967). The persistent dilemma of Protestantism was always twofold: to advance a general education as a foundation to a developing Republic, yet to ensure that religious training infuse that education. The search for a religious synthesis to bind the diverse Protestant denominations contributed, as Smith asserts (p. 679), "to the movements which gave rise to the nation's system of public education." The synthesis was forged during the late nineteenth century at the national level, infusing a Protestant heritage into an American nationality. It represented the achievement of a loyalty superior to kinship or local community.

What is noteworthy is the instrumental role attributed to Protestant denominations in the evolution of a common schooling. Rural schooling was always inseparable from its particular community, and within each a common education was conducted within the "district school." Protestant denominations were often the means by which new communities were organized and provisions set out for a common schooling. Schooling was the extension of parochial controls, yet these controls meant a common accessibility, because community and congregation were most often the same. With the development of the Republic, Protestant groups retained controls over both common and private schooling, and in so doing they "stamped upon neighborhood, states and nation an interdenominational Protestant ideology which nurtured dreams of personal and social progress'' (Smith 1967, p. 680). Private and common schooling successively overlapped, and yet Protestant denominationalism remained the catalyst in the evolution of the latter. What we are given is an outline of the transitions in schooling, a *historical sequence* from "parochial, to humanitarian to nonsectarian Protestant programs of public education" (Smith, p. 681).

This Protestant ideology of parochial control was extended across new territories as the West was settled and linked to the Northeast. Throughout the early nineteenth century, evangelical Protestantism joined the entrepreneurial ethic, placing the freedom of the individual against the prospect of a strong and intrusive state. Such a value was a mark of small-scale capitalism inhabiting and controlling new territories and markets. Critical to this was the role of the American farmer ''as the carrier of capitalist culture, involved in rational calculations in a world market eager to maintain free action in a free society'' (Meyer et al. 1979, p. 601). The common school, set among small-holding farmers, would transmit those values compatible with a republican polity and those moral virtues consonant with Protestant denominations. The effect of an evangelical Protestantism upon school enrollment lay primarily in its capacity to effect an ''awakening'' in new territories (Tyack 1966), to lend an order to new markets, and to mobilize numerous groups efficiently. This it did with success, for high levels of school attendance antedated the formalization of schooling as a system. As Meyer and his associates (1979) demonstrate, levels of school enrollment for the late nineteenth century were positively associated with evangelical Protestantism and Republican Party dominance.

The link between a rural, Protestant society and voluntary school attendance underscores the comparative weakness of economic class divisions as major determinants of early school enrollment. American society was still rural at the end of the Civil War and was nearly three decades away from closing the Farwest as its unsettled frontier. Yet this weakness should not mask the extent to which American rural society diverged from the agrarian culture typical of western Europe and was a nascent reflection of expanding urban centers. The turn away from industrial capitalism to rural culture as unique in its contribution to voluntary schooling can overstate the homogeneity of rural America. Hofstadter (1955, p. 43) captured this difference when he noted:

In a very real and profound sense, then, the United States failed to develop a distinctively rural culture. If a rural culture means an emotional and craftsmanlike dedication to the soil, a traditional and pre-capitalist outlook, a tradition-directed rather than career-directed type of character, and a village community devoted to ancestral ways and habitually given to communal action, then the prairies and plains never had one.

Hofstadter's point is a useful corrective to the presumption of a common rural culture transformed by industrialization. American rural culture was indeed exceptional, for in the period of early industrialization there was both a scarcity of labor and an availability of open lands to stimulate continuous migrations away from industrial centers. Yet at the same time these very conditions linked agricultural pursuits, shaped largely by geographic region, to specific industrial centers that provided the capital and were the receiving markets for commercial agriculture. This made for an affinity between various rural communities and the prospects which common school attendance symbolized. At the same time, urban school reformers could spread their ideas to a variety of places, for rural cultures were never fully isolated from dominant economic centers.

With the rapid growth of cities as industrial centers and with the close of the frontier by 1890, schooling became compulsory and institutional. The setting for this change was largely, but not wholly, urban.

Urban America, Cultural Diversity, and the Formation of School Systems

What is broadly understood as the origin of school systems occurred when schooling ceased to be confined within autonomous social groups and became the responsibility of the state. The formation of school systems illustrates a dominant trend of the late nineteenth century, what Coleman (1974) terms the rise of "juristic persons" empowered as corporate entities. The decades that saw the emergence of juristic persons experienced shifts in the economy that began to sharpen class divisions and to take away the flexibility that open lands gave to newly arriving immigrants. The expansion of industrial capitalism, now largely unrestrained by 1870, implicated increasing numbers of groups in urban, wage-labor economies that redefined the intent of and returns from voluntary school attendance (see Hogan 1978). The systematization of schooling was at once a response to problems of social control encountered in expanding cities and a mark of changes which were then altering the relation of groups to oc- cupational mobility.

The rise of juristic persons was not a swift change brought in by industrial capitalism. In the historical sequence, the transition from "humanitarian" school- ing to public systems of education exemplifies the persistent overlap between private and public during the nineteenth century. A diversity of humanitarian schools had proliferated from the end of the eighteenth century, providing with success and efficiency a means of education in cities. Whether "dame" schools sponsored by women in their own homes or charity schools conducted by various religious denominations, these modes of schooling extended rudimentary instruc- tion to the increasing numbers of "churchless poor" (Kaestle 1983, p. 41). Paralleling the charity schools were the privately controlled academies, which offered secondary instruction and preparation for higher education. Often in- corporated by the state yet maintained by a self-perpetuating board of trustees, these schools were able to meet a broad range of public needs. Insofar as it was successful, humanitarian schooling contained its own momentum that pressed beyond denominational boundaries and private controls.

With increasing population and industrial expansion, the inability of "paternalistic voluntarism'' (Katz 1971) to meet the public need became evident. Within this context, a centralization of supervision was particularly adaptive to the diversities of immigrant groups and to the panoply of schools vying for enrollments. Case studies of states and city school systems converge in their interpretations of a centralized bureaucracy as suited to the problems of urban poverty and cultural diversity. The precursor of the bureaucratization of urban schools and the competitor with humanitarian schooling was the Lancasterian model of instruction. As a hierarchical school organization, the Lancasterian model employed older students as monitors of larger groups of younger students. Widely successful in England, the mode of instruction was introduced into northeastern cities in 1805 by Joseph Lancaster himself. It was soon communicated as superior to charity schooling because of its demonstrated efficiency and nonsectarian instruction. By mid-nineteenth century it had become the most widely diffused and practiced model of school organization (see Ellis 1907; Kaestle 1973; Knight 1948). As a means of centralizing supervision, it could unify schools that otherwise would continue to serve private interests at great expense.

The terminus to this historical sequence is exemplified by the passage of compulsory school attendance laws. These laws signified state commitment to the financing and supervision of a common education. Enactment of these laws, coming as it did at the end of the nineteenth century, is variously interpreted as a point of culmination, as the formalization of already high enrollment levels (Landes and Solmon 1972; Fishlow, 1966a), as the perceived greater economy of state-financed education over private schooling (West 1967), or as the triumph of an "institutionalized" education (Everhart 1977). Empirical studies suggest only indirect effects of enactment on enrollment levels (Chiswisk 1969) and a limited impact on income inequality (Solmon 1970), and thus compulsory school laws may be assigned a more passive than active place in the evolution of common schooling. Yet emphasizing such evidence overlooks their political intent, as declarations of intended systems of schooling, needing only to await enrollments and personnel. In this vein, compulsory attendance laws were instruments of nation building, the means whereby citizens were incorporated into the broader Republic (Tyack 1976, p. 365; also Burgess 1976).

It is critical that compulsory school attendance not be reduced to a uniform historical event. It is the variation in timing of enactment that gives the greater insight into the processes of school system formation, for it reveals the full spectrum of the historical sequence. The fact that most northeastern states led in the passage of these laws underscores the importance of developmental changes internal to states that made enactment politically feasible and organizationally practical (Richardson 1980). Yet the parallel fact that several farwestern states and territories, underpopulated and latecomers to industrial expansion as they were, nonetheless enacted along with these northeastern leaders suggests how compulsory attendance was a means whereby traditional barriers to the formation of school systems could be overcome. It was a means, in effect, whereby progress through the historical sequence could be hastened. During those decades of the late nineteenth century, a nation was being stitched together, and a representative symbol of this was the mandate of a state-financed and state-supervised system of common schooling. Lacking that mandate, states remained dependent upon voluntary schooling and susceptible to parochial or private controls.

We have identified a historical sequence of schooling marking transitions from parochial to humanitarian to nonsectarian systems of public education. This sequence is analytically useful, for it captures broad movements of changes in the direction taken by states. The empirical substance of this sequence is given by the pattern of conformity or divergence by states. Yet this was not a random pattern, bound ultimately to the peculiarities of individual states. Rather, the pattern of conformity and divergence was defined by regions, their patterns of historical settlement and modes of interdependence. We now specifically consider how this historical sequence was woven into and forged by the settled regions and moving sections which, as Turner argued, were the most important underlying forces in American history.[1]

The Northeast and the South: The Resolution of Social Divisions

The ruling fact about the northeastern states is that they led most others in extending education as part of the common welfare and initiating legislation that ensured it as part of state responsibility. Some minimal level of schooling had been integrated into towns of New England since their inception. Providing some common schooling was an outcome of the adaptation to a harsh and menacing environment, as well as to the political origins of New England towns. The fear of native populations and the difficulty of securing supplies of food contributed to the compactness of early settlement. To reinforce this cohesion, the church assumed a central ecological position, and religion was the ideological mainstay of the settlements. The churchhouse was simultaneously the schoolhouse. This fact established an intimate tie between religion and schooling, in turn shaping the subsequent view that establishing school systems severed that tie. In early northeastern settlement, schooling was indeed parochial, yet this parochialism originated from constraints necessitating a collective conformity through both physical proximity and ideological commitment to the strictures of Puritanism.

The compactness of New England towns cannot be traced wholly to conditions of environmental adaptation. Towns did not originate fortuitously, nor did they grow organically. Rather, they were constituted as "cells" of the broader colony and underwent growth after their existence was decreed. This is a significant, if often overlooked, fact, for it emphasizes how delineation of the colonial boundary preceded its constituent elements. As original settlements expanded, antagonisms of socioeconomic divisions contributed to the formation of new towns organized around a church-school nexus.

These two features of early settlement distinguish the Northeast in a way that helps us to understand the greater speed with which humanitarian schooling was transformed into a school system in that region than in others. The compactness of early settlement and the generation of new towns around a church-school link provided the historical antecedents to the school district, the unit common throughout the Northeast by the eighteenth century. As an outgrowth of early patterns of settlement, the school district reinforced the continuation of private or parochial holds over schooling. The overlap between school district and parochial interests widened the accessibility of groups to schooling, in part because schooling remained primarily a local enterprise. Such conditions favored the consolidation of common schools around an ideology of nondenominational supervision and their subsequent integration to secondary instruction.

The ideology of nondenominational supervision did not signify the decline of Protestant influence. Indeed, the sequence of schooling from parochial to a public education is clarified within the Northeast by understanding the strategic position of Protestant groups at each point in the sequence. The political instrumentalism of Protestant denominations is best exemplified by the New York School Society. The Society began initially in 1805 to parallel the churches as a supplier of common schools to the nondenominatinal poor. Yet by 1825 it led the campaign against sectarian use of state funds and initiated a plan to forge a public system of education (Bourne 1870; Culver 1929). The struggles between the Public School Society and the Catholic hierarchy reflected the changing climate then critical to private controls over schooling and their access to public funds for education. The intent to establish a nondenominational, yet essentially voluntaristic, system of common schools mirrors the sequence of schooling because such an administration would terminate the sectarian conflicts over school enrollment while representing the Protestant ideal of a general education for a developing Republic.[2]

Unification of common schools received more approval than opposition in putting this ideal into practice (Kaestle 1973, p. 161). Yet the consensus which underlay this triumph of a nondenominational system of schooling was intertwined with the complexities of social class. For many northeastern cities, a dynamic of educational reform was the contrast in social origins between school reformers and the incoming foreign-born populations. Many who led in the formation of school systems were themselves from rural, old middle-class backgrounds for whom the "harmonious rural ideal" was a remembrance shaping pedagogic philosophies and providing a model for the strategy to consolidate urban common schools (Lazerson 1971, pp. 24–30; also Tyack 1974, p. 6). As the main architects of urban school systems, reformers from this once propertied and native-born class felt very keenly the instabilities of the new urban, industrial environment. Their own backgrounds led neither to manual nor to business occupations, but to those independent professional careers whose social and economic standing was not as yet established. To these reformers, the Lancasterian model of instruction not only was superior to the humanitarian charity schools on practical grounds, but also offered means to contrapose the rigidities and inequalities brought in by industrial capitalism. While schools might transmit values compatible with large-scale economic production and correspond in structure to the setting of workplaces (Bowles and Gintis 1976, pp. 131–41), it was a correspondence forged with little direct knowledge. Systems of common schooling might direct the course of economic change, for in addition to a certain inevitable origin to urban school systems, the ascendancy of a *public* system over private controls implied a structure wherein upward movement would be determined by criteria of merit and not inherited status. In northeastern cities, school systems implied a diffuse egalitarianism while at the same time structuring the mobility paths of immigrant groups (Smith 1969, p. 525; also Thernstrom 1969, pp. 50–51).

Whereas regional leadership in extending schooling and forming school systems marks the Northeast, southern states are commonly cited as the least responsive to the development of public education. The causes of this resistance are most often seen as being rooted in the "peculiar institution," where the combination of rural class relations and racial divisions led inexorably to the dual school systems found within most southern states. While no doubt true, this explanation can obscure such evidence that "in both 1840 and 1860 Southern expenditures per student—apart from variations in per capita income and urbanization—were significantly greater than in any other area" (Fishlow 1966b, p. 60). Moreover, for these dates there is evidence of a vitality to the southern cotton economy: the region's share of the nation's income was higher than that of the northern "frontier" (Engerman 1967). While school enrollment levels remained lower than in other regions, high expenditures demonstrate a responsiveness to education, despite the impending Civil War. The significant point, therefore, is the inability of southern states to *sustain* the antebellum support of education and to formalize school systems in some concert with other regions.

Despite the sharpness of the South's contrast to other regions, the sequence of schooling was woven into the southern social structure. From colonial settlement, most southern states had a form of humanitarian schooling in apprenticeship systems whereby poor and dependent children could be bound over to parish overseers often until the time of their marriage. The tradition of English poor-relief was the foundation of much subsequent legislation which had a public educational aspect (Knight 1916; 1922). This original tie between education and poor relief differed from New England, where the extension of education emanated from the physical and ideological cohesion of communities. The settlement in southern states was not in compact towns, but dispersed across expansive parishes or counties (Richardson 1984a). Moreover, the settlers who came to Virginia and elsewhere were not simply counterparts to those who settled New England, for they differed in the localities from which they emigrated, and they brought strikingly different values and expectations. Their values were decidedly more individualistic, and their expectations were of immediate gain from a plantation economy (Breen 1980, p. 111). In contrast to the Northeast, the extension of education was founded in community settlement but was a charge that fell upon a reluctant, powerful, and self-protective planter class. The role of this class in determining the South's transitions in schooling was evident up through the turn of the century.

In the sequence of schooling, the significnat barrier in the South lay in the transition from humanitarian to state-supported, public education because that point made most evident those class and sectional conflicts which set southern states apart. Those factors that contributed in a direct way to the rise of school systems in the Northeast had only a marginal effect in the South. Specifically, both Protestantism and cities were not as experienced in other regions. Whereas in the Northeast and West, evangelical Protestantism contributed to the high levels of voluntary school enrollment, because of slavery, "Protestantism could never be wedded to republicanism and to education as vitally in the South as in the North" (Kaestle 1983, p. 206). If an evangelical Protestantism were the bulwark of a republican ideology stamping dreams of personal and social progress upon neighborhoods and states, southern evangelical Protestantism was confiningly pessimistic, isolating the individual and blunting efforts to change the real-world conditions of class and racial division. The other worldly tenor of southern Protestantism permeated southern urbanism in that even the largest of cities remained intimately linked to rural culture. Southern cities were not industrial centers compounded by the influx of diverse peoples. Rather, for both the antebellum and the postbellum periods, the southern city retained its "orthogenetic" character, marked by the infusion of rural folkways and institutions into an urban environment (Goldfield 1981, pp. 1019–23). Southern Protestantism and urban culture were, thus, mutually reinforcing. The southern city did not break sufficiently from the dominant fact of the region, the impact of a plantation economy, and the rule of its planter class.

Against this background of regional conservatism, the transition from charity schooling to public school systems was forged. Within the southern city, however, charity schools did not assume the impracticality they did in northeastern cities because the diversity of foreign-born groups and industrial poverty were not at the base of educational reform. As with the northeastern states, educational reform was intertwined with the complexities of social class. Yet the specific form of class relations and the additional factor of race gave to southern educational reform a difference in content and direction.

As with the Northeast, those who led in the forming of public school systems were from the new middle class of independent professions. Unlike their northern counterparts, however, they faced the politically coercive planter class whose base was not urban industrialism, but landed property and tenant labor. The extension of public expenditures for common schooling was not sought through land reform, for these middle-class progressives shared a greater identity with the planter class than with those below them. In their programs for public school systems, the barriers to both educational and industrial modernization were located in enfranchised blacks and lower-class whites. The political disfranchisement of blacks met with wide consensus, and some educational reformers formulated the plans that led to the restriction of suffrage for blacks. Yet the social control of blacks was not so critical as the problems of poor whites, a group described by the leading educational reformer in North Carolina, Walter Hines Page, as "the Forgotten Man" (Page 1897). Poor whites were a broad group of illiterate, small farmers. They formed a fundamental problem of the region, and the public school systems were designed around them.

Although the architects of public school systems in the northeastern and southern states were from similar social backgrounds and were members of the weakly established new middle class, they differed significantly in the broader context of relations. The presence of a landed, planter class and its potential for antagonistic relations to poor white farmers underlay the essentially conservative intentions of southern educational reform. In his study of the continuity of planter control in North Carolina, Billings (1979, p. 20) observes that "the small professional middle class that included a number of important southern reformers allied itself with the landed upper class that sponsored industrialization and, after 1900, expanded the range of state activity, thereby exchanging the right to rule for the right to teach school." For southern educational reform, the systematization of schooling was entrapped by the politics of class and race which led inexorably to the construction of dual systems separating whites and blacks.

While the design and content of both northeastern and southern school systems were motivated by pressing needs for social control, the "universal education movement" of the South spoke more openly of the need to design a common education in the service of industrialization (Dabney 1936, pp. 156–76, 205–17). In this respect, the content of school reform differed between the Northeast and the South. The absence of a landed class in the North enlarged the flexibility of school reformers. Educational systems in the Northeast originated from substitutive strategies where school reformers were able to erect an institutional structure upon already established local instructional networks. This enabled them to link more closely the conduct of instruction to the character and occupational futures of the new middle class, evident in curricula stressing a denial or escape "from the ethos of the industrial system and its traditional asceticism" (Cohen and Lazerson 1977, p. 380). In contrast, southern educational reform originated from partial restrictive strategies, restrained by the continuity of political power based in a landed, planter class. Here educational reform was "from. above," defining the public realm by the extension of common schooling to the broad base of poor whites.

The Two Wests: Anticipatory Settlement and School Systems

If compact settlement is a key to the origin of school systems in the Northeast, such conditions cannot be found in the Midwest and Farwest regions. These regions provide a sharp contrast to conditions of the Northeast and represent a check upon tendencies to project the Northeast's conditions as underlying the origins of school systems elsewhere.

The midwestern ("Old West") and farwestern states stood apart from other regions in two significant respects. The first, characterizing the midwestern states more specifically, was the impact of planned settlement through the Ordinance of 1787. The second, typifying the Farwest, was low population density. While the latter dominated the farwestern territories, it was a feature of early midwestern states as well. Contrary to predictions from experiences of northeastern states, both characteristics *assisted* the early development of school systems, in that many states consolidated common schools, linked them to secondary instruction, and, in specific cases, mandated compulsory school attendance at the same time or earlier than some northeastern states. In important respects, both regions reversed the sequence of schooling, for many states *began* by establishing school systems in anticipation of the requisite school-age population. Whereas school systems in the Northeast "extended downward before [they] extended upward because that is where the problems lay" (Kaestle 1973, p. 173), school systems in the midwestern and farwestern states more often extended upward before they extended downward.

The concept that unites both regions and that helps to explain the early construction of school systems is *anticipatory settlement*. The concept was used to much advantage by Fishlow (1965) in his analysis of the spread of the American railroad. Specifically, the anticipation of later railroad expansion explains much of the earlier migration to the western interior and the "immediate economic pay-off in the agricultural sector" (p. 215). In a similar respect, state and territorial governments proceeded to legislate an institutional framework in anticipation of later migrations and subsequent economic growth. These procedures were often more imitative than innovative, for these regions were intimately linked to the Northeast, from which settlers brought models of political and social institutions (Meinig 1979, p. 240). Thus, along with state and local governmental structure, these states superimposed the structure of school organization and governance across their yet unpopulated lands, awaiting the migration of families and school-age population.

The Ordinance of 1787 had a direct impact on the meaning of schooling and on the organization of school systems in midewestern states. This legislation divided the lands into townships of 6 miles square which were further divided into lots that were 1 mile square, or 640 acres, and numbered 1 through 36. The sixteenth lot, or section, was mandated as reserved for schools, and the adjoining section, numbered 22, was reserved for the church. Significantly, however, the final Ordinance of 1787 amended the legislation of 1875 to abolish the section for religion. In effect, these midwestern states did not have to sever a church-school nexus; it had been severed by legislative mandate from the beginning (Richardson 1984a).

The significance of this orderly division of the public lands into townships was that it set a structural ceiling on the intrusions of entrepreneurial or private controls into the organization of schooling. A township that did not set up a school, employ a teacher, and ensure some minimal level of attendance would relinquish its share of revenue to other townships. This "involuntary contribution'' elevated township benefits over the gains of particular groups, thereby forcing parochial interests either into the *public* system of schooling or to peripheral schools removed from collective sources of support. Again, in contrast to the Northeast, the effect of township divisions was to attribute a greater collective respect to a common education, reinforcing a conception of public over private control. The transitions from parochial to humanitarian schooling were thus bypassed because the specific design of territorial divisions contributed to the early consolidation of common schools, the establishment of a public secondary level, and the integration of that public secondary level to common schools.

The absence of population was a paramount constraint upon the states of the farwestern region. Although the census of 1870 shows only California with a population above 100,000, these states nonetheless established offices of territorial and county superintendencies of education, delineated school districts, and built schoolhouses even in areas that lacked sufficient students or teachers. Moreover, of the eleven states which constitute the farwestern region, Nevada, Washington, California, and New Mexico enacted compulsory school attendance laws before 1875 and Wyoming enacted in 1876. In these instances, the formal constitution of a school system was an evident means by which a corporate existence could be declared in the absence of a sustaining population.

The state of Washington illustrates this reversed sequence of schooling most clearly. Washington became a territory in 1854 with only 3,956 inhabitants, 1,682 of whom were voters (Meany 1910, p. 159). Probably no other territory was formed with so small a population or with such aspirations. In 1870, speculators trying to attract a population base large enough for statehood tried to draw settlers into ''paper towns'' which were projected on the map (Bowden 1935, p. 7). Schoolhouses were cited as a major attraction, and in some instances, teachers were hired to teach in imaginary schoolhouses. A law designating the legislature to appoint a territorial superintendent was enacted in 1861 in order to collect the necessary census data to arrange for and distribute the ''immanent'' school fund. While school laws existed during the territorial period and were essentially the same as the ones adopted in the state constitution (Miles and Sperlin 1940, p. 154), their strength in defining a school system was contingent upon anticipated settlement. Thus the laws of 1877 created a Board of Education, required certification of teachers, provided for the consolidation of small districts, set out courses of study, and provided for graded schools. By statehood, in 1889, there were 1,044 schools, but the enrolled school population was only 14,780.

The very fact that the Farwest was linked to the Northeast through lines of migration and economic exchange meant that the character of individual states would be shaped by the particular ties to the East. Yet, beyond this, the pressing need was to affirm the boundaries of the territory or state, and central to that affirmation was the existence of a school system. Schooling under entrepreneurial or private control symbolized an inchoate, pioneer status. Much of territorial government was designed to achieve statehood; the persistence of private or entrepreneurial schooling would simply delay this. As a result, those who advanced the leadership of a territory or state were necessarily the promulgators of the system of common schooling.

Although the governmental leadership of western territories constituted a political and economic elite, the pursuit of private schooling was not a viable structural alternative. This was further strengthened by the structure of territorial politics resulting from thinly populated areas. The pattern of most farwestern states was either a single political party expressing a dominant majority with local patronage, as in Oregon, Washington, or Dakota, or a nonparty structure, characterizing Montana, Utah, Wyoming, and New Mexico (Owens 1970). In these latter states, territorial government expressed local interest groups which cut across party lines. Thus, although the interests of economic elites were upheld, they required a broad-based support. One avenue critical to this was the political affirmation of a system of common schooling. In this way, the building of school systems in many western states and territories was an effort designed to legitimize the moral standing of these regions relative to the national collectivity. This *anticipatory schooling* finds some parallel in contemporary movements by newly independent nations to expand schooling well before they possess a modernized economy or society. For both the western regions of nineteenth century America, and many contemporary new states, the institutional structure that is adopted reflects a wish to align with a broader imperative. For the American wests, it was the commitment to a new nation being stitched together; for much of the Third World, it is the institutional form defined by the larger world system (see Boli and Ramirez, Chapter 3 of this book).

The Legacy of Regions: From Private Academy to Public High School

The patterns of regional difference and similarity return us to the historical sequence with an established qualification: the transitions in schooling were neither causal nor strictly evolutionary. Among regions, the specific character and magnitude of parochial or humanitarian forms varied, as did the length of time they persisted before common schools were centralized. Moreover, it is clear that the parochial or humanitarian patterns were not preconditions to the rise of systems of common schooling, for many of the western states skipped these transitions.

The forming of school systems did not cease with the consolidation of elementary grades. Nor did the antecedents to common schooling linked historically to entrepreneurial or private interests lose their influence. Indeed, if regional differences are to have more than a narrative importance, their effects on the growth and direction of school systems is a pertinent issue. One measure of regional influence is the rise of secondary schools. The rise of the public high school was the organizational complement to the consolidation of common schools. In this respect, the relation of private secondary schools to the public high school is a particularly good measure of the historical sequence and of the legacies of regional differences forging that sequence.

The evolution of secondary instruction closely paralleled that for the common school. The historical antecedent to the public high school was the private academy, the predominant form of secondary instruction from the late eighteenth century. The academy was preceded by the grammar school, a colonial institution designed to impart a classical instruction, distinctly preparatory to higher education "intended for students who were fitting themselves for a profession or a government career" (Brown 1905, p. 553). The academy reflects the transition from humanitarian public instruction to nonsectarian public instruction, for it was a private incorporation, yet it was designed to provide a broad, public function. Moreover, the academy was, initially, as much a rural institution as an urban institution. It was constructed with elaborated design to instill a Christian education while preparing gentlemen (McLachlan 1970, pp. 19–48). It was not until this capacity of the academy was narrowed by many of the same forces which led to the consolidation of common schools that the public high school earned the exclusive designation as the source of public secondary instruction.[3]

Academies were of two kinds: those begun and maintained by a religious denomination and those of nonsectarian status. A nonsectarian status did not preclude a religious influence, but it did signify a greater interdenominational standing or a particular socioeconomic base. As forms of the private academy, both religious and nonsectarian academies were evident in many states from the beginning of the nineteenth century. Yet records of state school systems kept from 1870 show a rise in the numbers of these schools from then until 1895, when the numbers started declining steadily as academies were replaced by the public high school.

Analysis of reports of state and territorial school systems between 1880 and 1895 reveals a distinct regional pattern in the distribution of number and type of private secondary school. For the North and South, the nonsectarian school predominates over the sectarian, while the reverse pattern is found for the Midwest and Farwest. The Northeast and the South experienced sharp increases in the overall number of schools, while the rise in number of schools for the Midwest and Farwest was modest. In addition, the regions diverge sharply in the type of school which accounted for the increase. Specifically, for the northeastern and southern states, the nonsectarian school increased, while for the midwestern and farwestern states, the increase was primarily in denominational schools.[4]

The historical sequence has been conceptualized as a means to identify broad and cumulative changes in the evolution of common schooling. Measurement of the determinants of private and public secondary schools should consequently provide some evidence for the substantive differences elaborated for each region. The rise of the nonsectarian private academy in the North and the South and its only minimal presence in the Midwest and the Farwest underscore the contention that regions stood in different relations to the historical sequence. Nonsectarian status has been used as an indicator of the transition to a public system of schooling. The similarities between the North and the South provide an opportunity to explore the determinants of the number of nonsectarian schools as well as the substantive differences between the two regions. Many midwestern and farwestern states, in contrast, ought to have moved unimpeded to the public high school without having to disestablish the nonsectarian private academy. Beyond the problems of population and immediate resources, territorial settlements presented few barriers to the formation of public secondary schools. For our purposes, the formation of public high schools is a most definitve criterion of a school system insofar as high schools lent an organizational strength to the common school and symbolized the change in the relation of groups to occupational mobility.

Empirical tests of the determinants of private secondary schools in the North and the South, which we take up next, demonstrate the regional differences in the formation of public high schools.

Formation of Private and Public Secondary Schools: Some Empirical Tests

The data for the number of private and public secondary schools are taken from the Reports of the Commissioner of Education for 1880 and 1895 (Reports 1882, 1896). The measurement of the number of schools in 1880 permits the analysis of the rate of change in the generation of schools. The 1895 date measures the number of schools at the peak of their increase. The number of students attending common schools in 1880 and 1890 is included among the set of independent variables to control for the effects of population levels as a base from which schools are generated. It is important to note that this measure of school attendance is independent of the proportion of the school-age population to which a state has extended common schooling. This latter measure of school enrollment is the variable most commonly cited as marking the rise of common schooling and of defining the origins of school systems. We test the effects of this measure in the analysis of public high schools, and in so doing we test the theoretical significance commonly attributed to it.

The data for the measures of regional differences are drawn from the U.S. census for 1880 and 1890 (U.S. Bureau of Census 1883; 1896). The prior theoretical formulation of substantive differences within regions imposes a specific constraint upon any empirical test, for the influence of one or more of the determinants would be expected to be different within a given region. Thus, for the North, urbanization and the presence of foreign-born populations are discussed as the underlying determinants of the transition to school systems. They ought, then, to have contributed to the formation of nonsectarian private academies as predecessors to the public high school. For the South, cities were the extensions of a dominant plantation economy controlled by a landed planter class. While the census for the decades of the late nineteenth century provides data on the proportion of northern and southern state populations residing in urban areas, the meaning and effects of this measure upon the formation of schools would be different. Similarly, while the census provides data on the number of agricultural workers engaged as planters and farmers, the meaning and effect of this measure would differ qualitatively between the South and the North. The percentage of the population that was urban and the proportion that was foreign-born are identified as the variables of theoretical interest for the Northeast. The segment of the work force engaged as planters and farmers is tested as the variable of theoretical interest for southern states.

To test for the effects of theoretically relevant variables within the regions, a series of regression analyses are performed. What is crucial is a term that can detect whether a variable has a greater influence within a specific region than it does across other states. The term best suited to this is a *slope dummy variable*, which is created by multiplying the regional dummy variable (North/South) times the variable of theoretical interest (see Hanushek and Jackson 1977, pp. 107–108). The measure is an interaction term and is most consistent with the core theoretical idea advanced in this chapter, that the determinants of schooling and school systems had different effects within regions. For the North, the term measures the interaction of urbanization (and foreign-born) with states in that region, specifying an effect of urbanization in the North only; for the South, it measures the interaction of the percentage of planters with region, specifying an effect only among states in the South. The results of the regression analyses are presented in hierarchical form, where the base model begins with the control term of school attendance (Attend) and the regional dummy variable. From that model, the theoretically relevant measure is added, followed by the interaction term. The measure of a greater effect of urbanization in the North and of planters in the South is demonstrated by a statistically significant increase in R^2.[5]

Table 2.1 gives the results of the hierarchical tests for the North and the South. The proportion of a state's population which was foreign-born has a significant effect for 1895 but does not significantly influence the increase in the number of private secondary schools after 1880. Therefore, only the results of urbanization are reported. The table reveals that for both the North and the South, the models that contain the interaction terms increase R^2 significantly beyond that for models that contain the regional dummy variable and the variable of theoretical interest. For the North, the results indicate that the generation of nonsectarian private schools was a regional phenomenon yet was accelerated by urban growth. The conditions of northeastern cities narrowed the capacity of charity schools to remain adequate suppliers of instruction and led to the consolidation of common schools. The evidence for private schools suggests a similar dynamic. For northeastern states, nonsectarian status held a meaning that was defined less by the structure of class relations and more by the constraints of urban expansion. Within the context of northeastern cities, the combination of population growth and of cultural diversity enhanced the efforts by school reformers to define the school as the agent of a common, nonsectarian instruction.[6] This may have been spurred by perceived threats to the middle-class belief in

Table 2.1
Regional and Interactional Effects on Private Nonsectarian Schools–1895

Attend	North	Urban	South	Planter	Inter	1880	R²
.59	.26						.47
.61	.37	-.17*					.49
.59	-.18*	-.43			.78		.55
.59		-.39			.59		.55
.24	-.05*					.65	.70
.26	-.12*	.12*				.64	.70
.27	-.25*	-.31*			.57	.60	.75
.28		-.26*			.30	.59	.74
.63			.33				.51
.67			.44	-.24			.56
.64		-.25*	-.38		.78		.62
.65			-.35		.54		.61
.26			.24*			.62	.76
.29			.28*	.07*		.49	.77
.29		-.25*	-.19		.62	.59	.80
.30			-.16*		.37	.57	.80

*less than twice SE (standardized coefficients reported)

cultural homogeneity (Bidwell 1966, p. 86), yet school reform was freer to complete a transition to the public high school. For the South, however, the generation of nonsectarian secondary schools was linked more directly to its distinct set of class relations. The traditional dominance of a landed upper class was not minimized by the growth of urban areas. For this region, nonsectarian status did not so much represent a transition point in a historical sequence as it remained an educational means for the continuity of planter interests and control.[7]

Insofar as nonsectarian private schools had different sources and meaning in the North and the South, such differences would affect the transitions to the public high school. The academy provided not only the organizational model for the public high school, but its physical structure as well (Smith 1916, pp. 330–31). The relation of regions to the historical sequence offers a vantage point to measure the rise of the public high school. Although public high schools had antebellum origins, with the first begun in Massachusetts in 1821, their increase commences largely from 1880.

The regional effects on the number of public high schools for 1880 and 1895 are given in Table 2.2. What is initially found is that no region has a statistically significant effect for 1880. Yet for this early date, the direction of the coefficients indicates that the Northeast had a greater number of schools than expected by its enrollment base, while the South had the reverse. Although the Northeast led in the number of public high schools and the South had comparatively few in 1880, specific midwestern and farwestern states had by this date a greater number of schools than expected relative to their enrolled populations. The factor which these particular states had in common, independent of their regional membership, was an early enactment of compulsory school attendance. If the generation of

Table 2.2
Regional Effects on the Number of Public High Schools—1880, 1895

Year	Attend	North	South	West	Enroll	Date	R^2
1880	.62	.13*	−.16*	.04*			.52
	.62				.16*		.48
	.64				−.06*	−.39	.60
1895	.75	.05*	−.13*	.26			.83
	.75	.01*	−.03*	.27		−.14*	.83

*less than twice SE (standardized coefficients reported)

public high schools was linked to enactment of compulsory school attendance, it was so as the culmination of the historical sequence or as the anticipation of transition to a system of common schooling.

To test the effect of compulsory school attendance on the formation of public high schools, the date at which states enacted the compulsory attendance law was entered into the analysis for 1880 (Date). The proportion of the school-age population enrolled for 1880 (Enroll)) was tested also, for it is commonly proposed that public high schools arose primarily as a function of the expansion of common schooling to the age-eligible population. As shown in Table 2.2, only the date of enactment of compulsory school attendance is significant and raises R^2 by nearly 10 percent. The strength of this term reinforces the theoretically relevant effect of compulsory attendance laws. As territorial governments sought to affirm a corporate existence in anticipation of population, the generation of public high schools represented that corporateness. The failure of the proportion of a school-age population to be a predictor of the number of public high schools demonstrates that formation of these schools did not have to await a sufficient volume of a school-age population. The significance of the timing of compulsory attendance legislation lies in its theoretical interpretation, for while these laws may have formalized what was already an observed fact, they also formalized an anticipated fact. While the Northeast and Farwest are most geographically removed and distinct by age of settlement, they converged through a similarity in the timing of state-mandated school attendance at close to the same time. For the Northeast, enactment followed a century or more of population and institutional growth; for the Midwest and much of the Farwest, the framework committing resources to a state school system was superimposed in advance of both population and institutional growth. For the latter, enactment was a spur to consolidation of common schools, to the establishment of public high schools, and to the integration of the two. These defining criteria of a school system were set in place and awaited the school-age population to sustain them.

A final measure of regional effects for 1895 points to movement by regions in regard to the formation of public high schools. Relative to 1880, by 1895 the Northeast had moved to a stabilization in the ratio of high schools to enrolled school population. The South, in contrast, remained with a lower number of schools to enrolled population. The significant effect for the Midwest suggests both a regional dynamic of movement and a distinctiveness to that region as well. From 1880, the Midwest had moved to a point where the number of high schools significantly exceeded that expected from the enrollment base. The majority of midwestern states enacted compulsory school attendance laws during the 1880s, accounting in part for this evident surge in the number of schools. Yet, in addition, the region was unique in its organization of common schooling.[8] These states skipped transitions in the historical sequence, and thus this region presents a set of conditions inhibiting the intrusion of private interests into the conduct of public schooling. Such conditions depressed the number of private or parochial schools before that expected for a given population base. The parochial schools that did arise reflected a greater impenetrability of the common school system, forcing private interests to take a more separatist alternative. For this region, parochial interests arose *alongside* the establishment of nonsectarian programs of education. The township bounded the population which would be served by the public school, and the school's ecological location was maximally favorable to enrollment, affirming a greater public access and public control (White and Harvey 1876, pp. 133–34). The generation of public high schools was an extension of these conditions, a regional legacy of anticipatory enrollment in already-established schools.

CONCLUSIONS

In this chapter, a proposal is made that the study of historical origins of common schooling in the American states requires explicit attention to the role of geographic region. Accepting Turner's thesis, we argue that regions were the defining forces giving meaning to voluntary schooling and organizational shape to school systems. The substantive differences between the Northeast, the South, and the Midwest and Farwest were not simply confined to historical backgrounds; nor were they erased by the outcome of the Civil War and the unrestrained diffusion of industrial capitalism. On the contrary, the substantive differences between regions account for the alternative modes taken in the evolution of common school systems.

Examining regional differences in relation to the historical sequence reveals a fundamental contrast between two basic explanations for the origins of common school systems. The first, traditional theory, gives primary importance to the level of voluntary school enrollment. It views school systems as eventual outcomes of a sufficient volume of growth, defined by the extension of schooling to an age-eligible population. To this measure of school enrollment is attributed the broadest of meaning; often it is taken as the marker of nationhood itself. Evidence for this explanation is readily accessible, and almost any measure of national development is correlated with achieved enrollment levels within states. Yet variant cases are more than statistical deviations from this thesis. The evidence of high enrollments in predominantly rural, yet economically underdeveloped, states presents instances partly, though not sufficiently, explained by extending the thesis into the character of American rural culture. Indeed, the specifics of the variant cases provide the very means for a reconceptualization of the origins of school systems advanced in this chapter.

The second approach is alternative to the first primarily because it subordinates school enrollment as a causal factor of common school systems. It does so on both theoretical and empirical grounds. The approach gives a central place to the *timing* of a school system's formation independent of achieved enrollment levels. Specifically, enactment of compulsory attendance is seen as marking the origins of a state school system, for it signified a commitment to a common schooling which was state-centered, rationalistic, and long term (Richardson 1984b). Enactment by states and territories with small sustaining populations nonetheless alerted local communities to the state level, giving to that level the only real means to unify communities and local districts. Enactment was rationalistic because the relations among school units and personnel became defined as more formal and accountable. Enactment was long term precisely because compulsory attendance marked the state's commitment to the progressive expansion of the system. The formal declaration of a state school system initiated a momentum of its own, and its effects are demonstrated independent of a volume of school enrollment deemed necessary to sustain a system.

The exploration of a historical sequence of schooling through the analysis of regional differences suggests that the sequence is a dialectic of change with a continuing legacy within the American states. The manner in which states made the transition to common school systems provides a persisting precedent defining educational alternatives to common schooling. For southern states, private schooling is a potentially viable alternative to public education precisely because the historical origins of the latter never fully subordinated the former. The systems of common schooling in the South retain an element of impermanancy, a disposition of system illegitimacy, and thus weakness. In contrast, systems of common schooling in midwestern states resolved the question of private alternatives very early, thereby endowing public education with an organizational and ideological obduracy. Inasmuch as the strength of alternatives to common school systems was based more on their meaning than on their number, the conditions of regional historical origins to common school systems defined a trajectory of change for states. The substantive differences between regions that this chapter has explored constitute legacies that may impede or hasten that trajectory.

NOTES

1. The states which compose the northeastern, southern, midwestern, and farwestern regions are identified in earlier research (Richardson 1984a).

2. The New York School Society did not advance a pure form of voluntarism. It was notably bureaucratic in specific ways; by the time its control of schooling was relinquished, in 1841, it had laid the foundation for the centralization of common schools. This point

emphasizes that transitions in the sequence of schooling were not distinct, but overlapping. Indeed, as Culver (1929, p. 217) noted for Massachusetts: "If there were cases where sectarian instruction existed in the schools, it is certain that in a considerable portion of the community it had largely disappeared before 1837."

3. Cremin (1970, p. 505, ftn. 24) provides a conceptually useful description of the academy as a form of schooling which "confirms and symbolizes the widespread move toward general schools, essentially a movement toward intrainstitutional undifferentiation." As he suggests, the very origins of the academy were institutionally rooted in the grammar school, and thus the academy remained essentially similar to the grammar school in form. The transition to the public high school would, therefore, represent a qualitative transformation insofar as it brought in a broader public base and was internally differentiated by grade level.

4. The regional pattern may be best expressed in the mean nonsectarian and sectarian private secondary schools for the North, the South, and the Midwest. Because the Farwest had relatively few schools, their numbers are not given.

	Nonsectarian/Sectarian	
	1880	1895
North	28.7/24.4	60.2/24.1
South	16.8/12.5	42.5/21.1
Midwest	6.1/12.4	10.2/18.8

5. The measure for a statistically significant change in R^2 can be found in Bohrnstedt and Knoke (1982, p. 391).

6. The interpretation that urbanization in the Northeast provided a context more favorable to the rise of systems of common schooling than did the context within southern cities is one which may be enhanced by drawing the parallel to the argument advanced by Weber on the Occidental city (Weber 1958). In his explanation for the success of Occidental cities in developing a political autonomy separate from the countryside, and the failure of cities in the Orient to do likewise, Weber emphasized the role of *fraternization*, the formation of associations that cut across kin loyalties and class divisions and made possible the recognition of a communal "polis" (Weber 1958, pp. 96–104). In contrast, such formations were inhibited in China by the retention of clan loyalties that never permitted the break of city life from village organization. The strength of Weber's thesis lies in its demonstration of the affinity between economic or material changes and symbolic, normative influences. These normative influences were largely religious: the abstract concepts of Christianity served to break down the particular loyalties of kinship and to forge a broader constituency as an oath-bound association. The historical sequence of schooling as outlined here attributes that normative influence to Protestant denominations. In northeastern cities, those became the active instruments behind the formation of "public" institutions. The southern city of the late nineteenth and early twentieth centuries did not bear the same influences as found in Weber's Occidental city, for it did not sever the link to the countryside precisely because of the retention of planter controls in city life and organization. The role of religious or normative influences that we may cite for northeastern cities cannot be extended to the southern city insofar as

Protestantism in the South reinforced particular loyalties and thereby weakened the authority of a "common schooling."

7. These findings may be more suggestive than definitive. It is clear that the *urban* and *planter* terms tap a contrast between the midwestern and southern states. Nonetheless, these very contrasts form the core theoretical idea. While these results support those in case studies of the urban origins of common school systems, the negative sign for the urban coefficient more accurately describes the minimal number of nonsectarian schools in the Midwest along with the higher number of such schools in the predominantly rural South. Similarly, although the number of planters within southern states has an effect beyond membership in the region, the negative sign for "planters" again contains the regional difference between the Midwest and the South, with the Midwest characterized by many farmers and few nonsectarian schools. In this regard, it is important to emphasize that this analysis does not seek the most parsimonious model to explain the maximum variation in private secondary schools across states. Rather, the models tested are of primary theoretical interest. The addition of the Midwest as a dummy variable raises R^2 and eliminates the observed effects of the interaction terms. However, no theoretical knowledge is gained by doing so.

Further, it must be noted that the basis for planter control did undergo change with Reconstruction, specifically by the increased number and wealth of merchants (Wiener 1975). Nonetheless, the pertinent issue is the retention of a political and cultural influence by this "planting class" in the face of post–Civil War economic changes (see Wiener 1976, p. 256; also Anderson 1981, pp. 13–19). As Wiener notes, the persistence of this segment was a structural continuity, not necessarily maintained by the same individual planters. This fact reinvokes the "meaning" of Turner's concept of frontier as a property of geographic settlement that can explain the patterns of institutional difference between regions. While the Midwest and the South had sizable numbers of planters, the difference in conditions of settlement set structural limitations upon the exercise of political democracy. The multiplicity of immediate tasks facing settlers in the Midwest contrasts with the "limited range of opportunities" in the South, reinforcing a more collective and democratic involvement in the former, while solidifying sectional and class divisions in the latter (Elkins and McKitrick 1954, p. 567; see also Barnhart 1953, pp. 3–19). These regional differences shaped the range and means of access to occupations and in so doing impinged upon common and secondary schools. For the Midwest, the regional conditions which strengthened political democracy accelerated the transition to the public high school. The regional conditions of southern states more narrowly circumscribed the public arena, and private secondary schools remained alternatives for the continuity of planter interests and control.

8. In this analysis of regional effects on the number of public high schools for 1880 and 1895, the dummy variable for the Farwest was left out. When it is tested individually, it has a negative coefficient. This is probably because several of the states had so few public high schools because they virtually lacked the school-age population. However, inspection of individual states reveals that the internal difference among the states was the timing of enactment of compulsory school attendance. The strength of this variable captures those farwestern states that enacted early and in so doing commenced to establish public secondary schools.

Moreover, the distinctiveness of the Midwest in regard to its form of school organization is upheld by the finding that inclusion of date of enactment of compulsory attendance (Date) for 1895 does not alter the strength of the dummy variable for the Midwest (West).

In addition to these states having enacted compulsory laws during the 1880s, their distinctive township structure contributed independently to the formation of public high schools in greater numbers relative to their enrolled school population than in other regions.

REFERENCES

Anderson, James D. "Ex-Slaves and the Rise of Universal Education in the New South, 1860–1880." In *Education and the Rise of the New South*, edited by Ronald K. Goodenow and Arthur O. White. Boston: G. K. Hall and Co., 1981.

Archer, Margaret S. *Social Origins of Educational Systems*. Beverly Hills, CA: Sage Publications, 1979.

Bailyn, Bernard. *Education in the Forming of American Society*. New York: W. W. Norton, 1972.

Barnhart, John D. *Valley of Democracy: The Frontier versus the Plantation in the Ohio Valley, 1775–1818*. Bloomington: Indiana University Press, 1953.

Bidwell, Charles E. "The Moral Significance of the Common School: A Sociological Study of Local Patterns of School Control and Moral Education in Massachusetts and New York, 1837–1840." *History of Education Quarterly* 6 (Fall 1966): 50–91.

Billings, Dwight B., Jr. *Planters and the Making of the "New South."* Chapel Hill: University of North Carolina Press, 1979.

Bohrnstedt, George, and David Knoke. *Statistics for Social Data Analysis*. Itasca, IL: F. E. Peacock, 1982.

Bourne, William O. *History of the Public School Society of the City of New York*. New York: William Wood & Co., 1870.

Bowden, Angie B. *Early Schools of Washington Territory*. Seattle: Lowman & Hanford Co., 1935.

Bowles, Samuel, and Herbert Gintis. *Schooling in Capitalist America*. New York: Basic Books, 1976.

Breen, T. H. *Puritans and Adventurers: Change and Persistence in Early America*. New York: Oxford University Press, 1980.

Brown, Elmer E. "Secondary Education." Ch. 12, vol. 1. *Report of the Commissioner of Education for the Year 1903*. Washington, DC: U.S. Government Printing Office, 1905.

Burgess, Charles. "The Goddess, the School Book and Compulsion." *Harvard Educational Review* 46 (1976): 199–215.

Chiswick, Barry R. "Minimum Schooling Legislation and the Cross-Sectional Distribution of Income." *The Economic Journal* 79 (September 1969): 495–507.

Cohen, David K., and Marvin Lazerson. "Education and the Corporate Order." In *Power and Ideology in Education*, edited by Jerome Karabel and A. H. Halsey. New York: Oxford University Press, 1977.

Coleman, James. *Power and Structure in Society*. New York: W. W. Norton, 1974.

Cremin, Lawrence. *American Education: The Colonial Experience, 1607–1783*. New York: Harper & Row, 1970.

Culver, Raymond B. *Horace Mann and Religion in the Massachusetts Public Schools*. New Haven, CT: Yale University Press, 1929.

Dabney, Charles W. *Universal Education in the South*. Vol. 2. Chapel Hill: University of North Carolina Press, 1936.

Elkins, Stanley, and Eric McKitrick. "A Meaning for Turner's Frontier." *Political Science Quarterly* 69 (December 1954): 565–602.

Ellis, Charles C. *Lancasterian Schools in Philadelphia.* Ph.D. diss., University of Pennsylvania, 1907.

Engerman, Stanley L. "The Effects of Slavery upon the Southern Economy: A Review of the Recent Debate." *Explorations in Entrepreneurial History* Ser. 2, 4 (Winter 1967): 71–97.

Everhart, Robert B. "From Universalism to Usurpation: An Essay on the Antecedents to Compulsory School Attendance Legislation." *Review of Educational Research* 47 (Summer 1977): 499–530.

Field, Alexander J. "Educational Expansion in Mid-nineteenth Century Massachusetts." *Harvard Educational Review* 46 (November 1976): 521–52.

———. "Economic and Demographic Determinants of Educational Commitment: Massachusetts, 1855." *Journal of Economic History* 39 (June 1979): 430–58.

Fishlow, Albert. *American Railroads and the Transformation of the Ante-Bellum Economy.* Cambridge, MA: Harvard University Press, 1965.

———. "Levels of Nineteenth-Century Investment in Education." *Journal of Economic History* 26 (1966a): 418–36.

———. "The American Common School Revival: Fact or Fancy?" In *Industrialization in Two Systems: Essays in Honor of Alexander Gerschenkron*, edited by Henry Rosovksy. New York: John Wiley & Sons, 1966b.

Goldfield, David. R. "The Urban South: A Regional Framework." *American Historical Review* 86 (1981): 1009–34.

Hanushek, Eric A., and John E. Jackson. *Statistical Methods for Social Scientists.* New York: Academic Press, 1977.

Hofstadter, Richard. *The Age of Reform.* New York: Vintage, 1955.

Hogan, David. "Education and the Making of the Chicago Working Class, 1880–1930". *History of Education Quarterly* 18 (Fall 1978): 227–70.

Kaestle, Carl. *The Evolution of an Urban School System: New York City, 1750–1860.* Cambridge, MA: Harvard University Press, 1973.

———. *Pillars of the Republic: Common Schools and American Society, 1780–1860.* New York: Hill & Wang, 1983.

Kaestle, Carl F., and Mark A. Vinovskis. *Education and Social Change in Nineteenth Century Massachusetts.* Cambridge, MA: Harvard University Press, 1980.

Katz, Michael B. *The Irony of Early School Reform: Educational Innovation in Mid-nineteenth Century Massachusetts.* Boston: Beacon Press, 1968.

———. "From Voluntarism to Bureaucracy in American Education." *Sociology of Education* 44 (Summer 1971): 297–332.

———. *Class, Bureaucracy and Schools: The Illusion of Educational Change in America.* New York: Praeger, 1975.

Knight, Edgar W. *Public School Education in North Carolina.* Boston: Houghton Mifflin, 1916.

———. *Public Education in the South.* New York: Ginn & Co., 1922.

———. "Interest in the South in Lancasterian Methods." *North Carolina Historical Review* 25 (July 1948): 377–402.

Landes, William W., and Lewis G. Solmon. "Compulsory Schooling Legislation: An Economic Analysis of Law and Social Change in the Nineteenth Century." *Journal of Economic History* 23 (March 1972): 54–91.

Lazerson, Marvin. *Origins of the Urban School: Public Education in Massachusetts, 1870–1915*. Cambridge, MA: Harvard University Press, 1971.

McLachlan, James. *American Boarding Schools: A Historical Study*. New York: Charles Scribner's Sons, 1970.

Meany, Edmond S. *History of the State of Washington*. New York: Macmillan, 1910.

Meinig, D. W. "American Wests: Preface to a Geographical Interpretation." In *Geographic Perspectives on America's Past*, edited by David Ward. New York: Oxford University Press, 1979.

Meyer, John W., et al. "Public Education and Nation-Building in America: Enrollments and Bureaucratization in the American States, 1870–1930." *American Journal of Sociology* 85 (1979): 591–613.

Miles, Charles, and O. B. Sperlin. *Building a State, Washington, 1889–1939*. Vol. 3. Tacoma: Washington State Historical Society Publications, 1940.

Owens, Kenneth N. "Patterns and Structure in Western Territorial Politics." *Western Historical Quarterly* 1 (October 1970): 373–92.

Page, Walter Hines. "The Forgotten Man." *State Normal Magazine* 1 (1897): 74–88.

Reports of the Commissioner of Education. Washington, DC: U.S. Government Printing Office, 1882; 1896.

Richardson, John G. "Variation in Date of Enactment of Compulsory School Attendance Laws: An Empirical Inquiry." *Sociology of Education* 53 (July 1980): 153–63.

————. "Settlement Patterns and the Governing Structures of Nineteenth-Century School Systems." *American Journal of Education* (1984a): 178–206.

————. "The American States and the Age of School Systems." *American Journal of Education* 92 (1984b): 473–502.

Schultz, Stanley K. *The Culture Factory: Boston Public Schools, 1789–1860*. New York: Oxford University Press, 1973.

Smith, Frank W. *The High School: A Study of Origins and Tendencies*. New York: Sturgis & Walton, 1916.

Smith, Timothy L. "Protestant Schooling and American Nationality, 1800–1850." *Journal of American History* 53 (March 1967): 679–95.

————. "Immigrant Social Aspirations and American Education, 1880–1930." *American Quarterly* 21 (Fall 1969): 523–43.

Solmon, Lewis C. "Opportunity Costs and Models of Schooling in the Nineteenth Century." *The Southern Economic Journal* 7 (1970): 66–83.

Soltow, Lee, and Edward Stevens. "Economic Aspects of School Participation in Mid-nineteenth Century United States." *Journal of Interdisciplinary History* 8 (1977): 221–43.

Thernstrom, Stephan. *Poverty and Progress*. New York: Atheneum, 1969.

Troen, Selywn. *The Public and the Schools, Shaping the St. Louis System, 1838–1920*. Columbia: University of Missouri Press, 1975.

Turner, Frederick Jackson. *The Significance of Sections in American History*. New York: Henry Holt & Co., 1932.

Tyack, David. "The Kingdom of God and the Common School: Protestant Ministers and the Educational Awakening in the West." *Harvard Educational Review* 36 (Fall 1966): 447–69.

————. *The One Best System: A History of Urban Education*. Cambridge, MA: Harvard University Press, 1974.

————. "Ways of Seeing: An Essay on the History of Compulsory Schooling." *Harvard Educational Review* 46 (August 1976): 355–89.

U.S. Bureau of Census. "Statistics of Population of the United States." Tenth Census, vol. 1. Washington, DC: U.S. Government Printing Office, 1883.

————. "Report on Population of the United States." Eleventh Census, vol. 1, Pt. 2. Washington, DC: U.S. Government Printing Office, 1896.

Weber, Max. *The City.* New York: The Free Press, 1958.

Weiner, Jonathan M. "Planter-Merchant Conflict in Reconstruction Alabama." *Past and Present* 68 (1975): 73–94.

————. "Planter Persistence and Social Change: Alabama, 1850–1870." *Journal of Interdisciplinary History* 7 (Autumn 1976): 235–60.

West, E. G. "The Political Economy of American Public School Legislation." *The Journal of Law and Economics* 10 (1967): 101–28.

White, E. E., and T. W. Harvey. *A History of Education in the State of Ohio.* Columbus, OH: Gazette Printing House, 1876.

3

JOHN BOLI AND FRANCISCO O. RAMIREZ

World Culture and the Institutional Development of Mass Education

INTRODUCTION

Virtually all macrolevel research in comparative education has operated under the assumption that the nation-state is the fundamental unit of comparison. Regardless of the perspective—conflict theory (Bowles and Gintis 1976), status competition (Collins 1971; 1979; Bourdieu 1971), functionalism (Foster 1977; Dreeben 1968), or social control (Katz 1975; Carnoy 1974), comparative education researchers generally have accepted national units as the entities to be analyzed and compared (for some fruitful exceptions, see Collins 1977; Arnove 1980). This largely unexamined methodological practice and metatheoretical assumption has produced fairly curious results. For one thing, comparative studies typically confine their scope to no more than two or three countries (see the review in Ramirez and Meyer 1981), so that generalizations about educational development across a large number of nations can rarely be justified. This custom reflects the difficulty of understanding the detailed history and structure of the educational system of more than a very few countries. At the same time, only a few countries have been studied extensively—the major nations, including England, Germany, France, the United States, and some of the smaller European countries. The result is a field that can say a great deal about a few cases but rather little about educational development and structure in general.

Comparative education is also impaired by the unwillingness of most researchers to operate from a historical perspective. Histories of education probe the origins of school systems and educational theory, of course, but they tend to slight the more general, transnational aspects of educational development while becoming obsessed with the details of parties, legislation, and personalities (see, e.g., Archer 1979; Bowen 1981; Bantock 1980). Nonhistorical research, on the other hand, implicitly assumes that the modern situation has always existed and is a natural state of affairs. In short, it is difficult to get an overview of the development of education as a major social institution that is not severely limited in scope, mired in historical detail, or uncritically focused on the recent period (Durkheim's 1938 effort remains one of the most useful, though it is hardly comprehensive; see also Craig and Spear 1978). And little work has been done on the *sociological* aspects of educational history, that is, the characteristics of education as an institution linked to the central ideological and organizational features of changing societies. We attempt to provide such an overview in this chapter.

Our perspective rests on the following foundation. Education as a social institution is a transnational, or "world cultural," phenomenon, in precisely the same sense that science, technology, political theory, economic development, and a host of other phenomena are transnational in nature. By this we mean that what education is (its ontology), how it is organized (its structure), and why it is of value (its legitimacy) are features that evolve primarily at the level of *world* culture and the world economic system, not at the level of individual nation-states or other subunits of the overarching system. The most appropriate analogy we can offer is that of Christianity, which evolved as a transnational and, indeed, transimperial religion in conjunction with the changing political, ideological, and economic conditions of western Europe, the Middle East, and North Africa (and, eventually, the entire globe). What Christianity became was worked out not simply as a separate religion in each of a number of different countries, but as the central institution in a "civilizational network" (Cohen 1970) in which such events as the collapse of the Roman Empire, the invasions of the Germanic and Norse tribes, the development of Renaissance humanism in the twelfth and fifteenth centuries, and the rise of a system of national states strongly influenced its meaning and role in society. None of these events can be understood as being at all "national" in character. To be sure, the nature of Christian doctrine and the church (or churches) has varied greatly from country to country, especially since the Reformation, but the core phenomenon of Christianity that has meaning and important social implications in all corners of the globe can best be studied not at the level of individual nations, but as a transnational phenomenon. Education is transnational in the same sense.

Education as a World Cultural Institution

Let us explore the perspective of education as a world cultural institution more fully by explicating its components in the contemporary world.

Ontology. What is the nature of social reality that underlies mass education? The following elements are essential, though we do not pretend that this brief description is complete. First, the primary social unit is the *individual*, not the family, the village, or other collective unit. The individual exists and has meaning apart from all other considerations; without the individual, education makes no sense. A related ontological unit is the *child*, a being whose nature is different from that of adults and peculiarly suited to being educated according to various psychological and pedagogic theories. Second, organizational units called *schools* exist in which education is carried out (education having been reduced largely to formal schooling, despite the lip service given to such notions as "all life is education"). Third, within schools there are people occupying the roles of *teacher, student, principal,* and so on—roles that make the process of educating students a socially intelligible activity despite the fact that what actually goes on in schools is often quite nonsensical. Fourth, there is the organizational unit called the *state* and its institutional counterpart, the *nation.* The former is responsible for funding and operating education, while the latter provides several of the purposes of the educational system, that is, its legitimacy. Finally, we should mention the ontological status of God in this modern schema. As Berger (1967) notes, God is no longer an active force in human history; there is no clear-cut public organizational domain identified with God. Absent from the public social stage, God is able neither to interfere with nor to legitimate large-scale human activity. Though God's presence may be intensely experienced by individuals, in the modern world, God has become almost exclusively a private affair.

Without this ontology, mass education is neither conceivable (as prior to the sixteenth century) nor realizable (as prior to the nineteenth century). As we shall show, ontological change is related to both institutional and organizational change, and it is a crucial element in the development of mass education.

Structure. Mass education is organized in school systems. It is primarily for children, and it is conducted on a free, egalitarian, compulsory, and rational basis; that is to say, in practical terms, the state controls the schools. Education is thus organized as a public good, available to all and dispensed on the basis of merit, not position. It is conducted by teachers, who are themselves highly educated (schooled) and certified as competent by the state. It is largely autonomous from parents, whose participation is regulated and rendered largely ritualistic through official organs of the schools. What educational systems produce, finally, is certificates of competence (i.e., credentials; Collins 1979) that define the occupational and social potential of students.

At the national level, education is a key part of the techno-industrial enterprise and has multiple interconnections with all of the other organizational complexes of modern society. It constitutes a large segment of national economic activity, and its representative bodies (national teachers' unions, administrators' associations, ministries of education, etc.) wield a considerable political power. The health of the educational system is a continual concern of all other major organizations, and in times of crisis education it is likely to be seen as the most important structure in society (Ramirez and Boli 1982b).

Legitimation. The legitimacy of education is provided by justificatory ideologies at a number of levels. At one level, education is justified because of its practical utility. Education creates good workers; it makes people more productive contributors to the economy and enables them to meet their own financial needs adequately. Education creates good citizens; it makes people loyal members of the national polity. And education creates good persons; it enables people to develop their self-potential fully and thus leads them not only to be just, humane, and tolerant toward their fellow citizens, but also faithful, resolute, and courageous in dealing with enemies of the public good. Note that, in the modern view, education's utility no longer includes creating good Christians; despite the importance of the Reformation for the development of the modern institution of education, salvation is no longer a concern of education.[1]

The ideology supporting mass education also emphasizes certain *social* utilities. Education provides a better work force to further economic development. It creates a happier, more satisfied population, both as an end in itself and for social and political stability. It contributes to the cultural growth of society. It makes the country strong in the external world. These examples could be multiplied many-fold.

But legitimation operates at a deeper level as well. Education is legitimated through its consonance with the fundamental elements of cultural ideology. Education is a part of progress. The history of the West is one of continual uplifting of humanity, and mass education makes that uplifting a universal process. Education makes democracy possible; the key ingredient in a true democracy is an educated and informed citizenry.[2] Education is at the root of technological development, providing the scientists, engineers, and technicians necessary for technical advance. Education is a vital methodology of equality, overcoming background differences and putting every individual on an equal footing with all others. In short, education derives its legitimacy from its purported importance for reaching virtually all the goals of modern society.

This is the contemporary world cultural view of education. Our purpose in this chapter is to analyze the origins of this view at the institutional level. From this perspective, the events and agents of change in particular countries can be used as examples to show how transnational processes take distinct forms in different countries in response to both their internal conditions and their roles in the larger external world. But our overriding interest lies in showing how the larger cultural environment has shaped the ontology, structure, and legitimation of education to produce the enormous organizational endeavor that education has become in the twentieth century.

The Dialectics of Modern Western Development

We organize our discussion of the rise of mass education around four dialectical relationships of central importance in the West.[3] Two of these dialectics pertain to the sphere of institutional or ideological reality, while the other two pertain to the sphere of social organization.[4] The institutional dialectics:

1. individualism/collectivism (especially nationalism); and

2. faith/rationalism.

The organizational dialectics:

3. state organization/transnational (international) organization; and

4. economic expansion/impoverization.

The contradictory yet complementary development of these dialectical pairs led to mass education. The interplay between the opposing forces of these dialectics was made manifest primarily in the two central struggles of the modern period (up to about 1880). These consisted of the conflict between church and state, or the struggle for organizational supremacy, and the conflict between the aristocracy (usually including the monarchy) and the bourgeoisie, the struggle for estate (and later class) supremacy. Both conflicts will appear repeatedly in the discussion that follows.[5]

The four dialectical pairs cannot be discussed in isolation from one another. They are intimately connected, and we realize that our analytical scheme at times makes distinctions and separations that do violence to the historical situations we cite. For example, the rise of individualism is in fact an integral part of the expansion of economic exchange relations, not reducible to the latter, but certainly indispensable for it (Polanyi 1944). Similarly, the development of the bureaucratic state was necessarily related to the ascendancy of rationalist modes of thought and organization, though again the two are not equivalent (Anderson 1974b). We cheerfully admit that there is a certain degree of arbitrariness in our explanatory scheme, but we hope it will be justified by the light it sheds on our problem.

Individualism and Collectivism

We view the individualist/collectivist dialectic as the most important for the rise of mass education. Mass education is meaningless and in fact practically inconceivable where the primary social unit is the family, clan, village, or other group collectivity. The operation of the individualist/collectivist dialectic led to a shift in Western ontology such that small and medium-sized collectivities of this sort became socially unimportant compared with two emerging ontological units: the autonomous individual and the independent nation-state. Once the individual and the nation had taken on primary importance, theories of the usefulness and, indeed, indispensability of mass education could become both attractive and compelling.

The Rise of the Individual. The rise of individualism can be sketched as follows. An initial burst of humanism in the "first Renaissance" of the twelfth century, which Morris (1972) attributes to the social differentiation brought by economic growth and Ullmann (1966) lays at the door of the personalization of political relations under feudalism, brought an interest in persons not solely as members of groups or characters in social roles, but as unique human beings. The concept that developed at this time was a far cry from modern notions of individuals with rights and inborn capacities and potential, but the individual took on much greater social importance. It became possible to discuss the individual's inner needs and character (in modern times, personality) independent of the corporatist family and village.

A deepening of humanism in the fifteenth-century Renaissance continued this line of development, as epitomized by, for example, Shakespeare's post-Renaissance plays, in which individuals could defy their families for purely selfish reasons. Building on Thomas Aquinas's theological separation of church and state from the thirteenth century, this later humanist explosion legitimated the view that many aspects of human activity could be considered completely autonomous from divine concerns, and humanity became an object of intense study for its own sake (Ullmann 1966). Under these conditions, a growing concern for individuals apart from larger social groupings became quite normal.

At the same time, and as part of the rise of economic exchange and the commercialization of production, notions of rights vis-à-vis the monarchy appeared. Initially, these rights were corporate in nature. The twelfth and thirteenth centuries saw the nobility join together to place restrictions on the arbitrary exercise of kingly power through such mechanisms as judicial process and judgment by peers (Boli-Bennett 1981), restrictions formalized in such early documents as the Magna Carta (1215) and the Hungarian Bulle d'Or (1222). Here civil rights were at issue. Among the bourgeoisie, demands developed for more concrete social and economic rights, such as the freedom to pursue an occupation of one's choosing (in opposition to the monarchical monoploly of various activities), the right of property (to prevent arbitrary seizures), the right of movement, and so on (Ritchie 1894; Ellul 1967; Pirenne 1936). The granting of such rights usually occurred on a limited and corporate basis: the right of occupational choice would be granted to all bourgeois members of a given town or league of towns but not as a universal principle applying to all individuals nor even to all bourgeois.

For these highly concrete rights, the exercise of which was restricted by class and status considerations, to take on a universal form, it was necessary to await the Reformation and its political consequences. Dumont (1965) sees the notion of freedom of conscience that grew out of the right to religious freedom as the most fundamental of all rights and traces its development to the religious wars of the sixteenth and seventeenth centuries, in particular to the civil wars that saw the same national people divided into separate religious camps. The majority faith might well demand restriction of conscience, but the minority faith fought hard for religious tolerance.

The Reformation had other, equally crucial implications for individualism, these of a more purely ideological character. In his call for a return to the original Pauline view, Luther emphasized that salvation was a matter of each individual's *personal* relationship with God. The mediating role of the church was both unnecessary and in fact erroneous; the individual was responsible for his or her own spiritual condition, and no collective entity or organization could possibly have the sort of direct, personal relationship with God to which the faithful

Christian was called. Of special significance for the rise of mass schooling was the fact that, for Luther and most of the other Reformers, literacy was an essential requirement for the true Christian because study of the Bible was necessary in order to come to know Christ and seek to know God's will. It was for this reason that Luther and his contemporaries devoted so much of their time to translating the Bible into vernacular languages and seeing to it that their translations were published in what were, by historical standards, quite enormous editions (Bainton 1956).[6] Latin was the language of only the privileged few; the vernacular was the language of all, from the point of view of a given society.

The universalist personalism of Luther's and Calvin's thought implied that *all* individuals were to stand in a personal relationship with God. Hence the rights and responsibilities of all individuals *as individuals*, not as members of collectivities, became a legitimate moral concern. From here it was but a short step to the development of the abstract Individual as a social construct taking the place of concrete individuals; when a principle applies to all, it becomes divorced from social reality and applies to no one as a unique entity, being replaced by its idealized social construct. This step was facilitated by both the rise of the state and the relegation of God to a quite subsidiary place after Kant's demonstration that the question of God's existence could be settled only on the basis of faith, not reason (Witcutt 1958). By the time of the French Revolution, the abstract Individual had been fully formed in the Western mind and could be used as a legitimating myth for all sorts of revolutionary (and, eventually, reactionary) activity.

With the rise of the abstract Individual, a great deal of social reality had to be restructured, and much of world history since the eighteenth century (including the extension of the franchise, women's and minority group movements, and even the rise of Third World nationalism) has involved the laborious task of institutionalizing the Individual throughout the social fabric. For our purposes, the most important consequence of this process was the construction of the concept of the child as a distinct form of human with unique characteristics and the concept of childhood as a distinct part of the life cycle.

Childhood and Children as Social Constructs. While the Christian church had shown considerable concern for the welfare of children from its beginnings (Held et al. 1983), through the Middle Ages, children were socially conceived as miniature adults, having essentially the same properties as adults (Aries 1962). Once again the Reformation played a crucial role in social development: the religious struggles of the sixteenth and seventeenth centuries centered on the competition for human souls (Jolibert 1981; Sommerville 1982). As Milton was to express it in 1671, the notion that "the childhood shews the man" took hold as it was realized that children raised as Protestants were likely to remain Protestants, and the more thorough their Protestant upbringing, the less likely they would return to the fold of the Catholic church. We thus find that child-rearing manuals, sermons on children and their socialization, and concern for the moral character of children appeared much sooner and in more systematic form among the Protestant sects, especially the Puritans, than in Catholic countries (Sommerville 1982). This concern was quickly linked to education, leading to the first compulsory school attendance law in 1642 in the Puritan colony of Massachusetts (Jolibert 1981). The Catholic counter-attack implicitly accepted this new view of children despite its inconsistency with the bureaucratic and liturgical nature of the church. The spearhead of the Counter-Reformation, the Society of Jesus, wrote into its founding charter of 1540 the intention to work for the education of "children and the ignorant" (Jolibert 1981). The Jesuits went on to become the most significant single force in Western education until their expulsion from France in 1774, and their developments in pedagogy and teacher training served as a model for both Catholic and Protestant educators well into the nineteenth century. The Catholics also accepted the universalism of Protestant individualism, as was demonstrated by the founding and rapid growth of religious orders devoted to the education of girls, especially the Ursuline Sisters (founded in 1537) and the Order of Notre Dame (founded in 1628).

Another important element deriving from the Reformation, the notion of the innocence of the child, helped to stimulate the movement toward socialization theories and universal education. The Protestants were led to this view because of their insistence on the importance of a personal relationship with God for salvation. Since young children could not reasonably be expected to have developed such a relationship, it became necessary to reject the Catholic view of original sin and child depravity; otherwise, salvation would be unavailable for children who died at an eary age. The injustice inherent in this theological view led directly to an insistence on the innocence of children, thereby restoring the possibility of salvation even to unborn souls (Jolibert 1981). This line was well established by 1700 among the Neoplatonists at Cambridge and was invoked innumerable times as a motivation for universal education independent of state action, especially among such moralistic sects as the Puritans of England and the American colonies and the Anabaptists of Germany.

The seventeenth century found social philosophers giving increasing attention to the nature and upbringing of children. What is important in the social philosophers' work is not so much the relative merits of, for example, Locke's *tabula rasa* theory as contrasted with Rousseau's insistence on the natural goodness of children, as the very fact that children became the subjects of intensive thought and analysis. There was a parallel movement to study and understand children and the socialization process as a practical, empirical matter on the part of such educational innovators as Francke of Prussia, Ratke of Holstein, and Comenius of Moravia (all Protestants), and for the first time, children became the subjects of more or less systematic investigation (Curtis and Boultwood 1977). In short, in the seventeenth century, theories of socialization and pedagogy began to arise.

Developments in the political economy of western Europe contributed greatly to this process. In the eighteenth and nineteenth centuries, two important factors were the rise of powerful national states and the development of the ideology of progress in the minds of such thinkers as Spinoza, Leibniz, and Vico (Nisbet 1980). The concept of progress provided a link between children and the society that was to come (Boli-Bennett and Meyer 1978); if children were to face a world that was different from that of their parents, it became necessary to socialize them on a wholly new basis that was not bogged down in the traditions of the past.

At the same time, as the national polity supplanted more intermediate groups as the primary collective entity in society and became a major source of individual identity, there was a growing realization that national success in the European state system depended on full utilization of the nation's resources. The days were numbered when a charismatic general or elite corps of hardened cavalry could suffice to determine the outcome of battles and wars. National success could no longer be defined solely in terms of military prowess; economic development and technical change began to have direct implications for military capabilities, and warfare was moving more and more toward the mass model that the French Revolution brought into being. This development meant that all people, and in particular all children, were potential contributors to national success, and the state that excluded a portion of its population from the normal social experiences that lead to productive economic activity and loyalty to the state did so at its own peril. Hence there was a radical shift in the legal status of bastard and abandoned children, who constituted a sizable proportion of the population in many countries (Jolibert 1981). The state began to take an active interest in these underutilized resources, and rather quickly the legal rights and status of illegitimate and parentless children were brought close to those of other children. State financing of orphanages, hospitals, and other institutions was initiated. Further, these institutions served as natural breeding grounds for the development of practical knowledge about both child development and pedagogy, pushing forward the developing theories of socialization and child psychology. Such developments occurred under private auspices as well; in some Protestant countries, such as England, private efforts in this direction far outstripped public ones.

The eighteenth century was marked by the triumph of the innocence of the child and the importance of child socialization for individual development, culminating in Rousseau's *Émile* as the most popular and widely discussed written work founded on these ideas. Child-oriented organizations arose, including the toy industry, children's medical clinics, publishing ventures devoted to literature written explicitly for children, and so on (Sommerville 1982). Underlying all this activity was the development of numerous ideologies making universal education ever more desirable. Chief among these were moralist concerns for the spiritual condition of children and the adults they would become and political concern about the apparently rising rates of criminal and antisocial activity among the poor. Once these were joined by a more positive attitude on the part of states—that children were the source of future national success in the interstate system—the soil had been fully prepared for involving masses of children in homogeneous educational systems under centralized control.

The State and Nationalist Collectivism. We can hardly hope to summarize the rise of the state and nationalism here (the best recent studies include those of Lubasz 1964; Anderson 1974a, 1974b; Tilly 1975; Poggi 1978), but several of the most important factors leading to the development of the centralized national state and the coherent national polity require discussion. As a preliminary remark, we stress that, with respect to the ontology of social reality, the major consequence of the development of the state is the reification of both the national polity and the individual through the state's nation-building efforts (Bendix 1964; Rubinson 1974; Tilly 1975). The state constructs, simultaneously, the national polity, as a larger and all-encompassing collectivity with respect to which citizens are to find their primary source of identity and their strongest sense of loyalty, and the individual, who as a citizen is freed from the bonds of village, family, regional, or other corporate identity. The important historical observation is that national polities are not simply naturally evolving entities based on clear ethnic identities, but the result of long and often bloody struggles to establish territorial integrity, political control, and cultural homogeneity.[7]

Four factors involved in the rise of the state and nationalism are of interest: the bourgeoisie, the exchange economy, the struggle with the church, and the interstate system. The first two of these are best discussed together.

First, the bourgeoisie and the exchange economy. From early times, the bourgeoisie was centrally involved in the expansion of state power and the development of effective administration (Lubasz 1964). On the one hand, the bourgeoisie offered a source of revenue for the monarchy that, unlike land and agricultural products, was both relatively expandable and highly mobile: money, initially in the form of taxes on trade and domestic manufacturing and later in the form of loans. As the exchange economy expanded, the wealth that could be siphoned off and employed for royal purposes also expanded; and because kings almost invariably expanded their ambitions faster than the commercial economy expanded, loans to the state became a regular and indispensable feature of European politics. On the other hand, the bourgeoisie became increasingly important as a supplier of educated professionals to staff and fashion the burgeoning state bureaucracies that developed from late feudal times onward (Fischer and Lundgreen 1975; Rosenberg 1958). In contrast to the aristocracy, for whom education was useful primarily as the prerequisite to enter the clerical order and was therefore necessarily religious, the bourgeoisie supported and relied upon secular education, using it as a means of upward mobility. It was thus among the educated bourgeoisie that the ideology of the value of education for both professional life and social status arose, and it was with the *embourgeoisement* of all of society after the seventeenth century that this ideology permeated the entire social fabric (cf. Ellul 1967). Because the bourgeoisie was so central to state administration, the emerging states were in effect naturally favorable to education where it was needed. For states to support universal education, the only ideological element lacking was a convincing theory as to why education was needed by all members of society.

This analysis is not meant to imply that the bourgeoisie steadfastly supported universal education. In the latter half of the nineteenth century, the central class struggle became that between the bourgeoisie and the working class (proletariat). Much recent scholarship has been devoted to showing that the bourgeois classes of that period, having gained political ascendance, fought against both the extension of the franchise and the expansion of schooling (Archer 1979; Hobsbawm 1962; Moraze 1957). The bourgeoisie sought restrictions on the size of the educational system and the creation of separate schooling tracks, with the higher-status academic track reserved for the middle classes and the lower-status vocational system reserved for the working classes. But with respect to primary education, even the vigorous efforts by the bourgeoisie to keep education a prerogative of the upper and middle classes were insufficient, for by this time the ideologies of progress, nationalism, and universalist individualism, in conjunction with the increasing autonomy of the state, had become too powerful to be overcome by the class that had been primarily responsible for their creation. It was only at the upper levels that the bourgeoisie successfully resisted mass education.

Second, the struggle between church and state. The struggle with the church (Tierney 1964) was probably the most decisive factor leading to the rise of the state. At the theological level, the triumphant return of Aristotelian thinking epitomized in Aquinas's work cleared the way for state control of secular affairs, but this ideological development was actualized only much later, after intense conflict. It was not until the Reformation that the church's grip on Europe as a whole was definitively broken. The universal church of the post-Roman era was replaced by national churches that were closely allied to their respective states, and even in several Catholic countries, the church was more national than universal, especially in France. The long struggle boosted state power both by virtue of the economic (and even military) competition that it involved and by the model bureaucracy that the church represented; for a millennium after the collapse of Rome, the church was the only extant formal organization in Europe (cf. Strayer 1970). Its administrative procedures and structure were widely copied by monarchs, particularly their control and financial aspects. The nationalization of religion in the sixteenth and seventeenth centuries also added considerable legitimacy to states, making possible the absolutist state with the king as God's appointed.

Third, the rise of the interstate system. The final factor, the emergence of an interstate system, has been analyzed by Wallerstein (1974) and his colleagues. Because Europe was composed of a multiplicity of relatively autonomous political centers, a system of intense interstate rivalry appeared. Competition led to the success and increased power of some units and the collapse and absorption of others, and it was largely on the basis of the outcomes of the wars fought along the way that the boundaries of the emerging national units were determined. As with the struggle between church and state, competition itself induced expanded state power. But another, and probably more important, consequence of interstate rivalry was the legitimation it provided for the construction of the national polity and the identification of the individual with the nation (Reisner 1922). It is often held that nationalism crystallized as a sociological phenomenon with the reign of Napoleon and the long series of wars following the French Revolution (Kohn 1962). The mass army made virtually every French person concerned about the survival of the nation, either directly as a combatant or indirectly as a producer, a soldier's relative or concerned friend, or a mourner.

The nation-building process involves the deliberate destruction of intermediate group identities and loyalties and the strengthening of the national polity composed of relatively unattached individuals. European states typically strove to eliminate local systems of weights and measures, regional dialects, multiple and overlapping jurisdictions for law enforcement and the collection of tolls, regional variations in customary law and agricultural practices, and a host of other characteristics that maintained the distinctiveness of local regions and the identity of local inhabitants (Tilly 1975; Lubasz 1964). Education became a central part of the nation-building process in the nineteenth century. As the state expanded its control of schooling, the diversity of schools, curricula, and pedagogic methods was diminished and more standard models of childhood socialization were instituted. Even though a differentiated system linked to class identity became common, the nationalist character of schooling permeated all branches of the system and an underlying uniformity replaced earlier diversity of experience.

Some intermediate forms of identity and corporate organization persisted, of course, especially ethnoreligious ones. Until the twentieth century, state action was often formulated in terms of the family, not merely individuals, so that the family remained as a corporate group with meaningful ontological status. In the present century, however, as individualism has been extended to women, children, and other formerly excluded categories, even ethnoreligious identity has lost its significance except as a symbol around which to organize in order to demand political and economic benefits. Participation in the national polity is the primary goal, and it translates into the goal of improving the status of disadvantaged groups, not as corporate entities, but as individuals. Meanwhile, the family has been transformed from a coherent unit symbolized and controlled by the patriarchal father to a composite of unique individuals whose interests and needs are often in conflict (Shorter 1975). In its extreme form, fairly typical of the social democracies in northern Europe, the family is no longer a meaningful social unit with respect to any state-regulated activity (including income tax collection or inheritance laws); the state rejects the legitimacy of all forms of ontological entity except the individual and the polity, with intermediate groups reduced essentially to the status of voluntary associations.

These developments, so crucial to the rise and expansion of mass education, render the fact that children spend most of their waking hours in state-directed educational systems a matter of course. The nation is the primary collectivity of ontological significance; the individual is the primary unit at the other end of the scale, and the individual as citizen has an obligation to participate as a willing and active member of the state-directed polity. It is through the notion of citizenship that the dialectical opposition between state-sponsored nationalist collectivism and the individualism of the autonomous person is resolved (Ramirez and Boli 1982a; see also Spring 1972).

Faith and Rationalism

Faith and rationalism constitute the second great institutional dialectic of significance for the rise of mass education. We will not attempt to summarize the history of this dialectic, but only to show its role in the development of an institutional framework within which mass education would arise. This dialectic has troubled the heart of the West throughout the Christian era with two primary forms of spiritual and political tension. One is the tension *within* the church between the Reformers of all eras who clung to one or another version of primitive, Pauline Christianity and the bureaucratized religious institution that presented a rationalized form of faith offering salvation through prescribed conduct and ritual. The other is the tension between the church, as the guardian of faith, and the secular powers (the state), as claimants to the throne of worldly activity.

The first of these tensions followed a highly cyclical course, with repeated waves of powerful reform movements that sometimes led to a revitalization of the church, as with the Franciscan and the Dominican Orders of the thirteenth century (Little 1978), and at other times ended in denunciation as heresy, as with the Arians, the Cathars, and Martin Luther. The great schism provoked by Luther centered very much on this issue: could the true path to salvation be the bureaucratic rationalism of Aquinas, or was it not instead the piety of Luther's individualistic faith? Over the long run, it was bureaucratic rationalism that prevailed as the organizational model followed by the Catholic church, while more fundamentalist and nonritualistic organization could be maintained only within the Protestant camp.

The dominance of the bureaucratic/rational model within the church was important for mass education because it served as a model for the state/citizen relationship that gradually displaced it from the center of social life. The individual parishioner's relationship to the church is that of a subordinate and loyal member subject to the authority of a powerful and often distant bureaucracy. Both body and soul are at stake; parishioner and citizen alike must yield a portion of their economic resources to the bureaucratic organization, while the parishioner seeks spiritual salvation through Christ and the citizen seeks existential release through nationalism. In short, as the state replaced the church as the dominant organization in society, a powerful legitimating ideology was taken over by the state in establishing nationalism as a secular Christianity.

Though the church's bureaucratic organization survived the Reformation, the expansion of individualism even within the Catholic sphere reveals the ideological triumph of the Reformers. The strenuous Jesuit efforts to develop a strong schooling system reflected the realization that souls—*individual* souls—had to be captured early through proper socialization. The institutionalization of this individualized approach to social control constituted another important legacy that facilitated the expansion of state power.

In those Protestant countries in which state churches replaced the Catholic church (notably, in Scandinavia), the bureaucratic rationalism of Catholicism was supplanted by a similar form of Lutheranism or Calvinism—somewhat less ritualized, to be sure, but still the model for state organization. And it was in these places that compulsory state education developed first (the first such regulation appeared in Weimar in 1619), because here the combination of the Catholic organizational model of the bureaucratic church and the Protestant emphasis on individual salvation was strongest. Where Protestantism did not take the form of a monopolistic state church, as in the United States, religious organizations did not provide such a powerful unitary model. This helps to account for the peculiarly fragmented nature of the American state and the piecemeal approach to mass education that developed there (cf. Meyer et al. 1979).

The second form of the dialectic between faith and reason involved the struggle between church and state or, more generally, the religious and the secular. The cyclical nature of this dialectic paralleled that of the struggle within the church, as the main impetus to intrachurch conflict derived from the society outside. The waves of humanist thought that helped to construct the modern individual also activated the issue of the religious *versus* the secular, with the recurrent expansion of the claims and legitimacy of secularism apart from the active intervention of the religious. From this perspective, the Reformation was the culmination of the humanism of the two Renaissances that preceded it, for the establishment of national Protestant churches signified not only the end of Catholic universalism, but also the subordination of religious organizations to the state. With the rise of the absolute monarch as God's appointed on earth, God became a less powerful figure and no longer could play an active role in the affairs of humanity.

This removal of God from earthly affairs marked a major ontological shift. With God out of the way, the Individual, as an abstract entity, could complete its ascendance to the primary place in social reality, accompanied by the nationalist collectivity as its dialectical counterpart.[8] With Kant's philosophical rationalism that made God an article of faith, and with the establishment of freedom of religion that made religious affiliation a matter of personal preference, by 1700 the faith/reason dialectic had seemingly been resolved quite neatly in favor of rationalism on earth and faith in heaven.

Such an analysis is too simple, of course. What developed in succeeding centuries was a more complementary relationship between faith and reason that found religious sentiment transformed into modernizing ideologies that helped

facilitate the rationalization of economy and society (Thomas 1979), while the
conflictual dialectic between reason and faith was supplanted by that between
the rational and the irrational. This opposition became aligned with the notions
of the public sphere and the private sphere, where the former is the realm of
rational, purposive action relating the individual to the collectivity, while the
latter is the realm of individualistic expression and freedom of choice in which
the collectivity is supposedly unimportant (cf. Schelsky 1958). The continuing
rationalization of collective social reality helped to reinforce the sanctity of
private activity and the legitimacy of irrational (i.e., faith-based or purely whim-
sical) behavior in the private sphere.

With this development, which was well underway by the end of the eighteenth
century but did not become institutionally elaborated until the twentieth, the
legitimacy of state control of the educational system becomes an unquestioned
fact of life. The schools, the army, economic organizations, the state are all part
of the public realm, where rationaliity and bureaucratic control are deemed
inevitable (Zijderveld 1970). As compensation there is the private life of hobbies,
clubs, fads, and cults, and these private activities have become the "real" life
of the individual; our avocations have become our vocations. Thomas's (1979)
ineffectual individual, what Rieff (1966) calls the "therapeutic" personality type,
reigns supreme, and the legitimacy of state-controlled mass education is not an
issue because it is part of the relatively distant, abstract public realm over which
the individual cannot exercise any control (cf. Bell 1973; Berger et al. 1973).

Nation-State Organization versus Transnational Organization

As Wallerstein (1974, 1980) has argued at great length, the development of
industrial capitalism in western Europe could not have taken place solely within
a single nation. Rather, it required a differentiated structure in which some areas
or nations played the leading role in shifting to secondary and tertiary production,
while other areas or nations supplied primary products to the developing center
and served as markets for finished products. In other words, national development
in the core was predicated on the existence of numerous relatively distinct political
units engaged in complex relationships of trade, dependence, and interdependence. Taking this view a step further, Meyer (1980) and his colleagues have
stressed the importance of the *transnational* structure that developed along with
the system of international production and exchange. The international, or world,
system is not simply a collection of nation-states engaged in exchange, but also
an overarching social system of institutional rules and structural properties. These
rules define the parameters within which nations operate and strongly influence
the behavior of nations. At the same time, the behavior of nations helps to shape
the institutional structure and push its evolution in new directions.

As with economic development, mass education could not have arisen in the
absence of an international system of this sort. At the organizational level, the
intensely competitive state system that dominated European politics by the eight-

eenth century provided a strong impetus to state efforts to make schooling universal. As we have shown elsewhere (Ramirez and Boli 1982b), for most nations, the initial commitment to mass primary education followed on the heels of a crisis of national integrity in which the status and power of the nation in the state system was in doubt. Education was seen as the route to national salvation in Prussia following the defeat by Napoleon at Jena in 1807; in Denmark following the loss of Norway to Sweden in 1809; in Britain following the Paris Exhibition in 1867, when British superiority in manufactured goods and technological achievement was seriously challenged; and so on. Without the competitive state system, the motivation to bring all citizens into close, extended, and subordinated contact with the state would have made no sense. In addition, interstate competition was largely responsible for the great increase in state power and state command of resources in the centuries leading up to the educational revolution of the 1800s, and without relatively powerful states, a mass educational system would have been a practical impossibility.[9]

The transnational aspects of the world system were of greatest importance at the institutional level. The development of Western ontology and social structure is itself largely a feature of the transnational cultural environment, and it is quite unlikely that Western individualism and nationalist collectivism could have become such powerful forces in the absence of the transnational structure. Small-scale, locally oriented economic and political units would have remained the rule, instead with their tendency to reify intermediate ontological entities rather than those at the extreme ends of the scale. Further, in the absence of transnational institutions, the compelling nature of educational ideology could not have been established, and we would not have seen the emergence of education as the *sine qua non* of nation-state organization in the twentieth century (Meyer 1977).

The dialectic between nation-state and transnational structures has seen both of these levels of social reality become immensely more powerful over the past two centuries: states have become by far the most dominant organizations in national societies, and transnational culture and ideologies have become extremely influential in determining the behavior of states. While the tension between the two levels has greatly stimulated their development, it is important to remember that at both levels the indispensability of mass schooling is highly institutionalized. Even if, in the long run, nation-state organization gives way to a world state and transnational reality triumphs over nationalism, we should not expect education to become a less central element of the ideological universe. The forms of legitimation and ontology may be altered, but the institutionalization of education has gone so far now that it is bound to persist into a new world organizational form (cf. Ericson 1982).

Economic Expansion versus Impoverization

The final dialectic of importance is that between the expansion of economic production and exchange and the increasing numbers of impoverished people in the world system. We have seen this dialectic at work throughout the history of capitalist development, from the brutal treatment of native African and American populations during the Age of Exploration to the severe exploitation of displaced peasants in nineteenth-century industrialism to the emergence of huge numbers of homeless urban villagers in most capital cities outside of Europe today. The impoverization that has accompanied economic growth has been of two kinds: an absolute impoverization, in which the poor are actually worse off than they or their immediate ancestors were (a development that has characterized the capitalist system throughout its history, especially affecting newly urbanized populations), and a relative impoverization ("relative deprivation") that is of more recent vintage. Both forms of impoverization increase with economic development. As the long line of economic-dependency research has shown, development in the core of the system relies on the underdevelopment of peripheral areas (Frank 1967; Emmanuel 1972; Amin 1974). This structural differentiation develops both within and between nations, and even in nations that have reached a high level of economic exchange, the developmental period was fraught with extraordinary impoverization of a large proportion of the population. The populations of those countries that become peripheral suppliers of raw materials and agricultural products are more or less permanently poor, locked into the exchange economy through capitalist control relations (so that a return to subsistence production is impossible) and unable to share the benefits of economic growth because of their lack of political power.

Relative impoverization is a rather new phenomenon. It arose only as Western individualist ideology, especialy the ideology of equality, became truly universal in the twentieth century. When non-European peoples were considered heathen, uncivilized, savage, and the like, from the point of view of Western ontology, they were not really human. It was impossible to speak of their rights, of an obligation on the part of the conquerors and traders to treat them fairly, humanely, as equals. Owing largely to the universalism of Christian doctrine and the triumph of nationalism and the ideology of national self-determination, by the nineteenth century, the situation began to change such that the concept of all human beings belonging as equals to a single collective entity, *humanity*, began to haunt the ontology landscape. By the end of World War II, these developments created the ideological imperative that all peoples, regardless of historical background or even their own value systems, had the right and indeed the obligation to participate equally in the modern technological economic system (whether of the capitalist or the socialist model). Poverty then became a relative, not only an absolute, matter: traditional peoples living tribal ways of life are poor, whether they think so or not, because they do not have the same high standard of consumption as people living in the capitalist or socialist core. Taken one step further, practically everyone not living the life of luxury associated with the rich can now experience feelings of poverty, and impoverization became a nearly universal phenomenon.

We have stressed the impoverization process because it is generally given less heed than its dialectical counterpart, economic development, and the importance of economic development for mass education has been widely discussed (see Archer 1979). Economic development as a historical phenomenon was important primarily through its connection with the rise of the powerful state,[10] although perhaps it was of even greater importance as a source of ideological legitimation for education through the supposed connection between education and both national economic success and individual upward mobility (i.e. "progress"). These legitimating ideas are a legacy of the bourgeoisie, whose formal training proved to be of great value for the development of effective administrative and accounting structures (hence for an active state role in economic development) and for whom education was indeed essential to individual success.

The role of impoverization in mass education was more ambiguous, at least in the early stages. One of the more powerful arguments against mass education in the eighteenth and early nineteenth centuries was the claim that educating the rude, violent, criminally inclined poor would result in revolt and a threat to the entire social order (see, e.g., Warne 1929). Only gradually did this view give way to the argument that violent revolt by the poor could be avoided through education; in England especially, this latter view was advanced quite explicitly after about 1850 (Jones 1977), and in Sweden it was a major factor in the eventual acquiescence of the clergy to a state system of schools (Isling 1980). The shift in position occurred because of the ascendance of the ideology of equality and the resulting democratization of Western nations in the nineteenth century. As individualistic citizenship became available to a large proportion of people, even the beastly poor were seen as beginning to assume the qualities of authentic personhood that made their inclusion in the modern system imperative. As Rubinson (1974) has argued, education becomes a crucial instrument of political incorporation when citizens have to be created.

In the twentieth century, impoverization has become an irresistible force in expanding mass education. True impoverization, where living standards and life chances are declining, serves as a powerful stimulus to states and other large-scale institutions to expand education under the theory that progress (economic growth) depends on a schooled labor force (for a striking example of this theory in action, see World Bank 1980). Relative impoverization, on the other hand, serves as a stimulus for individuals to seek education as a means of upward mobility. It can affect persons at any level of the social hierarchy. And both forms of impoverization lead to demands for expanded education in the name of equality, which has become one of the central purposes of the modern state. Meanwhile, any thought that impoverization cannot or should not be ameliorated through education has all but vanished from the social arena, even in countries where the rugged individual is still a major component of cultural expression.[11]

SUMMARY AND IMPLICATIONS

In Table 3.1, we present a summary of the arguments made in this chapter describing the institutional shifts that have occurred in the rise of mass systems

Table 3.1
Models of the Institutional Structure of European Society in the Fifteenth and Twentieth Centuries

Fifteenth-Century Model	Twentieth-Century Model
	Ontology
	Primary Social Units
Family/Clan	Individual
Estate	Nation
Other intermediate groups	
	Nature of God
Active in history	Removed from history
Relationship mediated by church	Relationship direct for person
Source of meaning in public affairs	Source of meaning on private basis only
	Nature of the Child
Small adult	Distinct type of person
Identity defined through family	Identity defined through personality and environment
Depraved character (original sin)	Innocent character
	Dominant Social Organization
Universalist Church	Nation-state
Specific purposes: salvation	Diffuse purposes: welfare
Duffuse responsibilities	Specific responsibilities
Normative control	Legal control
	Class Structure
Aristocracy	Ruling elite
Capitalists	Technocrats
Bourgeoisie	White-collar workers
Peasantry	Working class
	Class Struggle
Aristocracy v. bourgeoisie	Ruling elite v. working class; gradually replaced by non-class struggle (special interest politics)
	Structure of Education
	Schools
Wide variety of types	Relatively few types
Differentiation strongly linked to class structure and occupations	Differentiation limited and weakly linked to classes and occupations
Weak links among levels	Strong links among levels
	Controlling Organizations
Church	State
Local communities (towns)	Some autonomous units linked to voluntary associations
Trades and professions	
Some autonomous units (e.g., faculty controlled)	
	Social Product
Specifically trained persons:	Occupationally diffuse training certificates of competence
Clergy	
Professionals	
Artisans	
	Prominence in Society
Relatively marginal social sector	Major social sector
Highly limited clientele	Universal clientele
	Legitimation of Education
Provides servants of God	Enhances labor productivity
Creates good Christians	Creates good citizens
Creates skilled workers	Provides opportunities for self-fulfillment
Meets the needs of the monarchy	Increases national well-being, security, political stability
	Facilitates democracy, progress equality, and technical development

of formal education. The figure is necessarily too general and brief; the two
models of society it depicts are only ideal types, in Weber's sense, and we do
not claim that they fully describe the empirical reality they reflect.

As Table 3.1 suggests, the rise of mass education in western Europe was
conditioned by and related to all of the major changes in the institutional structure
of the European civilizational network. In this extremely complex historical
situation, it is extremely difficult to untangle the web of causal processes that
led to these changes. We have identified four major dialectical axes by which
the changes occurred: individualism/nationalism, faith/reason, transnational or-
ganization/nation-state organization, and economic expansion/impoverization.
Of course, the dialectical development associated with each of these axes has
been strongly conditioned by and related to each of the others; they constitute,
as it were, a coherent bundle of sociological forces whose full development
depended on the presence of all four axes simulataneously. We therefore conclude
that the rise of mass education was itself dependent on the interplay among these
four pairs of forces, and a full understanding of the rise of mass education
requires a much deeper penetration of the development of each of these pairs.

What are the implications of this line of work for research in comparative
education in the contemporary world? First, it is crucial that comparative researchers consider educational development from the view of the world cultural
system, as a whole, not simply on a country-by-country basis. What happened
in France and the Netherlands in the nineteenth century was conditioned both
by developments in other countries (the usual borrowing and diffusion ideas)
and by the evolving cultural framework overarching European societies as a set
of institutional definitions of reality, purpose, and value. Similarly, what happens
in contemporary Nigeria or Mexico is conditioned by the overarching cultural
framework that now contains the institutional definitions of reality, purpose, and
value for the entire world, beyond the specific borrowing and imitation that occur
between these countries and others. Thus research on particular countries needs
to be tied into a larger framework that puts the particularistic findings into context.

Second, we hope to have shown that a long historical perspective is essential
for understanding the foundations for educational development and that understanding the foundations helps make sense of education's role in the modern world.
If we consider only the postwar world of the past forty years, the time period commonly analyzed by cross-national researchers, we are likely to consider mass education a natural, necessary, and irreplaceable aspect of any social system.
Education appears to have diffused from the developed center of the world system
to the underdeveloped periphery, and all countries, no matter what their political
system or economic capabilities, strive toward universal, compulsory systems. A
historical perspective reveals that this situation is in fact rather odd and depends
on the legitimating myths that tie education to the central axes of the modern world
cultural system, making of education a mythical being worthy of universal wor-
ship and sacrifice. In short, a historical perspective facilitates a critical posture.

Finally, we strongly urge that more attention be given to the institutional aspects of educational development, that is, to changes in the ontological and legitimational components of the world social system. We moderns live lives that are no less regulated and controlled by myth and symbol than those of our ancestors of a hundred, a thousand, or even five thousand years ago, and it is tragic that we are unable to accept analytical approaches to understanding contemporary society that are hailed as widely illuminating and revealing when applied to societies more distant in time. Part of our unwillingness to accept them is itself determined by one of our most powerful myths, that of materialism and the ontological primacy of the materially concrete.

In more specific terms, we suggest that comparative research attempt to explain variations in the development of educational systems in terms of variations in the ontological and legitimational structure of society. For example, it is quite clear that the individualistic/nationalist dialectic is heavily tipped in favor of individualism in the United States but heavily tipped in favor of nationalist collectivism in, say, Sweden. Hence, while solutions to social problems that operate through the state are somewhat suspect in the United States, where individualistic market-based mechanisms have great legitimacy, in Sweden the only solutions to social problems that are given serious attention are those that operate through the state. Market-based mechanisms have little legitimacy there and are themselves rather suspect. One fruitful study might trace the history of the individualist/nationalist dialectic in Sweden to determine both the reasons for the dominance of the collectivist pole of the axis and the implications this different form of institutional structure had for the Swedish educational system. A typical research question might then be, how are the factors that account for the dominance of nationalist collectivism over individualism in Sweden related to the relatively early expansion of the Swedish school system and the particular positions taken by the various estates in the debate over the school reform bill of 1842? Or, in a more comparative vein, how does the dominance of different poles of this dialectic account for similarities and differences in educational development in the two countries in the crucial period from 1880 to 1910?

This type of question has received virtually no attention in comparative education (and here comparative education is hardly alone!). We are gratified to find that researchers more and more are looking at the historical and institutional dimensions of social change, and we hope this chapter makes a contribution in stimulating them further.

NOTES

1. The salvation of *souls* is no longer a concern of education; that archaic notion has been replaced by the more modern concern for the salvation of the *nation*. Consider, for example, Shils's (1971) article, "No Salvation Outside Higher Education," or the recent explosion of anxiety about the inadequacies of American education in preparing the work force to compete with the Japanese.

2. To quote Tanzania's Julius Nyerere: "If I leave to others the building or our

86 The Social Origins of Education

elementary school system, they [the people] will abandon me as their responsible national leader" (quoted in Thompson 1971, p. 153).

3. In our usage, a dialectic is a pair of historical processes, or "forces," that develop in opposition and serve to reinforce each other such that both forces increase (or decrease) in importance simultaneously. The contradiction between the opposing forces is necessary to their continued development, and generally, no "synthesis" or resolution of the contradiction emerges; instead, the nature of the dialectic is transformed into a different set of opposing forces. This is not to say that synthesis is impossible, but as an empirical matter, it is rarely observed. For further discussion, see Boli-Bennett (1980, pp. 170–77).

4. This distinction is false, of course, in that organizational reality *is also* an aspect of institutional reality; that is, the way that organizational reality is understood and depicted is equally a matter of the social construction of reality (Berger and Luckman 1966) and can function as sociological myth equally well. We retain the distinction nonetheless in order to stress different aspects of institutional order.

5. In the United States, of course, these conflicts took a quite diminished and altogether different form from that characterizing the European countries. There was no established church, so the principle of religious freedom and state control of the secular realm was established early on and with little argument. Similarly, true classes in the European sense, deriving from the former estates of society, never developed in the United States. These factors help explain the peculiar path toward mass schooling taken in the United States, where the central state was only rather loosely linked to education and the principle of universalism was instituted more quickly and thoroughly than in Europe. For an excellent discussion of the limited impact of the class system on educational struggle in the United States, see Rubinson (1983).

6. Because of the early Protestant emphasis on literacy, we find that Protestant countries generally had more expanded schooling prior to the massive entry of the state in the nineteenth century (Craig 1981). As the universalist ideology of individualism took root in Catholic countries, their educational efforts increased and literacy rate differentials began to diminish, though they were not eliminated until after state systems were developed.

7. Developments in the United States again took a rather different form, with the state playing a less central role in nation building and the creation of the individual. While the federal state actively helped to forge the national economic market (Burlingame 1949), thereby indirectly furthering construction of the national polity, the excessive strength of individualism in the United States from the beginning led to a more privatized form of nation building on the part of voluntary associations, both economic and religious (cf. Thomas 1979). It is important not to let American exceptionalism distort our understanding of the more general processes.

8. Goffman (1956, p. 501) expresses this idea by saying that "many gods have been done away with, but the individual himself stubbornly remains a deity of considerable importance." The individual as a sociological entity has *become* God, so that all of his social interactions are now imbued with extraordinary significance, and social organization is increasingly restructured to deal with the heightened status of the individual.

9. We are well aware that the United States had a highly expanded school system in the presence of a relatively weak state in the nineteenth century. But the federal U.S. state was weak only relative to the level of bureaucratic power and organization attained in such countries as Germany and France at that time. By historical standards, even the U.S. state was immensely strong by 1900, both internally and with respect to its ability to exert power in the external world.

10. The two conventional arguments about economic development—that it provides the resources necessary to build a mass educational system and that it demands a literate, informed work force that can be produced only by mass schooling—have little validity. In recent decades we have seen the rise of mass education in poor countries with only weak exchange economies, demonstrating that constructing a school system is largely a political, not an economic, process (cf. Meyer et al. 1977); on the other hand, training the work force during the heavy industrialization phase in the West occurred far more through the apprenticeship system than through schools (Hobsbawm 1962), and even today it is commonplace that highly schooled college graduates learn what they need to know in order to work effectively only after they have found jobs (Berg 1971).

11. The recent concerns about educational inflation and the possible economic disadvantages of too much time spent in school by no means represent general rejection of the belief in education's primacy for economic development. Educational inflation is seen as a problem insofar as it suggests that the quality of the educational system is declining; the proposed solution is stricter standards and greater discipline in the schools (cf. Thurow 1975). As for the concern about the income foregone while in higher education ("opportunity costs"), this line of thought has been generated primarily to bolster the standard American myth of the "self-made man," who succeeds without education, and to suggest that certain (lower-class) groups may be overstepping the bounds of proper behavior by seeking too much education. Studies of the issue show that the economic returns of education *for the individual* generally remain quite high (Pace 1979; Blaug 1968, 1969), and none of the propagators of this perspective suggests that the educational system be disbanded or even seriously curtailed.

REFERENCES

Amin, Samir. *Accumulation on a World Scale*. New York: Monthly Review Press, 1974.
Anderson, Perry. *Passages from Antiquity to Feudalism*. London: New Left Books, 1974a.
———. *Lineages of the Absolute State*. London: New Left Books, 1974b.
Archer, Margaret S. *Social Origins of Educational Systems*. Beverly Hills, CA: Sage Publications, 1979.
Aries, Philippe. *Centuries of Childhood*. New York: Vintage, 1962.
Arnove, Robert F. "Comparative Education and World-Systems Analysis." *Comparative Education Review* 24 (February 1980): 48–62.
Bainton, Roland H. *The Reformation of the Sixteenth Century*. Boston: Beacon Press, 1956.
Bantock, G. H. *Studies in the History of Educational Theory*. Vol. 1, *Artifice and Nature*. London: George Allen & Unwin, 1980.
Bell, Daniel. *The Coming of Post-Industrial Society*. New York: Basic Books, 1973.
Bendix, Reinhard. *Nation-Building and Citizenship*. New York: John Wiley & Sons, 1964.
Berg, Ivar. *Education and Jobs: The Great Training Robbery*. Boston: Beacon Press, 1971.
Berger, Peter. *The Sacred Canopy*. Garden City, NY: Doubleday, 1967.
Berger, Peter, and Thomas Luckmann. *The Social Construction of Reality*. Garden City, NY: Doubleday, 1966.
Berger, Peter, Brigitte Berger, and Hansfried Kellner. *The Homeless Mind*. New York: Random House, 1973.
Blaug, M., ed. *Economics of Education*. Vol. 1. Baltimore: Penguin Books, 1968.
Blaug, M., ed. *Economics of Education*. Vol. 2. Baltimore: Penguin Books, 1969.
Boli-Bennett, John. "Human Rights or State Expansion? Cross-National Definitions of

Constitutional Rights, 1870–1970.'' In *Global Human Rights: Public Policies, Comparative Measures, and NGO Strategies*, edited by Ved Nanda, James Scarritt, and George Shepherd. Boulder, CO: Westview Press, 1981.

———. "The Absolute Dialectics of Jacques Ellul." *Research in Philosophy and Technology* 3 (1980): 171–201.

Boli-Bennett, John, and John W. Meyer. "The Ideology of Childhood and the State: Rules Distinguishing Children in National Constitutions, 1870–1970." *American Sociological Review* 43 (December 1978): 797–812.

Bourdieu, Pierre. "Systems of Education and Systems of Thought." In *Knowledge and Control: New Directions for the Sociology of Education*, edited by Michael Young. New York: John Wiley & Sons, 1971.

Bowen, James. *A History of Western Education*. Vol. 3, *The Modern West, Europe and the New World*. New York: St. Martin's Press, 1981.

Bowles, Samuel, and Herbert Gintis. *Schooling in Capitalist America*. New York: Basic Books, 1976.

Burlingame, Roger. *Backgrounds of Power*. London: Charles Scribner's Sons, 1949.

Carnoy, Martin. *Education as Cultural Imperialism*. New York: David McKay Co., 1974.

Cohen, Yehudi. "Schools and Civilizational States." In *The Social Sciences and the Comparative Study of Educational Systems*, edited by J. Fischer. Scranton, PA: International Textbook 1970.

Collins, Randall. "Functional and Conflict Theories of Educational Stratification." *American Sociological Review* 36 (1971): 1002–19.

———. "Some Comparative Principles of Educational Stratification." *Harvard Educational Review* 47 (February 1977): 1–27.

———. *The Credential Society: A Historical Sociology of Education and Stratification*. New York: Academic Press, 1979.

Craig, John. "The Expansion of Education." *Review of Research in Education* 9 (1981): 151–210.

Craig, John, and Norman Spear. "The Diffusion of Schooling in Nineteenth-Century Europe: Toward a Model." Paper presented at the annual meeting of the Social Science History Association, Columbus, Ohio. Department of Education, University of Chicago, 1978.

Cubberley, Ellwood P. *Readings in the History of Education*. Boston: Houghton Mifflin, 1920.

Curtis, S. J., and M.E.A. Boultwood. *A Short History of Educational Ideas*. 5th ed. Slough, England: University Tutorial Press, 1977.

Dreeben, Robert. *On What Is Learned in School*. Reading, MA: Addison-Wesley, 1968.

Dumont, Louis. "The Modern Conception of the Individual." *Contributions to Indian Sociology* 8 (October 1965): 13–61.

Durkheim, Émile. *L'Evolution Pedagogique en France*. 2 vols. Paris: Felix Alcan, 1938.

Ellul, Jacques. *Métamorphose du Bourgeois*. Paris: Calmann-Levy, 1967.

Emmanuel, Arghiri. *Unequal Exchange: A Study of the Imperialism of Free Trade*. New York: Monthly Review Press, 1972.

Ericson, David P. "The Possibility of a General Theory of the Educational System." In *The Sociology of Educational Expansion*, edited by Margaret S. Archer. Beverly Hills, CA: Sage Publications, 1982.

Fischer, Wolfram, and Peter Lundgreen. "The Recruitment and Training of Administrative and Technical Personnel." In *The Formation of National States in Western Europe*, edited by Charles Tilly. Princeton, NJ: Princeton University Press, 1975.

Foster, Philip. "Education and Social Differentiation in Less-Developed Countries." *Comparative Education Review* 21 (1977): 211–29.

Frank, Andre Gunder. *Capitalism and Underdevelopment in Latin America.* New York: Monthly Review Press, 1967.

Goffman, Erving. "The Nature of Deference and Demeanor." *American Anthropologist* 58 (June 1956): 473–502.

Held, Thomas, Francisco Ramirez, and John W. Meyer. "Violence and Abuse in the Family." Paper presented at the annual meeting of the American Sociological Association, Detroit. Department of Sociology, Stanford University, 1983.

Hobsbawm, E. J. *The Age of Revolution, 1789–1848.* New York: New American Library, 1962.

Isling, Ake. *Kampen För och Mot en Demokratisk Skola* (The Struggle for and against a Democratic School). Stockholm: Sober Förlags AG, 1980.

Jolibert, Bernard. *L'Enfance au XVIIᵉ Siècle.* Paris: Librairie Philosophique J. Vrin, 1981.

Jones, Donald K. *The Making of the Educational System 1851–81.* London: Routledge & Kegan Paul, 1977.

Katz, Michael B. *Class, Bureaucracy and Schools: The Illusion of Educational Change in America.* New York: Praeger, 1975.

Kohn, Hans. *The Age of Nationalism.* New York: Harper & Row, 1962.

Little, Lester K. *Religious Poverty and the Profit Economy in Medieval Europe.* Ithaca, NY: Cornell University Press, 1978.

Lubasz, Heinz, ed. *The Development of the Modern State.* New York: Macmillan, 1964.

Meyer, John W. "The Effects of Education as an Instsitution." *American Journal of Education* 83 (September 1977): 340–63.

———. "The World Polity and the Authority of the Nation-State." In *Studies of the Modern World-System,* edited by Albert Bergesen. New York: Academic Press, 1980.

Meyer, John W., et al. "The World Educational Revolution, 1950–1970." *Sociology of Education* 50 (Fall 1977): 242–58.

———. "Public Education as Nation-Building in America." *American Journal of Sociology* 85 (1979): 978–86.

Moraze, Charles. *Les Bourgeois Conquérants, XIXᵉ Siècle.* Paris: Armand Colin, 1957.

Morris, Colin. *The Discovery of the Individual, 1050–1200.* London: SPCK, 1972.

Nisbet, Robert. *History of the Idea of Progress.* New York: Basic Books, 1980.

Pace, C. Robert. *Measuring Outcomes of College.* San Francisco: Jossey-Bass, 1979.

Pirenne, Henri. *Economic and Social History of Medieval Europe.* New York: Harcourt, Brace, 1936.

Poggi, Gianfranco. *The Development of the Modern State.* Stanford, CA: Stanford University Press, 1978.

Polanyi, Karl. *The Great Transformation.* Boston: Beacon Press, 1944.

Ramirez, Francisco O., and John Boli. "Global Patterns of Educational Institutionalization." In *Comparative Education,* edited by Philip Altbach, Robert Arnove, and Gail Kelly. New York: Macmillan, 1982a.

———. "On the Union of States and Schools." Paper presented at the annual meeting of the American Sociological Association, San Francisco, San Francisco State University, Department of Sociology, 1982b.

Ramirez, Francisco O., and John W. Meyer. "Comparative Education: Synthesis and Agenda." In *The State of Sociology: Problems and Prospects,* edited by James Short. Beverly Hills, CA: Sage Publications, 1981.

Reisner, Edward. *Nationalism and Education Since 1789.* New York: Macmillan, 1922.

Rieff, Philip. *The Triumph of the Therapeutic: The Uses of Faith after Freud*. New York: Harper & Row, 1966.

Ritchie, David G. *Natural Rights*. London: George Allen & Unwin, 1894.

Rosenberg, Hans. *Bureaucracy, Aristocracy, and Autocracy: The Prussian Experience, 1660–1815*. Boston: Beacon Press, 1958.

Rubinson, Richard. "The Political Incorporation of Educational Systems." Ph.D. diss., Stanford University, 1974.

―――. "Class Formation and Schooling in the United States". Unpublished manuscript, Department of Social Relations, Johns Hopkins University, 1983.

Schelsky, Helmuth. *Die Skeptische Generation*. Dusseldorf-Köln: E. Diederichs Verlag, 1958.

Shils, Edward. "No Salvation outside Higher Education." *Minerva* 6 (1971): 313–21.

Shorter, Edward. *The Making of the Modern Family*. New York: Basic Books, 1975.

Sommerville, John. *The Rise and Fall of Childhood*. Beverly Hills, CA: Sage Publications, 1982.

Spring, Joel. *Education and the Rise of the Corporate State*. Boston: Beacon Press, 1972.

Strayer, Joseph. *On the Medieval Origins of the Modern State*. Princeton, NJ: Princeton University Press, 1970.

Thomas, George M. "Institutional Knowledge and Social Movements: Rational Exchange, Revival Religion, and Nation-Building in the U.S., 1870–1896." Ph.D. diss., Stanford University, 1979.

Thompson, Kenneth. "Universities and the Developing World." In *The Task of Universities in a Changing World*, edited by Stephen Kertesz. South Bend, IN: University of Notre Dame Press, 1971.

Thurow, Lester. *Generating Inequality*. New York: Basic Books, 1975.

Tierney, Brian. *The Crisis of Church and State, 1050–1300*. Englewood Cliffs, NJ: Prentice-Hall, 1964.

Tilly, Charles, ed. *The Formation of National States in Western Europe*. Princeton, NJ: Princeton University Press, 1975.

Ullmann, Walter. *The Individual and Society in the Middle Ages*. Baltimore: Johns Hopkins University Press, 1966.

Wallerstein, Immanuel. *The Modern World-System*. Vol. 1. New York: Academic Press, 1974.

―――. *The Modern World-System*. Vol. 2. New York: Academic Press, 1980.

Warne, Albin. *Till Folkskolans Förhistoria i Sverige* (Early History of the Folk School in Sweden). Stockholm: Svenska Kyrkans Diakonistyrelsens Bokförlag, 1929.

Witcutt, W. P. *The Rise and Fall of the Individual*. London: SPCK, 1958.

World Bank. *Education: Sector Policy Paper*. Washington, DC: International Bank for Reconstruction and Development, 1980.

Zijderveld, Anton C. *The Abstract Society*. Garden City, NY: Doubleday, 1970.

PART II

Socialization Processes and Educational Outcomes

4

ALAN C. KERCKHOFF

Family Position, Peer Influences, and Schooling

INTRODUCTION

This chapter's focus is on two kinds of major social relationships experienced by school-age individuals, which affect the educational process. Families and peers, primarily same-age peers, constitute the primary, universally found social relationships that impinge on the educational process in all industrialized societies. While most of the literature to be cited here uses the American case as the source of data, the effects to be discussed can reasonably be assumed to be similar in any society in which a formal educational process occurs in separate institutions called schools. At least such an assumption will be made here.

The approach taken here views the individual's involvement in both family and peer relationships as a potential source of formative experiences, experiences which can influence values, opinions, attitudes, and skills relevant to the formal educational process. At the same time, the individual is not viewed as a passive recipient of that influence. All social relationships are reciprocal, and the individual's effect on the "other," whether peer or family member, is as great as the "other's" effect on the individual. For good methodological reasons, that reciprocality is not always reflected in the research arena, but it is important to be aware of the limitations of our knowledge when it is not taken into account.

From the perspective of the individual child's development, however, family members and peers are potent sources of influence. They contribute significantly to what is referred to as the socialization process. All theories of socialization recognize that the individual is influenced by a series of meaningful social relationships. In the normal course of events, the individual spends the first few years of life largely within a rather narrow and intense network of relationships, almost exclusively made up of relationships with family members. By the time the child goes to school (either nursery school or elementary school), he or she has already learned a great deal that will have significant implications for the school experience. To the extent that children have been exposed to different early experiences, the effect of entering school will vary.

After entering school, the matrix of social relationships expands rapidly, and the potential sources of socialization influence increase greatly in number and type. A major factor in determining the nature of this expanded matrix is the organizational structure of the school which normally provides a relatively large number of same-age peers with whom the individual is expected to develop effective relationships. However singular in significance the family may have been during the preschool years, the immersion of the individual in a sea of peer interactions during a large part of the day presents another powerful source of potential influence.

The general theoretical perspective on the socialization process adopted here is shared by many behavioral scientists. It defines socialization as "the process by which persons acquire the knowledge, skills, and dispositions that make them more or less able members of their society" (Brim 1966, p. 3). Socialization does not include all formative processes experienced by individuals. It is limited to those associated with *acquired* characteristics (and thus it excludes qualities evolving through biological maturation) which have *social* significance (and thus it excludes individual differences that are not systematically relevant to social functioning.)

While the specific "knowledge, skills, and dispositions" required to make a child "a more or less able member" of the school community may be defined somewhat differently by different analysts, there would be little disagreement that cognitive skills and social relations skills are central and that motivation to do well in academic pursuits relative to others is highly functional. Families contribute to the motivational and cognitive skill levels exhibited by their children when they first enter the educational system, and they continue to influence these qualities throughout the children's school experience. It is equally apparent that the kinds of experience a child has with the peer group can also significantly affect cognitive and social skills and academic motivation. The fact that family and peer influences occur simultaneously throughout much of the pre-adult period also provides the opportunity for various kinds of interactions (in the statistical sense) among those influences.

It will be apparent throughout this chapter that it is impossible to examine the individual's family and peer relationships, as they impinge on the schooling process, without taking into account the other central figure(s) in the process— school personnel, especially the classroom teacher. Much of what we know about the effects of family-child and peer-peer relationships becomes meaningful only when those relationships are viewed in combination with the individual's relationships with school personnel. Although the student-teacher relationship is not a central concern here, the discussion necessarily requires repeated reference to it.

The first two sections of the chapter deal with the educationally relevant effects attributed to the family and to peers. A duality of research is noted in both of these areas of inquiry. The two traditions may be thought of as treating social relations either as contexts or as processes. The theoretical foundations of these two approaches are essentially the same. When social relations are treated as contexts, their effect on the individual is assumed to occur through processes which are more fully considered in other research. And when social relations are treated as processes, their significance in the individual's socialization is implicitly assumed to be due to their omnipresence. Thus the two kinds of research, though formally different, are at least potentially complementary, although they are not always viewed in that way. A third section focuses on some of the conceptual and methodological issues these bodies of research raise. A final section provides a summary and an overview.

Family Socialization and the Educational Process

My interest in this section is directed toward specifying how, during both the preschool and the school years, families influence the individual's responses to school experiences. Approaches taken to the general question of the relationship between family influences and the educational process vary considerably, and it is not always possible to combine them coherently. I have adopted the general stance of socialization theory outlined earlier and then attempted to state how various bodies of literature provide suggestive clues to understanding the processes involved.

Rollins and Thomas (1979) review an extensive body of literature which takes a process approach to the analysis of family relations. They report that particular types of parent-child interaction patterns (in particular, inductive control) appear to be most conducive to the development of socially competent behavior in the children. By *inductive control* they mean persuasive methods which seek the voluntary compliance of the child; the parent provides sufficient information about the consequences of behavior so that the child chooses to behave as the parent wishes. Inductive control involves the use of explanation and reasoning rather than coercion. *Socially competent behavior* is a general term Rollins and Thomas use to encompass a range of socially valued behaviors and characteristics, including cognitive development, internal locus of control, instrumental competence, and conformity to parental standards. The important point of their analysis for present purposes is that the pattern of parent-child interaction seems to have a predictable effect on the child's development of characteristics that are valued within the school setting.

The *confluence model* of intellectual development (Zajonc and Markus 1975) is conceptually consistent with Rollins and Thomas's generalizations and with basic socialization theory, but it adds a contextual dimension. Zajonc and Markus argue that intelligence in children is increased to the extent they interact with persons more mature than themselves. Thus the more younger siblings a child has, the more he or she interacts with less mature persons, and the less intellectual development can be expected. Other things being equal, the more adults and the fewer the younger children in the family, the greater the intellectual development. The child's intellect is seen as a function of the average of the intellects of the family members. Since this view emphasizes the importance of verbal interaction, it would be expected that verbal intelligence would be affected more than non-verbal intelligence. A number of research findings are at least consistent with the Zajonc-Markus confluence model, especially as it applies to verbal intelligence (see Mercy and Steelman 1982 for a recent example).

Both patterns of parent-child interaction and the verbal context provided by the family are thus expected to influence the development within the child of characteristics valued in school: intellectual capacity and social competence. These sources of influence presumably continue to be effective after the child enters school, but the school experience combines with (and may even conflict with) the home experience. Another possible source of family influence on the child's school experience is more direct, involving parent visits to the school, explanations of the child's school experiences, help with homework, and so on. There is little doubt that there is a great deal of variation among parents in the degree of direct involvement (Gildea et al. 1961; Hess and Shipman 1965).

The complexities of the multiple social relationships experienced by children when they enter school make it difficult to take them all into account simultaneously and to assess their relative importance. One attempt to take several sources of influence into account during the early school years is reported by Entwisle and Hayduk (1982), who followed a number of entering first graders into the third grade. Through complex multivariate statistical models, Entwisle and Hayduk show how parental expectations of their children's school performance, as well as the children's own expectations, interact with teachers' evaluations (the assignment of grades), each tending to influence the other over time. They also show how children vary in their responsiveness to these sources of influence, in particular by adjusting or not adjusting their expectations so as to be consistent with the teachers' earlier expectations. Thus children vary in how well they "learn" in school, both in the usual sense of mastering the academic material and in the sense of "learning the system." Entwisle and Hayduk do not analyze the family interaction patterns of their subjects, but their children seem to vary in the kinds of "social competence" Rollins and Thomas associate with inductive control.

Another approach to the kinds of possible combined effects of family and school influences is taken by Epstein (1983) in her study of older children. Following students from the eighth to the ninth grade, she assesses the effects of the kinds of social relations they experience at home and in the school. She conceptualizes both home and school experiences according to the degree of the child's participation in decision making, viewing those in which there is greater participation by the child as more democratic. She reports evidence that both family and school democratic patterns (a) increase the degree of independence shown by students, (b) are associated with more positive attitudes toward school, and (c) are associated with higher school grades. She also reports interaction effects: a democratic school structure has more effect on students from families with low child-participation rates. Although not all such research shows significant interaction effects (see Epstein 1980), the fact that both family and school structures affect student attitudes and performances well into the adolescent years is a significant finding.

Another extensive body of literature is relevant to the issue of the importance of the family in the educational process, that which deals with what has come to be called the *status attainment process.* As an outgrowth of an interest in social mobility patterns, multivariate models of the movement of people from an origin to a destination in the social stratification system have developed in increasingly complex forms over the past two decades. Since it was noted early in this research period (Blau and Duncan 1967) that educational attainment is the major link between social origin and destination, the more elaborate models have included representations of factors influencing educational attainment. Family social position and family process or influence have been important components of these models.

The so-called Wisconsin model of educational and occupational attainment (Sewell et al. 1969) has been the most influential in this body of literature. A schematic representation of the relevant parts of that model is shown in Figure 4.1. This model represents family influences in three ways.

First, the socioeconomic position of the family is represented by the occupational status and educational attainment level of the individual's father and (sometimes) mother. Second, the nature of the family structure is represented by the number of siblings the individual has and (sometimes) by whether one or both parents are present. Third, the direct educationally relevant influences of the parents are represented by the individual's report of whether they encouraged him or her to go to college (included in "significant others' influences").

In effect, the first two of these kinds of family characteristics (socioeconomic status and family structure) are indications of the family context in which the individual matured, while only the third (encouragement to attend college) is concerned with the actual process of parent influence. At the same time, the inclusion of these measures in the model is founded on the same general socialization theory as the more in-depth studies of family-school relations. As Haller and Portes (1973, p. 69) put it: "Well-established theories of interpersonal influence in social psychology are supported empirically by the strong direct paths [effects] from significant others' influence to status aspirations." Even the socioeconomic measures are interpreted in this way: "The effect that family's socioeconomic status has on a person's educational and occupational attainment is due to its impact on the types of attainment-related personal influences that the person receives" (p. 62).

The findings reported in this body of research tend to support the same view of the significance of the family in the educational process as the findings do from research more directly focused on family and school processes. Parents with higher levels of educational attainment, for instance, have a positive effect on their children's educational attainment, and the fewer the number of children in the family, the higher the individual's educational attainment, holding constant

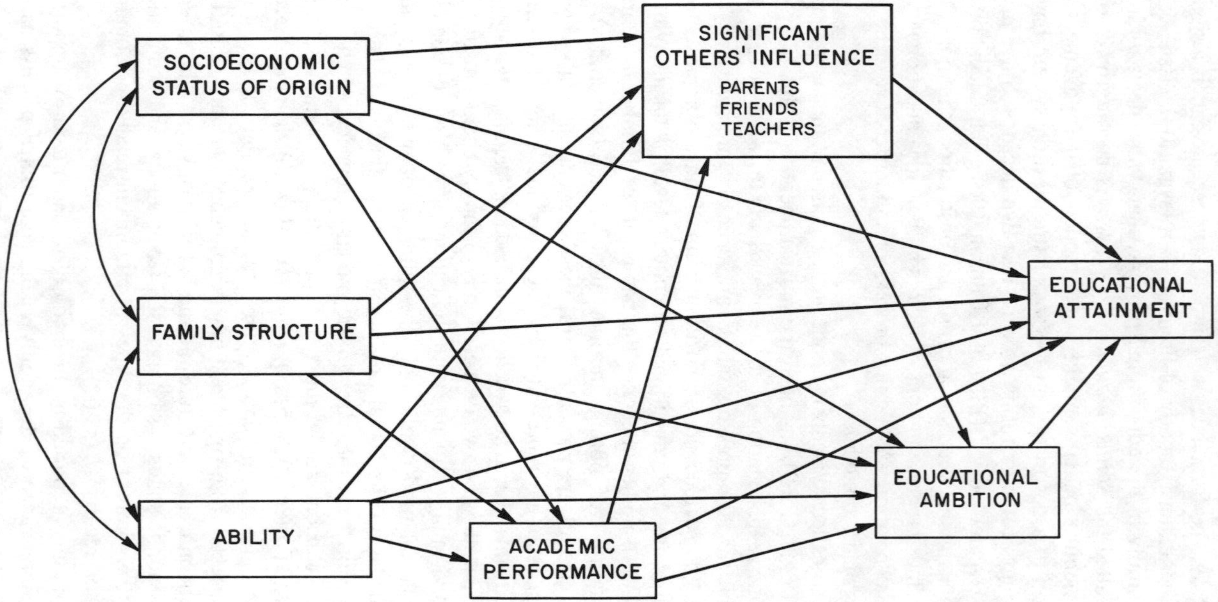

Figure 4.1 Schematic Model of the Educational Attainment Process

the other variables in the model. Also, the fact that the individual's own level of educational ambition and attainment are responsive to parental encouragement suggests a continuing parental influence well into adolescence (see Kerckhoff 1980 for reviews of many of the studies using this general approach).

Some studies have attempted to combine the analysis of abstract models of the educational attainment process, such as shown in Figure 4.1, and more detailed analyses of family relations. In effect, these studies have taken a more in-depth approach to one or more of the paths (represented by the arrows in the figure) between pairs of elements in the model. For instance, the recent Southern Occupational Goals Study collected data on fifth- and sixth-grade students and their mothers and then recontacted both students and mothers six years later (Howell and Frese 1982). While studies in the status attainment tradition have used samples of different ages and locations, followed varied research designs, and focused on different specific questions, they have left no doubt about the importance of family influences on both the school performance and future orientations of students throughout the school years.

Overall, from these several bodies of literature, it is clear that families influence the educational process in two ways: (1) They provide the kinds of interpersonal stimulation that leads to the development in the child of characteristics that are functional in the school setting. (2) They guide, coach, explain, encourage, and intercede on behalf of their children in reference to the school experience. They clearly help children to "acquire the knowledge, skills, and dispositions that make them more or less able members of their [school] society."

Peer Influence and the Educational Process

Socialization theory suggests that, potentially, all significant others have an influence on the individual's development of characteristics relevant to effective social functioning. While the family is crucial due to its intense and early interactions with the individual, many other social relations are also important. In the school setting, teachers and classmates are the most consistently encountered and potentially most significant. The organization of schools ensures that children will spend a large proportion of their waking hours in close association with a group of other children of approximately the same age and intellectual development. Because that collective experience is essentially universal, it is impossible to determine its overall socialization significance. Also, since the child's experience with classmates occurs largely within a setting which also includes one or more teachers who are in a supervisory or controlling position, it is often difficult to differentiate between effects of peers and effects of teachers with any precision. However, in this section I will review briefly a number of findings suggesting that variations in peer relationships are significant factors in the educational process.

As with the research on family influences, there are two types of investigations into the importance of peers in the educational process: those focusing on interpersonal processes and those concerned with social contexts. Peer process studies generally deal with the dynamics of the relationships within the classroom or in the overall student population. They tend to focus on friendship choice and sociometric position as factors associated with academic performance or attitudes toward school. Rather than viewing the peer group as a whole, these studies examine differentiation and patterns of interpersonal relations within it.

A consistent finding is that friends tend to be more similar on attitudes toward school, educational ambitions, and even academic performance than are random pairs within the classroom. This greater similarity is found at both the elementary and the secondary levels (Kerckhoff 1974). The basic question raised by this observation is whether that similarity is due to criteria of selection of friends or to interpersonal influence between friends. There seems little doubt that both selection and influence are involved (Cohen 1977; Kandel 1978), although only a few studies which collect true longitudinal data are able to differentiate between the two processes with any confidence.

The nature of the school setting needs to be taken into account if influence from peers is to be fully understood. Since students are generally divided into separate classrooms, it is not surprising that most friendship choices are made within the same classroom. Other organizing principles also narrow the range of probable choices. The differentiation of separate high school curricula, for instance, means that even if students move from one classroom to another for different subject lessons, they are likely to move together, and limited subsets of students spend most of their school time together (Rosenbaum 1975). Even the organization of the individual classroom can affect the patterns of friendship choice. For instance, Hallinan (1976) has shown that friendship patterns differ in traditional and open classrooms. Open classrooms have more evenly distributed friendship choices, presumably due to greater opportunities to interact with a larger proportion of the class. Also, to the extent that a classroom is divided into subgroups (e.g., reading groups), the kinds of opportunities peers have for interaction and the bases upon which they can judge similarity between themselves and others are altered.

Whatever the variation owing to the structure of the institutional setting, the general finding has been that friendship relations in schools tend to reflect both selection and socialization. Even after holding constant the friends' prior similarities (some of which can be attributed to family influences), the fact of friendship leads students to become more similar, and some of the ways in which they become more similar are directly relevant to their responses to the educational process. For instance, Kandel (1978) estimated degrees of homophyly of adolescent friendship pairs at the beginning and end of the academic year. She found evidence of both selection and socialization effects on a number of measures of similarity, including educational aspirations, in which case the two effects were essentially equal.

The status attainment literature has also repeatedly shown the importance of friends in the explanation of adolescents' ambitions and educational attainments. The ''significant others'' noted in the schematic representation of the Wisconsin model in Figure 4.1 includes friends, and numerous studies have shown that the plans or ambitions of the individual's friends make an independent contribution to understanding his or her own ambitions and attainments (for instance, see

Rehberg and Rosenthal 1978). While these analyses have the same limitations noted earlier (in that only crude indices of peer influence are used), the consistency of the findings leaves no doubt of the educational significance of peers during the high school years.

The nature of these peer influences seems to differ by age, or level in school. There is a general observation that peer relations increase in importance through the childhood years, especially in relation to the importance of adults (Rosenberg 1973). At the same time, the kinds of influence peers have change through the same period. The broadened range of activities away from school and family during the pre-adolescent and adolescent years makes the peer group in general (and friends in particular) a source of influence in kinds of activities not relevant in the early childhood years. Peer influence is found to be particularly strong during adolescence in relation to dating and other newly emerging social activities. There may be some general decline in parental influence during later childhood and into adolescence, but so far as educationally relevant issues are concerned, parental influence continues to be strong (Brittain 1963; Kandel and Lesser 1969; Smith 1981).

The fact that adolescent peer relations are so heavily concerned with nonacademic issues might lead some to be skeptical about the educational relevance of peer influences during the period of development. However, the interrelatedness of adolescents' activities and the probable effects of nonacademic activities on the educational process also need to be considered. Certainly extracurricular involvements (both in school and outside) often affect the individual's interest in and ability to perform adequately in school.

Simmons and co-workers (1979) and Blyth and co-workers (1978) report on a particularly interesting study of the importance of the general social context on personal development in the period of transition into adolescence. They analyze developmental changes of students as they pass from the sixth to the seventh grade in two kinds of school system, those with a K-6 organization and those with a K-8 organization. Since students in the former kind of system change schools and become the youngest students in their new school, while the latter remain in the same school, where they are among the more mature students, the effects of social context can be observed. Among the findings reported are the tendencies for those who change schools (a) to be more future-oriented so far as their academic goals are concerned (even before the move), (b) to experience a greater sense of anonymity in seventh grade, and (c) to participate less often in extracurricular activities in seventh grade. Simmons and others also report a lowering of self-esteem on the part of girls who change schools, especially if they have reached puberty and have begun dating. While it is difficult to disentangle the effects of system organization from peer influence in such an analysis (the former actually determines the possible nature of the latter), kinds of peer context need to be considered in any analysis of peer influence.

These studies of system effects are similar to another major form of structural analysis of peer influence during adolescence, what has been called *contextual effects analysis.* Beginning with the major study by Coleman and his associates (1966), a number of investigations have been concerned with the effect on the individual attending a school with a particular kind of student body. In that early analysis, Coleman and his colleagues showed that black students who attended schools whose students were predominantly white had higher levels of academic performance than those who attended predominantly black schools. While that analysis has been subject to some sharp criticism (Mosteller and Moynihan 1972), the same general approach has been used in more recent studies of the effects of student body composition.

The overall thrust of these studies has been to argue that if the student body has an average high level of academic ability, a student of any given ability level will tend to receive lower grades than he or she would have received in a school with a less able student body, although that same high-ability context may tend to raise the individual's performance on a standardized test. The lower grades, in turn, will tend to lower the individual's academic self-esteem and thereby lower his or her educational goals. Although it is sometimes only implicit, such a conceptualization involves an assumption about the competitive and comparative nature of the academic evaluation system. It essentially assumes that teachers "grade on a curve," making comparisons among the students before them rather than using a universalistic standard. However valid that assumption might be, there are several studies, including the original Coleman investigation, that are consistent with this contextual interpretation (Campbell and Alexander 1965; Davis 1966; Meyer 1970).

What is not always clear from these investigations, however, is how the ability level and the socioeconomic level of the student body are interrelated in the process leading to a contextual effect on individuals' self-evaluations and ambitions. The most explicit examination of the effects of these two definitions of peer contexts has been conducted by Alexander and Eckland (1975). They argue that the academic ability and social status composition of the student body both affect educational outcomes, but they do so in opposite directions. They argue that ability composition has the effects just outlined, but they view social status composition as having the opposite effect. That is, student bodies with relatively high socioeconomic status will, other things being equal, have more members oriented toward post–secondary education. This will thus tend to raise the level of educational expectations of individual students. One of the mechanisms by which this occurs is through a greater proportion of students in high–status schools being in the college preparatory curriculum. Alexander and Eckland's analysis does exhibit these counteracting effects of ability and status contexts, and they are able to show that if they had looked at only one of these contextual effects, without dealing with the other at the same time, a significant pattern would not have been found. For our purposes, it is also important to recognize that what might be viewed wholly as a form of peer influence cannot be fully understood without taking institutional factors into account. Teacher grading practices and the organization of the high school into separate curricula (varying in relative size across schools) are important factors in producing these effects.

This type of contextual effect analysis is a refined and special example of a more general interest in the nature of the school setting. What has been called the "climate" of the school has been a focus of investigation, at least since Coleman's early analysis in *The Adolescent Society* (1961). McDill and associates (1969) have shown that variations in educational climate (defined in terms of the degree of emphasis on intellectual matters) in high schools influence both academic performance and educational plans of students, with relevant individual measures controlled. Of particular significance for present purposes, they also show that the degree of parental involvement and commitment to the school is the best single explanation of school climate. Such an analysis seems to link family and peer influences, as well as school structural factors, in ways which may be difficult to disentangle but which also testify to the significance of all three.

The literature on the significance of peers, in both its process and context forms, points up the dual nature of significant others in the educational setting. Peers act both as sources of interpersonal influence and as a reference group in comparison with which the individual makes self-evaluations. In both these respects, the effects of peers are clearly a function of the individual's own contribution. The choice of friends from among those available and the definition of the appropriate reference group with which to compare oneself are not simply externally determined. Equally apparent, however, is the significance of institutional patterns in establishing the boundaries of the potentially influential groups. To that extent, the individual's own contributions are circumscribed.

SOME CHALLENGING PROBLEMS

While the effects of family and peer influences on the educational experiences and performances of young people can be observed throughout this extensive literature, there are some significant problems faced when one attempts to integrate them into a coherent conceptualization. These problems are both conceptual and methodological in origin, and they involve both the process and the context approaches to family and peer influences. I will review some of the more important ones here before turning to a summary statement.

Conceptual Problems

The conceptualization of the socialization process that implicitly or explicitly underlies all of these studies of family and peer influence recognizes that the social relationships involved are *interactive*. While the research is concerned with the developmental processes undergone by the young people studied, it must recognize that they are active participants in those processes. Thus what

parents do in relation to their children is, to some significant extent, in response
to whatever behaviors the children have engaged in, as well as a reflection of
how the children have responded to previous parental behavior. Similarly, the
nature of an individual's reaction to a friend's behavior or expressed ambition
will depend on the history of the friendship. Obvious as this is, it is difficult to
take it into account in studies of family or peer influence.

We always tap into the flow of a relationship and attempt to capture its quality,
based on a limited set of observations. Our analyses may treat one measure as
an independent variable and another as a dependent variable, but that is more a
convenient convention (however analytically necessary) than a veridical representation of the process involved. The artificiality of the convention is clearest
in the status attainment type of research. If we record a parent's aspiration for
a child or a friend's own educational plans and interpret these as representing
influences from parent or peer, we are ignoring that these measures of "significant
others' influence" are also tapping the results of the individual's influences on
the parent and friend. Most parents' aspirations for their child respond to the
child's earlier performances and expressed aspirations, and the flow of influence
between two friends is in both directions.

Even the process studies pose this conceptual problem. For instance, if parents
who engage in induction tend to have children who have more advanced cognitive
development, it requires a fundamental assumption about the direction of causality to conclude that induction "produces" cognitive development rather than
that advanced cognitive development makes induction feasible. Although longitudinal studies help to clarify some of the questions of directionality, we are
often left with the need to interpret our findings more fully than the data justify.
We need at least to consider alternative interpretations under those conditions.

A second conceptual problem relates to the reflexive nature of human interaction. Many studies of the family and peer influence obtain information from
students about their parents' or their friends' views on various issues, in particular
on goals. It can be shown that if this is done, the views of others reported by
the students differ to some extent from those which would be given by those
others themselves (Kerckhoff and Huff 1974). As a result, the associations
between these two kinds of measures and any third measure (say, the student's
academic performance) will differ. The conceptual problem is to decide whether
a parent's "actual" view or the view as perceived by the student is the proper
measure. Ideally, of course, a full analysis of the influence process might include
both, as well as some indication of the bases for the differences, but this is
seldom possible. Since it is likely that somewhat different conclusions would
be reached depending on which is used, the decision is a conceptual, rather than
a methodological, one.

Finally, studies of family and peer influences on the educational process
involve a distinction that is seldom explicitly made between the form and the
content of the influence process. Much of the literature reviewed by Rollins and
Thomas is wholly concerned with the structure of the parent-child relationship

as it affects the child's development of particular characteristics. Induction, for instance, refers to *how* the parent attempts to go about controlling the child's behavior. It does not refer at all to *what* the parent is trying to accomplish. Similarly, many studies of peer relations in school are concerned with the distribution of friendship choices, how popular various individuals are, and so on and have little, if any, concern with the bases of friendship or the kinds of activities friends engage in. Other research, on the other hand, either explicitly or implicitly assumes a form of the relationship while being wholly concerned with a particular content. The status attainment research tradition generally does this. It is simply assumed that parents and peers transmit influences of a particular type, given some characteristic of the parent or peer. The form of the transmission process is not considered as part of the investigation.

However, the research reviewed here suggests that it may be possible for the methods parents use, or the very form of the social relationships an individual has with peers, to have an effect on the individual that is distinct from the effect of the content of the interactions involved. In fact, one would expect the two kinds of effects to "interact" (in the statistical sense). There are few investigations that attempt to combine these two views of interpersonal influence. Unfortunately, some that do combine them (by investigating whether the quality of the parent-child relationship affects the degree of adoption of parent values by children) have not been successful in finding the expected outcome (Kandel and Lesser 1969; Sandis 1970; Kerckhoff and Huff 1974). Unless we are to assume that form and content have wholly independent effects on the child's development, however, further clarification needs to be sought.

Methodological Problems

One of the major difficulties encountered in attempting to make generalizations based on studies ranging across the full pre-adult period is that the methods used in the studies vary according to which part of the period is being investigated. In general, the younger the children involved, the more homogeneous the sample. Studies of relatively young children, even in the early grades in school, tend to be based on observation, interviews, and, sometimes, experiments. They usually involve collection of data from both children and adults (parents and/or teachers) as well as from institutional records. In contrast, studies of older children, especially adolescents, are usually based on questionnaires, with most of the data being collected from the children themselves and little, if any, collected from parents.

Correlated with this basic difference in data collection techniques and variation in the kinds of data that can be collected with the different techniques are the size and distribution of the samples studied. Elementary-school student studies are inevitably restricted to a few classrooms or schools, while studies of secondary-school students more often include much larger and more diverse samples. Thus it is often difficult to estimate how relevant the more demographically restricted but more in-depth studies of family influences during the elementary-school years are in relation to the more representative but more data-restricted studies of the secondary-school years.

Closely related to this problem is the fact that the institutional settings are significantly different in the two kinds of studies, but the research designs are not adequate to determine the extent of the effect of that difference. The elementary school tends to be smaller and more homogeneous in its student body than the secondary school. Unless the structures of the school are included in the research design, some of their effects (possibly including interactions with family characteristics) may be overlooked or misinterpreted. To the extent that elementary-school students are homogeneous with respect to social background and kinds of parent and peer characteristics, any investigation of a limited number of such schools is likely to underestimate the extent of parent and peer influence in the overall population. Even crude indices of parent and peer influence at the secondary-school level may exhibit stronger associations with the schooling process simply because of the greater range of kinds of parents and peers represented in a broader-based sample of secondary-school students.

A third methodological problem is probably the most troublesome of all. It is the specification problem, and it is found in studies of all age levels, although it tends to differ by level. By specification problem, I mean the problem of specifying the sources of influence on whatever outcome is being investigated and the distortions in findings that result from improper specification. Several examples come readily to mind. For instance, studies of secondary-school students have often failed to take into account the curriculum the students were in (college preparatory, vocational, etc.). When that is the case, students from various socioeconomic levels are seen to exhibit greater performance differences than they do when curriculum is taken into account. Because lower-status students are less likely to be found in the college preparatory curriculum, and because college preparatory students tend to perform at higher levels than other students, the differences that could be attributed to curriculum placement come to be attributed directly to socioeconomic position when curriculum is left out of the analysis.

However, inclusion of curriculum in an analysis can also lead to misinterpretations. As Alexander and Cook (1982) have shown, if pre-high school performance data are included in the analysis, the specific effects of being in one curriculum or another are sharply reduced. Those who are in the college preparatory curriculum not only perform at higher levels when in that curriculum, but they also have performed at higher levels before coming to high school. Thus, to some extent, differential performance by curriculum is due as much to the selection process that places students in a curriculum as it is to the fact of being in that curriculum.

Entwisle and Hayduk (1982) show that this same problem is found in analyses of children's school experiences in the first years of elementary school. In their study, they recorded the grades received at two points in each of the first three years of school. If the full set of grades is included in a multivariate analysis, continuity from one measurement point to the next accounts for much of the variance in the later grades. However, if the earlier grades are omitted from the analysis, two things happen. First, and most obviously, it is possible to explain much less of the variation in later grades. But more important here, of the variation that is explained, a much larger proportion is explained by family characteristics than if the full range of performances is taken into account. In a similar fashion, other kinds of measures can be included or excluded from the analysis and thereby alter the observed effects of family or school influences. One such measure, discussed earlier, is the characteristics of the school's student body. If the socioeconomic status of the school's average student is made part of the multivariate analysis, this will tend to reduce the magnitude of the effect of any individual student's family characteristics on whatever school outcomes are being studied. This would be especially likely if a large number of elementary schools were included in an analysis and most of those schools had student bodies that were relatively homogeneous in socioeconomic status.

Concern with the specification problem necessarily involves us in attempts to be more specific about the multiple factors involved in producing any particular outcome of interest, say, educational ambition. It means attempting to take into account both family and peer influences but also the nature of the educational process itself. Any multivariate analysis, using a conceptualization of a flow of influence over time, must recognize that factors experienced early may have effects later on and that such effects may be indirect, through intervening factors. It is because of such complexities of relationships that schematic models such as Figure 4.1 have been developed to help the researcher clarify the processes involved. Attempting to deal with the specification problem usually involves inserting more factors into such a diagram, factors that are thought to intervene between any two of the factors already being considered. It also raises the necessity of differentiating between the direct effects of one factor on another and any indirect effects due to a flow of influence through one or more intervening factors. For instance, in Figure 4.1 the full effect of socioeconomic status on an individual's level of aspiration cannot be understood without taking into account the mediating functions of academic performance and significant others' influence.

Actually, the specification problem is both a methodological and a conceptual problem. It is usually treated as a methodological problem because it is assumed that the conceptualization of the influence process being studied is clearly recognized and the only problem is in operationalizing it in the analysis. In fact, all too often we fail to conceptualize the influence process clearly at the outset, and it is only when we begin to interpret our results that we (or others) recognize that we might be attributing effects to particular factors because of misspecification.

CONCLUSION

The fact of influence on the educational process by family and peers is apparent from the kinds of research reviewed earlier. The nature of the patterns of inter- action with these significant others, as well as the kinds of characteristics they exhibit, have repeatedly been linked with variations in educational performance, attitudes toward school, and future educational orientations. Families and peer groups provide contexts within which socialization processes occur. They both provide and delimit important formative types of interpersonal relationships in which young people participate. Both the form and the content of that interper- sonal influence has educationally relevant effects.

At the same time, our knowledge of these familial and peer influences is limited and somewhat disjointed. While most of the literature reviewed here can be linked by means of a general conceptualization of the socialization process, there remain conceptual and methodological issues which are challenging, per- haps even intractable. It seems unlikely that they will be adequately dealt with unless we broaden our perspective on the processes involved beyond what is usually foud in the literature reviewed. Almost all of the studies dealing with these issues have focused on a particular substantive question, relevant to only a limited part of the age span during which individuals are in school. One of the more difficult metatheoretical issues posed by this literature is how to link these pieces together into a coherent whole. In this chapter, I have adopted a general socialization perspective in order to show how various rather different types of investigation are relevant to one another. But this is, at best, a crude beginning.

What is needed is a perspective on the entire period of schooling which takes into account both the family and peer factors discussed here and the processes occurring within the school itself. Most important is to recognize that the influ- ences occur over time and that the kinds of processes and the nature of the individuals involved in them change over the school years. While there are undoubtedly some similarities, the peer relations of the first grader are quite different from those of the high school senior—they are different in both form and content, and they are engaged in by people with quite different personal characteristics. Yet there is continuity as well as change. Early experiences have effects which are likely to be apparent many years later. It is not surprising that none of the research reviewed here attempts to encompass the entire period of schooling, since the methodological difficulties are awesome. However, unless we at least organize our observations of parts of this period within a concep- tualization of the whole, it is unlikely that we will be able to understand the parts very well.

The kind of perspetive needed here is beginning to evolve in the social and behavioral sciences under the general heading of "life course analysis." It attempts to view the trajectory of an individual's life as a whole, as a patterned sequence of steps or stages or events. While much of the recent writing which has used this perspective has focused on adulthood and old age, the perspective is equally appropriate (perhaps more appropriate) for an analysis of the first two decades or so of life. If nothing else, there is a greater uniformity of sequential stages during childhood and adolescence than during adulthood and old age, and the stages are institutionally organized largely within the two settings of the family and school. While I have not been able to organize my present discussion in any systematic way within a life course perspective, the life course literature at least suggests some promising ideas. In closing, I will note a few of these.

Nearly two decades ago, Brim (1966) discussed the differences between the socialization process in childhood and in adulthood. He argued that socially appropriate role performance requires knowledge of what is expected, the ability to do what is expected, and the motivation to do it. Essentially, he argued that socialization in childhood is largely directed toward developing appropriate motivation, while adult socialization assumes motivation and focuses more on the development of knowledge and skill. Clearly, this kind of shift occurs during the school years, and it is equally clear that families and peer groups play important roles in facilitating (or retarding) these kinds of individual development. If we accept this conceptualization as relevant to the present discussion, it suggests that what is an important outcome and an important kind of family or peer influence during the early years of schooling may be much less important later on. Equally obvious is the conclusion that new factors assume significance as the child matures.

If one is to go beyond such broad generalizations about the kinds of influence or kinds of change associated with different periods in the life course, there is need for a conceptualization of the different types of trajectories the life course can take. How those trajectories are defined will, of course, depend on the substantive area of interest. For instance, if we focus on academic performance, it would be possible to define trajectories as varying in three essential ways: according to their average level (high or low), consistency (stable or varied levels over time), and length (time in school). It seems likely that different trajectories not only lead to different later outcomes, but that they also are influenced by different early or contemporary factors. Thus, in addition to charting the forms of life course trajectories, we will want to investigate what factors help explain those forms.

Clausen (1972) discusses a number of ways in which trajectories might be represented and investigated while at the same time acknowledging the problems involved. Some of his discussion is at least implicitly relevant to an interpretation and further elaboration of some of the research discussed earlier. For instance, he notes that many life course transitions are culturally defined in terms of age or sequence, and deviations from those definitions can have significant effects on the individual. Being "early" or "late" is itself an important fact for the individual to contend with. The research of Simmons and co-workers (1979) and of Blyth and co-workers (1978) suggests that this can be so with respect to such a basic matter as the timing of puberty. There are also many other experiences which, while not culturally defined, are not easily controlled by the individual and which can have a deflecting effect on one's trajectory. The divorce of one's parents (or the death of one of them) and a shift of peer contexts through a residential move are contingencies which may have far-reaching effects.

Finally, when considering the idea of life course trajectories, it becomes apparent that we normally think in terms of continuities over time. The trajectory is a line (straight or curved) which is connected from beginning to end. If the shapes of trajectories differ, one way in which they may do so is to diverge at some point after having been similar earlier. If we find that to occur, it becomes crucial to examine the branching point for clues to the reasons for the divergence. Clausen (1972) notes that adolescence is a time of divergence, a point at which "alternate tracks" are taken. However, the analysis of Alexander and Cook (1982) suggests that this branching (at least academic branching) has its origins much earlier. It may be, therefore, that the search for explanations of varied life course trajectories will need to include consideration of many aspects of the earlier part of the life course as well as contemporary factors.

Conceptualizing the research reviewed here within a life course framework increases the need for a dynamic view of the individual. Not only do such sources of influence as families and peers (and schools) have effects throughout the period of schooling, but they also interact with each other. In addition, the individual contributes to the process throughout, not only because of the knowledge, skills, and dispositions already acquired, but also because of the choices continually made. There are both regularities in the form and sequencing of these interacting factors, largely owing to institutional patterns, and variataions, owing to contingencies and the blending of the several sources of influence. The combination of regularities and variations produces a number of possible trajectories. The kinds of research discussed earlier should provide a basis for initial efforts to conceptualize some of those trajectories and the processes that produce them. This would be a major step forward toward a coherent view of the significance of families, peers, and other sources of influence in the educational process.

REFERENCES

Alexander, K. L., and M. A. Cook. "Curricula and Coursework: A Surprise Ending to a Familiar Story." *American Sociological Review* 47 (1982): 626–40.

Alexander, K. L., and B. K. Eckland. "Contextual Effects in the High School Attainment Process." *American Sociological Review* 40 (1975): 402–16.

Blau, P. M., and O. D. Duncan. *The American Occupational Structure*. New York: John Wiley & Sons, 1967.

Blyth, D. A., R. G. Simmons, and D. Bush. "The Transition into Adolescence: A Longitudinal Comparison of Youth in Two Educational Contexts." *Sociology of Education* 51 (1978): 149–62.

Brim, O. G., Jr. "Socialization through the Life Cycle." In *Socialization after Childhood: Two Essays*, edited by O. G. Brim, Jr., and S. Wheeler. New York: John Wiley & Sons, 1966.

Brittain, C. V. "Adolescent Choices and Parent-Peer Cross Pressures." *American Sociological Review* 28 (1963): 85–90.

Campbell, E. Q., and C. N. Alexander. "Structural Effects and Interpersonal Relationships." *American Journal of Sociology* 71 (1965): 284–89.

Clausen, J. A. "The Life Course of Individuals." In *Aging and Society*, vol. 3, edited by M. Riley, M. Johnson, and A. Foner. New York: Russell Sage Foundation, 1972.

Cohen, J. M. "Sources of Peer Group Homogeneity." *Sociology of Education* 50 (1977): 227–41.

Coleman, J. S. *The Adolescent Society*. New York: The Free Press, 1961.

Coleman, J. S., et al. *Equality of Educational Opportunity*. Washington, D.C.: U.S. Government Printing Office, 1966.

Davis, J. A. "The Campus as a Frog Pond." *American Journal of Sociology* 72 (1966): 17–31.

Entwisle, D. R., and L. A. Hayduk. *Early Schooling: Cognitive and Affective Outcomes*. Baltimore: Johns Hopkins University Press, 1982.

Epstein, J. L. *A Longitudinal Study of School and Family Effects on Student Development*. Center for Social Organization of Schools, Johns Hopkins University, Report No. 301, 1980.

———. "Longitudinal Effects of Family-School-Person Interactions on Student Outcomes." In *Research in Sociology of Education and Socialization, Personal Change over the Life Course*, vol. 4, edited by A. C. Kerckhoff. Greenwich, CT: JAI Press, 1983.

Gildea, M., J. Glidewell, and M. Kanter. "Maternal Attitudes and the General Adjustment in School Children." In *Parental Attitudes and Child Behavior*, edited by J. Glidewell. Springfield, IL: Charles C. Thomas, 1961.

Haller, A. O., and A. Portes. "Status Attainment Processes." *Sociology of Education* 46 (1973): 51–91.

Hallinan, M. T. "Friendship Patterns in Open and Traditional Classrooms." *Sociology of Education* 49 (1976): 254–65.

Hess, R., and V. Shipman. "Early Experience and the Socialization of Cognitive Modes in Children." *Child Development* 36 (1965): 869–86.

Howell, F. M., and W. Frese. *Making Life Plans: Race, Gender and Career Decisions*. Washington, D.C.: University Press of America, 1982.

Kandel, D. B. "Homophily, Selection, and Socialization in Adolescent Friendships." *American Journal of Sociology* 84 (1978): 427–36.

Kandel, D. B., and G. S. Lesser. "Parental and Peer Influences on Educational Plans of Adolescents." *American Sociological Review* 34 (1969): 212–23.

Kerckhoff, A. C. *Ambition and Attainment: A Study of Four Samples of American Boys*. Washington, D.C.: American Sociological Association, 1974.

———, ed. *Research in Sociology of Education and Socialization: Longitudinal Perspectives on Educational Attainment*. Vol. 1. Greenwich, CT: JAI Press, 1980.

Kerckhoff, A. C., and J. L. Huff. "Parental Influence on Educational Goals.' *Sociometry* 37 (1974): 307–27.

McDill, E. L., L. C. Rigsby, and E. D. Meyers. "Educational Climates of High Schools: Their Effects and Sources." *American Journal of Sociology* 74 (1969): 567–86.

Meyer, J. W. "High School Effects on College Intentions." *American Journal of Sociology* 76 (1970): 59–70.

Mercy, J. A., and L. C. Steelman. "Familial Influence on the Intellectual Attainment of Children." *American Sociological Review* 47 (1982): 532–42.

Mosteller, F., and D. P. Moynihan. *On Equality of Educational Opportunity.* New York: Random House, 1972.

Rehberg, R. A., and E. R. Rosenthal. *Class and Merit in the American High School.* New York: Longman, 1978.

Rollins, B. C., and D. L. Thomas. "Parental Support, Power, and Control Techniques in the Socialization of Children." In *Contemporary Theories About the Family* vol. 1, edited by W. Burr et al. New York: The Free Press, 1979.

Rosenbaum, J. E. "The Stratification of Socialization Processes." *American Sociological Review* 40 (1975): 48–54.

Rosenberg, M. "Which Significant Others?" *American Behavioral Scientist* 16 (1973): 829–60.

Sandis, E. E. "The Transmission of Mothers' Educational Ambitions, as Related to Specific Socialization Techniques." *Journal of Marriage and the Family* 32 (1970): 204–11.

Sewell, W. H., A. O. Haller, and A. Portes. "The Educational and Early Occupational Attainment Process." *American Sociological Review* 34 (1969): 82–92.

Simmons, R. G., et al. "Entry into Early Adolescence: The Impact of School Structure, Puberty, and Early Dating on Self-esteem." *American Sociological Review* 44 (1979): 948–67.

Smith, T.E. "Adolescent Agreement with Perceived Maternal and Paternal Educational Goals." *Journal of Marriage and the Family* 43 (1981): 85–93.

Zajonc, R. B., and G. B. Markus. "Birth Order and Intellectual Development." *Psychological Review* 82 (1975): 74–88.

5

CARL H. SIMPSON AND
SUSAN J. ROSENHOLTZ

Classroom Structure and the Social Construction of Ability

INTRODUCTION

Much research recognizes that schools reproduce in microcosm the culture (e.g., Dreeben 1968) and structure (e.g., Bowles and Gintis 1976) of the larger society. That is to say, each school socializes and allocates individuals, acting not simply as an isolated local social system, but as part of a larger social institution. Schools are created on the basis of institutionalized knowledge and gain their legitimacy in part from their isomorphism with beliefs and structures institutionalized within the society rather than simply as effective or ineffective local organizations (Meyer 1977). In short, schools mediate institutionalized reality to individuals. Much as religion in pre-modern society mediated between the individual and the social and metaphysical cosmos, schools now mediate to each new generation of children much of the basic structure and culture of our modern society/cosmos.

Ability formation theory addresses one intersection between the cultural macrocosm and the school microcosm, that concerning the socialization of successive generations of students to a conception of intellectual ability isomorphic with that institutionalized in the larger society. The nature and distribution of intellectual ability appear so consistent that they impel study of the conditions under which the obvious and the commonplace occur: individuals' ability levels vary widely; ethnic minorities perform less well in school than others; measured IQ stabilizes at about the time school begins; children overestimate their abilities when they begin school but gradually make more accurate judgments.

Indeed, the dominant interpretation of such findings is sociologically adrift. It is reductionist, seeing no role of context (Rosenholtz and Simpson 1984a): when children arrive at school, they possess inherent levels of ability, approximating a normal and stable distribution; during the early years of schooling, students mature cognitively and receive feedback from teachers, leading them to "learn" about the ability which inheres within them (see Frieze 1981; Stipek 1984). This conventional developmental explanation recommends itself because

of its parsimony. Moreover, the popular culture readily accepts such a formulation because of its compatibility with the use of ability differences to legitimate
inequality (Fass 1980).[1]

However, the economy of such an explanation must be questioned when
differences in classroom context are shown to affect the distribution and interpretation of ability among students. In this chapter we (a) summarize our theoretical approach, which we have called *ability formation theory*; (b) summarize
previously published findings testing ability formation theory; and (c) discuss
the most recent developments of the theory, supported by new research findings.

THEORETICAL BACKGROUND: THE SOCIAL
CONSTRUCTION OF REALITY

While the beginning point of most reductionist explanations is the reification
of the individual, we work instead from the assumption that individual abilities
and performance behaviors are in part socially constructed and as such are subject
to variation across classroom contexts. The best-developed formulation of the
reality construction approach also provides the origin of the name: *The Social
Construction of Reality* by Berger and Luckmann (1966). Berger and Luckmann
propose connections at the metatheoretical level between macrocosmic structure
and culture and microcosmic structure and culture by way of the sociology of
knowledge approach. They argue that a gradual, reciprocal evolutionary process
leads local and societal structure and culture toward consistency. The larger
culture influences the structure of daily activities by establishing what is feasible
(real) and what is acceptable (cognitively and morally legitimate). In turn, locally
structured daily activities provide plausibility for institutionalized beliefs, reinforcing those beliefs by allowing us to see that they accurately reflect our daily
experience. In stable societies, this mutually reinforcing interplay produces unchallenged knowledge of what is real.

The process of reality construction is essentially unobservable in the short
term, except in the case of the socialization of new generations to embrace
already institutionalized knowledge. In the Berger and Luckmann view, socialization is primarily accomplished indirectly, through individuals' interpretations
of patterns and typifications emerging fro the patterns of daily activities. Individuals being socialized actively seek information to learn about their environment and how they are situated within it. The patterns they locate during their
search are normally consistent with a particular interpretation of reality. Interpersonal conversation concerning the shared experience of daily activities moves
these interpretations out of the private, subjective realm into the public, objective
realm of knowledge (i.e., interpretations are objectivated as real). At this point,
the knowledge which local actors have helped to re-create is projected outward,
to be viewed as entirely and permanently external to the control of those very
actors.[2]

In stable situations, the local interpretations most likely to be reified in this way will be identical to those already institutionalized. It is here that the end points of reality construction theory and developmental theory are identical: the individual accurately reports the facts of his or her ability. However, the reality construction approach also allows another possibility: where local organization of daily events varies from traditional forms, local knowledge may depart from institutionalized knowledge. Thus different facts may be "accurate" in different local systems. If so, the inevitability of institutionalized knowledge must also be questioned.

Ability Formation Theory

Despite conventional interpretations, the reconstruction of ability in elementary schools is a phenomenon which plausibly fits the social construction approach. The larger society contains institutionalized ideas about ability. Indeed, intelligence occupies a nearly sacred mythic stature in U.S. society (see Rosenbaum in this *Handbook*). Schools have close connection to the development and measurement of students' abilities. And, most important, schools provide a continual flow of daily activities involving academic ability. In the context of these recurrent daily activities, teachers and students come to make judgments about self and others and to interpret those judgments in conversation with other classroom actors (Bossert 1979).

The study of students' introduction to intellectual ability as a social construction requires first that we specify the nature of institutionalized conceptions of ability. Daily classroom experience which locally constructs that conception, and the process of conversation, information exchange among actors in the classroom, can then be pursued.[3]

Institutionalized Conceptions of Ability

We take as a model of the institutionalized conception of intellectual ability the standardized IQ test. IQ has the following qualities salient to our analysis.

1. IQ levels are stratified. Each individual has a single level, with all levels normally distributed so that as many individuals score low as score high.
2. IQ is general. Each individual receives a single IQ score which is believed to indicate the individual's ability to learn and therefore to perform nearly any task.
3. IQ is stable over time.
4. IQ is a consensual fact. It is a reliably measurable (i.e., objective) quality of individuals which may be accurately perceived by others and by the self.
5. A secondary quality of IQ is its association with ethnic and socioeconomic status. While this quality is not inherent to the definition of IQ, as are the first four, it is a deeply ingrained element of our knowledge about IQ (see Fass 1980). Our approach argues that these closely associated differences emerge from the same roots as the individual stratification of ability levels and will therefore accompany ability formation.

The above five qualities constitute the dependent variables in our reality construction argument that classroom daily activities socialize students to accept the institutionalized conception of ability. We will say that ability formation has taken place to the extent that students' conceptions of ability are individually and collectively isomorphic to this institutionalized conception, that is, when students' reported ability levels are *stratified, general, stable,* and *consensually "accurate"* and when these reports reflect ethnic and social status levels. We identify these aspects of ability because they are susceptible to variations in degree; they can be translated into measurable variables.

Given this institutionalized conception, our next task is to specify precisely how school experience constructs it. Our basic argument is straightforward. As students seek to make sense of their school world, several analytically distinct processes will occur. First, intellectual ability is a relative concept that will be formed comparatively. Second, students will perform academic tasks, providing the basic data for the comparison process. Third, students will receive feedback from teachers and peers, influencing their ability perceptions. Fourth, the structure of students' academic tasks symbolically will imply conclusions about the abilities believed to influence task outcomes. That is, the way daily academic activities are organized will in and of itself imply how ability is structured. Fifth, the way in which performance evaluations are organized and interpreted will provide a language (e.g., letter grades) within which to cast interpretations of ability. Finally, accumulated school experience will gradually lead students to adopt as factual knowledge the institutionalized conception of their own and others' abilities.

Each of these processes has to do with gathering and interpreting information relevant to intellectual ability. The amount of feedback students receive, the consistency of that feedback, and the ease with which it can be gathered and compared will all affect ability formation. In the following section, we examine classroom organizational conditions that underlie the construction of institutionalized ability conceptions among new student recruits.

Qualities of Local Classroom Organization: Deep Structure

We believe that one reason studies of classroom effects on students' self-evaluations of ability have been largely inconclusive is the absence of convincing theory directing choice of sample, comparison groups, and measures. Instructional forms which appear very different, for example, use of ability groups versus individually paced standardized learning materials, may have identical effects regarding a particular phenomenon such as ability formation. One must look to deeper structures to identify differences that are likely to affect such basic outcomes as the distribution of performances or the conception of ability developed within a classroom.

Ability formation theory argues that students actively participate in their own socialization. They seek interpretation, and they make interpretations in comparison with other students in their cohort. Institutionalized interpretations are, by their nature, always available. Students' interpretations will come to mirror those particular conceptions to the extent that (a) daily academic performances are consistent with the model of stratified, general, stable ability levels and (b) classroom performance and evaluation structures facilitate comparison but inhibit multiple or indeterminant comparisons.

The quality of classroom structure that is most likely to affect the extent to which these conditions are met is the *dimensionality* of classroom organization during instruction. In particular, the more closely all surface activities within the classroom imply a single, underlying academic performance dimension, the sooner and more fully students should mirror institutionalized ability conceptions. That is, *unidimensional* classroom organization facilitates ability formation. Unidimensional classroom organization, where the performance structure is singular and consistent across time and task areas and where the evaluation structure maximizes the comparability of performances, is most likely to imply that ability is a *single dimension* along which individuals are differentiated into singular, general, dispersed, and stable scores.

On the other hand, where the task and evaluation structure is *multidimensional*, implying many distinct performance dimensions, ability formation will be inhibited. Inevitable differences among individuals' skills and experiences in specific task areas mean that shifts among performance dimensions will be accompanied by changing performance levels. Global inequality is constructed unidimensionally; yet where multiple types of performances and evaluations exist, each student will perform better at some types than at others. The resulting inconsistency of performance levels inhibits ability formation in several ways.

First, the changeable or inconsistent evaluations stemming from individuals' differential ranks on the various performance dimensions will produce an internally contradictory or obscure information flow, undermining classroom actors' ability to agree about any specific formulation. Peers may average out these different ranks, perceiving little overall stratification among individual students, or each peer may choose which performances to emphasize, producing lack of consensus among peers. With several alternative performance levels to choose from, students will tend to emphasize their strongest performances both when developing personal learning styles and when reporting their own ability levels. Thus the stratification pattern in such classes should "accurately" find many students reporting a medium–range ability but few reporting the lowest ranges. Further, students of different ethnic, cultural, or socioeconomic backgrounds should be more likely in such classes to locate methods of learning suited to their own backgrounds. Therefore, ability should show less correlation with these factors in multidimensional classes.

In addition, in multidimensional classes, ability will tend not to be viewed as general or stable. Performance levels change with changing performance dimensions. Therefore, if ability is general, it cannot be stable; if it is stable, it cannot be general. Indeed, less reason exists in such classrooms to assume it is either stable or general.

We think that most research in ability and educational stratification, as well as much in developmental psychology, attribution, and social psychology of status relations, has taken place in social systems constructed so as to produce relatively unidimensional status comparisons. Indeed, despite all manner of innovation, Goodlad (1983), in one of the most comprehensive studies ever undertaken, reported that traditional instructional organization occurred in nearly all the 1,041 classrooms sampled. The bulk of our findings remains accurate within the scope condition that the setting be unidimensional. However, we find the picture different enough in multidimensional settings to argue that these findings emerge not from individual qualities alone, but from individual qualities in conjunction with the structures of the social setting.

Specific Indicators of Classroom Organizational Dimensionality

In three empirical investigations, classroom dimensionality has been in operation in the following ways:

1. Performance structure is *unidimensional when tasks are relatively undifferentiated*, as indicated by few different types of materials or instructional media which might provide optional learning methods or reward diverse learner experience or skill. Multidimensional classes use many different materials for different learners and augment traditional methods with manipulative experiential learning, multimedia presentations, computer-assisted instruction, and the like.

2. Performance structure is *multidimensional when student grouping patterns are complex*. Whole class instruction and ability-grouped instruction unidimensionalize the classroom by increasing comparability and by implying a single stratification dimension for all. Flexible grouping and nonprogrammed individual learning time disrupt unidimensional comparisons.

3. Performance structure is *unidimensional when student autonomy is low*. If students are able to make independent choices about what work to do or when to do it, they are likely to increase the number of options (dimensions) in the classroom, disrupt comparability, and make choices favoring positive self-perceived ability.

4. The evaluation structure is *unidimensional when grades are assigned*. Formal symbolic letter or number grades can override multiple performance dimensions to create global stratification. Frequency, visibility, comparability, and singularity of performance evaluations are increased by grades. Further, grades carry compact symbolic meanings. They can be averaged, giving the appearance of unidimensionality, and they symbolically increase the salience of ability in the classroom.

In sum, we argue that unidimensional classroom organization produces a set of daily performances and evaluations which implies a single underlying dimension of ability. As classroom actors—teachers, peers, and selves—observe performances in such settings, they will be drawn toward judgments congruent with institutionalized ability conceptions. Individuals will stratify themselves, as they are consensually forced to take positions on a relatively singular scale. Positions on the scale will correspond to major divisions of the social structure. And students will come to perceive ability as something objective (fact-like and external to their control), global, and stable.

A REVIEW OF FINDINGS FROM TESTS OF ABILITY FORMATION THEORY

Ability formation theory, as developed above, stipulates a number of differential outcomes resulting from variations in one basic aspect of classroom structure. To illustrate the versatility of this perspective, we briefly review findings from previous tests of ability formation theory. Again, we choose to emphasize in this chapter the diversity of surface manifestations derived from this one deep structure. This involves summarizing results published elsewhere, without repeating references, and mentioning results of our most recent work, without reporting detailed quantitative analysis.[4] Three studies have been explictly constructed to test this theory. Two are described elsewhere (Rosenholtz and Rosenholtz 1981; Simpson 1981). The third, a study of twenty-four classrooms, grades one through six in two schools, is described later in this chapter. In addition, we have reviewed elsewhere a large body of research we find compatible with this theoretical view (Rosenholtz and Simpson 1984a).

Findings Concerning Classroom Stratification Outcomes

In the following pages, we summarize the results of our tests of a series of research hypotheses drawn from ability formation theory. We begin with findings concerning stratification outcomes. All the findings reported have withstood statistical tests for alternative interpretations, such as arguments that family social status or tested ability upon entering school might account for observations.

1. Students' self-perceived ability levels are widely dispersed and closely approximate a normal distribution in unidimensional classrooms. In multidimensional classes, self-perceptions are less dispersed, with a concentration in the average to moderately-above-average range. We find statistically reliable evidence supporting this conclusion consistently in three separate samples, in grades one through six, for various academic subject areas as well as for global self-ratings. The pressure upon students to stratify themselves on a single dimension versus the freedom to choose options which enhance self-perceived ability is illustrated by the fact that in each of three studies, at least twice as many students in unidimensional classrooms as in multidimensional classrooms report for themselves below-average academic ability.

2. Peers' ratings of individual students' ability levels are more widely dispersed in unidimensional classrooms than in multidimensional classrooms. Our

previous studies offer indirect support for this finding. The most recent study provides a direct test and shows support in academic subjects (e.g., reading and math) as well as in global ratings (e.g., "smart" and "all classwork").

3. In the one clear test case to date, we found a reliably greater performance deficit among minority children in unidimensional classrooms than among such children in multidimensional classrooms. In reading and social studies, the distance between minority and nonminority students' performance levels, as estimated by teachers, was nearly three times as great in unidimensional classes. Preliminary analysis of our most recent data set shows the same pattern of results for both teacher and peer perceptions. Indirect support is also provided by Cohen's (1976) use of multidimensional curricula during an attempted black/white status intervention field experiment and by Mercer's (1971) conclusion that fewer black students are labeled retarded when screening is multidimensional (when more than one screening device is used).

However, the distribution of *self-perceived* ability levels is affected by neither ethnic status nor classroom organization interacting with ethnic status.

4. One of our two tests of family socieconomic status shows closer association between status and classroom performance in unidimensional classrooms. In the other study, no reliable interaction between social status and classroom organization was located. This discrepancy is probably due to measurement difficulties in the first, smaller study. Our most recent study used participation in the school lunch programs to identify reliably families with very limited resources versus others. Here we find higher correlations in unidimensional classes between status and performance in academic subjects and in global ratings, as reported by teachers and peers. We also find a smaller but reliable difference in the case of self-perceived ability.

5. A large number of nonacademic qualities of students are more closely dependent on academic ability in unidimensional classes than in multidimensional classes. These correlates of ability occur as unintended consequnces of the classroom stratification process in unidimensional classes, where performance information is more public, more salient, and more consensual. We have found at least some evidence of the following correlates, although none of our studies was directed primarily toward this issue.

Student power is slightly more stratified and substantially more closely linked to academic ability level in unidimensional classes than in multidimensional classes. Also, we can borrow Hallinan's (1976, 1979) findings to suggest that friendship choice is more affected by academic status in unidimensional classes than in multidimensional classes. When these findings are combined with our finding that unidimensional classes stratify academic performance according to social status, the greater popularity and power of those with higher social status can be derived for unidimensional classes. That prediction is fully supported by research findings (for reviews see Cohen 1984; Patchen 1982; Schofield and Sagar 1983).

Although classroom dimensionality does not consistently affect students' net liking for school or engagement with school, we have some evidence that liking for school is more dependent on ability level in unidimensional classes, and our recent research offers strong evidence that effort engagement varies significantly with ability level in unidimensional classes. Finally, we also find moral self-censure more closely associated with academic self-concept in unidimensional classrooms.

These findings cumulate to support our general contention that the stratification order in unidimensional classes is more global (singular) and that academic ability is more salient in these settings.

Findings Concerning Nonstratification Outcomes Expected under Ability Formation Theory

Aside from stratification outcomes, we have stipulated three major qualities of ability that we expect to be reproduced more fully in unidimensional classrooms than in multidimensional classrooms: consensus, generalization, and stability.

1. We consistently find high peer consensus about classmates' relative ability levels in all classrooms, and we find equally consistently that consensus is higher in unidimensional classes.

2. We also find consistent evidence that peers and teachers agree more closely about individuals' ability levels in unidimensional classrooms.

   It is to be expected from attribution research findings that judgments coming from an outside objective viewpoint would reflect more consensual facts, even when unpleasant for individuals, than would be the case for individuals' perceptions of self. In addition, we observe these external judgments converging on consensual facts more closely in unidimensional classrooms than in multidimensional classrooms.

3. We predict that performance levels and ability conceptions will be stabler in unidimensional classrooms than in multidimensional classrooms. Panel data are required for a full test of this hypothesis. However, we have included in our research some questions tapping students' perception of the variability of their ability levels. In one study, we found no differences in perceived stability. Our most recent study included more sensitive indicators, clearly illustrating greater stability among students in unidimensional classes: students in these classes less often feel that they can alter their math and reading performance levels "if I tried harder" and express much greater agreement that "there are some things you won't be good at no matter how hard you try."

4. We also predict that students' ability, as perceived by self or others, will be more general in unidimensional classes. In multidimensional classes, we expect ability to be conceived as a multifaceted phenomenon. Experimental studies by Cohen (1980), Tammivaara (1982), and Rosenholtz (1985) confirm this possibility. Explicitly multiple-abilities curricula significantly reduced the generalization of global ability ranks of interaction, power, and future task performance expectations.

Our most recent research was structured to provide multiple tests of this prediction. We find markedly higher correlations among various academic self-ratings in unidimensional classrooms. Also, although all peer ratings are remarkably highly correlated (indicating high generalization), those in unidimensional classrooms are even higher than those in multidimensional classrooms. Further, as an explicit test of generalization from global ability, we asked students to rate selves and others on probable ability to perform an entirely new type of task. Associations between this measure and reports of academic ability are reliably higher in unidimensional classes. Finally, we asked students directly how true they felt it was that "there are many kinds of smartness. If kids aren't smart in one thing, they might be smart in another." Agreement is reliably higher in multidimensional classes. At the other end of the scale, we asked whether "some kids are smart in everything" and found greater agreement in unidimensional classrooms.

Findings Concerning Interpersonal Process in Ability Formation

Teachers are in the position to initiate the information exchange and comparison process in the classroom. However, it is peers who, through their comparisons and conversation, make ability "real." We argue that peers are in several ways pivotal to the ability formation process. These, along with findings on teacher behaviors, are summarized below.

Key differences in teacher behavior have been included as indicators of classroom dimensionality. In particular, teachers who use grades or other public tools for differentiating students increase the salience of academic ability in the classroom and the amount of highly comparable information available (see Stipek 1984). They therefore increase their power to define students' ability levels. We find peer ratings, and to a lesser extent self-ratings, more closely linked to teacher reports of performance levels in unidimensional classrooms than in multidimensional classrooms (see also Brattesani et al. 1981; Blumenfeld et al. 1983).

On the other hand, students' self-perceived ability shows remarkably weak association with teachers' assessments of their performance levels. This is no doubt, in part, because teacher feedback often masks the teacher's assessment of the student's ability. For example, 85 percent of seventy-two first-grade through sixth-grade teachers we interviewed disagreed at least slightly that "it is unfair to praise students who are in fact performing poorly."[5] Further, teachers in multidimensional classrooms include more diverse criteria in their formal feedback to students, including in particular, greater emphasis on student effort.

The first way in which peers are pivotal in the ability formation process is that they mediate teacher evaluations to individual students. We find no "direct" impact of teacher assessment on students' self-reported ability levels. Instead, the path is indirect, through peer ratings. To the extent that peers perceive the same performance reality that teachers see, students' self-perceived ability levels more closely approximate teacher assessments. In multidimensional classrooms, where peer consensus about ability levels is relatively low, peers mediate less of teachers' evaluations to individual students, giving teachers less power.

The second way in which peers are pivotal involves the presence or absence of alternative identities for individual students. With the extremely high peer consensus which arises in unidimensional classrooms, optional self-definitions are cut off and with them the freedom to maximize self-perceived ability and the tendency to see ability as multidimensional (see also Strang et al, 1978).

The third way in which peers are pivotal involves their perspective as external judges. As attribution researchers note (Stipek 1984; Jones and Nisbett 1971), one's self-judgments are more complex because one has access to the full complexity of one's motives, engagement, options, etc. But external judges tend to see only bold patterns and highly salient dimensions. They are also more willing to include negative judgments in their evaluations. In both these respects, students move through the ability formation sequence earlier in their role as peers than in their role as self-perceivers. Thus, at any given grade level, we find greater stratification and greater generalization among peer judgments than among self-judgments by these same students. On the short term, the self is spared the stress of negative appraisal. However, on the longer term, ability formation, the reproduction of institutionalized ability conceptions, has been facilitated. Each individual, in the role of peer, has experienced making highly unidimensional judgments about ability. This finesse, the transition from external to internal ability formation, occurs in all classrooms. However, in unidimensional classrooms it is accelerated. Peer judgments are more unidimensional and have greater power over individual judgments.

Finally, evaluations of ability made by all actors in a classroom may correspond more or less closely with standardized test scores. We are accustomed to using standardized test results as "true" scores against which to measure student progress or the accuracy of students' perceptions. In the reality construction view, however, these standardized tests reflect a particular construction of ability. They are, by the nature of their construction, unidimensional in extreme. We therefore expect, and we find, that performance levels approximate standardized test scores more closely in unidimensional classrooms than in multidimensional classrooms. We find this true not only for subjective self-ratings, but also for peer ratings and teacher ratings. Daily academic activities and evaluations in multidimensional classrooms are less standardized. Therefore, performance levels and the ability levels they imply match standardized measures less well.

This finding offers insight into the greater correspondence between ethnic and socioeconoic status and ability in unidimensional classes. We find the greater minority student performance deficit statistically explained by the greater correspondence between standardized measures of ability and students' performance levels in these classes. Minority students score lower on standardized tests to an equal extent under both types of classroom organization. However, the local classroom performance reality in multidimensional classes departs from the standardized form, giving standardized tests less predictive power and allowing minority students options to improve their relative performance levels.

New Theoretical Development and Research Findings
Regarding the Ability Formation Process over Time

Ability conceptions and performance distributions consolidate accumulatively. Research in developmental psychology shows repeatedly that students gradually increase the accuracy of their self-reported academic performance (the correspondence between self-reports and teacher reports or standardized test reports) (Frieze 1981; Stipek 1984). We also argue that the full set of patterns constituting ability formation will emerge gradually, as students accumulate greater experience with daily school activities. We therefore expect to see an increase with grade level in the isomorphism between institutionalized ability conceptions and classroom ability distributions and conceptions.

At the same time, we expect two types of differences to emerge between unidimensional classrooms and multidimensional classrooms. First, ability formation should be accelerated in unidimensional classrooms. We argue that unidimensional inequality is constructed, not natural and inevitable. Our research compares classrooms which vary *in degree*, rather than being totally distinct species. Some ability formation should therefore occur in multidimensional classes also—but more slowly.

Second, to the extent that we have located genuinely multidimensional classrooms, the conception of ability implied within the classroom should remain qualitatively different over time. That is, instead of simply following the same sequence but in later grades, multidimensional classrooms should produce enduring differences in the nature of ability constructed there. Finding such differences in empirical research depends on the degree of difference in the organization of classrooms in a sample. Locating such differences marks an important theoretical development for this work, because differences which are consistent over time, rather than those that are simply lagged, demonstrate most clearly that the effect of multidimensional classroom organization is not simply to obscure truth temporarily, but to construct a truth somewhat alternative to that most usually seen.

Our most recent research provides our first systematic examination of the unfolding pattern of ability formation throughout the elementary-school years as affected by classroom dimensionality. Because this research has not been described elsewhere, we preface this section with a description of our sample and research procedures.

The Sample

We sampled students from two elementary schools within a large metropolitan district of Tennessee. Both schools exhibited highly stable student and teacher populations, above-average achievement test scores, and unusual internal consistency in teaching approaches. Reputationally, the two schools were considered contrasting yet exemplary alternatives. Teacher reports certify that the two quite consistently represent the two poles of the unidimensional/multidimensional dichotomy. Lee School, serving primarily a white-collar community, was showcased for its diversity of instructional methods and materials, its utilization of open space, and its attention to the motivational needs of the child. Grant School, serving a middle-class and professional community, was known for its rigorous attention to academic content, its achievement test scores—which frequently led the district—and its traditional emphasis on basic skill acquisition. While Lee School held as an explicit schoolwide goal the nurturing of student responsibility for learning, Grant School's emphasis was clearly on teacher control of the learner's experience.

Two examples make graphic the schools' instructional differences. First, microcomputer technology had come to both schools through fund-raising efforts by their PTAs. While computers were put to creative use in Lee School, by integration into the teaching of art, Grant School used their computers in basic skill drills. A second illustration is found in the teaching of social studies. Lee School relied on storytelling, dramatic play, and multimedia material to teach content; the approach at Grant School was testbook-based and called almost exclusively for written activity.

Here, then, we find organizationally distinctive schools occurring in a naturalistic setting but as well matched to our research design as if they had been experimentally manipulated. Especially critical to our purpose of examining cumulative effects is the fact that both schools exhibited high internal consistency instructionally. Moreover, despite the instructional differences between the two schools, all teachers were excellent classroom managers, and we found student commitment to both schools' moral orders was equally unwavering.

The internal instructional consistency of these schools combined with their highly stable populations permit a quasi-longitudinal examination of how ability perceptions unfold over time under different instructional conditions. In essence, students in each grade level may be treated approximately as a synthetic cohort passing through a consistent style of instruction. The great similarity between the schools in areas other than the organization of instruction eliminates many possible alternative explanations, allowing us to present confidently results expressed by bivariate statistics.[6]

Research Procedures

Students completed a questionnaire/interview in late spring of the 1983–84 school year. At least two classrooms per grade level were sampled in each school, for a sample of 641 students in twenty-six classes. The questionnaire was administered in two parts, during two sittings, each taking twenty to twenty-five minutes. Questions were read aloud to avoid student reading difficulties. In the first and second grades, the research staff administered questionnaires in small groups of three to five children to ensure that directions were understood and that pacing was appropriate. In later grades, classes were divided by gender, with each group supervised by at least one staff member.

The first segment of the questionnaire asked students to evaluate themselves and like-gender classmates on several dimensions of classroom performance, including intelligence ("how smart are they"), reading, math, all classwork, effort ("how hard they try"), and a new activity ("something that you have never done before"). Students responded to a quasi-magnitude estimation scale by marking one of fifteen circles arranged in a vertical column with top and bottom anchors of "top of the class" and "bottom of the class."

Results: Cumulation toward Normally Distributed Perceived Ability Levels

Consistent with previous work, means and standard deviations of self-ratings are revealing measures of stratification. Means are lower and standard deviations higher among students at Grant, the unidimensional school. Beyond that, we are now able to test whether ability formation occurs identically in the two settings, except that the sequence occurs later in multidimensional classes, or whether multidimensional classes move toward a stable distribution, which reflects a different conception of ability. We can also ask at which grade level we are first able to observe the effects of classroom organization.

We find modest differences between students in the two schools at the end of their first-grade year. Mean ratings for each dimension we measured are slightly lower in Grant, but variances are approximately equal.[7] For Grant students, mean ratings drop and dispersion scores increase monotonically over the grades, with standard deviations for "smart" increasing from 2.6 for first graders to 4.6 by fifth grade. Students at Lee also reduce mean self-ratings but lagged behind for their first three or four grades. In "all classwork" self-reports, for example, third graders at Lee exhibit mean ratings nearly identical to those of second graders at Grant. However, students at Lee reach their lowest mean ability reports by grade three or four, as shown below in Table 5.1. Further, they exhibit no consistent trend toward increasing the dispersion of their ratings, instead clustering in the moderately high range rather than the extremely high range after third grade. Thus, for example, the highest standard deviation at Lee for "smart" is 3.4 in fourth grade, a nonsignificant increase from 3.0 at first grade.

We found in our previous work that unidimensional classrooms considerably increase the proportion of students who report very low ability levels. Here we see that pattern unfolding over time. At Grant School, only 4 percent of first graders report for themselves a level of "smart" at or below 8, the midpoint of our 1 to 15 scale. By sixth grade, 35.3 percent do so. The number giving themselves the highest possible rating, 15, drops from 75.5 percent in grade one to 6 percent in grade 6. At Lee, the multidimensional school, the proportion

Table 5.1 Mean Ability Self Ratings*, by Grade and School

	"SMART"		ALL CLASSWORK		NEW ACTIVITY	
Grade	Lee	Grant	Lee	Grant	Lee	Grant
1	13.8	13.3	13.2	12.2	13.6	11.3
2	13.7	12.3	14.5	13.6	13.7	12.7
3	12.9	10.7	13.4	12.0	12.8	10.9
4	11.4	10.7	12.1	12.6	12.2	10.5
5	11.9	9.3	12.6	9.9	12.0	9.0
6	11.7	9.0	12.8	9.3	12.8	8.5

Highest = 15; lowest = 1.

reporting 8 or below does not change significantly from first to sixth grades, moving from 14.6 percent to 15.0 percent. The proportion giving themselves the highest possible rating falls from 79.2 percent to 12.2 percent. Thus the difference between the two types of classrooms is that by sixth grade, students in multidimensional classes cluster in the range moderately above average, while students in unidimensional classes distribute themselves across the entire scale, top to bottom. In multidimensional classes, 63 percent of sixth graders fall between 11 and 14 on our 1 to 15 scale, while in unidimensional classes, only 35.4 percent do so.

In sum, the developmental perspective, that student ability reports become more realistic over time by decreasing from early overestimations, occurs in both types of classrooms in our sample but differs markedly by instructional setting. As they progress through the elementary grades, Grant students increasingly report their ability in normalized form, with means close to the center point of the answer scale and with wide dispersion. By grade five, these students' reports closely resemble the IQ model of intelligence. Lee students, on the other hand, stabilize perceptions portraying a more self-enhancing distribution of ability. Table 5.1 portrays these patterns for three measures of self-reported ability.

A noteworthy point shown in Table 5.1 is the pattern of decline in self-perception of ability for a new activity. We asked students to rate themselves on some unknown new task to test the degree to which their academic ability perceptions had established generalized expectations of performance. In Lee School, where curricular diversity and multiple opportunities to demonstrate competence abound and where student autonomy is high, students report greater success in their previously assigned school subjects than in Grant, where only a narrow band of performance dimensions is tapped. Even more marked, however, is the fact that at Lee, greater diversity of performance opportunity translates into far greater optimism about the ability to succeed at a task never before encountered. These ratings stabilize earlier and higher than ratings for areas of past performance, even at Lee. At Grant, however, students come to predict future task success as identical to their highly stratified perceptions of success

Table 5.2 Pearson's R's between Self Ratings, by Grade School

Grade	READING AND "SMART"		ALL CLASSWORK AND "SMART"		NEW ACTIVITY AND "SMART"	
	Lee	Grant	Lee	Grant	Lee	Grant
1	.67	.78	.68	.50	.70	.66
2	− .07	.61	.28	.62	.21	.76
3	.62	.91	.54	.85	.24	.86
4	.70	.85	.53	.79	.39	.69
5	.54	.96	.56	.97	.34	.95
6	.72	.90	.63	.87	.25	.73

with academic subjects. Indeed, their predictions about performance on some unknown future task are the lowest of any rating that Grant students provide for us. Reduced optimism about future performances evokes the possibility of self-defeating reduction in effort or risk taking, an unintended consequence of the generalized stratification of ability within unidimensionally structured classes.

Findings: The Development of Generalized Ability Conceptions

We confront more detailed evidence of this trend toward greater generalization at Grant than at Lee by comparing Pearson correlation coefficients between self-ratings on "smart" with self-ratings on other performances. Table 5.2 shows the trends over grade levels for three pairs of self-perceived ability ratings.

We encounter in Table 5.2 another monotonic increase (albeit somewhat less consistent) in the associations among self-perceptions as Grant students accumulated experience in school.[8] Table 5.2 also documents far stronger associations among self-ratings in Grant School than in Lee. That difference is established early, builds momentum rapidly through third grade, and then appears to have hit a ceiling, with correlations varying in the .9 range.

In Lee School, on the other hand, generalization is lower, does not increase in any regular fashion, and displays the somewhat erratic pattern which might be expected on the basis of differences in the composition of particular classes. Only two of the correlations Table 5.2 shows for Lee reach the .7 level—one in first grade and one in sixth. Only in the case of correlations between "smart" and "new activity" does Lee exhibit any here, as in the case of dispersion, that Lee not only exhibits lower ability formation at any given grade level, but also shows little lagged cumulative trend. Instead, a relatively stable alternative pattern is presented.

These findings augment our earlier tests of ability formation theory by showing three clear indicators of greater generalization at Grant, with unidimensionally organized classrooms, than at Lee, with multidimensionally organized classrooms. First, the similarity of performance reports in different spheres of classroom is greater at Grant. Second, that similarity becomes greater with cumulated experience at Grant but not at Lee. Third, students at Grant, much more than those at Lee, generalize from academic ability to predict performance for themselves on new and different tasks.

Results: Stabilization of Ability as an Unchangeable Aspect of Self

An important explanation for performance success or failure which may serve as an alternate to unchanging ability is effort engagement. This dichotomy between ability and effort as explanations for performance offers us an entry point to observe the process through which students' perception of ability moves from one of internal control to one of external, unchangeable fact. Attribution theorists distinguish between attributions to internal causes and attributions to external causes. Level of effort, clearly an internal cause, carries with it the implication of control (and therefore changeability) by self, of responsibility, and therefore blame. Purely external attributions—for example, luck and teacher favoritism— exist outside the individual and therefore carry none of these implications. Ability, however, is neither of these. It is presumed to be a quality internal to the individual, but the fully institutionalized conception implies no control or changeability by self, nor internal responsibility or blame. Indeed, lack of ability acts as a legitimate "external" excuse for poor performance, preventing teacher censure among students who perform poorly despite exerting effort (Weiner and Kukla 1970).

During elementary-school years, ability moves from relatively internal interpretation to relatively external interpretation. Stipek (1981) found that the majority of kindergarten and first-grade students she interviewed cited effort as an indicator of smartness. Further, some first graders believed that effort is the actual cause of intelligence (Harari and Covington 1981; Stipek 1981).

By third or fourth grade, students no longer expressed the idea that effort causes or defines ability (Harari and Covington 1981; Karabenick and Heller 1976; Kun 1977; Nicholls 1978). Indeed, the definitional association between effort and ability becomes reversed, with intelligence proven by an absence of need to exert effort. In these later grades, ability becomes seen as a stable cause of performance. Effort can perhaps partially offset the effect of ability, but it does not alter the ability itself.

Thus students come to adopt this most fascinating quality of ability, that it is internal to each of us as individuals and yet is beyond our control. It is not my teacher's fault that I perform poorly, yet it is not my "fault" either. My low ability is beyond the control of my teacher, my school, and myself. It is stable, unchangeable.

Our research adds to the literature in this area findings which provide a preemptory challenge to the "obvious fact" that ability is stable. We studied two types of reports concerning effort: descriptions of perceived level of effort compared with peers and attitudinal statements indicating the definition of ability stable or as tied to effort. Level of effort was measured on the same one to 15 scale used

Table 5.3   Linkages between Ability and Effort, by Grade and School

| | Correlations: Self Ratings on: | | | |
| | Effort and All Classwk | | Effort and Smart | |
Grade	Lee	Grant	Lee	Grant
1	.35	.50	.42	.47
2	.19	.49	.38	.68
3	.32	.82	.33	.83
4	.61	.49	.41	.47
5	.51	.87	.32	.85
6	.66	.81	.63	.70

to measure perceived ability levels. For attitudinal measures, we asked students to indicate their level of agreement with several statements: "Smart kids try the hardest"; "smart kids get the right answers without trying"; "I could do better in math if I worked harder"; and "I always work as hard as I can in math." Table 5.3 reports correlations between self-perceived levels of effort and self-perceived ability levels and reports mean responses to attitudinal statements for each grade level.

Certainly other studies of effort and ability led us to expect a monotonic decline in the degree of association between effort and ability with age. Instead, the patterns presented by our two types of measures run in opposing directions. In Grant school, students' attitudinal statements match previous findings: effort is disassociated from ability as grade level increases. However, over those same grade levels, the association between self-reported ability level and self-reported level of effort *increases*. Students appear to be indicating that smart ones *need not* work hard, but the smarter the student, the higher the level of actual effort. The objective connections among behaviors and perceptions lead to a conclusion which is the polar opposite of students' statements of belief concerning effort and ability. Table 5.3 illustrates by counterposing selected findings of each type.

The correlations reported in Table 5.3 show an early and strong connection between effort and ability among students at Grant, where we find all aspects of ability formation progressing rapidly. The association does not decline in later grades, but remains constant and high after fourth grade. At Lee, the correlations between effort and "smart" remain much lower, and with the exception of sixth grade, they show no tendency to rise with grade level. However, the correlation between effort and performance in all classwork does increase with grade level at Lee. Thus at Lee also, effort is more positively associated with perceived school performance at higher grade levels, although the association never reaches the strength of that at Grant, and most revealingly, the association does not generalize from achievement behavior to "ability" at Lee.

From the standpoint of student motivation, we see a consistent decline in the reported level of effort expenditure precisely because student effort levels become so closely associated with their ability levels, which drop over grade levels. This is much more the case at Grant than at Lee because (a) perceived ability reports decline further there and (b) the generalization of ability and effort is greater there. Greater stratification of effort levels and net decline of effort in the uni-dimensional classrooms may be seen as unintended consequences of the ability formation process that bear directly on student learning potential.

Despite the objective association between effort and ability, our tests using direct measures of attitudinal perception produce a pattern much like that expected from previous literature. In Grant School, students show declining use of effort cues in determining classmates' abilities, moving instead toward acceptance of the interpretation that task success given little effort reveals intelligence. While in the earliest grades, students agree that smart kids try the hardest and disagree that smart kids get the right answers without trying, by the later elementary grades, their responses point toward reversal. Moreover, reported levels of personal effort expenditure also differ by grade level for Grant students. In the earliest grades, students report working as hard as they can and in a statement reflecting naive optimism, they report that they could do even better if they worked harder.[9] In the later grades, students at Grant report less effort expenditure and less optimism about the possibility of greater success with increased effort. That is, they express, in varying degrees, a stance which at its extreme is labeled *learned helplessness*, companion to the acceptance of ability as stable.

Although Lee students exhibit these same tendencies, their subtle transition in beliefs comes nowhere near the dramatic shift of Grant students. Indeed, Lee students in sixth grade retain faith in the efficacy of effort and personal sense of engagement greater than that expressed by Grant students in third grade. Given that correlations show the association between ability and effort *higher* in later grades, we ask why children's responses to belief statements reflect the *disassociation* between ability and effort. Further, both these contradictory trends are much more marked in unidimensional settings than in multidimensional settings. We explain the apparent divergence between these two sets of findings with reference to Berger and Luckmann's concept of the "alienation" of human constructions from their source.

As students at Grant move through the grade levels, they come to almost completely confound effort and ability. Their behavioral descriptions of their own and of others' levels of ability and effort are nearly identical. (For peer ratings, this correlation reaches .98 at sixth grade.) This makes it impossible to disentangle these two determinants of school performance level reliably. Yet students' early exertion of effort, combined with unidimensional performance and evaluation experiences, has led them to *perceive* only one of these two as the cause of their school performance. They move toward seeing their ability as a fixed attribute which they cannot change and which determines their school performance, quite apart from the effort they exert. Since they exert effort in precise proportion to their perceived ability levels, the effects of the two factors—

ability and effort—are never tested separately. It could be that relative performance levels become stable either because of ability differences or because of
effort differences. As perceived, the two produce identical predictions and are
therefore equally accurate attributions. One indicator of successful ability formation in unidimensional classes is students' failure to recognize possible dis-
junctures between effort and ability; instead, they attribute performance entirely
to ability. It is probable that relative performance levels, and therefore perceived
ability levels, are in part reenacted daily through a matching application of effort.
Yet the accomplished acceptance of ability as objective, stable determiner of
nearly all valued performances blinds students to such an interpretation.

Once again, we find this aspect of ability formation unfolding to a much
weaker degree in multidimensional classes. Ability and level of effort are less
closely linked. The belief that effort can change performance is retained. There
is no movement toward seeing intelligence as indicated by performance without
effort. And we see only a slight reduction in the belief that smarter kids try
harder. In short, by sixth grade, students at Lee School are not experiencing
ability as a reified, externalized construct.

Results: The Role of Peers

We have argued that the external viewpoint of peers leads students to adopt
institutionalized ability conceptions earlier in their role as peers than in their role
as observers of self. Our past research has documented the pivotal role of peer
consensus and peer conversation in the ability formation process. Our latest
research allows us to add sequencing comparisons. How soon do student reports
reflect institutionalized ability conceptions when students act in their role as
peers? Table 5.4 illustrates by offering representative findings. The clear answer
is "almost immediately." Mean ratings by peers at the end of first grade are as
low as self-ratings reached only at fourth grade. Similarly, at Grant, correlations
for peers begin much higher and increase until they essentially reach identity by
third grade. Further, lest our reverie over the fit of these data to ability formation
theory become too sanguine, levels for Lee are only slightly lower. Although
the direction of difference between Lee and Grant is consistent, the margin is
small at all grade levels.

While our intent was to capture the process of ability formation unfurling over
time, in the case of peer ratings, we discover surprisingly that by the end of the
first-grade year, we are already too late. Both for dispersion and for generalization, ability formation from the peer perspective is nearly complete by the end
of the first grade, and little difference between unidimensional and multidimensional classes is located. Peers receive only partial performance information and
judge from the external viewpoint, without knowledge of internal states and
without motivation to weigh positive performances more heavily than others in
the averaging process. Thus, while very young students and those in multidimensionally organized classrooms are buffered against generalized negative self-

Table 5.4   Mean Level and Generalization of Peer Ratings, by Grade and School

Grade	Mean Ratings On "Smart"		Correlations of "Smart" With:					
			All Classwk		New Activity		Effort	
	Lee	Grant	Lee	Grant	Lee	Grant	Lee	Grant
1	11.0	10.1	.91	.93	.88	.90	.77	.95
2	11.0	11.8	.86	.88	.87	.90	.79	.76
3	11.7	10.3	.94	.97	.92	.94	.89	.93
4	11.1	10.4	.94	.99	.93	.98	.83	.89
5	11.1	9.1	.94	.99	.92	.98	.90	.86
6	10.4	8.8	.96	.99	.97	.99	.88	.98

perceived ability, classmates are not. This means that children accept the idea of general, stratified ability long before they must admit such a state for themselves.

Further, we find here that students in multidimensional classrooms do exhibit high levels of ability formation when making external judgments about their classmates. This finding underscores the degree to which ability formation theory concerns the social construction of *factual knowledge*. Multidimensional classroom structure apparently prevents full ability formation at the individual level by failing to force young students to perceive this quality of themselves as objective (external, unchanging) fact. They retain the optimism of subjective knowledge that they could change effort levels, that they sometimes perform better, and the like. In unidimensional classrooms, these "internal" attributions are truncated. Whether students in multidimensional classes err by being naively optimistic, or students in unidimensional classrooms err by prematurely reducing effort because they believe that their ability levels prevent improvement, is perhaps the subject for future work. Here we note the addition to ability formation theory of this critical *peer objectivation* stage.

Finally, we note that the association between ability and effort occurs for peers as well as for individuals. As with other correlations, this one begins high and becomes higher over grade levels, with unidimensional settings higher than multidimensional settings.

CONCLUSIONS

Ability formation theory generates a large number of specific hypotheses concerning the distribution and conception of ability in elementary school classrooms. These stem from two rather basic notions: that schools will typically reproduce institutionalized patterns of ability and that classroom unidimensional organization during instruction constitutes a "deep structure" condition required for that reproduction. The value of the approach is also the factor which generates the greatest skepticism before the empirical results are viewed: predicted outcomes are usually assumed to be invariant qualities of individuals; and many different outcomes are predicted, each having less-than-obvious connection to the others aside from the connections drawn by ability formation theory. Since the original development of the theory, all the original hypotheses save one have been empirically validated.[10] We think that this occurs because the theory specifies structural determinants at the appropriate level for the types of outcomes studied: deep structures affecting many daily activity and interaction patterns to predict patterns of students' knowledge regarding a basic school-based reality.

In this chapter, we can for the first time also report tests of the ability formation sequence from grades one through six. Three patterns emerge which are particularly useful in the further development of theory regarding the social construction of ability.

First, we observe repeatedly qualitative differences between ability reports in multidimensional and unidimensional settings, in addition to time lag differences. Not only do these settings differ at any given grade level; in addition, passage of time in school has different effects in the two settings. Grade level and classroom organization interact to affect ability formation. Ability formation occurs more rapidly and far more completely in unidimensional classes.

Multidimensional classes exhibit two patterns most commonly. In one, the most common, similar beginning points in first grade are followed by movement toward ability formation at a slower pace than in unidimensional classrooms, reaching a ceiling level at third or fourth grade. Thus, while students in unidimensional classrooms continue to move toward full ability formation through grade six, time in school appears to stop affecting students in multidimensional classes at grade three or four. In the second pattern, students in unidimensional classes move through the expected ability formation stages, but those in multidimensional classes show no trend across time, failing to exhibit any evidence of ability formation.

The fact that both these patterns show more than time-lagged differences caused by classroom dimensionality adds confidence to the interpretation that multidimensional classes tend to produce a conception of ability divergent from that produced in unidimensional classes. Multidimensional organization does not simply delay ability formation by obscuring information flow. That flow, and consequent comparisons, is obscured, but beyond that, the information flow is qualitatively different enough that the distribution and conception of ability which emerges there is different from that expected on the basis of institutionalized beliefs about ability.

The second sequence pattern of note involves the objective perspective of peers. Peers move rapidly and extremely toward a relatively normal distribution of ability perceptions, perceptions quite closely aligned with teachers, and highly general conceptions of ability. Even at the end of first grade, we have missed much of whatever ability formation process occurs among peers. This illustrates the error of developmental explanations that young children are incapable of interpreting feedback. It also reinforces the central place of peers as mediators of ability formation. Peers collectively direct individuals' perceptions, depending on consensus. Further, each student experiences making relatively unidimensional ability comparisons and judgments in the role of peer well before ego enhancement would allow the same self-perceptions.

The third sequence pattern which we find especially valuable is the gradual growth of association between perceived ability and effort, which occurs during precisely the same period when students' belief systems are disassociating ability and effort. The behavioral overlap between the two means that engagement differences help to maintain the appearance of stable ability differences. The attitudinal result of ability formation directs all attribution of causality toward unchangeable ability rather than toward engagement of effort, over which both schools and individual students exercise some control.

NOTES

1. Indeed, it is for this reason that much of the debate concerning IQ is informed by ideological support for or opposition to current stratification patterns. Our work is not directed toward that political debate, although it carries some implications for it.

2. The recent popularity of ethnomethodology has led some to confuse the social construction of reality theory with the ethnomethodological contention that all reality is continuously re-created in reactive interaction. Based on this error, some argue that reality construction can be studied only through in-depth ethnographic research. Nothing could be further from the truth. The end result of the process Berger and Luckmann posit is the actors' individual and collective perception of being acted upon by an external reality over which they have no control. Indeed, the great power of the reality construction approach lies in the irony that we create what eventually returns to control us as external facts not subject to renegotiation.

3. Ability formation theory has been described elsewhere (Rosenholtz and Simpson 1984a, 1984b; Rosenholtz 1982; Rosenholtz and Rosenholtz 1981; Simpson 1981, 1982; Rosenholtz and Wilson 1980; Rosenholtz 1977; Simpson 1975.) In this chapter, we offer a summary of the basic elements of the theory, without extended discussion or justification and without reference to other work which guided its formulation. In this respect, the intellectual heritage extends into the classical sociological tradition, particularly with affinities to Weber's meaning of *legitimation*.

4. To illustrate the major strength of this type of theory we are exposed also to a major weakness: the difficulty of explaining and reviewing evidence for a great variety of hypotheses derived from one deep structure. For more thorough exposition, the reader is referred to our earlier work.

5. It is not teachers in multidimensional classes who most often approve of masking their feedback. Instead, they are slightly more often committed to accurate feedback. This observation is important, for it counteracts a potential alternative explanation for the lower consensus in multidimensional classes. Ability formation is not delayed in these classes because students are being protected from accurate knowledge, but because the nature of accurate knowledge departs from that in other classes.

6. The similarity of these two schools conveniently eliminates two possible rival explanations for certain of our findings. Stratification findings could be affected by the mix of students' family status or of tested ability level. Happily, Grant and Lee are nearly identical in these respects. They have statistically indistinguishable proportions of eco-

nomically disadvantaged students and of ethnic minority students. Standardized tests of
students' school preparedness in math and reading show both schools above average,
with Grant students scoring slightly higher at school entry and at each grade level.
However, students' self-perceptions are lower at Grant. More important, the dispersion
of tested ability, measured as standard deviations, is virtually identical at the two schools,
so that Grant's greater stratification of self- and peer ratings cannot be explained by greater
differences in "actual" ability.

The second rival explanation is that Lee students are less serious about classwork or
evaluations of it. Lee's greater emphasis on student self-direction and lesser emphasis
on basics may reduce student commitment to the school's moral order. However, data
on level of effort (see Table 5.3) as well as several attitudinal measures (liking for school
subjects, feeling bad if not doing one's best work, caring about one's grades, being good
at following rules, wishing for better performance) show equal, and sometimes *greater*,
levels of moral commitment among Lee students.

7. These lower ratings occur despite the higher mean first-grade scores at Grant in
reading and math.

8. The exuberant participation of first graders sometimes led them to unusual extremes
in completing the questionnaire. Therefore, correlations for this grade show inflated
estimates sometimes deviant from the monotonic patterns of second grade upward.

9. When informally asked about this apparent contradiction, two first graders explained that there was much knowledge to be gained in succeeding grade levels, but that
to learn it would be a difficult undertaking, requiring great effort. As one responded,
"Ya don't learn everythin' here, but ya try hard to git it."

10. The hypothesis not confirmed was that self-perceived ability would show greater
association with ethnic status in unidimensional classes than in multidimensional classes.
It turns out that self-reports are unrelated to ethnicity in any type of classroom. Apparently,
students adjust these perceptions on other bases.

REFERENCES

Berger, P., and T. Luckmann. *The Social Construction of Reality*. Garden City, NY:
    Doubleday, 1966.
Blumenfeld, P.C., et al. "Teacher Talk and Student Thought: Socialization into the
    Student Role." In *Teacher and Student Perceptions: Implications for Learning*,
    edited by J. Levine and M. Wang. Hillsdale, NJ: Lawrence Erlbaum Assoc.,
    1983.
Bossert, S. T. *Tasks and Social Relationships in Classrooms: A Study of Classroom
    Organization and Its Consequences*. ASA Arnold and Caroline Rose Monograph
    Series. New York: Cambridge University Press, 1979.
Brattesani, K. S., et al. "Using Student Perceptions of Teacher Behavior to Predict
    Student Outcomes." Paper presented at the Annual Meeting of the American
    Educational Research Association, Los Angeles, April 1981.
Bowles, S., and H. Gintis. *Schooling in Capitalist America: Educational Reform and
    the Contradictions of Economic Life*. New York: Basic Books, 1976.
Cohen, E. G., M. E. Lockheed, and M. Lohman. "The Center for Interracial Cooper-
    ation: A Field Experiment." *Sociology of Education* 49 (1976): 47–58.
Cohen, E. G. "Design and Redesign of the Desegregated Schools Problems of Status,
    Power, and Conflict." In *School Desegregation: Past, Present and Future*, edited
    by W. G. Stephan and J. R. Feagin. New York: Plenum Press, 1980.

————. "Sociology of the Classroom: 1972–1984." Paper presented at the Annual Meeting of the American Educational Research Association, New Orleans, 1984.

Dreeben, R. *On What Is Learned in School*. Reading, MA: Addison-Wesley, 1968.

Fass, P. S. "The IQ: A Cultural and Historical Framework." *American Journal of Education* 88 (1980): 431–59.

Frieze, I. H. "Children's Attributions for Success and Failure." In *Developmental Social Psychology, Theory and Research*, edited by S. S. Brehm, S. M. Kassin, and F. X. Gibbons. New York: Oxford University Press, 1981.

Goodlad, J. I. *A Place Called School*. New York: McGraw-Hill, 1983.

Hallinan, M. T. "Friendship Patterns in Open and Traditional Classrooms." *Sociology of Education* 49 (1976): 43–54.

————. "Structural Effects on Children's Friendship and Cliques." *Social Psychology Quarterly* 42 (1979): 43–54.

Harari, O., and M. V. Covington. "Reactions to Achievement Behavior from a Teacher and Student Perspective: A Developmental Analysis." *American Educational Research Journal* 18 (1981): 15–28.

Jones, E. E., and R. E. Nisbett. "The Actor and the Observer: Divergent Perceptions of the Causes of Behavior." In *Attributions*, edited by E. Jones. New York: General Learning Corp., 1971.

Karabenick, J. D., and K. A. Heller. "A Developmental Study of Effort and Ability Attributions." *Developmental Psychology* 2 (1976): 559–60.

Kun, A. "Development of the Magnitude-Covariation and Compensation Schemata in Ability and Effort Attributions of Performance." *Child Development* 48 (1977): 862–73.

Mercer, J. "Institutionalized Anglocentrism: Labeling Mental Retardates in Public Schools." In *Race, Change and Urban Policy*, edited by Peter Orleans and W. R. Ellis, Jr. Beverly Hills, CA: Sage, 1971.

Meyer, J. W. "The Effects of Education as an Institution." *American Journal of Sociology* 83 (1977): 55–77.

Nicholls, J. G. "The Development of the Concepts of Effort and Ability, Perception of Academic Attainment, and the Understanding That Difficult Tasks Require More Ability." *Child Development* 49 (1978): 800–14.

Patchen, M. *Black-White Contact in Schools: Its Social and Academic Effects*. West Lafayette, IN: Purdue University Press, 1982.

Rosenholtz, S. J. "The Multiple Abilities Curriculum: An Intervention against the Self-fulfilling Prophecy." Ph.D. diss., Stanford University, 1977.

————. "Organizational Determinants of Classroom Social Power." *Journal of Experimental Education* 50 (1982): 83–87.

————. "Changing Performance Expectations in the Traditional Classroom." In *Research in Expectation States Theory: Pure and Applied*, edited by J. Berger and M. Zelditch, Jr. San Francisco: Jossey-Bass, 1985.

Rosenholtz, S. J., and S. H. Rosenholtz. "Classroom Organization and the Perception of Ability." *Sociology of Education* 54 (1981): 132–40.

Rosenholtz, S. J., and C. Simpson. "The Formation of Ability Conceptions: Developmental Trend or Social Construction?" *Review of Educational Research* 54 (1984a): 31–63.

————. "Classroom Organization and Student Stratification." *The Elementary School Journal* 85 (1984b): 21–37.

Rosenholtz, S. J., and B. Wilson. "The Effect of Classroom Structure on Shared Perceptions of Ability." *American Educational Research Journal* 17 (1980): 75–82.

Schofield, J. W., and H. A. Sagar. "Desegregation, School Practices and Student Race Relations Outcomes." In *The Consequences of School Desegregation*, edited by C. Rossell and W. Hawley. Philadelphia: Temple University Press, 1983.

Simpson, C. "The Social Construction of Ability in Elementary School." Ph.D. diss., Stanford University, 1975.

———. "Classroom Structure and the Formation of Ability Conceptions." *Sociology of Education* 54 (1981): 120–32.

———. "Classroom Organization and the Gap between Minority and Non-Minority Performance Levels." *Educational Research Quarterly*, Special Issue on Multicultural Education 6 (1982): 43–53.

Stipek, D. J. "Children's Perceptions of Their Own and Their Classmates' Ability." *Journal of Educational Psychology* 73 (1981): 404–10.

———. "Young Children's Performance Expectations: Logical Analysis or Wishful Thinking?" In *The Development of Achievement Motivation*, edited by J. G. Nicholls. Greenwich, CT: JAI Press, 1984.

Strang, L., M. S. Smith, and C. M. Rogers. "Social Comparison, Multiple Reference Groups, and the Self-concepts of Academically Handicapped Children before and after Mainstreaming." *Journal of Educational Psychology* 70 (1978): 487–97.

Tammivaara, J. S. "The Effects of Task Structure on Beliefs about Competence and Participation in Small Groups." *Sociology of Education* 55 (1982): 212–22.

Weiner, B., and A. Kukla. "An Attributional Analysis of Achievement Motivation." *Journal of Personality and Social Psychology* 15 (1970): 1–20.

6

JAMES E. ROSENBAUM

Institutional Career Structures and the Social Construction of Ability

INTRODUCTION

Toward a Sociology of Ability

Norms not only tell us how to act, but they also tell us how to see the world, and when they succeed in that, they also reassure us that things are as they should be. Consequently, sociologists' efforts to delineate social norms, which have sometimes been directed to justifying social reality, can also be used to discern the myths which give unjustifiable and misplaced certainty to society's members.

This chapter seeks to understand an important myth in American society: the myth of ability. Obviously, ability is a valued and important conception in American society, so the importance of the topic is assured. By labeling this a myth, I do not intend to assert that it is demonstrably untrue. Rather, it is its very untestability which makes it a myth in the sense suggested by the dictionary: "Myth . . . a thing having only an imaginary or unverifiable existence . . . that serves to unfold part of the world view of a people or explain a practice, belief, or natural phenomenon" (*Webster's New Collegiate Dictionary* 1976). This mythological character of ability—by which it is both central to normative descriptions of societal outcomes and unverifiable and irrefutable by empirical examination—has confounded our understanding of selection systems in social institutions and generated numerous unresolved theoretical debates in the social sciences. This chapter contends that this mythological character of ability not only beclouds understanding of the determinants of selections in social institutions, but it also prevents us from seeing the ways that selection systems actually affect inferences about ability and the properties attributed to ability.

As every schoolchild knows, ability is one of the main determinants of success in American society. This view is pervasive among social scientists too. Psychology, economics, sociology, and education offer ability-based theories which are founded upon this premise. Structural sociologists are the main holdout, maintaining that social barriers often prevent the most able individuals from getting ahead. Despite extensive controversy and research, the issue remains no closer to resolution, largely because structuralists generally concede that imprecision in the measurement of ability prevents them from knowing to what extent ability might account for the results they identify as structural ones.

Everyone acknowledges that the measurement of ability is imprecise and subject to error, that ability is an inference from various cues, that the particular cues chosen are somewhat arbitrary, and that the inference is imperfect. What is mystifying about these problems is not only that they are ignored and assumed to be soluble in principle, but also that they are used to make ability-based theories impregnable to attack, instead of being utilized in an attack upon those theories.

Obviously, it matters very much which cues are selected to ascertain ability. While most of the discussion of the discrimination focuses on overt discrimination, it seems likely that some kinds of discrimination may be hidden within ability inferences. This may be particularly the case for statistical discrimination, in which evaluators take sex and race cues and infer ability implications (Thurow 1975). This chapter extends this contention by suggesting that individuals' histories of social attainments also affect the ability attributed to them.

Structuralists may have conceded too much on this issue. Rather than conceptualizing the issue as a conflict between ability and structure this chapter suggests a new conception: that ability itself is determined by institutional career structures. Rather than being an unchanging attribute of individuals—like eye color—ability is in part a social status conferred to individuals based upon a multitude of social cues, including cues derived from individuals' positions in institutional career structures in schools and workplaces. As a derivative of institutional career structures, ability can be understood only after analyzing these career structures in schools and workplaces.

Obviously, this analysis does not deny that individuals differ in ability: this fundamental premise is irrefutable. However, the present analysis raises new issues about how school staff and corporate managers infer which individuals have more ability, and it suggests that institutional career structures may have a major influence on these inferences and, consequently, on the properties which are atrributed to ability.

We begin by reviewing some conflicting conceptions of career structures and presenting research evidence to help us choose among these conceptions. This review indicates that a new version of signaling theory, which suggests the structural sources of ability, explains much of the available evidence. To describe the cumulative impact of signaling theory in an entire career system, the tournament model of careers is proposed. This model is evaluated in terms of empirical evidence on career mobility in schools and workplaces. The final sections of the chapter explore some implications of the tournament model for understanding how career structures affect the conceptions of ability held by school staff and corporate managers and the properties they impute to it.

The point of this analysis is not merely to stress that ability inferences are imperfect, but to make four other points. First, social structurally determined outcomes are important determinants of ability inferences.

Second, customary analyses of discrimination which consider discrimination as "departures from ability" may be oversimple. The present analysis suggests that if discrimination is built into a career system so that it is hidden or unrecognized, then it will become part of the ability signals conferred by the system and these signals of ability will themselves contribute to discrimination. In such cases, discrimination will not be a departure from ability; it will be an intrinsic part of the way ability is operationalized.

Third, if one accepts the premise of the tournament model—that previous losses signal lesser ability—then age may even be considered a meritocratic selection criterion, and age discrimination will be difficult to discern or even to conceptualize.

Fourth, if career systems in schools and workplaces do indeed operate according to the tournament model, as this chapter asserts, then information about the nature of career systems is imperative for efficient and equitable selections. This suggests that it is of paramount importance that social scientists pursue this line of inquiry and that schools and workplaces make this kind of information widely available.

Two Conflicting Models of the Opportunity Structure

There is a strong ambivalence between the perceived efficiencies of early selection programs and the concern that early selections may be seen as curtailing opportunity. The basis of this conflict is described by Turner (1960) in a classic paper. Turner describes two normative systems which stand as ideal types in our society: the contest and the sponsored mobility norms.

Individuals in the United States grow up believing that everyone has the opportunity to advance, and that, as "the land of opportunity," the United States has no policies or practices which curtail anyone's advancement opportunities or which protect any elite from downward mobility. Turner calls this the *contest mobility norm*. In a selection system which follows the contest mobility norm, selections are delayed and individuals are allowed complete freedom for mobility through most of their careers. Of course, even in a contest system, selections must sometimes occur; but the contest system delays selections and minimizes their consequences. It instills an "insecurity of elite position. In a sense, there is no final arrival under contest mobility, since each peson may be displaced by newcomers throughout his life" (Turner 1960, p. 860). Nor are there any final losses, since everyone is kept in the running and offered another chance to qualify for advancement (p. 861).

A selection system following the contest mobility norm embodies several desirable features. In permitting late mobility, such a system helps to maintain motivation and morale by continually holding out the possibility that one's efforts may have a payoff. Moreover, such a system is quite consistent with Americans' long-standing mistrust of selection criteria. If selection criteria are mistrusted, then a selection system which makes few selections and delays them as late as possible will be relatively less objectionable. Moreover, it would leave maximum opportunity for "late blooming" or late failing to alter individuals' destinies. Such a system also minimizes the chances of errors. Of course, this minimizing of errors also has its costs, for the later that selection occurs, the less time individuals have to acquire specialized training. Normative ambivalence emerges here because the loss of adequate specialized training is seen as inefficient and, consequently, undesirable.

In contrast, the *sponsored mobility norm* stresses efficiency. It prescribes that selections occur as early as possible so that the system can maximally benefit from the efficiencies of specialized training and socialization. In a selection system which follows the sponsored norm, individuals are selected for their ultimate careers very early, and departures from these early assigned careers are not permitted. Those who are selected for elite status are maximally separated from others, given specialized training and socialization, and guaranteed that they, and only they, will attain elite status.

Although Turner attributed this sponsored norm predominantly to Britain, it is clear that there are elements of this norm in the United States as well. Surely the United States is a country that values efficiency. The widespread existence of ability grouping and curriculum grouping in public schools (Findley and Bryan 1971; Rosenbaum 1976) and of manpower planning in industry suggests the importance this notion attributes to efficiency in the selection of individuals for specialized training. The early selection systems of Plato's *Republic* and Young's (1958) "meritocracy" have a great deal of utopian appeal for Americans.

Which of these normative models is the best description of the opportunity structure in society? Strong beliefs in opportunity and efficiency coexist; yet the two often conflict. Schools and other institutions rarely give explicit attention to this conflict, how it might be resolved or, indeed, how their policies and practices deal with it. This conflict is clearly manifest in descriptions of personnel policies in some leading corporations (Shaeffer 1972). Their policies ostensibly seek to create a sponsored system in which the organization would capitalize on the efficiencies of early selection and specialized training. Yet these organizations could not let their commitment to the contest norm be questioned, so their program descriptions are qualified by contest mobility protections: there are no guarantees for those who are selected for these programs, and there are no barriers for those who are not selected.

This ambiguity and ambivalence in policy statements is similar to the way high school administrators describe selection procedures for ability and curriculum grouping. In a study of a high school, I found that administrators were reluctant to admit that their system of grouping students by ability and curriculum might affect students' opportunities to move up to a higher track, and they stressed examples of students who had moved into higher tracks (Rosenbaum 1976). Yet systematic analysis of the school's records showed that only a negligible portion of the students actually moved into a higher track. Administrators' evasiveness about this is apparently widespread, for the Coleman report study of a national sample of schools found that school administrators' responses often directly contradicted the responses of a majority of the teachers and students in the same schools (Coleman et al. 1966, p. 569; Jencks et al. 1972, p. 97).

SOCIAL SCIENCE THEORIES ABOUT OPPORTUNITY

While the contest-sponsored typology poses the normative constraints on organizational selection procedures, social science theories provide more detailed models and causal mechanisms. Human capital theory in economics and structural theories in sociology and economics (i.e., internal labor market theory) offer counterparts of the contest and sponsored models, respectively, in their emphasis on opportunity or structure. But these theories also go beyond these norms; they elaborate the underlying processes and provide specific hypotheses for empirical study of the issues. These theories provide the basis for a great deal of current research on labor markets and social mobility generally, and they are the basis for much of the research reported in this study.

Human Capital Theory

Human capital theory in economics proceeds from the same assumptions as the contest mobility norm. It posits that schools and work organizations offer open opportunity, and that individuals' attainments are largely a function of how hard they work and the ability, education, and training they possess. This theory conceptualizes the latter factors—ability, education, and training—as *human capital*. Like physical capital, human capital is increased by investments, and education and training are the primary investments individuals can make in their human capital (Becker 1964; Blaug 1976; Mincer 1974).

Individuals are the primary causal forces in the model. Individuals' productivity is the basis for compensation, and individuals' productivity is determined by the ability they possess and by the investments they make in themselves.

In this model, the job world is assumed to act like a perfect market. It is not structured, and it does not impose restrictions on individuals' careers. Individuals alone are the main actors in this model. They choose whether and how much they will invest in themselves: how much effort they will expend and how much immediate earnings they will sacrifice to get better training. No barriers exist for able individuals if they choose to make the sacrifices and efforts to acquire the skills necessary for advancement.

The human capital theory is very much the embodiment of the contest mobility model. Individuals' opportunities are not predetermined; opportunity remains open to those who have ability and are willing to make the investments required to get ahead. There are no structural barriers to advancement. Although human capital theory notes that later investments have lesser payoffs since less time remains to amortize investments, the fall-off in returns would not prevent individuals from having second and third chances to advance.

Structural Theories

Structural theories posit mobility patterns similar to those described in the sponsored mobility norm. In describing mobility within the educational system and mobility from schools into the work world, structuralists posit a predetermined mobility structure in which individuals' early status classifications strongly determine their later status attainments. In effect, structural theories contend that underlying social structures exist in institutions, and these structures are formed by the strong influences that institutional classifications impose upon mobility patterns. Instead of ability, effort, or performance affecting mobility, institutional classifications largely constrain mobility within narrowly defined mobility paths.

Structural theories were first developed to explain employees' career patterns in workplaces. The most commonly applied version, *internal labor market* (ILM) *theory*, provides a highly articulated model of the fine-grained structure of mobility within organizations.

ILM theory posits that organizations, not individuals, make the most important investments in individuals, and that these investments segment the work force into separate opportunity circumstances (Doeringer and Piore 1971; Spilerman 1977). Individuals in the primary labor market receive investments from their employing firms and, as a result, receive advancement opportunities. Individuals in the secondary labor market do not receive such investments, and even if they invest in themselves, the firm will not respond to these investments. Such individuals have no advancement opportunities. In effect, employees in the primary labor market are sponsored by the firm, and those in the secondary labor market are deprived of sponsorship.

Like Caplow's (1954) description of the bureaucratic labor market, internal labor markets are characterized by fixed ports of entry, by internal promotions as the main way of filling vacancies, and by normatively approved, established procedures for hiring, firing, and promoting. Doeringer and Piore (1971) describe what they call the "promotion unit" in which "each job in the progression line develops skills requisite for the succeeding job and draws upon the skills required on the job below it" (p. 21).[1]

As a result, after individuals are assigned to entry jobs, their subsequent careers are largely determined, since entry jobs lead into predetermined progression systems. This view differs radically from human capital theory, for it assumes that individual attributes have no influence after they determine initial job assignments. Thereafter, entry jobs lead to distinctive career lines within which future mobility is constrained (Doeringer and Piore 1971). After an individual enters an organization through a particular entry job, the key decisions about his career follow. The occupational decisions that he made earlier will be of relatively little significance (see Ginsberg 1971).

Structural theories have also been used to describe educational selections into groupings within classrooms, into classes within schools, into different schools and colleges, and from schools into different kinds of jobs. Although schools have no counterpart to economic "demand" to create a *need* for high-ability students, a number of recent studies suggest that structural and organizational factors affect the formation and stability of ability groups and curriculum groups. Hallinan and Sørensen (1983) provide the most detailed structural model of educational grouping and its relationship to structural models of work organizations. They propose conceiving of pupils' opportunities in educational grouping systems:

as vacancies in positions in the social structure. . . . The timing of such vacancies that provide opportunities for change will not in general coincide with whatever changes take place in individual performance. . . . The importance of vacancies for the attainment process in vacancy competition assumes that filled positions are closed to outsiders. Systems in which this is the case may be called closed position structures and contrast to open position systems, in which there are no constraints on the availability of positions. . . . Closed position labor market structures include internal labor markets and similar bureaucratic structures. . . . Educational systems may also be conceived of . . . as a vacancy competition process. These allocations in turn . . . form career lines in the educational system. (pp. 838–39).

Hallinan and Sørensen (1983) spell out the notion that ability groups within classrooms are closed-position structures, with positions determined more by structural factors than by individual atrributes. Following Eder (1978), they contend that teachers establish groups of approximately the same size for a number of practical reasons, including the distribution of instructional time and curriculum materials, spatial constraints, and control of behavior. Moreover, they suggest four reasons why the concern to maintain equal-sized groups leads to stability of group placements: (1) Moves would require corresponding moves in the opposite direction to maintain equal sizes; (2) downward moves generate parental resistance; (3) upward moves require extra time for remediation; and (4) all moves disrupt students' friendships. The findings of their study generally support these expectations of stability over the course of a school year.

What remains unexamined in their work, though, is the longer-term implications of group placements. While Hallinan and Sørensen do not extend their analysis to educational careers longer than a year, their analysis might be interpreted to predict stability over longer time periods. Rist (1970) found stability between children's group placements in a kindergarten class and their group placements in first and second grades, and he concludes that kindergarten classifications confer different status labels which preclude subsequent reclassifications. Schafer and Olexa (1971) found high school curriculum–tracking placements to be highly stable, and they attribute this stability to structural effects. Moreover, studies indicate a continuity from junior high school tracking to high school tracking to college attendance, even after controlling for individual attributes and performance (Alexander and McDill 1976; Rosenbaum 1976, 1980). Indeed, some structuralists have suggested that colleges sponsor graduates into elite occupational positions irrespective of ability (Collins 1971, 1979; Kamens 1974).

Structural theories, whether applied to work organizations or to schools, have several distinctive features. First, they suggest that individual attributes and performances are relatively less important determinants of careers than are structural factors. While human capital theory stresses the influence of individual factors, structural theory contends that administrative rules, institutional customs, and structural barriers will determine which individuals will be selected for advancement and how far they will be allowed to advance.

Second, they suggest that selections will resemble the sponsored mobility model. Structural theories generally suggest that selections are made at an early age, and that the individuals selected will be sponsored to high attainments. Implicit in most structural accounts is the sponsored mobility assumption that early selections will foster efficiencies by allowing more time for differential socialization and training for individuals' future attainments.

Third, structural theories also imply that careers are ahistorical: career history is irrelevant because present jobs embody the entire effect of job history on future job opportunity. Stated in operational terms, early attainments have no effects on future attainments, after controlling for intervening attainments. Ahistorical effects are posited by vacancy models (Hallinan and Sørensen 1983; White 1970), Markov models (Bartholomew 1967; Mayer 1972), status attainment models (Kelley 1973a, 1973b), and internal labor market models (Doeringer and Piore 1971).

This ahistorical feature of careers in internal labor markets is most graphically captured in the concept of the job ladder, which allows entry only at the bottom and movement up this ladder, associated with a progressive development of knowledge or skill (Althauser and Kalleberg 1981, p. 130). The implications conveyed by the ladder image are precisely those suggested in most discussions of job structures. Like a physical ladder, a job ladder poses barriers to entry except at the bottom and constrains individuals on any particular ladder to remain on the same ladder; jumping from ladder to ladder is a risky trick on job ladders, just as it is on physical ladders. Consequently, the job ladder model implies that all individuals at a given position have the same career history (on the same ladder) and, as a result, that career history is irrelevant, net of present position, in predicting future attainments.

Fourth, structural theories imply that career advancement patterns are relatively unresponsive to changes in external social and economic circumstances. Structural theories contend that administrative rules, institutional customs, and basic features of hierarchies tend to be unresponsive to most external forces. Structural theories portray change as unlikely to occur, and whatever changes that do occur must be explained by processes outside of structural theory.

Beyond Human Capital and Structural Theories

Both human capital and structural theories are likely to be too simple. In its pursuit of parsimony, human capital theory ignores many social structural realities which have obvious relevance. Human capital theorists explain inequality only in terms of individuals' attributes, while ignoring the influence of social structures. For instance, the human capital model, if taken literally, implies that wage and status attainments would increase without limit if individuals would merely increase their education, an unbelievable outcome which has been contradicted with declining growth in the 1970s (Sørensen 1977, p. 966; Thurow 1975). Studies carried out since 1970 have incorporated social structural measures into their analyses, and they reveal the influence of occupations, industry, firms, and social class which were ignored in the former research (Baron and Bielby 1980; Beck et al. 1978; Bibb and Form 1977; Grandjean 1981; Spence et al. 1982; Stolzenberg 1975; Talbert and Bose 1977; Wright and Perrone 1977).

Even economists who take the notion of human capital seriously have begun to note the possibilities of incorporating structural influences into the model. One theoretical analysis shows that wages can grow with experience, even if productivity does not, because giving overpayment to senior workers creates incentives for all employees (Lazear 1979), and this predicted lack of association of experience and productivity is supported by empirical work (Medoff and Abraham 1981). In effect, this analysis provides an economic rationale for wage structures which depart from human capital considerations. Another analysis shows that individuals can be compensated in terms of the rank order of their performance, not in terms of the dollar value of their performance (marginal product), and they may receive salaries that are assigned in advance without regard to the dollar value of their productivity (Lazear and Rosen 1982). These analyses are remarkable because they use economic principles to extend economic theory in the direction of structural theory.

On the other hand, structural theory has difficulties with social change. As Granovetter (1981) and Jencks (1980) have noted, advocates of social structural theory concede that social structures must eventually change in response to economic and social forces; however, these theories rarely have mechanisms which describe how change occurs or under what circumstances it occurs. The fundamental contention is structural rigidity, and change is not explained by the structural theories.

For our purposes, the key limitation of both theories is their neglect of ability. Structural theory has difficulty accounting for the widespread perception that selections are meritocratic and that they involve time-consuming and deliberative assessments of candidates' abilities. Institutional actors engage in extensive activities to assess candidates for a selection. College admissions officers and corporation promotion committees expend enormous efforts to assess applicants and assure selection of the most able candidates, and all parties concerned report that these are good-faith efforts and that the outcomes are meritocratic in most cases. Structural theory's stress on early sponsorship of selected individuals is consistent with some reports of favoritism, but it conflicts with another perception that no guarantees are offered to anyone and that candidates' abilities are continually being tested. Structural theory's emphasis on ahistorical effects also seems to conflict with selectors' perceptions that they base their assessments on candidates' complete career histories when they review school transcripts or résumés. Are these actions and reports totally a facade? If not, then how are they reconciled with structural theory?

Interestingly, ability is also largely neglected in human capital theory. While human capital theory makes ability a central component of human capital, it also defines ability in such a way as to make it unmeasurable. Ability is the capacity to contribute to present and future productivity (controlling for education and experience), a definition which makes human capital theory tautological. Ability test scores cannot be used to assess employee ability because these tests measure academic ability which is not necessarily the same as the abilities needed in jobs. Some educators and psychologists even have doubts about whether these tests adequately measure the kinds of ability needed for success in school, particularly for ethnic minorities (Kagan 1973; McClelland 1973). When pressed, human capital theorists state that employers (and teachers) have better indicators of individuals' abilities than researchers possess, so the best operationalization of individuals' abilities are these evaluations. This answer merely begs the question, for it ignores the possibility of inaccuracies and biases in assessments. Although human capital theory places paramount importance on ability, its definition of ability either makes ability unmeasurable or makes it inseparable from evaluators' biases.

Ironically, while human capital theory disputes the structural theory contention that ability is irrelevant, both theories ignore ability in their empirical studies. Moreover, neither theory provides any conceptualization of what ability is, how it is inferred in practice, or what properties it has.

A Signaling Theory: Reconciling the Conflict between Human Capital and Structural Theories

Although human capital and social structural theories neglect ability, a third theory, *signaling theory*, makes ability its central concern. According to signaling theory, as it was originally proposed (Arrow 1973; Spence 1974; Stiglitz 1975), employers seek to make employee selections conform to human capital theory; but contrary to the assumptions of human capital theory, employers have difficulty knowing which individuals have the most ability. The expense and difficulty of getting information about employees' abilities induce employers to use certain social attributes and accomplishments of individuals as signals of their abilities.

Signaling theory is usually applied to explaining hiring decisions, since that is the prototypical case in which employers have little information about individuals. Signaling theory contends that employers use educational credentials as signals of individuals' ability in deciding whom to hire for demanding jobs, and this is why college graduates—and graduates of better colleges—are given preference for these jobs. However, the problem continues to exist after employees are hired. Particularly in large organizations, large numbers of employees must be evaluated and compared, and these individuals often occupy very different jobs with incomparable products and are evaluated by different supervisors (whose judgments may be based on different criteria and have different distributions). In addition, most candidates for promotions are in white-collar jobs, for which job peformance is difficult to evaluate. While extensive efforts have been made to develop assessment tests and procedures, these have generally been found to have limited validity (Campbell et al. 1970) and are regarded with mistrust by managers (Shaeffer 1972). A few large corporations have devised elaborate assessment programs (notably Uniroyal and AT & T; see Bray et al. 1974); but only the largest companies can afford such programs, and even they cannot afford to implement them for more than one stage of the promotion process. Clearly, promotion committees face a scarcity of information about ability, which suggests the relevance of signaling theory.

To discover how promotion committees deal with these issues, I interviewed several managers who had served on promotion committees at several levels in a large corporation (Rosenbaum 1984). They reported that although supervisors' ratings are the main factor determining promotion outcomes, promotion committees have difficulty comparing candidates who are rated equally highly by different supervisors, particularly when the candidates occupy jobs with very different task demands. In response to these problems, managers reported that promotion committee discussions rely upon objective comparable indicators of job demands—particularly job status and earnings—to distinguish among the abilities of several highly rated candidates. The managers explained that since the compensation system assigns job status and pay levels to jobs based on a thorough analysis of the difficulty of their tasks, job status and earnings are considered to be good indicators of job demands.

What is noteworthy in these managers' reports is not that these social attainments affect promotion decisions, but also that they do so because they are thought to be "signals" of candidates' abilities. The rationale for this inference is most crisply stated in the maxim which is frequently stated in this corporation: "the cream rises to the top." In effect, this maxim seems to be a shared informal theory about how to detect ability: when it is hard to distinguish among candidates, then their past attainments can be used as signals of their abilities.

Educational institutions face similar problems of assessing students' abilities, and they respond in similar ways. Although ability and achievement test scores can be used for educational selections, these scores are widely mistrusted, and few American educational institutions give such tests the kind of absolute influence that the Eleven-Plus exams have in Britain.

Cicourel and Kitsuse (1963) provided some of the seminal ideas about the social construction of ability, and their research identified a number of social factors which affect the ways guidance counselors evaluate the ability and achievement of students. Even grade performance is not necessarily accepted at face value, and counselors report labeling a student an "underachiever" based on "the estimation of parents, teacher, [or] counselors, that he isn't measuring up to his potential" (Cicourel and Kitsuse 1963, p. 99). Their research repeatedly found that counselors often emphasized differences of family social background and track placements in evaluating students. The authors conclude:

The rationalization of the school system through the incorporation of the concepts and methods of psychiatry, psychology, and the social sciences has legitimized the relevance of personal and social factors for the interpretation of the "objective" measures of the student's ability and performance. Such factors are explicitly acknowledged as educationally relevant and incorporated into a complex system of organizational policies and procedures. Thus, although testing procedures are extensively employed and course grades are routinely reviewed, the information they provide are in some instances the sole basis for organization decisions, but in other instances their significance is qualified by considerations of personal and social factors. (Cicourel and Kitsuse 1963, p. 138).

The limited influence of test scores in determining track placements and college attendance is further indicated in the common finding by large-scale survey studies across many schools that ability explains only a small (though often significant) portion of the variance in these outcomes (Alexander and McDill 1976; Jencks et al. 1972). Of course, this limited explanatory power across schools may only reflect different allocation rules in different schools; however, studies within single schools arrive at the same conclusion. Such studies find that ability and achievement test scores are only moderately related to ability and curriculum group allocations, even when official school records are analyzed (Cicourel and Kitsuse 1963; Rosenbaum 1976; Schafer and Olexa 1971). These studies also indicate the underlying processes contributing to this outcome. Rosenbaum (1976) finds that a multitude of factors influence curriculum track placement and that ability (whether measured by objective tests or by teachers' subjective evaluations) has less influence on track placements than do indicators of effort (attendance and teachers' evaluations of student industry and deportment). As noted, Cicourel and Kitsuse (1963) identify the ways in which guidance counselors reinterpret these scores and take other factors into account in evaluating students.

Besides using test scores, counselors assess students' abilities based upon students' histories of performances and attainments. Just as the contest norm implies, counselors consider ability to be multifaceted and composed of nonacademic elements. Consequently, there is no better indicator of the ability to succeed than a record of past successes. In the high school I studied, counselors reported that several kinds of school classifications affected their judgments of students' abilities (Rosenbaum 1976). They reported that academic ability was inferred if students were admitted to high-ability groups; if students avoided low-ability groups; if students avoided shop, home economics, and typing courses; and if students were permitted to take "academic" foreign languages (French and Latin versus Italian and Spanish, which were considered to be ethnic, non-academic languages). According to reports by high school counselors, students were assigned to these courses and groupings based on junior high school coun-selors' assessments of students' abilities. Consequently, these classifications were considered to be good signals of students' abilities, and they were used as such in assessing students' abilities.

Signaling theory reconciles much of the conflict between human capital and structural theories by allowing structural attainments to be viewed as signals of ability. If ability, which is a key component of human capital theory, is signaled by structural attainments, then the conflict between human capital and structural theories largely disappears. Signaling theory provides a mechanism by which ability acquires a specific operational meaning from its social context.

Career Systems in Schools and Workplaces: Structure or Signaling?

Although signaling theory resembles elements of human capital and structural theories, it differs from each in important respects. This section evaluates the usefulness of structural and signaling theories in explaining the available evidence on career systems in schools and workplaces. Human capital theory is not con-sidered because of the difficulties of testing its predictions; it is addressed in detail elsewhere (Rosenbaum 1984).

Structural and signaling theories are similar in some respects. One defining characteristic of structural theories—that structural factors are more important determinants of careers than are individual attributes—is also a feature of sig-naling theory, so this provides no test between the two theories. However, the theories do differ in three other respects. First, the two theories differ in the mechanism they posit and in the extensiveness of its effects. Second, the theories differ in the complexity of the career results that they posit. Third, the two theories differ as to whether they posit historical effects. Evidence on these three points is reviewed below.

First, at the most manifest level, the two theories differ in the mechanism they posit and in the extensiveness of its effects. Structural theories posit that careers are determined by institutional rules and customs which confer advantages to certain groups and impose barriers against others. Moreover, they suggest long-term categorical outcomes, similar to those suggested by the sponsored mobility mode. The concept of fixed career ladders emanating from certain jobs is a common feature of structural theories. In contrast, signaling theory posits that careers are determined by the way past structural attainments are interpreted as ability signals, and as a result, the categorical "all-or-nothing" character of sponsored asurances and barriers will be absent.

The available evidence suggests that structural and signaling patterns both occur. Workplaces often identify certain jobs as offering no promotion opportunity (the "secondary labor market") and other jobs as offering "fast-track" career advances (Doeringer and Piore 1971; Kanter 1977). However, many jobs offer neither guarantees nor barriers to mobility; they offer an intermediate probability of promotion, and they do so fairly stably over various time periods. These promotion probabilities do not resemble the all-or-nothing character of sponsorships; they suggest a probabilistic process like the one suggested by signaling inferences.

Schools also show both patterns. In my study of a high school, students who did not enroll in a foreign language in junior high school were never allowed into college track in high school (Rosenbaum 1976, p. 39). Foreign language constituted a structural barrier which was absolute. However, students taking Italian or Spanish as their language, though they had a lower probability of entering college track than did students taking French or Latin, were not excluded from the college track option.

Moreover, people in these two kinds of settings perceive both kinds of processes operating. While managers and high school counselors acknowledge some kinds of structural barriers and advantages, they also note some ways that structural attainments are taken as signals. When doubts are raised about students' abilities, high school counselors report that early ability group and language classifications are used to help in assessing ability (Cicourel and Kitsuse 1963; Rosenbaum 1976). Similarly, managers serving on promotion committees report that early promotions help them infer employees' abilities (Rosenbaum 1984).

Second, more specifically, the structural theory prediction of job ladders suggests a simpler model than is predicted by signaling theory. The job ladder notion implies that employees fill higher-level jobs from a limited number of specific lower-level jobs. In contrast, signaling theory implies no such simple relationship; it posits only that individuals will come from jobs of equivalent "ability status," which may include a wide range of positions.

The corporation I studied actually investigated this question. Suspecting that distinct career ladders emanated out of particular jobs, the personnel department tried to map out the pattern of career ladders. After a year's effort, the project concluded that no such clear structure existed, and the effort was abandoned. My own quantitative analyses of employees' careers drew a similar conclusion. Rather than careers being determined by a simple career ladder emanating from an employee's present job, careers are affected by present and past jobs and by the timing of advancements among jobs, and each of these has an impact independent on the others (Rosenbaum 1984, chap. 6).

Similarly, in high schools, no single selection criterion and no set of criteria could be identified as explaining students' track placements (Cicourel and Kitsuse

1963; Rosenbaum 1976). Numerous factors went into these selections, and counselors combined, interpreted, and utilized these many factors in different ways for determining track placements for different students.

As noted earlier, structural theories imply that careers are ahistorical. The job ladder notion implies that employees are constrained to remain on the same job ladder. In contrast, signaling theory implies historical effects. It suggests that career history, because it communicates additional information, will affect future careers, independent of present attainment. If, instead of imposing social structural barriers, past social attainments convey information, then the signaling process will carry forward these old signals which would affect subsequent selection decisions. Just as a candidate's résumé is presumably evaluated by a complete reading of the candidate's entire history (with increasing weight given to most recent attainments), signaling theory posits that past signals affect present selections, independent of intervening attainments.

Research findings again support the prediction of signaling theory. For instance, in counseling college-track students, particularly those with modest achievements, counselors looked back over the students' previous records. A student's previous ability group classifications and previous language courses affected the counselor's decision about whether the student was able to handle college. (Since this finding is based only on counselor reports, analyses of school records would be useful in supporting his conclusions.)

Analyses of records was possible in the corporation I studied. These analyses found that an employee's entry job status continued to have an influence on later careers, even after the employee had moved on to a subsequent job, and this effect remained significant even after controlling for employees' education, experience, and a proxy measure of ability (college quality) (Rosenbaum 1984).

While none of these considerations totally precludes a structural model, the weight of all these considerations is difficult to assimilate in a structural model without profound alterations of the model. Even if such alterations were made, they would create a structural model which was so complex as to make it lose its original elegant simplicity. In contrast, these complexities are easily incorporated in a signaling theory which specifies a dynamic process by which the status and timing of individuals' past attainments affect ability inferences about individuals.

The Tournament Model: How Signals Cumulate to Create Career Patterns

While signaling theory describes a specific mechanism by which structural attainments affect particular selection decisions, it doesn't give an overview of the selection system. Signaling theory tells us what cues are used at any time, but it does not indicate how they cumulate over time, whether they have different effects at different times (career stages), or how selections of various employee subgroups throughout an institution are interrelated.

The tournament model has been proposed to describe the way that signals cumulate over time to create careers (Rosenbaum 1984). The tournament model describes a career selection system as a series of implicit meritocratic competitions which progressively differentiate a cohort of individuals as their careers unfold. Each competition identifies further differences among individuals, and each selection creates ability signals which in turn affect subsequent selections.

Indeed, this is the purpose of tournaments. In sports events, tournaments identify and communicate individuals' ability relative to their competitors (both those against whom they have been pitted and, by extension, everyone else in the tournament). Tournaments imply that the losers at any stage are less able than the winners at that stage. The statement that an individual "survived the semifinals" implies that the individual is more able than those who did not. By pitting winners at each stage against one another, tournaments can differentiate ever more finely among degrees of ability. This procedure is prevalent in sports tournaments, and it is implicit in the "social Darwinism" of the business ethos.

Like the contest mobility model, a win in the tournament does not guarantee ultimate attainments; it only gives one the right to advance to the next competition for further advancement. Like the sponsored mobility model, a loss in the tournament removes one from the competition for top positions. Thus the tournament model provides a partial resolution of the conflict between opportunity and efficiency by offering initial opportunity to all individuals while fostering efficiency by increasingly winnowing down the number of winners.

Thus the normative power of the tournament model arises from its success at encompassing and seeming to reconcile major elements of the two conflicting norms which guide the thinking about selections in American society. In dictating that selections should operate like a tournament, the tournament model provides a simple ideal to follow and use in judging the legitimacy of past and future selections. Obviously, the paramount difficulty is in justifying negative decisions to losers, and tournaments are a widely accepted way of doing this in American society.

The tournament also serves quite well as a descriptive model of careers. As a descriptive model, it gives an overview of the ways that organizations make selections as the individuals in a cohort progress through their careers. The tournament model extends signaling theory by specifying the timetables that define ability signals and the ways that combinations of signals cumulate over time. The tournament model describes individuals' careers as part of career systems, and it stresses that timing is a crucial dimension of career systems.

The tournament functions the same way in educational selections as it does in sports events. As students proceed through their educational careers, they face selections in a series of hierarchical educational classifications—reading groups in elementary schools, ability groups in middle schools, curriculum tracks in high schools, and various kinds of post-secondary schools, colleges, and graduate schools of differing status. As in sports tournaments, there are winners and losers at each stage of the competition in the educational tournament, and only the winners advance to compete for the top-status outcomes. Compared with the winners, the losers at each stage are declared to be less able, and as a result, they may be eliminated from competition for further selections or they may be relegated to minor tournaments in which their chances for the highest attainments are greatly diminished.

Although the primary utility of the tournament model is in providing a general normative and descriptive model which encompasses entire career systems, the tournament model extends the specific empirical predictions of signaling theory in an important respect. It suggests that mobility is primarily unidirectional; assignment to low groups is contingent on continual winning and any loss leads to downward mobility.

Pursuing the prediction of structural theories, most research has only investigated the stability of grouping placements. The research repeatedly finds high stability, both in ability groupings (Balow 1964; Barker Lunn 1970; Daniels 1961; Hallinan and Sørensen 1983) and in curriculum groupings (Jones et al. 1972; Rosenbaum and Velez 1978). Findings of less than 2 percent mobilty in a year (Balow 1964; Daniels 1961; Mason 1974) suggest strong support for inferring that early groupings have a strong impact on later groupings.

However, the few studies which have noted the direction of mobility support the tournament contention of one-directional mobility. While Mason (1974) finds a high degree of stability in elementary-school ability grouping (in a Canadian school), he also notes that what little mobility occurred was in a downward direction. Studies using school records of curriculum groupings also find that mobility is primarily downward (Jones et al. 1972; Rosenbaum 1976). Moreover, analyses of the Project Talent national survey find this same one-directional pattern (Evans and Galloway 1973), as do analyses of the Parnes longitudinal survey of American young men (Rosenbaum and Velez 1978). In contrast with our ideal of open opportunities for advancement, opportunity is predominantly unidirectional: it is easy to lose college-curriculum status and hard to gain it.

Selection processes resembling a tournament also operate within work organizations. Jobs in a large corporation are ranked in terms of status and authority, and careers are gauged in terms of their advancement in the status-authority hierarchy. Although stated organizational policies often suggest a resemblance to the contest model (Kanter 1977; Rosenbaum 1984; Shaeffer 1972), and although some research has observed that organizations create a sponsorship of employees from certain ethnic, class, or educational backgrounds (Collins 1979; Edwards 1979; Glaser 1964), a longitudinal analysis of the actual patterns of career mobility of an entering cohort over a thirteen-year span found neither the contest nor the sponsored pattern (Rosenbaum 1964). Careers in this corporation resembled the tournament model. The first employees to be promoted were inferred to be the most able (according to managers' reports), and the personnel records revealed that early promotees received the greatest subsequent career attainments, while members of the same cohort who were promoted later (even from the same jobs), having been losers of earlier competitions, were, consequently, inferred to be less able. These early attainment effects remain significant even after controlling for education, experience, and a proxy for ability (college quality: see Rosenbaum 1984, ch. 6). Since the organization posits that competitions for promotions occur continuously, early promotions become signals of greater ability, and failure to advance regularly is taken as a signal of lack of ability.

These mobility patterns differ from those predicted by structural theory in the lack of guarantees offered to winners. Unlike the sponsorship pattern, which is most often suggested by structural theories, these findings indicate no guarantees about ultimate attainments: one must continually compete for further advancement. However, losses do have permanent effects. Unlike human capital theory, which ignores structural influences, the findings indicate that individuals who do not receive early promotions are eliminated from the competition for the highest positions.

The descriptions of career mobility in schools and in corporations strongly support the tournament model. The tournament's prediction of a lack of guarantees for winners, of downward mobility for former winners who lose a competition, and of curtailed opportunity for individuals who have lost a competition is strongly supported in the empirical analyses. Although these patterns could conceivably be described by other models, the tournament model provides a simple mechanism to account for these results.

The tournament model not only describes mobility patterns, but it also imposes an interpretation upon these outcomes, which is fundamentally a signaling interpretation. It suggests that all contestants compete in a fair competition and that the winners emerge victorious because of their superior ability. Like the contest model, the tournament does not have to specify what abilities allowed individuals to win; this is not important. In truly pragmatic fashion, only performance counts, and it does not matter how one accomplished that performance. Of course, organizations must establish rules to assure fair competition, but the particular rules are secondary details. What is crucial is that there is general consensus that a fair tournament has occurred and that the tournament's outcomes identify the most able contestants. As long as these assumptions are believed to be met, the tournament inference can be made: abilities can be imputed to individuals based on their record of attainments. This brings us to the notion of the social construction of ability, the central contention of this chapter.

Ability: Property of Individuals or a Structurally Assigned Status?

Commonsense notions and pschological and economic theories conceive of ability as a property of individuals. By this notion, individuals possess high or low ability as personal qualities. Ability is an individual attribute, just as eye color is, and the social worlds of teachers and employers assess this property of individuals and respond to individuals accordingly.

But that is ability as an ideal concept. In practice, I would contend, ability is a social status conferred to individuals by their peers and supervisors, and attributes of the social system are likely to influence what social statuses are available and upon what criteria they are based. In particular, as the previous analysis has suggested, the tournament model asserts that the career system has a major influence in defining how the status of ability will be identified and assigned to individuals. Organizational members will rely on such signals because of the difficulties of measuring ability and of comparing different supervisors' evaluations of ability across different jobs.

According to the tournament model, ability is inferred from an individual's record of past attainments. Moreover, an ability status must continually be confirmed by repeated selections, for if an individual fails to continue advancing, the tournament indicates that the individual has lost a competition. Consequently, lack of future prospects is a sign of a tournament loss, and thus it signals a lack of ability.

In effect, tournaments confer ability statuses by two processes: retrospectively, from an individual's history of attainments, and prospectively, from the individual's future opportunities. However, each of these processes is subject to the constraints and opportunities imposed by structural factors.

Retrospectively assigned ability derives from individuals' personal accomplishments, but in part this is due to social system attributes and conditions which permitted their abilities to result in career advancements.

Prospectively assigned ability derives from the awareness that the system will have certain needs in the future. What happens when there is sudden organizational growth? The ability pool does not increase; if anything, it declines, because other firms are likely to be drawing away talent. But managers in the organization spend more time looking for ability. They give training and testing experiences to more individuals. And everyone knows that more individuals will be promoted and given the label of "high potential." The knowledge that a promotion will occur in the future creates a competition among those qualified to compete and creates a task for managers to find ability among the competitors. Ability is relative to the needs of the career system.

In the tournament, ability is a socially assigned status, and it is determined at least as much by the needs and properties of the career system as by the attributes of the individuals involved. When an organization has promoted many individuals quite rapidly in the recent past, then many ability statuses will have been assigned in the process, regardless of the actual distribution of ability. Similarly, when an organization needs to promote many individuals rapidly in the near future, then many ability statuses will be assigned.

We might wonder if such structural factors are important in determining ability signals in schools. The general availability of academic ability tests seems to obviate the need for signals, but as noted previously, these tests are widely mistrusted. Moreover, in contrast to the rigid structural constraints suggested in the foregoing analysis, which might be very pertinent to profit-maximizing corporations, ability and curriculum groupings in schools are generally believed to be responsive to individual students' needs, rather than vice versa. However, the previous review indicated that structural considerations about equal-sized groups and stable placements are serious constraints on the organization of groupings (Eder 1978; Hallinan and Sørensen 1983). Evidently, even in schools, to the extent that high-ability groups, curriculum tracks, or high-status colleges confer ability statuses as the tournament model suggests, high ability will be rationed by the availability of these positions.

The career system in educational systems and work organizations defines how many winners there will be at any particular time, how quickly they will be tested for further advancements, when—if ever—tournament losers will be offered subsequent competitions, and the positions for which they will be qualified to complete. The career system's rules define the ways that ability labels will be assigned and even what ability labels individuals may subsequently compete for.

The conception of ability as a *status* resembles the conceptions of social labeling in symbolic interactionist analyses. Although that literature mostly discusses deviant labels, "high ability" or "high potential" can be considered positive labels that organizations confer on their most valued members, and the career system regulates how many and which individuals are assigned this status.

The conception is most similar to what Meyer (1977) describes as "legitimation theory-which treats education [or other institutions] as both constructing or altering roles in society and [as] authoritatively allocating personnel to these roles" (p. 56). According to Meyer, while the evidence regarding education's effect on competence is mixed, education still constitutes a system of "institutionalized rites" which define "new roles and statuses for elites and members" (p. 56). Moreover, different schools receive distinct social "charters to define people as graduates and therefore as possessing distinctive rights and capacities in society" (Meyer 1977, p. 59; also see Kamens 1971, 1974, 1977). However, Meyer's notion can apply to other institutional contexts besides education (Meyer and Rowan 1977), and the differentiation of roles and statuses not only occurs between institutions, but also within institutions, with high school tracking being a noteworthy example (Meyer 1977, p. 61; see also Rosenbaum 1976).

The tournament is a particularly effective way of legitimating selections in work institutions and in schools (Rosenbaum 1976). As in Meyer's conception of an allocation system, the tournament makes selections and assigns new roles and statuses, but the tournament provides an additional source of legitimation— the presumed open competition which gradually winnows down the winners' cohort by successive competitions. While Meyer's conception explains how the outcomes of selections at any point in time are legitimated, the tournament explains how patterns of career mobility are legitimated.[2]

What is noteworthy here is that relationships between macrolevel career systems and microlevel social interactions are posited, with each reinforcing the other (see also Collins 1981). The career system defines how many individuals and which individuals receive ability status, and these ability assignments in turn tend to legitimate the career system as meritocratic.

Career systems specify that a certain number of individuals must be identified as appropriate for high-status classifications (e.g., a high-ability group or a promotion to a higher-status job), and consequently, they create a need for conferring the high-potential labels that justify these selections. Even if talented employees did not exist, organizations would have to invent them to fill the high-ability groups in schools and the fast tracks of corporate career systems. And while talent cannot be created, signals of talent can be, and the tournament model contends that this is done by conferring better social positions and rapid advancements. Moreover, by maintaining fixed mobility paths, the career system guarantees that the organization will have a pool of individuals designated with the status of "high potential" from which to recruit its future top executives.

If this is so, then human capital theory may have the facts right for the wrong reason. High pay is associated with high ability not only because talented people advance, but also because most people tend to see the world in that way. Consequently, high-ability labels are imputed to individuals who have high pay, high status, and fast-rising career trajectories. If career histories are commonly used to signal ability, then the human capital prediction of ability affecting earnings attainments becomes true by a process of reverse causality: managers infer that an employee is bright if he has quickly attained a good job and a good salary.

Structurally Determined Properties of Ability Signals

A career system does more than merely respond to vacancies. It defines patterns for career advancements, and in the process, it presumes certain properties of ability. A career system based on the sponsored mobility norm specifies that early selections have permanent effects in differentiating individuals' subsequent career trajectories. To the extent that sponsored systems presume to be based on ability, they assume that ability can be detected very early and that it will be very stable over the duration of an individual's career. In contrast, in a career system based on the contest mobility norm, individuals are allowed great flexibility for changing their attainments over time. Such a system conceives ability as being transitory and subject to change; high-ability individuals may falter, while initial losers may be "late bloomers." That is why the contest system delays making final selections as long as possible, even though considerable costs arise from deferring selections.

A tournament system is more complex. It sets a "ceiling" on ability for individuals after they lose a competition and a higher "floor" on ability for individuals after they win a competition. A decision to move a student to a lower track or not to promote an employee to higher status communicates the message that the individual lacks the requisite ability, and this social fact has irreversible consequences in limiting the individual's maximum attainment. Those who lose an early selection are assigned a low-ability status, which sharply limits their future opportunities. The tournament implies that there are no late bloomers. Nonetheless, the contest and sponsored norms present conflicting conceptions about ability. Almost by default, individuals are forced to draw their own conclusions about ability, and career selection systems provide the social arena from which most individuals draw their inferences about ability.

Thus, for instance, guidance counselors had good reason to suppose that students choosing an easier foreign language were avoiding the top competition in the high school tournament, and this would be a reasonable inference in many, or even most, cases. However, the unfortunate student who chose Spanish as a commercially valuable or personally important language would suffer a low-ability status unless he had a strong record to prevent this inference.

Similarly, the corporation study found that individuals who do not advance in their first three years are less likely to do so subsequently. We might infer that any manager who noticed the regularity of this pattern might also infer that it made little sense to look for ability in such individuals. Indeed, in a system which rations promotability ratings (i.e., if no manager could give top ratings to more than 25 percent of his subordinates), a manager would be wasting his scarce top ratings to give one to individuals who had not been promoted in their first three years. This could be true even if diminished company growth or temporary family difficulties were the reason for the employee's lack of advancement.

Although the tournament sets a higher floor for ability when individuals win a competition, it does not define an upper limit for the individual's ability or an ultimate career attainment for the individual. A tournament is far more pragmatic than a sponsorship in this respect. A sponsorship makes far-reaching decisions about which students are destined for the best colleges and which employees are destined for top executive positions because it considers ability permanent and easy to detect. In contrast, the tournament makes incremental decisions at each stage in the process (see Lindblom 1959), for like all signaling theories, it considers ability difficult to detect and assess accurately. The tournament continually asks, "What have you accomplished recently?" Each win connotes somewhat more ability than the previous win indicated, but a win never guarantees more than one advancement, nor, consequently, does it irreversibly confer a signal of very high ability. For instance, college-track students in Grayton had no guarantee of staying in that track (Rosenbaum 1976). Each year they were reassigned, some were declared not able to handle college track, and they were removed from this track (with no option to return to it). Similarly, in the corporation, employees who began in high-status jobs and received a promotion in their first three years have the best chance of attaining middle management, but even they are not guaranteed such attainment. Thus the tournament career system implies a conception of low ability as permanent, which irreversibly eliminates the individual from competitions for top positions; high ability is conceived as unspecified and subject to change, requiring continual reaffirmation by continued winning.

These presumptions about ability are not merely of theoretical interest; they are likely to be part of the social conceptions of actors in these career systems. Individuals' social conceptions about the properties of ability will be derived from the nature of the career selection systems in which they participate. Obviously, the direction of causality is always difficult to infer on such issues, and there can be no doubt that causality works the other way too: general social conceptions about ability may mold institutional career systems. Indeed, I have contended that the tournament model results from a need to reconcile the conflict between the contest norm and the sponsored norm (and the ability conceptions implicit in these normative systems).

Consequently, when managers have difficulty in inferring individuals' abilities, these patterns suggest that they could use individuals' job histories to assist in inferring their potential for future advancement, and managers report that they do indeed use these as signals. The tournament definition of the ability signal might be expressed as the quotient of job status divided by tenure and entry age. This quotient is similar to the signals that managers reported using in promotion committees. Based on observations of another corporation, Kanter (1977) has also suggested such a relationship. It is also consistent with descriptions of still other corporations. For example, based on observations of many firms, Kellogg (1972) notes that most employees expect that high-potential managers will advance every two or three years, a belief which implies that those who do not are not good candidates for advancement; and Ference (1979) notes that employees who "level off" are seen as failures with no abiliity to advance further.

The simple quotient expresses the net result of the tournament norm: ability is indicated by how high one has risen in a particular span of time. Other historical features of careers may also be taken into account—entry job status, subsequent job status and timing of selections—and these may be similarly used as signals of ability.

Critical Periods: Properties of Individuals' Abilities or of Career Systems?

Perhaps the best example of the tournament defining properties of ability signals is the critical-period conception of ability proposed by Berlew and Hall (1966). In a study which has become a cornerstone of the psychological study of organizational careers, Berlew and Hall found that the company's early expectations for a manager and the concomitant challenge posed by his first job were strongly related to his success five years later. The researchers conclude that the first year is a critical period for learning, a time when the trainee is uniquely ready to develop or change in the direction of the company's expectations. This year would be analogous to the critical period, probably between six and eighteen months, when human infants must either experience a close emotional relationship with another human being or suffer ill effects ranging from psychosis to an inability ever to establish such a relationship. (p. 221).

While noting that work orientation in unlikely to be "fixed" in the first year, and "corrective experiences are certainly possible," Berlew and Hall conclude that "probably never again will [a manager] be so 'unfrozen' and ready to learn as he is in his first year" (p. 222).

However, the tournament model raises the question of whether it is the person or the career system which becomes increasingly "frozen" over time. If the tournament career system—not individual development—is responsible for the greater changeability of career trajectories in early career, then the tournament career system may also explain this critical-period aspect of careers. Berlew and Hall's findings are certainly open to alternative interpretations, for they only study individuals and do not look at properties of the career system. Since Berlew and Hall do not analyze what stimulation or challenge employees are offered, their data do not define what it is that vanishes at the end of the critical period. Does an individual's ability to benefit from challenge vanish, or does the challenge from the environment vanish? If it is the former, as Berlew and Hall imply, then the critical period is a property of individual development; but if it is the latter, as the tournament model suggests, then the critical period is a property of the career system.

The tournament model advances a structural explanation of the critical-period notion. It suggests that there is a critical period during which organizational career systems will notice ability in individuals and will offer them challenge. After this critical period, the career system will no longer notice employees' ability and will no longer offer them challenge. Instead of the critical period being an attribute of individuals, the tournament makes it a property of the career system and what the career system allows individuals to do. Once the career system has determined that some employees have no potential for advancement, either it assigns them to jobs which do not permit them to manifest the skills needed for advancement or it does not notice those skills if exhibited. As a result, the abilities which individuals are allowed to manifest (or which are recognized by the career system) are limited by the jobs which the tournament has assigned them.

If a career system has critical periods for allowing individuals to demonstrate ability, then the career system can prevent individuals from manifesting ability after they have passed its critical period (i.e., after the organization stops paying attention and stops offering challenge). One's performance after being eliminated from the tournament is irrelevant, and consequently, it goes largely unnoticed.

Similar processes are evident in high school tracking. Students have a limited amount of time to show mastery of material in their classes. If they fail to show mastery in that period of time, they receive poor grades, and soon thereafter they must meet with the guidance counselor, who advises or compels them to transfer out of the college track.

Schools may differ in how quickly this happens, and they may differ in their propensity to use downward track mobility as opposed to other approaches (such as additional instruction, extended personal counseling, changing teachers, or changing ability groupings within college track).

In the working-class school I studied, counselors were quick to compel students to move to a lower track. In the upper-middle-class school Cicourel and Kitsuse (1963) studied, downward track mobility was rare and a matter of last resort after other approaches had been tried. These structural differences in track mobility are likely to have implications for the way that ability is conceived. The working-class school I studied encouraged a notion of critical periods for ability, while Cicourel and Kitsuse's school, by holding opportunity open longer, implied that the emergence of ability was not restricted to a narrow critical period. The educator's notion of late bloomers is the opposite of the critical-period concept, and school career systems are likely to differ in how receptive they are to discerning late bloomers.

Once a student was moved out of the college track in Grayton, second chances to reenter that track were virtually nonexistent. The track system operated as if the student had moved outside the critical period for showing college abilities, and students were given no opportunity to show such abilities. Late bloomers in this track system were out of luck; the track system permitted no way for late bloomers to become evident, and so it was widely assumed in this school that later blooming did not occur.

More subtle forms of career timetables are also evident in high schools. Grayton, like most high schools, had certain timetables about when students were expected to take particular courses. Students who failed to follow these schedules were considered to be "falling behind" expectations, and this tended to be interpreted as a sign of limited ability. For instance, college-track students normally took biology in ninth grade and chemistry in tenth grade. A student who deferred biology until tenth grade tended to be seen as "off schedule" and thus as less able. Of course, the signal conferred by being off schedule depended on what the student took instead of biology, but given the limited number of high-ability course alternatives, the alternative was likely to be a lower-status language (Italian or Spanish) or worse, a vocational course. However, even if the student took a high-ability alternative (e.g., an additional high-ability language), counselors would infer that the student had avoided the prescribed science course and that this signified some science deficiency in the student. The omission in itself was not terribly serious, but if the student subsequently showed difficulty in any of his other college-track courses, then counselors would point to the student's being off schedule on the prescribed college curriculum as an early sign of the student's limitations. Similar normative timetables existed for other subject areas as well, particularly math and language.

The concept of a career system which has differential responsiveness to individuals' performance makes it impossible to know whether limitations in performance are due to individuals' limited abilities or to limitations in the abilities which the career system permits individuals to manifest. This problem is not idiosyncratic to schools or to work organizations; it is true whenever ability is assessed. Ability is an inference from performance, and in all such inferences, doubts arise about whether the "testing" situation has allowed the individual ample opportunity to show the requisite ability.

Besides raising this question, career systems also raise the question of how long "tests" continue to occur. The contention here that career systems operate essentially like tournaments, with implicit competitions which determine subsequent job assignments, implies that the critical period for ability is determined by the career system, that an individual's critical period for showing ability remains open as long as he or she continues winning in the career tournament, and that a history which includes a loss will be taken as a clear signal of the limits of the individual's ability, justifying elimination from the major tournament for his positions.

It is ironic that human capital theory views the assessment of ability as a trivial problem. It makes ability central to its explanation, but it does not attempt to define or operationalize it, conveniently assuming that managers can easily assess it. The personnel literature on the assessment of managerial and professional ability makes it plain that managers do not know how to measure it, and the statements of managers (Rosenbaum 1984) confirm their confusion on the matter.

The answer proposed here to the human capital problem of ability is that the social structure determines it. The tournament career system determines the way ability is conceived and the way it is used to affect careers. It stipulates how ability can be recognized, where it is likely to be found, how long it takes to appear, and when to stop looking for it.

Policy Implications

The point of this analysis is not to deny that individuals differ in ability, or even to deny that some appropriate cues are available for inferring ability. Experienced teachers and supervisors may be reasonably good at evaluating abilities. But assessing ability is not an easy inference: one seeks to discover a fairly permanent underlying attribute for individuals from a series of performances in complex situations. Such situations usually present imperfect tests of ability, introduce a multitude of confounding influences on performance, and constrain how many individuals can manifest high ability.

The problem of assessing ability is particularly difficult at the systemwide level, as guidance counselors and promotion committees try to assess large numbers of individuals whose abilities were rated by different evaluators in different circumstances based on different standards. Problems also arise in deciding what properties are to be attributed to different abilities—particularly how long an individual is likely to maintain his or her current ability advantage over comparable peers. These are widely acknowledged to be difficult inferences, and even staunch advocates of ability-based theories admit that the various traditional approaches (tests, assessment centers, selectors' intuitions) have problematic features.

Traditional individual-based theories respond to the multitude of confounding influences by assuming that their influence is random and, consequently, that, on average, they have little net effect over many ability decisions. However, as this review has indicated, if one takes a larger view of the social context in which ability inferences take place, it becomes evident that institutional social structures impose systematic influences on ability inferences.

This chapter has presented an analysis of the social determinants of ability—what might be called the social construction of ability. Through a review of competing theories about organizational selections in schools and workplaces, we have concluded that available research findings provide support for the signaling theory of career selections and for the tournament model of career systems. This theory and model suggest that social structural circumstances might affect the ways ability signals are assigned and the properties attributed to ability signals.

The conclusions of this review cannot be considered definitive. The available evidence on career systems in schools and workplaces is too meager to permit certainty about the nature of these career systems or the processes that create them. Moreover, given the elusiveness of the concept of ability, it is not certain that any theory about the determinants of ability can ever be conclusively settled.

However, this review does raise the possibility that social structural considerations may affect the ability labels attributed to individuals and the properties attributed to ability. While confirmation of these contentions will not be possible until more research is done, even the possibility that these contentions may be true raises serious policy issues which organizational analysts must consider.

Race and Gender Discrimination. The notion of discrimination is generally conceived as a departure from selection based on ability. For instance, we speak of school tracking systems that are biased because they require racial minorities to show greater ability than nonminorities in order to qualify for high tracks. However, if ability itself is partially inferred from structural attainments, then past patterns of discrimination, if hidden or denied, create lower social attainments which confer inferior-ability signals to minorities. If minorities have been in the wrong ability groups, the wrong subject matter courses, or the wrong foreign languages, they will lack the social attainments which signal ability. In a workplace, past discrimination may prevent minorities from holding the right jobs, from moving on the right timetables, and from obtaining the right training experiences which signal ability in large organizations. After a long history of such practices, discrimination can no longer be considered as the simple notion of "departures from ability" because ability signals themselves will have been allocated in discriminatory manner.

Age Discrimination and Career Timetables. Age discrimination has special importance in a tournament system since age-based selections are an intrinsic part of such a system. The central principle of a tournament—that losers in a competition have irreversible consequences—inevitably makes age a negative signal. Among individuals in comparable positions, those who are older have taken longer to reach that attainment, and so one may infer that they must have lost some competition along the way and possess lesser ability than their peers. This type of inference might be used to stigmatize a student who is old for his grade level in school or a foreman who is older than other foremen.

If one accepts the premise of the tournament model—that previous losses signal lesser ability—then age may even be considered a meritocratic selection criterion. Those who are older have presumably had their chance to compete and have failed relative to their younger peers who hold positions similar to their own. In a fair tournament, selections based on age are no more discriminatory than the practice in tennis tournaments of eliminating the losers of the semifinals from competition in the finals.

Of course, a problem arises in the logic of the tournament if selection systems do not always offer equal opportunities in early competitions, as is likely to be the case. By placing irreversible importance on each selection, the legitimacy of the entire system rests on perfection in each and every selection, a standard impossible to satisfy. Consequently, when older individuals complain of discrimination because the tournament does not offer second chances, the customary counterargument, that they had their fair chance earlier, cannot be asserted with complete confidence.

Age discrimination contentions can be blunted by selection systems which offer ample opportunities for youth to demonstrate their abilities and advance. A selection system which offered second and third chances to compete for advancements would better satisfy this concern than a tournament in which each selection has lasting impact. However, even this reform would not totally remove the concern about age discriination. Even a modified tournament which allows second and third chances makes time a signal of lower ability. The problem of age discrimination is not easily solved in tournament systems; indeed, it is more difficult because age is so intimately implicated in ability inferences.

Misinformation and Mistaken Selections. Inadequate and incorrect information about the tournament selection process may be a serious problem in a career tournament. Students in high school and employees in a corporation do not always realize that they are competing in a tournament which will make irreversible decisions about their careers (Chinoy 1955; Goldner 1965; Rosenbaum 1976, 1984). Unlike a tennis tournament, in which the nature of the competition and its consequences are well known by all competitors, the fact that career systems in schools and workplaces are run as tournaments is not generally acknowledged or known. Students and employees make decisions about balancing their work efforts and the other demands in their lives without knowing the stakes for the rest of their educational or work careers.

At a minimum, this suggests that career tournaments would be more meritocratic and fairer if individuals were informed about the nature of the tournament so that they would know when selections were occurring and what was at stake. That would permit them to make appropriate decisions about how to allocate their efforts. Full disclosure of information about the nature of a selection system would improve the efficiency and fairness of its selections. Even this simple reform would reduce some of the concern about age discrimination. While older individuals would still suffer lesser opportunities than their younger peers, they could be considered to have had a fair chance at one time.

CONCLUSIONS

Information is a crucial ingredient for analyzing, assessing, and reforming career systems, and the next few years may be a time when information about career systems will increase. Social science has only begun to conceptualize and study these issues in recent years. Moreover, organizations also may be on the brink of addressing these issues. At the same time that schools are being required to provide full information to students being placed in special education programs, little information is being provided to students about the long-term implications of these placements, and no information is being provided about the long-term implications of ability group and curriculum placements. And while corporations are devoting significant resources to career counseling, they have not used the extensive information they have in their computerized personnel data banks to describe the nature of actual career patterns in their organizations. The importance of these issues has been increasingly realized, the resources for studying them are increasingly available in organizations' records, so the conditions may now be right for making important progress in this area.

NOTES

1. On-the-job training is often more economical than formal instruction, for it takes advantage of the physical proximity of workers, the use of free time and ideal equipment during a production break, the filling in by subordinates during a temporary absence of superiors, and the virtual absence of excess training since training is tailored to the learning capacities and needs of each trainee.

2. The tournament is particularly effective within institutions where career-history information about individuals can be preserved and easily communicated and where the status value of an individual's attainments is easily interpreted.

REFERENCES

Alexander, K., and E. L. McDill. "Selection and Allocation within Schools: Some Causes and Consequences of Curriculum Placement." *American Sociological Review* 41 (1976): 963–80.
Althauser, Robert P., and Arne L. Kalleberg. "Firms, Occupations, and the Structure

of Labor Markets." In *Sociological Perspectives on Labor Markets*, edited by Ivar Berg. New York: Acadeic Press, 1981.

Arrow, Kenneth J. "Higher Education as a Filter." *Journal of Public Economics* 2 (1973): 193–216.

Balow, I. H. "The Effects of Homogeneous Grouping in Seventh-Grade Arithmetic." *Arithmetic Teacher* 11 (1964): 186–91.

Barker Lunn, J. C. *Streaming in the Primary School*. London: National Foundation for Educational Research in England and Wales, 1970.

Baron, James N., and W. T. Bielby. "Bringing the Firms Back In: Stratification, Segmentation and the Organization of Work." *American Sociological Review* 45 (1980): 737–65.

Bartholomew, David J. *Stochastic Models for Social Processes*. London: John Wiley & Sons, 1967.

Beck, E. M., Patrick M. Horan, and Charles M. Tolbert. "Stratification in a Dual Economy: A Sectoral Model of Earnings Determination." *American Sociological Review* 43 (1978): 704–20.

Becker, Gary. *Human Capital*. New York: Columbia University Press, 1964.

Berlew, D. E., and D. T. Hall. "The Socialization of Managers: Effects of Expectations on Performance." *Administrative Science Quarterly* 11 (1966): 207–23.

Bibb, Robert, and William H. Form. "The Effects of Industrial, Occupational, and Sex Stratification on Wages in Blue-collar Markets." *Social Forces* 55 (1977): 974–96.

Blaug, Mark. "The Empirical Status of Human Capital Theory." *Journal of Economic Literature* 14 (1976): 827–55.

Bray, Douglas W., Richard J. Campbell, and Donald L. Grant. *Formative Years in Business*. New York: John Wiley & Sons, 1974.

Campbell, John P., et al. *Managerial Behavior, Performance, and Effectiveness*. New York: McGraw-Hill, 1970.

Caplow, Theodore. *The Sociology of Work*. Minneapolis: University of Minnesota Press, 1954.

Chinoy, Ely. *Automobile Workers and the American Dream*. New York: Random House, 1955.

Cicourel, A. V., and J. I. Kitsuse. *The Educational Decision-Makers*. Indianapolis: Bobbs-Merrill, 1963.

Coleman, James S., et al. *Equality of Educational Opportunity*. Washington, DC: U.S. Government Printing Office, 1966.

Collins, Randall. "Functional and Conflict Theories of Educational Stratification." *American Sociological Review* 36 (1971): 1002–19.

———. *The Credential Society*. New York: Academic Press, 1979.

———. "The Microfoundations of Macrosociology." *American Journal of Sociology* 86 (1981): 984–1014.

Daniels, J. C. "The Effects of Streaming in the Primary School. Part I: What Teachers Believe. Part II: A Comparison of Streamed and Unstreamed." *British Journal of Educational Psychology* 31 (1961): 69–78, 119–27.

Doeringer, Peter, and Michael Piore. *Internal Labor Markets and Manpower Analysis*. Lexington, MA: D.C. Heath, Lexington Books, 1971.

Eder, Donna. "Stratification within the Classroom: The Formation and Maintenance of Ability Groups." Ph.D. diss. University of Wisconsin, 1978.

Edwards, Richard C. *Contested Terrain: The Transformation of the Workplace in America.* New York: Basic Books, 1979.

Evans, R. N., and J. D. Galloway. "Verbal Ability and Socioeconomic Status of 9th and 12th Grade College Preparatory, General, and Vocational Students." *Journal of Human Resources* 8 (1973): 24–36.

Ference, Thomas P. "The Career Plateau: Facing up to Life at the Middle." In *Career Management*, edited by Mariann Jelinek. Chicago: St. Clair Press, 1979.

Findley, W., and M. Bryan. *Ability Grouping: 1970.* Athens, GA: Center for Educational Improvement, 1971.

Ginsberg, R. B. "Semi-Markov Processes and Mobility." *Journal of Mathematical Sociology* 1 (1971): 233–62.

Glaser, Barney. *Organizational Scientists: Their Professional Careers.* Indianapolis: Bobbs-Merrill, 1964.

Goldner, Fred H. "Success vs. Failure: Prior Managerial Perspectives." *Industrial Relations* 9 (1970): 453–74.

Grandjean, Burke D. "History and Career in a Bureaucratic Labor Market." *American Journal of Sociology* 86 (1981): 1057–92.

Granovetter, Mark. "Toward a Sociological Theory of Income Differences." In *Sociological Perspectives on Labor Markets*, edited by Ivar Berg. New York: Academic Press, 1981.

Hallinan, Maureen T., and A. B. Sørensen. "The Formation and Stability of Instructional Groups." *American Sociological Review* 48 (1983): 838–51.

Jencks, Christopher. "Structural versus Individual Explanations of Inequality: Where Do We Go from Here?" *Contemporary Sociology* 9 (1980): 762–67.

Jencks, Christopher, et al. *Inequality: A Reassessment of the Effect of Family and Schooling in America.* New York: Basic Books, 1972.

Jones, J. D., E. Erickson, and R. Crowell. "Increasing the Gap between Whites and Blacks: Tracking as a Contributory Source." *Education and Urban Society* 4 (1972): 339–49.

Kagan, Jerome. "What Is Intelligence?" *Social Policy* 4 (1973): 60–72.

Kamens, David. "The College 'Charter' and College Size: Effects on Occupational Choice and College Attrition." *Sociology of Education* 44 (1971): 270–96.

———. "Colleges and Elite Formation: The Case of Prestigious American Colleges." *Sociology of Education* 47 (1974): 354–78.

———. "Legitimating Myths and Educational Organization: The Relationship between Organizational Ideology and Formal Structure." *American Sociological Review* 42 (1977): 208–19.

Kanter, Rosabeth Moss. *Men and Women of the Corporation.* New York: Basic Books, 1977.

Kelley, Jonathan. "Causal Chain Models for the Socioeconomic Career." *American Sociological Review* 38 (1973a): 481–93.

———. "History, Causal Chains, and Careers: A Reply." *American Sociological Review* 38 (1973b): 785–96.

Kellogg, Marion. *Career Management.* New York: AMACOM, 1972.

Lazear, Edward P. "Why Is There Mandatory Retirement?" *Journal of Political Economy* 87 (1979): 1261–84.

Lazear, Edward P., and S. Rosen. "Rank-Order Tournaments as Optimum Labor Contracts." *Journal of Political Economy* 89 (1982): 841–64.

Lindblom, Charles E. "The Science of Muddling Through." *Public Administration Review* 19 (1959): 79–88.

Mason, G. A. "Ability Grouping: An Ethnographic Study of a Structural Feature of Schools." *Australian and New Zealand Journal of Sociology* 10 (1974): 53–56.

Mayer, Thomas. "Models of Intragenerational Mobility." In *Sociological Theories in Progress*, vol. 2, edited by Joseph Berger. Boston: Houghton Mifflin, 1972.

McClelland, David C. "Testing for Competence Rather Than for 'Intelligence.' " *American Psychologist* 28 (1973): 1–14.

Medoff, James L., and K. G. Abraham. "Are Those Paid More Really More Productive?" *Journal of Human Resources* 16 (1981): 186–216.

Meyer, John. "The Effects of Education as an Institution." *American Journal of Sociology* 83 (1977): 55–77.

Meyer, John, and Brian Rowan. "Institutional Organizations: Formal Structure as Myth and Ceremony." *American Journal of Sociology* 83 (1977): 341–63.

Mincer, Jacob. *Schooling, Experience and Earnings*. New York: National Bureau of Economic Research, 1974.

Rist, R. "Student Social Class and Teacher Expectations: The Self-fulfilling Prophecy in Ghetto Education." *Harvard Educational Review* 40 (1970): 411–51.

Rosenbaum, James E. "The Stratification of Socialization Processes." *American Sociological Review* 40 (1975): 48–54.

———. *Making Inequality: The Hidden Curriculum of High School Tracking*. New York: Wiley-Interscience, 1976.

———. "Track Misperceptions and Frustrated College Plans: An Analysis of the Effects of Tracks and Track Perceptions in the National Longitudinal Survey." *Sociology of Education* 53 (1980): 74–88.

———. *Career Mobility in a Corporate Hierarchy*. New York: Academic Press, 1984.

Rosenbaum, James E., and W. Velez. "Differential Selection Systems within Schools." Paper presented to the Eastern Sociological Society, Philadelphia, March 1978.

Schafer, W. E., and C. Olexa. *Tracking and Opportunity*. Scranton, PA: Chandler, 1971.

Shaeffer, Ruth G. *Staffing Systems: Managerial and Professional Jobs*. New York: The Conference Board, 1972.

Sørensen, Aage B. "The Structure of Inequality and the Process of Attainment." *American Sociological Review* 42 (1977): 965–78.

Spence, A. Michael. *Marketing Signaling: The Information Structure of Hiring and Related Processes*. Cambridge, MA: Harvard University Press, 1974.

Spenner, Kenneth I., L. B. Otto, and V. R. A. Call. *Career Lines and Careers*. Lexington, MA: D. C. Heath, Lexington Books, 1982.

Spilerman, Seymour. "Careers, Labor Market Structure, and Socioeconomic Achievement." *American Journal of Sociology* 83 (1977): 551–93.

Stiglitz, Joseph P. "The Theory of 'Screening,' Education, and the Distribution of Income." *American Economic Review* 65 (1975): 283–300.

Stolzenberg, Ross M. "Occupations, Labor Markets and the Process of Wage Attainment." *American Sociological Review* 40 (1975): 645–65.

Talbert, J., and C. Bose. "Wage Attainment Processes: Retail Clerk Case." *American Journal of Sociology* 83 (1977): 403–24.

Thurow, Lester. *Generating Inequality*. New York: Basic Books, 1975.

Turner, Ralph. "Sponsored and Contest Mobility and the School System." *American Sociological Review* 25 (1960): 855–67.

White, Harrison C. *Chains of Opportunity*. Cambridge, MA: Harvard University Press, 1970.
Wright, Erik Olin, and L. Perrone. "Marxist Class Categories and Income Inequality." *American Sociological Review* 42 (1977): 32–55.
Young, Michael. *The Rise of the Meritocracy*. Baltimore: Penguin Books, 1958.

7

CARL D. MILOFSKY

Special Education and Social Control

INTRODUCTION

Sociologists writing about special education programs in public schools have generally argued that these programs exist to further social control goals. They suggest that special education programs do not serve therapeutic purposes as their legislative mandates require. Enabling legislation in the United States requires that they provide services to children who suffer neurologic, physical, or personality disorders and who, therefore, cannot profit from the program of regular graded classrooms. It further forbids children being placed in special classes because they suffer from cultural deprivation or anti-social behavior. Thus the architects of the programs describe student problems as having biological origins. Educational handicaps are independent of the school or community contexts in which they are recognized. Sociologists have pointed out, sometimes politely (Ford et al. 1982; Tomlinson 1982) and sometimes belligerently (Mercer 1971, 1973), that student referrals to special classes, initiated as they usually are by teachers or by school principals, are socially motivated. The reasons which lead to student referrals usually have little to do with biology. Again and again, observers report teacher conflicts with principals or school discipline problems leading to special class referrals (McIntyre 1969; Milofsky 1976).

The social control argument is consistent with case studies of regular education programs which assert that discipline and maintenance of order are among the foremost concerns of teachers and principals. One of the benefits of research on special education, however, has been to provide a new angle in the argument that discipline is central to schooling. A shortcoming of past observational research on public schools is that it has focused on their core program, teaching in regular classrooms, to the exclusion of everything else. If maintaining authority is as important to schools and to teachers as sociologists from the time of Thomas and Thomas (1928) and Waller (1932) have claimed, then we should be able to show that aspects of school organization not involved with teaching regular students buttress social control efforts that go on in the regular programs. We should find that those programs which are peripheral (Shils 1975) to regular instruction sacrifice their own goals to enhance the social control efforts of the core program. We also should be able to describe an array of programs outside of regular class instruction which together make up a "social control apparatus" of the school. By focusing on its social control role, research on special education has furthered this agenda.

There is a flaw in this approach to special education. It implies that special educators abandon goals of their own programs because they are coerced. Social control is a powerful variable in explaining how schools are organized if it causes teachers to work together and to be mutually supportive. Earlier observational research suggested that this in fact happens in schools. In these studies, the need to maintain authority both motivates teacher behavior and helps to weld teachers into a cohesive work group. Teachers might coerce people working in less central school programs like special education to support their control efforts because they control essential school resources; access to children and the assignment of space are especially important. If regular program teachers are such a powerful force, we should find systematic evidence that children are referred to special education classes because they are discipline problems. The best study we have of referral procedures, one done in Chicago (Berk, et al. 1981), could demonstrate no such relationship. If special education serves social control purposes, we ought to see effects in an urban school district with many black students and chronic financial problems, like the Chicago schools. Failing to find an effect suggests that something is wrong with the control theory of schooling.

In this chapter, I argue that the problem is not that special education fails to perform social control functions for schools. Rather, the organizational forces which once made discipline and authority so powerful in encouraging solidarity among teachers have withered. Observational studies which find that special education serves social control functions report real findings. However, social control has become haphazard in schools. Because schools in the past two decades have become larger, more specialized, and more bureaucratic, teachers have become less concerned with controlling decision making at the school level. They still want special educators to perform social control functions, but they no longer enforce their wishes. Consequently, special educators have some freedom to be architects of their own roles. Because they are not coerced to act in particular ways, it is hard to find any variables which "cause" special educators' behavior. Unsupervised but not welcomed into the programs of many regular schools, special educators carry out their work in an idiosyncratic way which is statistically unpredictable.

This lack of regularity means that we need to revise the social control theory of special education. While special education may be oppressive to some students—particularly minority students—that oppression is not as tightly organized or as strongly "caused" as observers up to now have suggested. Rather, it happens because of the extraordinary diffusion of responsibility which typifies public schools today. Special educators tend to feel peripheral to the organization, unimportant, and unpopular with regular staff members. Few people in the regular program have much idea what special educators can or should do.

Lacking direction, special educators are marginal (Clark 1956a, 1956b; Milofsky 1974, 1976). They often try to please regular staff members or fall into a routinized, bureaucratic role which seems safe and noncontroversial. Newly employed by a school district, special teachers and school psychologists are inclined to accept special education programs as they are, to do their work uncritically, and to not challenge judgments made by regular educators. Lindblom and other investigators (1980; Lindblom and Cohen 1979; March and Olsen 1976) teach us that policymaking usually is governed by confusion and incrementalism rather than by rational design. Even knowing that most organizations are dominated by ambiguity and uncertainty, however, we see administrators or professionals struggling to create a role for themselves which allows them to do things they think are important (Bucher and Stelling 1969; Goldner 1967). Special educators tend to be passive in the face of standard operating procedures which have evolved within their school district to gain the force of law. If intelligence tests are abused, or if children are dumped into special classes for disciplinary reasons, special educators will not accept responsibility since in their view they do not control their own programs. Regular educators also do not accept responsibility for special education practices. In a sense, no one is responsible. But it is the same sort of irresponsibility that Everett Hughes (1964) described in explaining how ''good'' Germans could tolerate concentration camps. Rather than being an example of social control motivated by organizational maintenance or class domination concerns, special education provides a lesson in bureaucratic irresponsibility.

Social Control Theories

Those who argue that special education serves social control functions assert that the biological or medical model upon which these therapeutic special education programs are based is unrealistic. The medical model asserts that educational handicaps are a form of pathology, like a broken arm or cancer, which exist and are dysfunctional whether or not they are socially recognized or treated (Mercer 1973, pp. 1–19). The majority of students included in special education classes are hard to distinguish from normal students by way of a physical or psychological examination (Milofsky 1976, pp. 5–19; Sarason and Doris 1979, pp. 11–58). Special educators usually cannot diagnose students' physiological disabilities with any precision. Consequently, in most public schools, teaching programs cannot be designed in keeping with federal law (Bureau of Education for the Handicapped 1978a) to fill prescriptions that will remedy student problems. Yet children continue to find their way into special education classes.

Those who are sympathetic to educators suggest that special classes do serve important and legitimate functions for schools and for children. They provide a safety valve by which children and teachers who do not get along can be separated. They offer a protective setting for children who, for a time, have difficulties at home or who suffer some physical or cognitive problem which requires intensive assistance. Their teachers provide support and advice to the regular staff and thereby help to maintain children in regular classes (Ford, et al. 1982; McIntyre 1979; Milofsky 1976).

Even these optimists see a dark side to the social control functions of special education. They suggest that low-income and minority children are most likely to be candidates for placement in special classes. Harsher critics claim that special education is part of the machinery by which schools guarantee privilege to new generations of the middle and upper classes, while they oppress members of the lower classes (Kirp 1973; Williams 1971a, 1971b). In addition to institutional studies which trace these patterns in contemporary schools, historians have shown that, over the past century, the retarded have been used as an example in arguments to close off immigration (Kamin 1974) or to control the poor.

Whether one is friendly or hostile to schools, social control in special education is presented as a systematic force, shaping programs in definite ways. This is consistent with sociological theories in which social control is described as an instrument of system maintenance. One might describe this as a Durkheimian view. Any institution requires social control to maintain boundaries, to gain consensus about its mission or goals, and to achieve cohesion and solidarity among members. In this view, each social organization will generate mechanisms of social control, such as special education, which respond to distinct norms and to the particular historical conditions it confronts (Alschuler 1980; Metz 1978). Since in the Durkheimian view social control exists to achieve definite system maintenance goals, special education analysts in this tradition have concentrated on rewriting the goals of special education to give proper weight to the latent functions of programs.

One might also take a Marxian view, and argue that special education exists primarily to preserve and to replicate the class structure of society. This perspective is represented by revisionist educational historians (Katz 1971; Lazerson and Grubb 1974; Tyack 1974). In this view, one should never treat local organizational goals as complete in themselves (as the Durkheimians do). Those goals exist to give participants a rationale for involvement, and they help to legitimate programs before the public. But one cannot understand why programs exist or why they function as they do without placing them in the broader context of the class struggle in society and of efforts by elites and by the state to maintain a docile lower class (Bowles and Gintis 1976). Special education programs are important for two reasons. Special education is a way of directly controlling disruptive children by removing them from regular classes and by stigmatizing them with a negative label (mental retardate, learning disabled, behavior disordered). Special education programs also control the lower classes by strengthening a public belief that poor and minority people are not smart enough to achieve economic success in this society (Carrier 1983; Lazerson 1975, 1982). Special education is one of many devices at work in schools to demonstrate the stupidity of lower-class children and to convince them that inequality is just (Rosenthal and Jacobson 1968; Rubin 1976). Like Durkheimians, Marxists assert that systematic social control is going on in special education. To the latter, however, programs are shaped and directed to serve social class interests.

If the Marxists are right, a close look at special education in practice ought to reveal a bias to use special education classes to further social class domination goals. Following tracking studies like Rist (1970, 1973), Rosenbaum (1976), and Valentine (1971), one might expect research on school classification studies to show marked bias against minority children in referral practices because these students bring their lower-class culture to school, and this causes problems for educators. One might expect staff members to rationalize unequal treatment of children by talking about the disruptive, undisciplined qualities of poor children and the ways in which they were not prepared to learn. Alternatively, being unwilling to demonstrate racism and class bias overtly, school staff might talk about the difficulties of operating orderly schools in low-income areas and the necessity of using all available school services to maintain order and to give aid to teachers in the regular program. This ought to result in disciplinary referrals to special education classes.

The Disorderliness of Social Control

Despite the theoretical imperatives of Durkheimians and Marxists, social control is disorderly and unsystematic in special education programs. To be sure, special education does not often perform therapeutic functions in schools. It is easy to cite instances in which the children who find their way into special classes have arrived because people in the school the students attend see them as discipline problems. They may or may not suffer recognizable cognitive or physical disabilities. In either case, the overriding cause of their placement was the inability of regular teachers to tolerate them in class.

It also is easy to show that, despite legal reforms, minority children continue to receive lower-quality treatment in special education classes than do white children. A long-standing complaint is that intelligence tests are too heavily used to make decisions about placements in classes for the retarded and the learning disabled. Studies have reported that psychometric diagnoses completed by schools using only inteligence tests have up to 60 percent false positives (Garrison and Hammill 1971). PL 94–142, the federal law mandating special education, explicitly requires that measures other than IQ be used to evaluate children for placement (Bureau of Education for the Handicapped 1978b).

Despite this encouragement to use measures other than IQ, Berk and his associates (1981), in a study of classification practices in Chicago, report that intelligence test scores continue to be far and away the strongest predictor of whether or not children will be placed in classes for the retarded. A study I conducted of Illinois school psychologists shows that in Chicago, psychologists spend on average 3.6 hours carrying out the entire evaluation process—testing, writing reports, and attending decision meetings—whereas suburban and down-state psychologists spend upward of 6.5 hours for the same tasks. Since it takes about 2.5 hours (by my stopwatch) to give a full-scale intelligence test, the Chicago psychologists must be taking shortcuts—some of which I observed during the field portion of my study. These are likely to produce both greater dependence on tests and greater risk of test error. Since most black children in Illinois attend Chicago schools, the differences in testing rates between the city and other districts produce huge differences in selection practices where black children and white children are concerned (Milofsky 1983).

These findings support arguments for systematic social control in special ed-ucation. Yet it is hard to show that these results follow from anything systematic or intentional in the operations of the institution. In their study of Chicago classification, Berk and his co-workers (1981) examined the hypothesis that children placed in special education classes are severe discipline problems. Al-though theirs was a survey research project which depended on school records that might be inaccurate (but see Rosenbaum's 1976 assessment of school records on discipline), these authors could find no significant relationship between dis-cipline problems and special education referrals. Case study findings in particular schools do not generalize, according to their data. Similarly, while Chicago school psychologists test more briskly than do their suburban counterparts, it is hard to argue from my data that this represents any special prejudice against blacks. To the contrary, if one examines testing practices within regions—that is, within Chicago or within the suburbs—Chicago psychologists are less biased than those working outside the city. Blacks in suburbs receive substantially lower-quality testing than do whites. In Chicago, however, they receive slightly superior testing.

When we look at the entire school system, the pattern of bias is clear, but when we look at the level of individual practitioners, it disappears. How do we explain these differences? Part of the answer lies in differences between the old, bureaucratic, crisis-ridden school systems of cities and the newer, wealthier suburban districts. City school psychologists are pressured in various ways and so test faster than their suburban colleagues. The coincidence that more black children live in cities than in suburbs accounts for differences in the way their cases are handled during special education classification proceedings.

However, this explanation does not really tell us why we do not see clearer effects of social control. What difference does it make that urban school psy-chologists test more carelessly or mechanically than suburban psychologists? School psychologists and other members of the diagnostic team are supposed to be watchdogs, checking the inclination of regular educators to use special classes as they wish. As psychologists do their work in a more routine, less discrimi-natory fashion, regular educators should find it easier to place discipline-problem students in special education classes. In city schools, where school psychologists are least vigilant but where regular staff face the greatest teaching problems—low-income students, budget cuts, old buildings, bureaucratic school administrations, court-ordered staff integration plans—the pressure to use special classes as social control dumping grounds should be greatest. Yet we see from Berk and his associates (1981) that this does not happen. Having directly observed the same schools and personnel that they write about, I believe their conclusion.

Evidence for Orderly Social Control

While we know from the ethnographic literature that special education classes sometimes serve as devices to shore up the disciplinary apparatus of schools, they do so only occasionally. This haphazardness of use is a surprise, because the sociological literature on schools over the years has emphasized again and again the centrality of discipline and the maintenance of order to every aspect of school organization. Recently this orientation has gained attention from social scientists who wish to measure precisely the effects of school programs. Murnane (1975) found that in a sea of program-related variables that predict no variations in student achievement scores, one variable that does predict is a school principal's rating of which teachers are strong disciplinarians. The National Institute of Education (NIE) *Violent Schools—Safe Schools* (1978) project reported that achievement is higher in schools where students and staff believe that firm rules exist and that enforcement is consistent and fair. It is hard to know whether discipline causes learning in these studies or whether attributes of students cause both discipline and learning. Nonetheless, the findings confirm a conviction held by educational sociologists from Willard Waller (1932) forward that the central problem for schools and for teaching is achieving and maintaining authority over students. The central tensions in the institution revolve around struggles for control, according to generations of case study researchers.

A corollary of this perspective is that there exist in schools well-defined mechanisms by which schools and teachers enhance their personal authority and maintain order. The most systematically studied involve what Waller (1932) calls "techniques of control" exercised by teachers. More recent studies, like McPherson's (1972) ethnographic study of an elementary school, extend discussions of control mechanisms to analysis of the teaching group and to the role of the principal. Coleman's (1960, 1961) study of the adolescent subculture in high schools demonstrates the contribution interscholastic sports make to binding to schools those students who might not be attracted to the academic mission. Stinchcombe (1964) shows that the myth of universalistic competition in schools is a powerful source of conformity. He argues that high IQ, low socioeconomic status students—those most likely to be given a low-track assignment despite their ability—are the most rebellious. This suggests that the pattern of control and conformity is highly structured and predictable, not unsystematic and haphazard.

To the extent that studies of control in schools have measured the presence of a control orientation in a particular program and the contribution of control to outcome measures like achievement, studies have again and again demonstrated the explanatory power of these variables. They also suggest that the structure of control in schools, rather than being haphazard, is carefully constructed and an object of concern and attention by school staff members.

In this context, the mixed results on special education are a puzzle. We find examples of special education serving control goals. But in a school district where the effects of efforts to enforce social control should be strongest, namely Chicago, we find nothing measurable. To make sense of this we must examine the structure of social control in schools more carefully. In the sections which follow, we will first review the argument in the organizational theory of schooling which places discipline and authority at the center of the educational process. We then will consider evidence that in the past twenty years, schools, by becoming larger, more specialized, and more bureaucratic, have eroded organizational mechanisms which create and maintain a tightly structured system of authority. This accounts for widespread perceptions that schools have become more dangerous and students less serious over the past twenty years. It also explains why teachers, feeling less responsible for maintaining the control structure of their schools, are less aggressive than we would expect in making sure that special education serves their programmatic interests.

AUTHORITY AND THE COLLECTIVIST SCHOOL

According to institutional analysts, the central fact about schools is that they are collectivist, rather than bureaucratic, organizations. There is irony in this because in many ways schools are supremely bureaucratic. They are governed by boards of directors which appoint superintendents and which preside over a sharply defined, hierarchical structure. School administrations are notorious for promulgating rules and handing down to their school-level subordinates all manner of directives about how teaching should be carried out and about how students should be managed. Marxist analysts like Bowles and Gintis (1976) have argued that in fact the primary function of schooling is to provide children with a model for later life in bureaucratic work settings.

Despite all of this hierarchy and formal structure, teachers, though low in the administrative hierarchy, have substantial autonomy in making decisions about the details of instruction. This allows them to make local schools more like collectivist organizations than like bureaucracies. Teachers discipline children on their own and organize teaching materials within the local school by working as a group, dividing up extra work on an informal, ad hoc basis. While they recognize the power of the school administration, teachers generally resist close supervision or evaluation unless they explicitly ask for help (Lortie 1969, 1975). When they ask, their requests generally are informal and directed at their peers, rather than at their supervisors or at specialists like special educators. All of this makes the peer group of teachers important as a means for getting the work of organizational maintenance done, for defining what norms serve the school's interests, and for controlling people who violate them (McPherson 1972).

To the extent extra work has to be done so the school will work better, teachers traditionally have opposed creation of special, permanent roles but rather have rotated responsibilities so that everyone will share the burden. In presenting a theory of collectivist organizations, Rothschild-Whitt (1979) argues that these tendencies to share responsibilities undercut the specification of roles and of rules and the domination of organizational affairs by superordinate officials. Definite roles, written rules, and a sharply defined hierarchy are all characteristic of bureaucracies. An organization which lacks these qualities has little formal structure and tends to be democratically run or, in her terms, *collectivist.*

Collectivism and Street-Level Bureaucracy

Teachers gain autonomy because decisions about how discipline should be maintained and those about how particular children and classes should be taught are critical determinants of how well children will learn. What actions are proper depends on the context and cannot be well planned in advance. Lipsky (1980; also Weatherly and Lipsky 1977) suggests that teachers share this autonomy with other low-level social service personnel, people he calls "street-level bureaucrats." He argues that police, social workers, nurses, and other low-level functionaries of social service bureaucracies are autonomous because the following operating problems confront these institutions:

Undermanning. Staff members are badly outnumbered by clients. This means that it is difficult for them to provide in-depth, personal service to the people they serve. It also means that where the clientele is not completely willing, staff members can be overwhelmed and the institution threatened with violence and chaos. This is a special problem in institutions that manage crowds, like prisons (Sykes 1968), mental hospitals (Stanton and Schwartz 1954), and schools (Barker and Gump 1964).

Undersupport. Street-level bureaucracies generally are undersupported by the state or by their sponsoring agencies. Staff members receive low pay relative to their level of training and the responsibilities they assume. Institutions also can usually provide only some of the technical materials staff members desire to do their jobs properly. Given chronic shortages, staff members must substitute their own labor for support staff and innovativeness for established technology.

Client Acceptance. For street-level bureaucracies to achieve their technical goals, clients must accept and help to achieve institutional programs. Since clients often do not understand what the institutional program is, what it is supposed to do for them, why it is to their advantage to be served, and what they are supposed to do to be helpful, an important part of the program is to shape the values and attitudes of clients.

Imperfection of Technologies. Street-level bureaucracies generally have imperfect technologies in the sense that even the best practitioners and the most willing clients do not produce predictable results. The social psychological background of clients, peculiarities of their biological makeup, the mix of clients within groups that are served, goal conflicts, and limitations in scientific knowledge about how to best provide services all contribute to unpredictability.

Indivisibility of Work. While street-level bureaucrats usually work alone, it is often hard to separate the consequences of their work. If one worker is seen as illegitimate and unfair in the eyes of clients, all workers come under suspicion. If one police officer is violent or one prison guard dishonest or one teacher incapable of controlling a class, there is danger that all staff members will confront the consequences. Hostility and distrust among clients tend to be contagious. Thus provocative staff behavior tends to make the entire institution seem illegitimate to clients, threatening the social stability of the whole operation.

These conditions together require that the lowest-level personnel—the teacher, the prison guard, the police officer, the social worker, the nurse—have power to make the most important policy decisions for the institution. How innovative and individualistic teaching will be, whether or not police will be violent, whether nurses will intervene when patients exhibit unexpected symptoms, and whether or not welfare workers will grant aid to certain classes of clients all depend on decisions of those low-level personnel—the street-level bureaucrats. They have autonomy, in part, because they often are confronted with unique situations which demand judgmental responses and which supervisors cannot anticipate. They have autonomy because the compliance of clients flows from the quality of interactions with these staff members. Coupled with the necessary independence they must have in their work, street-level bureaucrats often feel abused and exploited by their superiors. They often are hostile to supervision and work to undercut efforts by higher-level administrators to control their work.

While teaching shares these characteristics with other low-level social service roles, two things work especially powerfully to make local schools collectivist organizations rather than simply collections of autonomous semiprofessionals (Etzioni 1969). First, teaching has definite products—the achievement level of students—which are inseparable from issues of social control. Second, teachers work in proximity with one another and share students. This gives them a stake in having their peers do their work well and in having the whole school run smoothly. These create incentives—not always pursued in practice—for teachers to work together and to go beyond the narrow work of classroom instruction to improve the operation of their local school. While some of this additional work has been institutionalized and provides teachers with extra pay—coaching is an example—much of the work is ad hoc and informally organized. In contrast to bureaucracies, much of this nonclassroom work is neither assigned to specialized staff nor routinized in the form of permanent administrative positions.

Teaching and Control

While all street-level bureaucrats have as one of their responsibilities the task of convincing clients to accept their orders or recommendations, teachers are especially vulnerable to having their work undercut by uncooperative students. This is partly because the mechanics of teaching make group management a matter of constant concern to instructors. Child care is a central requirement of the role. Teachers must supervise a large number of children in a confined space for many hours each day. Keeping students occupied, planning lessons so that they do not encourage disruptiveness, and arranging the instructional process so that teachers can give a little help to individuals without the rest of the class descending into idle chaos all require that teachers be ever conscious of the danger that their classes will go out of control (Smith and Geoffrey 1968).

There is a deeper control problem, however, which involves articulating the individual attitudes and motivations of children with the activities and goals of the class as a group. At the simplest level, this is reflected in an asymmetry between the role of teacher and that of student. Students must learn individually. Not only does the process of understanding go on inside their heads so that it is out of the public view. Public school instruction is relatively insensitive to the state of an individual child's understanding. Socrates led his students to knowledge by understanding the underlying assumptions implicit in their views of the world and by challenging those assumptions by asking leading questions which would break down false understanding and lead students to the truth. Nothing approaching this sort of individual appreciation of students happens in schools because teachers must work with too many children. Rather, we rely on formulaic styles of teaching which usually work with students. Teachers present their formulas to students, but it is up to the child to move from his present state of understanding to the understanding required by the lesson. As we teach, we rarely ask why a child made a mistake and what a mistake shows about his method of thought. Rather, we tell the child the right way to think or act and expect him to suppress those habits which lead to wrong answers. Feuerstein (1970) provides an extended discussion of the two approaches and argues that trying to understand why children make mistakes can lead to markedly more effective teaching with retarded children than the traditional method.

Standardized Teaching

What separates a socratic approach like Feuerstein's from the approach of most teachers is that the latter follow what Jensen (1969) calls an "average child" approach to teaching. Instructors assume that all children do or can learn by developing a standard progression of skills. This means that to teach reading, for example, the teacher must show children that reading is a decoding process which has a variety of regular rules. Most primers provide a logic for decoding written words which children memorize and apply repeatedly in drill exercises. The fact that the people who write reading curricula disagree about which rationale most effectively shows children how to read—phonics or word recognition or some other system—allows teachers to offer alternative methods to those students who do not learn in one system (Chall 1983a, 1983b).

While standardized reading curricula work with most children, there are some who simply cannot learn to read using them. We have all kinds of explanations for why these children do not learn to read; the newest and most elaborate explanation is the theory of learning disabilities. We do know that, in many cases, unsuccessful children can learn to read and that individualized instruction can help. It helps because teachers can diagnose student learning problems and suggest to pupils alternative strategies for carrying out literacy tasks. It also helps because teachers can explain what it feels like to read—they can explain that it is an intuitive, rather than a rote, process and that "failure" in school does not mean that one can never read.

Most children do not get this kind of help in schools unless they are placed in special education and unless, once there, they are lucky enough to get a good teacher. Their neglect in regular classrooms is not a criticism of the teaching that happens there. True, teachers may lack skills and time. However, regular class teachers I have interviewed argue that they *should* not be providing individualized help to children. Their job is to teach groups. Teaching children one by one is inefficient. It also is a denial of the fact that there always is a distribution of performance in classroom. When children do not learn, there will always be reasons for their failure, and probably there are always ways to teach them effectively. Were regular teachers to take responsibility for the achievement of every slow-learning child, their task would be endless. They often are willing to give slow-learning children a lot of individual instructional time. But most of that time involves drill or offering standard instructional materials. They draw the line at trying to diagnose learning problems and tailoring instructional programs for children, because that is outside of their domain (Milofsky 1976, pp. 68–93).

The Limits of Teaching

Teachers reading this essay might disagree with my argument that, as a group, they are unwilling to tailor teaching to the idiosyncratic needs of children. After all, *individualization* is one of the catchwords of public education. However, if one does not draw a line beyond which individualization efforts may go, there is danger a teacher will be drawn into a morass of student-family problems. When children fail to learn in school, it usually is not because they are physically incapable of learning. Often they are enmeshed in personal, home, community, or institutional problems which interfere with their schoolwork (Dexter 1964). Teachers might help children by trying to intervene in these extraschool problems. But doing so threatens to catch a teacher in a quagmire of frustration and personal demands on his or her time. Observing in schools, one occasionally finds a teacher who becomes so embroiled, and the consequences are the stuff of which school folklore is made (Milofsky 1976).

Teachers must draw a line at some point and simply decide that some children will be allowed to fail if those students cannot master materials with the benefit of the traditional methods of teaching. This is not to say that a teacher gives up on a child by setting limits on individualization. To the contrary, teachers often have available formidable resources to convince children to work hard at mastering material which to them is difficult. Teachers may provide tutors and other kinds of individual help. More important, teachers can use the social power of the student peer group to coerce a child to learn (Henry 1963, pp. 283–321).

Much is made of the competitive atmosphere of American public schools and of the negative stigma which adheres to the "dummies" in schools. Unpleasant though that stigma is and innocent though children might be, the threat of stigmatization and the barbs of other students sometimes can stimulate lagging students to improve their performance—particularly if they are given other kinds of help. The sociological literature on tracking and the emergence of failure roles in schools suggests that negative labels are persistent, deepening, and often inescapable. While that may be true for the lowest achieving group of children in school, it is likely that at the same time the performance of more successful students fluctuates. The danger of falling lower in the educational hierarchy provides a goal to children having bad years so that they will improve their performance.

The problem with relying on group pressures to stimulate performance is that to work, children must see their problems as personal, individual, and correctable. This may be a problem where mildly handicapped children are concerned because they are not allowed to do anything about their problems. As McIntyre shows (1969), teachers can be frighteningly destructive of a child's self-confidence if they continue to insist upon achievement when that is impossible given a child's cognitive ability.

More commonly, relying on group pressure to stimulate achievement eventually makes clear to students, especially low-income ones, that failure is not an individual affair. Many students fail. Often they "look" similar, and often they are together in schools. Insisting on group learning and ignoring class-based reasons for students not learning in school erodes the authority of teachers. To convince children to obey and to work on learning, analysts of authoritative leadership suggest, children must believe (a) that teachers are experts at the arts of instruction and (b) that teachers are fair and have the best interests of students at heart. Children must believe that the school, as an institution, rewards intelligence and effort through universalistic competition (Metz 1978; Selznick 1957). When groups of children begin to fail—all of the black students or all of the children from welfare families or all of the migrants from Appalachia—it becomes harder for children to believe in teachers or in school. This is partly because effort does not seem to pay off if one is the "wrong" sort of person, as Labov's (1972) Harlem teenagers claimed. More seriously, at the same time that most poor children or most blacks seem to fail, schools invariably promote and reward some low-IQ, unmotivated middle-class children, placing them in college tracks in violation of the rules of universalistic competition (Rosenbaum 1976). As Stinchcombe (1964) argues, high-IQ, low-SES students are especially likely to see public education as a lie and to rebel against it. This rebellion can take the form of a determined and subtle attack on the ability of teachers to lead in class (Milofsky 1976, pp. 94–117).

Thus authority is precarious in the classroom because the nature of the teacher role precludes socratic teaching. Teachers may simply demand less from their charges. They may also try to maintain control by exaggerating the differences between groups to convince the slower children that they are not capable of achieving. Doing this carries the risk of a rebellious student culture emerging. If students systematically try to undercut the authority of teachers, then all instruction can fail as the student group becomes an insurgent group. In this way, instruction is inextricably tied with control, from the standpoint of teachers, which is unique among street-level bureaucrats.

The Teacher Peer Group and Control

The struggle over teachers' authority is usually described as a personal battle within classrooms, between teachers and difficult children. This is reasonable since most of the contact time between instructors and students is within classrooms and most conflict-provoking issues arise there. Over the century of its existence, however, the institution of public education has evolved a variety of devices which support the authority of teachers in classrooms. By and large, they serve to place the authority of the whole school behind each teacher within his or her classroom. Historically, these devices have been of two main kinds: (1) means for making students and families see a united front when the teaching staff makes demands of students, and (2) programs outside of the regular instructional apparatus which provide students with an independent motivation to conform to the school regimen. Special education represents the institutionalization of a third device which historically has buttressed the authority of teachers— removal of students from school. We shall see that institutionalizing removal, rather than allowing it to happen through attrition, has serious consequences both for special education and for schools.

Teachers work closely together, and over several years they share the same children. This makes them interdependent and gives their collectivity greater power over students than they would have were they isolated. Classes are intensely personal.

By themselves, teachers have unique ways of relating to their students, and they usually have special relationships with different children. This allows children to decide that they are failing or that they seem to be out of favor because they have a personality conflict with the teacher. In this way it can become easy for them to dismiss punishment and lack of achievement. It is not a personal flaw. It is a social accident.

Teachers who work together and form a peer group discourage students from believing that their school problems come from personality conflicts with particular teachers. Emphasizing the generality of students' problems allows teachers to develop schoolwide rules and norms. These then will be followed in classroom after classroom as a student progresses through the grades. McPherson (1972) suggests that this pressure on students to see their failure as norm violation is double edged. As teachers work to convince students that their failures are part of some general pattern, teachers gain a stake in making sure that all instructors are sending out the same instructions and enforcing the same rules. This generates group pressure to monitor one another's performance, to apply group pressure when someone seems to be performing poorly, and to help one another out by discussing how to handle particularly difficult cases.

The principal may also be a powerful force for buttressing the authority of teachers in the classroom. Ideally, the principal is a rather shadowy figure whom children do not see very often and who seems distant and paternal (what is the equivalent female term?). A visit to the principal's office is frightening if the image is carefully cultivated, since the principal is the institution personified— impersonal, wise, fair. The principal also is the person most likely to contact parents in the event of serious disciplinary infractions. Being able to bring parents into a conflict and causing them to support the school can make the threat of a trip to the office frightening to a student.

Like the individual authority of the teacher, however, the additional strength provided by the teacher peer group and the principal are precarious because they require the school staff to close ranks. This is relatively easy as long as students are cooperative. However, overusing this collective apparatus of control can make the system of organizational supports for teachers fall apart. If children always seem to be disruptive, *esprit de corps* among the teaching staff can break down quickly, especially if members suggest that the incompetence of others as disciplinarians is to blame. To make matters worse, principals and teachers may also have a falling out, since the power for the former depends on infrequent use. "The threat is stronger than the execution," Aaron Nimzovich, the chess player, used to say. That rule certainly applies in schools. When children are too often sent to the principal's office, they begin to learn how limited are the coercive powers of that office. After several calls in close succession, parents begin to ignore the principal's demands for help. Children learn that there is little school officials can do once the ultimate (a trip to the office) has been tried.

As the cohesion of the school staff has cracks, the presence of critical peers and of a suspicious principal can make it even harder for a teacher to maintain authority than it might be were he or she to be working away from observers. McIntyre (1969) describes in one school the insecurity teachers felt about being able to maintain control of their classrooms and how their distrust was exacerbated by their hostility toward the principal. In a school I observed (Milofsky 1976), the principal felt overwhelmed by the students that teachers referred to him for punishment. When he suggested that some instructors were not controlling their classes, they retaliated by accusing him of poor playground management, of bad judgments in student class assignments, and of playing favorites with the teach- ers. Angry at the principal and worried that they would be accused of incompetence because of the disruptiveness of children in their classes, some teachers focused their anger on children they found especially difficult to teach; Coser (1956) calls this "scapegoating." In both McIntyre's and my research, scapegoating sometimes was directed with special intensity toward children who had been placed or who were candidates for special education classes. If the stigma of cognitive disabilities must be structurally created, as I have elsewhere argued (Milofsky 1978), scapegoating and staff conflicts are an important such structural source.

Just as the breakdown of staff relations can exacerbate discipline problems, staff cooperation in creating programs outside the classroom can tighten teacher authority and enhance the feeling of community in a school. As I noted earlier, there are a variety of traditional extracurricular programs in schools which have been institutionalized and recognized as important enough features of the school program for teachers to be paid for their participation. Coleman has demonstrated the power that interscholastic sports can play, increasing the cohesion of the student body and its commitment to the school. In schools with a strong sports culture, Coleman (1960) found that students achieving the highest grades had lower IQs than did students in schools with weak sports cultures. He interpreted this to mean that in schools with strong sports cultures, some of the students with high IQs were drawn away from the academic focus (or subculture) of their schools and invested their energy in sports achievement. Not working as hard at academics, they received lower grades. Students with lower IQs were attracted to the academic subculture, and they received the highest grades. When schools provide strong attractions other than academics, teacher authority in the classroom is relieved of the pressure to provide all of the justification for students to attend regularly and to work hard. The threat of being excluded from athletics can, if not force people to work up to their full potential, at least threaten students who might otherwise be laggards to be obedient students.

While athletics is perhaps the most widespread and successful extrascholastic program by which schools enhance the solidarity and commitment of their student bodies, there are other less structured ways schools solicit student interest. The open schools and schools-without-walls movements are examples, although perhaps extreme ones, of ways teachers can use resources from outside the traditional classroom to appeal to students. These schools appeal to children, in part, by structuring the curriculum or extracurricular activities to meet student interests and demands. Swidler (1979) suggests that free schools established in the 1960s and 1970s by some public school districts increased the allegiance of students by making schools democratic communities in which students were given the feeling that they had an equal role with teachers in making governance decisions. Involving students in school governance required that teachers invest private time in school activities, that they go outside their formal roles to become personally and emotionally involved with students, and that they take professional risks when students pushed for school policies which contradicted policies of the public school system. Teachers accepted these requirements because the solidarity of the school and of the teacher group was important enough for them to give more than required by the bureaucratically defined role of "teacher." Open schools like those Swidler describes have truly become collectivist organizations in Rothschild-Whitt's sense.

Schools are more successful at teaching students and maintaining order when teachers give one another moral support, when they work with the principal to create a consistent moral order throughout the school, and when they give time outside of class to create alternative sources of student allegiance to the school. However, these benefits which flow from the contiguity and interdependence of all school participants rest on the willingness of teachers to give their time and energy to building the collectivity. School solidarity is not something which can be bureaucratically mandated. It is, however, something which can be attacked and undermined when an ineffective principal or an excessively rule-bound administration convinces teachers that they will not benefit from extra effort or, worse, that they will be punished for trying to take control of their schools. When teachers become hostile to the administration, they are likely to become angry at those who would supervise or support them, and they may take out some of their anger on children. At the same time, they are likely to fight administrative efforts to control or direct activities within their schools. Teachers cannot, of course, prevent some kinds of local administrative action. They can, however, undermine and frustrate programs which require the cooperation of teachers. Special education is a prime example of a program which is easily undermined and attacked by the recalcitrance of teachers.

SPECIALIZATION AND AUTHORITY IN SCHOOLS

While there are numerous ethnographic descriptions of the authority structure I have described, that structure is not, and probably never was, universal. Institutional analysts have described an ideal type of organization which has some empirical support. Implicit in the school authority theory is an explanation of why schools today often seem disrupted. The authority model indicates that for a school to work, both children and teachers must accept the ideology of the school both as an institution of society and as a local organization. Acceptance makes the school a community and leads people at all levels of school organization to take on responsibilities that extend beyond a narrow definition of their roles. Teachers, recognizing the value of a cohesive school with a largely self-governing and collegial teaching staff, will take on a variety of nonteaching tasks. Students, recognizing the value of educational goals and activities, will be supportive of teachers and self-directed in their education, within the context of a prescribed educational program.

However, this spirit of good will requires that people in schools get to know and trust one another and that the organizational life of schools be orderly. Recent educational history has made such calm unusual. The assault has come from two directions. First, during the post-World War II period, but especially since 1960, there has been a national movement toward formal specialization in schools and toward creation of larger school units. Second, local governments—especially city governments—have in the past decade confronted a worsening fiscal crisis. There are a variety of contributors to this crisis: a broadened list of public programs, often inadequately supported by state and federal government; growth of unions in public service occupations which have increased pay and benefits for city workers; taxpayer revolts; and a decline in student populations which require that an inefficient ratio of students to capital resources be maintained in schools. A decline in discretionary school funding has required teacher layoffs. This often requires that teacher staffs be shuffled between schools to follow rules about seniority in layoffs and that extraschool programs, like interscholastic sports, be reduced.

Specialization and the Decline of Collectivism

Larger school units have undercut the traditional authority arrangements in two ways. Federal and state governments have systematically pressured small school districts to consolidate to make administration more efficient and to provide a wider array of programs to students (Rubin 1976). This means that there has been a reduction in the absolute number of school districts nationwide and especially of small schools and districts. As schools have become larger, it has become increasingly unlikely that, over their careers, students will have had in class all the teachers in the school. At the high school level, it is increasingly unlikely that students will have contact with their instructors for more than one or two semesters. A variety of studies have found that the more impersonal education becomes, the less orderly and authoritative schools appear to be. Rather than leading students to share organizational values which lead to orderliness, large schools are likely to impose formal rules on students which are passed down from department heads or from the principal. They have less moral force to control students than do those rules which grow out of student/teacher relationships in smaller, more collectivist schools (Abramowitz and Tenenbaum 1978; Barker and Gump 1964; NIE 1978).

Were the authority theory of school organization correct, one might expect that increased size and impersonality would produce chaos and a sharp increase in disruptiveness as the personal influence of teachers declines. The statistical data we have available suggest a weak relationship, however, although one which is still significant (Abramowitz and Tenenbaum 1978; NIE 1978). We have a weak relationship because size increases as specialization increases in schools. The desire to enrich school programs contributed to the increase in school size. Coincident with unification, school districts establish a variety of new administrative offices which are assigned technical functions previously handled informally (or ignored) by teachers. Thus, in addition to expanded special education programs, we see new programs for bilingual instruction, computer laboratories, school security offices, reading instruction centers, school libraries expanded into media centers, and more elaborate programs for teaching the arts.

Like the authority model of school organization, segmentation of school life— dividing it up into many functional parts—provides a method for gaining the interest and allegiance of students and for keeping them under control. Special education programs—mainstreaming notwithstanding—remove children who often are hard to teach and/or to control from the classroom. Other special instructional programs make school seem more relevant and more serious to children with unusual talents and interests. Remedial programs offer elaborate technology, individualized instruction, and greater contact between single teachers and students who need help. School security officers keep track of troublemakers and encourage reforms which eliminate physical settings in which disruptions tend to occur. Security officers also provide schools with flexibly scheduled staff who get to know the personal problems of troublesome students and who (if the staff are so inclined) can help teachers to understand why children are being difficult in classes.

All of this specialized help provides explicit organizational assignments to people so that work will be carried out which previously had relied either on voluntarism among teachers or on the goodwill and community feelings of the whole school population. Students get disciplined, planning is carried out, enriched teaching programs are provided, and the business of schooling goes on in a bigger and more expensive way. Specialization substitutes for authority and for the feelings of community that it fosters.

Though specialization gets the work of schooling done, it often does so with a loss of integration. The genius of the old authority model of schooling was that because teachers were so unspecialized (they did everything), all of the nonclassroom aspects of schooling evolved so that they would support teaching. Since teaching, by its nature, is context dependent, support for classrooms can happen only if teachers are involved intimately in planning and in administering nonclassroom programs. To be sure, this does not mean that specialized schools cannot achieve social integration or solidarity. This is the ideal of mainstreaming in special education, and sometimes it works beautifully.

In many schools, however, integration is lost. This might happen simply because the new schools are big, making it hard for busy people to know what everyone else is doing. More seriously, integration is lost because specialization is a result of administrative initiatives. Since teachers have a long tradition of battling against administrative controls (McPherson 1972), they tend to be suspicious of new programs which "come out of the central office."

Hostility may be simple parochial anger at anything the administration does. More likely, teachers become impatient with specialization efforts because they come at the expense of regular classroom programs. Teachers become most angry when they feel that their needs and those of the majority of children served by the schools are being neglected to serve a fraction of the school population. Thus one reason teachers have been hostile to special education programs is that while they expanded rapidly during the 1970s, teacher salaries stagnated, and there was a retreat from programs that earlier helped to enrich regular class instruction. In schools I observed, teachers left no doubt in special educators' minds that to be accepted by regular staff, they had to organize their programs to help meet the instruction and discipline problems of the regular staff. While not all schools are as explicit about this demand as the ones I visited, few special educators I have interviewed deny that they must address the institutional problems of the regular staff, thereby going beyond their narrow responsibility to diagnose learning problems or to teach with educational handicaps.

Special programs also anger teachers because special educators intrude into regular classrooms or claim responsibilities which regular teachers traditionally have controlled. Mainstreaming of special children, for example, can be inconvenient. Children are sent to special education classes because they do not work well in regular classrooms. Either they cannot do the work other children are doing or they pose discipline problems—they may be rebellious, hyperactive, or emotionally disturbed. When special classes are organized to keep those children in their regular classes a maximum amount of time, regular teachers often make plans so that special students do not interfere with the lessons of other students. In most places I have observed, special class students leave for the morning and return to the regular class in the afternoon. A teacher I recently interviewed complained that since the special education students assigned to her class could not read, it was difficult for her to have afternoon activities which required reading assignments. While supporters of mainstreaming would argue that this problem could be surmounted with a bit of imagination, many teachers seem to find it a barrier to academic instruction having special children in their classes. Thus, when I have observed special children during their hours in regular classes, teachers often have devoted those hours to gym, art, music, and other activities which do not require discipline or much intellectual skill. While they willingly arrange their schedule this way to avoid classroom management problems, many teachers grumble about their loss of flexibility in scheduling.

Where some special programs impose a burden, regular teachers may take advantage of other programs to avoid responsibilities. Where under the authority model their sense that they shared a collective fate convinced teachers that they should sometimes leave the classroom and altruistically do work for the good of the school, specialization convinces teachers to retreat and to leave problems to others. The best example of this perhaps is the retreat many teachers have made from taking disciplinary responsibilities outside their classrooms. Hallways, especially in high schools, have become no-man's-land. In earlier days, when there were no security guards and few special programs, teachers would leave their classrooms to restore order in the hallways or give up free time to patrol school grounds. Now that there are special people to do this work and given the extra headaches that administations have given classroom instructors, teachers give up their responsibility for making sure that the whole school is orderly.

Retreat from Responsibility and the Fragmentation of Control

I know of no studies which have carefully examined teachers' retreat from collectivist responsibility for running their schools. The scenario I have described is based on ad hoc observations in schools and indirect inferences in the literature. However, the story conforms to survey findings which suggest that schools have become increasingly fragmented administratively. Abramowitz and Tenenbaum (1978, p. 59), for example, summarize their findings in the NIE study *High School '77*:

The internal parts of high schools are not related to each other in ways that conventional organizational theory relates, and many of these "nonrelationships" violate the expectations of logic and reason. For example, where people are intensively involved in the process of evaluating teachers or principals, it seems reasonable that the frequency of evaluation might also rise—if only slightly. Analysis of the results, however, shows that where evaluations involve more people they tend to be less frequent. Equally puzzling nonrelationships lead to the general conclusion that important aspects of high school organization—administrative structure, and rules and other mechanisms for coordination—are not connected to each other. . . . Formal structure does relate to certain aspects of a school's instructional complexity. Schools with more varied courses, credit options, and services also have a more complex and differentiated staff, which exercises broader participation in school decisions. However, the coordination mechanisms we examined— the use of rules, evaluations and meetings—have little to do with how complex the school's instructional programs are. For instance, one might have reasonably expected that, in a school with numerous courses and nonclassroom arrangements, meetings and evaluations would occur more frequently, in the interest of control. However, they do not.

Abramowitz and Tenenbaum do not necessarily see the nonrelationships in large schools as a problem, anticipating the recent emphasis on loose coupling as typifying school organization (March and Olsen 1976; Weick 1976). Loose coupling allows low-level staff to take substantial responsibility for making decisions about how schools should be governed. However, if the loose coupling they observed encouraged greater democracy in school organization, one still would expect to see some articulation between programs. By emphasizing the nonrelationships between school personnel, *High School '77* suggests more a withdrawal from responsibility than the sort of democratic control one would expect in an authoritative school.

The Fragmentation of Control and Special Education

The retreat from responsibility also accounts for the confusing findings I reported at the outset of this chapter, that while special educators confront demands that they help to maintain social control through their programs, there is no systematic pattern of special classes being used for social control purposes on an aggregate level. Because teachers feel deprived by special programs, they tend to be hostile to specialists and indicate that they want special programs to aid the regular instructional program, even at the expense of achieving special program goals. However, because regular teachers are so alienated from the school, they do nothing to explicitly control special programs.

This confronts specialists with a supervision vacuum. In the survey I conducted of Illinois school psychologists in 1978, respondents said that, while a primary responsibility in their work is serving the needs of the regular program, they are not supervised, directed, or supported by either regular or special staff. No one wants to bother with them, so school psychologists are left to figure out on their own how they ought to spend their time (Milofsky 1984). There are certain tasks that special educators are expected to carry out—for psychologists, it is testing; for special class teachers, it is spending time with special students—but there often is substantial flexibility in how much time they give to these mandated tasks.

Confronted with a vacuum in supervision, specialists fill up their time in idiosyncratic ways. Some people I have observed go out of their way to help regular teachers with their classroom problems (Milofsky 1976), reasoning that their special programs can be effective only if they obtain cooperation from regular teachers. Here special programs may be taken over by regular school needs and may thus lose their "specialness" (Milofsky 1974). Others fall into alienated passivity. I interviewed a number of school psychologists who spent most of their time testing children because testing was the only thing anyone ever asked them to do. They were not inclined to think of things on their own that they might do around school. Still other specialists take a more confrontational approach. They decide what kind of program they wish to run and set out to implement it. Sometimes they confront hostile regular educators and force them to accept a genuinely *special* program. Other specialists take advantage of their organizational invisibility. They spend some of their time carrying out the functions that are stereotyped with their role. The rest of their time they free-lance in schools, looking for interesting problems to work on and help out with. These specialists (school psychologists especially fit this mold) may turn up anywhere in a school system. One person made himself into the most trusted adviser of the superintendent. Another became a computer programmer, overseeing the school tracking system. Another became a consultant on designing a new reading curriculum. Another introduced progressive relaxation techniques to a class for the trainable retarded at the same time he ran a support group for parents of adolescent delinquents.

Whether or not a specialist becomes passive or a free-lancer in schools depends in part on school district characteristics. People working in urban school districts feel more constrained (though no more supervised) than people working in nonurban districts. However, even in the most constrained situations, some individuals are effective at shaping their work environment and avoid total control by regular educators.

Procedures for assigning students to special classes do not show much evidence that social control concerns determine student classification practices, because teachers do nothing positive to enforce their demands on specialists. Teachers may be interested in eliminating some students from their classes and may go so far as to refer them for testing. However, the evaluation process takes time (often a year or more), and teachers cannot routinely monitor what is happening to children they have referred. Instructors could presumably pressure special educators to admit a particular child by regularly contacting psychologists and special teachers to check up on the progress of the evaluation process. But teachers are reluctant to do this, as they are reluctant to become involved in any of the administrative activities of schools. They complain about special programs not serving their needs and they regularly refer students, but they are enough confused by the administrative complexities of actually getting a child into a special class that usually they do not pursue the matter for long. When a difficult child is not removed, they just chalk it up to more inefficiency and administrative insensitivity. They do not go out of their way to make sure that special educators are helping to maintain control, and they rarely try to punish special educators who refuse to use their programs for control purposes.

The passivity of teachers in forcing special education to serve regular program needs, coupled with the idiosyncratic way specialists do their work, prevents control issues from dominating the organization of special programs. This does not mean that control concerns are not important, however. Special educators are marginal actors in schools. While no one tells them what to do, it is difficult for them to construct programs that meet the ideals set forth for them in their training programs. Regular teachers remain powerful in schools, and they control a strategic resource—children. Specialists end up being paralyzed. The content of their work tends to become dominated by the process of doing it. Psychologists test because they are supposed to test. Special teachers teach whomever is sent through the doorway of their classroom. No one anywhere spends much time figuring out what special education programs ought to do or thinking about how to be sure that actual programs work to achieve idealized goals. Each administrative operation is disconnected from each other operation. What emerges from the paralysis special educators feel, oddly, are rigid administrative procedures without any content. No one seems to care who actually gets placed in special classes. Because no one cares, control interests are not served any more than are instructional interests, and thus statistical studies do not show that they have an effect. Programs are empty motion.

Is There Redemption for Special Education?

Special education is the sort of topic which is embarrassing to sociologists. To the extent educational handicaps really are caused by physiological lesions which debilitate victims, there is nothing about the sociology of special education which makes it different from the sociology of physical therapy or the sociology of influenza therapy. We are not much interested in what the treatments are or in what administrative inconveniences trouble those who try to make programs run smoothly. The problems of special eduation might seem no different in kind from those of any program to remedy illnesses or disabilities which are carried out in a complex organization.

Those of us who have studied special education have argued that special education is worthy of sociological research because most children served do not suffer from identifiable lesions that cause handicaps. Rather, special education and assignments of children to classes are animated by problems of regular school programs. Special education provides a window through which we may observe the dynamics of the regular program in a new way. Special education teaches us about the social control apparatus of schools and about how attributions of intelligence or retardation are used to replicate the class structure.

I have argued, however, that these claims about the value of research on special education are misplaced because they assume a tightly structured school organization. That organization would require a strong, informal structure. In such an organization, it would be instructive to study the machinery which exists outside the classrooms for maintaining order; special education would be a prime candidate. However, survey research suggests that special education assignments are not heavily determined by disciplinary concerns. We might discount these findings, saying that one study is inadequate or that the measures used by Berk and his colleagues (1981) do not allow this sort of generalization.

I believe them, however, because I have been in the schools they studied, and because there is a substantial amount of data suggesting that the old collectivist model of school organization applies less and less in public schools. Our schools increasingly are large, bureaucratic, impersonal places where teachers have less and less power. Despite their declining power, teachers have the capacity to block or paralyze many programs, and special education is such a one. By controlling access to students, regular-class teachers can prevent special educators from obtaining the kinds of students who fit the learning disability model for treatment. Because regular teachers have become increasingly passive about trying to control their schools, however, they do not go out of their way to make sure that special educators actually are serving social control goals. Blocked from carrying out their formal goals but not forced to carry out any other functions, special educators live in purgatory. In many school districts, no one cares about or controls special education. It happens.

While this finding undercuts the old theory of how social control and school organization are related and about the contribution special education makes linking the two, it makes research on special education no less important. In some ways, the new perspective on special education I am suggesting is more disturbing in its image both of school organization and of special education than was the older one. If special education were a functional part of the social control apparatus of schools, we might instruct educators about how to play their roles more stategically, or we might attack social control functions as illegitimate—probably depending on the kinds of children special educators serve.

If special education operates in a vacuum, however, programs are beyond control. No one governs them—not even the people working in special education. School psychologists and special teachers guess what they are supposed to do and try to keep their regular-program patrons happy. Administration by impression management is beyond accountability, however. If special education is dangerous to children—leading to misclassification of black or Chicano children, for example—special educators plead that they are not responsible for decisions about how they are to work. However, no one in the regular school hierarchy would admit that they had ordered school psycholgists to examine children improperly. Catch-22.

Special education continues on because it is hard to kill off a department in a bureaucracy and because special education is symbolically powerful. It is politically convenient to have a school program which demonstrates that poor children more often are retarded than are middle-class children. It also is useful for schools to claim that every child, however physically handicapped, can receive a free education. In the absence of a strong lobby which demands program accountability, neither of these symbolic purposes demands that programs be rational.   This might finish off the discussion except that we do have ethnographic findings which show that, in many places, both in the United States and Great Britain, special education really does seem to work as a social control device in those schools that function on the collectivist principle. These examples are important because while the literature on educational administration reveals a fascination with the sort of disconnected, ambiguous administration I have argued exists in Chicago, there clearly are places where school administration is not disconnected. Do we just ignore those classes?

The problem with the whole analysis is that we pretend there is *one* school system (in the United States or in Great Britain) and one special education policy. Where special education is concerned, it is clear there are two. Urban special education nearly everywhere is a disaster. Outside of cities, however, quite a different situation prevails.

In my study of Illinois school psychologists (Milofsky 1984), people working in suburbs were sharply different from people working in cities in terms of professional background and work performance. Psychologists in cities tend to be promoted from the ranks of the regular teaching staff, whereas suburban psychologists tend to be recruited directly from psychology graduate schools. Urban psychologists on average spend about half as long administering each battery of tests as do suburban school psychologists, and they administer each year. I argue that these are just indicators of fundamentally different styles of school psychology. My findings are comparable to those produced in a study of Pennsylvania school psycholgists which, while not examining testing practices the same way, demonstrated similar urban/suburban differences in staff characteristics and work orientation (Kuriloff et al. 1979).

We have two special education systems, in part, for historical reasons. Urban special education generally is old. Its origins in Chicago date to the 1890s and in most cities date from well before World War II (Lazerson 1975, 1982; Slater 1980; Thomas and Thomas 1978). Attitudes about psychological measurement which prevailed half a century ago were institutionalized and have been frozen so that there is often considerable support for archaic testing techniques and contentless special education in cities. In suburbs, however, special education programs generally date from the 1960s. Staff hired to set up programs often were trained in post-World War II psychotherapeutic tradition, in which there is substantial skepticism about the accuracy of psychometric tests. Suburban districts, which serve wealthier families, are also likely to face pressure to provide technically sophisticated programs. It is not hard to find imaginative, therapeutic special education programs in suburban school districts. It also is not uncommon to find that the content of special education programs is in direct relation to the social class of students. The lower the parental income, the more special education is likely to serve social control purposes. Thus, in my Illinois survey, for example, where there is no bias against minorities *within* the Chicago public school district in terms of the rates at which psychologists test (my dependent variable measuring the quality of psychologists' practices), there is a significant correlation between race and testing speed in the suburbs. The social control model of special education works once one moves outside of cities.

We also have two special education systems for reasons rooted in the logic of organizational structure. In any school system, these programs are small and are viewed as special interest programs. They do not serve everyone, and they are not central to the political success of the school system within the community. This is disasterous in large school systems, where occupational groups like teachers, principals, and administrators form mass power blocs and where critical district decisions represent battles between these blocs that ignore small groups like special educators. In small districts, personal influence counts for more, and special educators can privately influence district decisions. They may, for example, make friends with the superintendent. Special educators can have proportionately more influence in a small school district than in a large school district.

Existence of two special education systems forces a further redefinition of the problem in special education. Those of us doing research in this area started off thinking that special education served social control functions. We assumed that it worked against the interests of minorities and low-income students, serving as an instrument of social class domination in schools. We then learned that schools are too disorganized to use special education as a device of social control. Receiving no reasonable direction or supervision, but prevented from doing what their professional ideas suggest is high-quality work, special educators become bureaucrats and avoid taking personal responsibility for program policies. This was not just a characteristic of special education, we learned, but increasingly characterizes public education as a whole. Following March and Olsen (1976) or Weick (1976), we might argue that special education is in purgatory because schools are unstructured and ungovernable by their nature.

That is not quite true, however. Urban school systems seem unstructured and ungovernable, at least from the standpoint of special education, because those systems are old, large, and politicized. Suburban systems are more flexible and innovative. Unfortunately, they also enroll most of the white students in a state like Illinois or Pennsylvania.

The denouement is that there is a subtle racism in pretending that there is one school system in this country when in fact there are two. In special education, there has been intense attention to guaranteeing children due process as they are reviewed for placement in special education classes precisely to protest against use of special classes for social control purposes. That due process sometimes works in suburbs as special educators fight against regular educators, trying to protect the right of psychologists and special teachers to admit to their programs only children who would profit from removal to a special class (Milofsky 1984). Due process does not work in cities because it requires that someone in the schools be administratively accountable and responsible. If no one is, then the system does not work. Due process controls just become a wilderness of irrelevant paperwork, and members of the special education evaluation teams—the school psychologists, social workers, nurses, and speech pathologists—simply become administrative functionaries who push papers. Since cities have the most children who are poor or members of ethnic minorities, the administrative ambiguity which prevails affects the children who need it most. Administrative rationality and accountable programs are provided to suburban children who are otherwise better protected by wealthy, informed, and caring parents.

REFERENCES

Abramowitz, Susan, and Ellen Tenenbaum. *High School '77: A Survey of Public Secondary School Principals.* Washington, DC: National Institute of Education, 1978.

Alschuler, Alfred S. *School Discipline: A Socially Literate Solution.* New York: McGraw-Hill, 1980.

Barker, R. G., and P. V. Gump. *Big School, Small School.* Stanford, CA: Stanford University Press, 1964.

Berk, Richard A., William P. Bridges, and Anthony Shih. "Does IQ Really Matter: A Study of the Use of IQ Scores for the Tracking of the Mentally Retarded." *American Sociological Review* 46 (1981): 58–71.

Bowles, Samuel, and Herbert Gintis. *Schooling in Capitalist America: Educational Reforms and the Contradictions of Economic Life.* New York: Basic Books, 1976.

Bucher, R., and J. Stelling. "Characteristics of Professional Organizations." *Journal of Health and Social Behavior* 10 (1969): 3–11.

Bureau of Education for the Handicapped. *IEP: Developing Criteria for the Evaluation of Individualized Education Program Provisions.* Washington, D.C.: U.S. Office of Education, 1978a.

———. *Due Process: Developing Criteria for the Evaluation of Due Process Procedural Safeguards Provisions* Washington, D.C.: U.S. Office of Education, 1978b.

Carrier, James G. "Masking the Social in Educational Knowledge: The Case of Learning Disability Theory." *American Journal of Sociology* 88 (1983): 948–74.

Chall, Jeanne S. *Learning to Read: The Great Debate*. New York: McGraw-Hill, 1983a.

———. "Reading and the Unconscious." A review of B. Bettelheim and K. Zelan, *On Learning to Read: The Child's Fascination with Meaning*. *Contemporary Education Review* 2 (1983b): 7–11.

Clark, Burton R. *Adult Education in Transition: A Study of Institutional Insecurity*. Berkeley: University of California Press, 1956a.

———. "Organizational Adaptation and Precarious Values." *American Sociological Review* 21 (1956b): 327–36.

Coleman, James S. "The Adolescent Subculture and Academic Achievement." *American Journal of Sociology* 65 (1960): 337–47.

———. *The Adolescent Society*. New York: The Free Press, 1961.

Coser, Lewis. *The Functions of Social Conflict*. New York: The Free Press, 1956.

Dexter, Lewis Anthony. *The Tyranny of Schooling: An Inquiry into the Problem of "Stupidity."* New York: Basic Books, 1964.

Etzioni, Amitai W., ed. *The Semi-professions and Their Organization: Teachers, Nurses, Social Workers*. New York: The Free Press, 1969.

Feuerstein, Reuven. "A Dynamic Approach to the Causation, Prevention and Alleviation of Retarded Performance." In *Social-Cultural Aspects of Mental Retardation*, edited by H. C. Heywood. New York: Appleton-Century-Crofts, 1970.

Ford, Julienne, Denis Mongon, and Maurice Whelan. *Special Education and Social Control: Invisible Disasters*. London and Boston: Routledge & Kegan Paul, 1982.

Garrison, M., Jr., and D. D. Hammill. "Who Are the Retarded?" *Exceptional Children* 38 (1971): 13–20.

Goldner, Fred. "Role Emergence and the Ethics of Ambiguity." In *Ethics, Politics and Social Research*, edited by Gideon Sjoberg. Cambridge, MA: Schenkman, 1967.

Henry, Jules. *Culture Against Man*. New York: Vintage Press, 1963.

Hughes, Everett C. "Good People and Dirty Work." In *The Other Side: Perspectives on Deviance*, edited by Howard Becker. New York: The Free Press, 1964.

Jensen, Arthur R. "How Much Can We Boost IQ and Scholastic Achievement?" *Harvard Educational Review* 39 (1969): 1–123.

Kamin, Leon J. *The Science and Politics of I.Q.* Potomac, MD: Lawrence Erlbaum Assoc., 1974.

Katz, Michael B. *Class, Bureaucracy and Schools*. New York: Praeger, 1971.

Kirp, David L. "Schools as Sorters: The Constitutional and Policy Implications of Student Classifications." *University of Pennsylvania Law Review* 121 (1973): 705–97.

Kuriloff, Peter, David Kirp, and William Buss. *When Handicapped Children Go to Court: Assessing the Impact of the Legal Reform of Special Education in Pennsylvania*. Washington, DC: National Institute of Education, 1979.

Labov, William. *Language in the Inner City*. Philadelphia: University of Pennsylvania Press, 1972.

Lazerson, Marvin. "Educational Institutions and Mental Subnormality: Notes on Writing a History." In *The Mentally Retarded and Society: A Social Science Perspective*, edited by Michael J. Begab and Stephen A. Richardson. Baltimore: University Park Press, 1975.

———. "The Origins of Special Education, 1890–1940." In *Special Education Policies:*

Their History, Implementation, and Finance, edited by Jay G. Chambers and William T. Hartman. Philadelphia: Temple University Press, 1982.

Lazerson, Marvin, and W. Norton Grubb, eds. *American Education and Vocationalism. A Documentary History: 1870–1970.* New York: Teachers College Press, 1974.

Lindblom, Charles E. *Policy Making Process.* Englewood Cliffs, NJ: Prentice-Hall, 1980.

Lindblom, Charles E., and David K. Cohen. *Usable Knowledge: Social Science and Social Problem Solving.* New Haven, CT: Yale University Press, 1979.

Lipsky, Michael. *Street-Level Bureaucracy: Dilemmas of the Individual in Public Services.* New York: Russell Sage Foundation, 1980.

Lortie, Dan C. "The Balance of Control and Autonomy in Elementary School Teaching." In *The Semi-Professions and Their Organization: Teachers, Nurses, Social Workers*, edited by Amitai W. Etzioni. New York: The Free Press, 1969.

———. *School-Teacher: A Sociological Study.* Chicago: University of Chicago Press, 1975.

McIntyre, D. "Two Schools, One Psychologist." In *The Psycho-Educational Clinic*, edited by F. Kaplan and S. B. Sarason. Boston: Massachusetts Department of Mental Health, 1969.

McPherson, Gertrude. *Small Town Teacher.* Cambridge, MA: Harvard University Press, 1972.

March, James G., and Johan P. Olsen. *Ambiguity and Choice in Organizations.* Bergen, Norway: Universitetsforlaget, 1976.

Mercer, Jane R. "Institutionalized Anglocentrism: Labeling Mental Retardates in Public Schools." In *Race, Change and Urban Society*, edited by P. Orleans and W. R. Ellis, Jr. Beverly Hills, CA: Sage Publications, 1971.

———. *Labeling the Mentally Retarded.* Berkeley: University of California Press, 1973.

Metz, Mary H. *Classrooms and Corridors: The Crisis of Authority in Desegregated Secondary Schools.* Berkeley: University of California Press, 1978.

Milofsky, Carl. "Why Special Education Isn't Special." *Harvard Educational Review* 44 (1974): 437–58.

———. *Special Education: A Sociological Study of California Programs.* New York: Praeger, 1976.

———. "Deviance versus Stigma: A Typology of Deviance in Special Education." Paper presented at the meetings of the American Sociological Association, San Francisco, 1978.

———. "Intelligence Testing and Race in the Public Schools." Paper presented at the meetings of the American Sociological Association, Detroit, 1983.

———. "Testers and Testing: School Organization, School Psychology and the Practice of Intelligence Testing." Unpublished manuscript, Bucknell University, 1984.

Murnane, Richard J. *The Impact of School Resources on the Learning of Inner City Children.* Cambridge, MA: Ballinger, 1975.

National Institute of Education. *Violent Schools—Safe Schools: The Safe School Study Report to the Congress.* Washington, D.C.: National Institute of Education, 1978.

Rist, Ray. "Student Social Class and Teacher Expectations: The Self-fulfilling Prophecy in Ghetto Education." *Harvard Educational Review* 40 (1970): 411–50.

———. *The Urban School: A Factory for Failure.* Cambridge, MA: MIT Press, 1973.

Rosenbaum, James E. *Making Inequality: The Hidden Curriculum of High School Tracking.* New York: John Wiley & Sons, 1976.

Rosenthal, Robert, and Lenore Jacobson. *Pygmalion in the Classroom: Teacher Expec-*

tation and Pupil's Intellectual Development. New York: Holt, Rinehart & Winston, 1968.

Rothschild-Whitt, J. "The Collectivist Organization." *American Sociological Review* 44 (1979): 509–28.

Rubin, Lillian B. *Busing and Backlash*. Berkeley: University of California Press, 1972.

———. *Worlds of Pain: Life in the Working Class Family*. New York: Basic Books, 1976.

Sarason, Seymour, and John Doris. *Educational Handicap, Public Policy and Social History*. New York: The Free Press, 1979.

Selznick, Philip. *Leadership in Administration*. New York: Harper & Row, 1957.

Shils, Edward. *Center and Periphery: Essays in Macrosociology*. Chicago: University of Chicago Press, 1975.

Slater, Robert. "The Organizational Origins of Public School Psychology." *Educational Studies* 1 (1980): 1–11.

Smith, L., and W. Geoffrey. *The Complexities of an Urban Classroom*. New York: Holt, Rinehart & Winston, 1968.

Stanton, A. H., and M. S. Schwartz. *The Mental Hospital: A Study of Institutional Participation in Psychiatric Illness*. New York: Basic Books, 1954.

Stinchcombe, Arthur L. *Rebellion in a High School*. Chicago: Quadrangle Books, 1964.

Swidler, Ann. *Organization without Authority: Dilemmas of Social Control in Free Schools*. Cambridge, MA: Harvard University Press, 1979.

Sykes, Gresham M. *The Society of Captives*. New York: Atheneum, 1968.

Thomas, William I., and Dorothy Swain Thomas. *The Child in America*. New York: Alfred A. Knopf, 1928.

Tomlinson, Sally. *A Sociology of Special Education*. London: Routledge & Kegan Paul, 1982.

Tyack, David. *The One Best System*. Cambridge, MA: Harvard University Press, 1974.

Valentine, Charles A. "Deficit, Difference and Bi-cultural Models of Afro-American Behavior." *Harvard Educational Review* 41 (1971): 137–57.

Waller, Willard. *The Sociology of Teaching*. New York: John Wiley & Sons, 1932.

Weatherly, R., and M. Lipsky. "Street-level Bureaucrats and Institutional Innovation: Implementing Special-Education Reform." *Harvard Educational Review* 47 (1977): 171–97.

Weick, Karl E. "Educational Organizations as Loosely Coupled Systems." *Administrative Science Quarterly* 21 (1976): 1–19.

Williams, Robert L. "Danger: Testing and Dehumanizing Black Children." *The School Psychologist* 25 (1971a): 11–13.

———. "From Dehumanization to Black Intellectual Genocide: A Rejoinder." *The School Psychologist* 25 (1971b): 21–24.

Educational Transmission and Reproduction

8

On Pedagogic Discourse

INTRODUCTION

It is a matter of some interest that the sociology of education has rarely turned its attention to the analysis of the intrinsic features which constitute and distinguish the specialized form of communication realized by the pedagogic discourse of education. Much of the analyses of the sociology of education, especially those carried out by the diverse group of theories of reproduction and transformation, assume, take for granted, the very discourse which is subject to their analysis. These theories, in particular, see pedagogic discourse as a media for other voices, class, gender, race. The discourses of education are analyzed for their power in the reproduction of dominant/dominated relations external to the discourse but which penetrate the social relations, media of transmission, and evaluation of pedagogic discourse. If the voice of the working class is the absent voice of pedagogic discourse, then what is absent from pedagogic discourse is its own voice. If theories of cultural reproduction or of transformation of culture formulate ordering or disordering principles, then these are *of the message of pedagogic discourse*, not of order/disordering principles *intrinsic* to its logic, as a specialized discourse. This chapter should be regarded only as a possible step toward the specification of ordering principles intrinsic to the production, reproduction, and change of pedagogic discourse. The basic concepts and rules for ordering are developed at length in Bernstein and Diaz (1984; applications may be found in Diaz 1983; Cox 1984; Moore 1983; and Tyler 1984). The work of Foucault (1972, 1977, 1982) has had influence upon our approach, but we should emphasize that our focus is very different. Indeed, we would consider that the articulation of the *specific* grammars of the pedagogic device is fundamental to much of Foucault's work. (For the relations between Foucault and the approach taken here, see Atkinson 1981, 1985; Diaz 1983.)

Although there is an extensive literature, if we examine the major texts within the sociology of education which give a definition of its range of concerns and, perhaps in particular, the most recent and detailed of these, *The Social Sciences in Educational Studies: A Selected Guide to the Literature* (Harnett 1982), we do not find any systematic account of the principles of the specialized communicative practice which is the distinguishing feature of the school's central activity, transmission/acquisition. From *Education, Economy and Society* (Halsey et al. 1961) to *Power and Ideology in Education* (Karabel and Halsey 1977), we have an important index of the transformation and development of focuses of interest within the sociology of education. Yet the question of the analysis of pedagogic discourse and its regulative practices receives little attention. However, in their introduction to *Power and Ideology in Education*, the editors noted that Durkheim looked at education in France from the period of the Primitive church to that of the Third Republic, exploring the history of what the French call *les idées pedagogiques*, a concept that includes not only the formal curriculum, but also the way in which the knowledge is transmitted and evaluated. Interestingly, the New Sociology of Education (see esp. Young 1971) took as its focus the problematic nature of knowledge and the manner of its transmission, acquisition, and evaluation in schools. Young states: "It is or should be the central task of the sociology of education to relate the principles of selection and organization that underlie curricula to their institutional and interactional settings in schools and classrooms and to the wider social structure" (1971, p. 24). However, this program, whatever else it produced, did not produce what is called for. General theories of culture reproduction (see Apple 1982a) again appear to be more concerned with an analysis of what is reproduced in and by education than with the medium of reproduction: the nature of the specialized discourse.[1] It is as if the specialized discourse of education is a voice through which others speak (class, gender, religion, race, region), as if pedagogic discourse is itself no more than a relay for power relations external to itself, a relay whose form has no consequences for what is relayed.

The perspective of the Center for Contemporary Cultural Studies at the University of Birmingham (Johnson et al. 1981 and Willis 1977 are two examples), in opposing the determination of French theories of cultural reproduction, has as yet produced no systematic analysis of the cultural practice intrinsic to the educational process. Nonetheless, this approach has attempted to create an active place and position for the working class in the shaping of the process.

Perhaps the most important attempt to formalize the role of education in the reproduction of class relations has been carried out by Bourdieu and Passeron (1977). While they are concerned with the analysis of the legitimation of structures of culture, principles of transmission/acquisition, communicative practices and their systems of meanings, together with an analysis of how their arbitrary features disguise the power relations which they transmit (through *méconnaissance* to *la violence symbolique*), there is little systematic and specific analysis of the principles whereby a specific discourse is constituted or of the principles of its transmission. Bourdieu and Passeron distinguish two forms of communication in very general terms: *magisterial* (language of the transmitter) and *popular* (language of the working class). They are more concerned with *relations to* pedagogic communication, that is, with the differential positioning of acquirers with respect to how they have been positioned in their relations to legitimate pedagogic communication, than with the analysis of the relations *within* pedagogic communication.

Finally, if we turn to more specific aspects of the school, we can find a diverse (not to say, perhaps, divergent) literature, from Waller's *Sociology of Teaching* (1932) to the major review of current empirical research by Tyler, in *The Sociology of the School: A Review* (1982). Here is perhaps a bedrock of the field of the sociology of educational, empirical studies of the school as an organizational structure and interactional practice, where curriculum, pedagogic practice, and modes of evaluation set the terms for the crucial encounters in the classroom context of teacher and pupils. Perhaps key new studies here are the studies of classroom language and the context and practices of its regulation and negotiation (Delamont 1976; Hymes et al. 1971; Stubbs and Delamont 1976; Edwards 1980, 1982). These studies, crucial as they are, presuppose a particular focus, a focus which is less concerned with the question of how the distribution of power and principles of control establish a regulating discourse but more concerned, and validly so, to articulate the principles of interactional communication and practice *within* the local context of the classroom. It is of little value to make a derogatory distinction between surface realizations and their underlying principles or grammar of realization, for what is one person's surface is another's underlying principles and vice versa. The body of work to which we have referred is of major relevance. Indeed, this body of work provides us not only with crucial points of reference and key concepts, but also has formulated the parameters for empirical research.

The Pedagogic Device

Our analysis will first outline what we take to be the internal orderings of the pedagogic device which we consider to be the condition for the production, reproduction, and transformation of culture. We consider that this device provides the intrinsic grammar of pedagogic discourse through *distributive rules*, *re-contextualizing rules*, and *rules of evaluation*. These rules are themselves hierarchically related, in the sense that the nature of the distributive rules regulates the re-contextualizing rules which in turn regulate the rules of evaluation. These distributive rules regulate the fundamental relation between power, social groups, forms of consciousness and practice, and their reproductions and productions. The re-contextualizing rules regulate the constitution of specific pedagogic discourse. The rules of evaluation are constituted by the specific pedagogic practice. The pedagogic device generates a symbolic ruler for consciousness. The question becomes, then, whose ruler, what consciousness? We shall see later in the chapter an attempt to construct a general model for the answering of such questions.

Distributive Rules. We shall start with a consideration of the means whereby a relation is constructed between power, social groups, and forms of consciousness. We can consider that this relationship is established through the controls on the specialization and distribution of different orders of meanings. These different orders/orderings of meanings can be said to create different knowledges/practices. The controls on the different specialization and distribution of principles for the ordering of meaning attempt to effect specialization and distribution of forms of consciousness and practice. From this point of view, if we wish to understand the production, reproduction, and transformations of forms of consciousness and practice, we need to understand the social basis of a given distribution of power and principles of control which differentially position, reposition, and opposition forms of consciousness and practice. We shall postulate that between power and knowledge and knowledge and forms of consciousness is always the pedagogic device (PD). We shall define the pedagogic device as the distributive re-contextualizing and evaluative rules for specializing forms of consciousness.

Fundamental distributive rules mark and specialize the thinkable/unthinkable and their entailed practices to different groups through the mediation of differently specialized pedagogic agencies.

In all societies, there are at least two basic classes of knowledge, the esoteric and the mundane, knowledge of the other and the otherness of knowledge, of how it is, the possible, as against the possibility of the impossible. We are well aware that the line between these two classes of knowledge/practices is relative to any given period and that the principles generating both classes are also relative to a given period. In small scale, nonliterate societies, with a simple division of labor, societies particularly studied by social anthropologists until fairly recently, the division between the thinkable and the unthinkable approximates to the distinction between the sacred and the profane. Essentially, the controls on the unthinkable and the practice of its management were effected by the religious system, its agents and their practices. Today the controls on the unthinkable lie essentially, but not wholly, directly or indirectly, in the upper reaches of the educational system, in that part more concerned with the production than with the reproduction of discourse. In contrast, the thinkable is a different power-regulated re-contextualizing in the lower reaches of the educational system, that is, in its reproductive levels rather than in its productive levels.[2]

In both simple and complex societies, a structurally similar distribution of forms of consciousness is to be found, differently specialized through different agencies and produced by differently specialized pedagogic discourses. The similarity is more profound; the system of meanings is structurally similar. We are not here referring to any similarity between magic and science or to, for example, sharing powers of complex navigation, but to the sharing of a particular order of meaning which establishes the particular relation between the material and the immaterial so relating one world to another, the mundane to the transcendental. This relation always, by definition, transcends the local and discrete. It is not that this order of relation is abstract, but more a question of the form taken by the abstraction. It is a form whereby there is an indirect relation between meanings and a specific material base (a given social division of labor and its social relations). Under these conditions, there is a potential discursive "gap," a "space" which can become the site for alternative possibilities, for alternative realizations of the relation between the material and the immaterial. This potential gap, space, the site of the unthinkable, the impossible can be both beneficial and dangerous at one and the same time. It is the meeting point of order and disorder, of coherence and incoherence; it is the crucial site of the "yet to be thought." In a fundamental sense, this potentiality is a potentiality of language itself. Any distribution of power regulates the realization of this potential for the social orderings it creates, maintains, and legitimates. In simple societies, this regulation was effected by the religious system and by the cosmologies to which it gave access and which it controlled.

In the language of codes (Bernstein 1981), we should make a distinction between elaborated orientations and an elaborated code. If the code is elaborated, then the principles regulating the realizations of the code are themselves the object of explicit principles of analysis. From this point of view, the cosmologies of simple societies are not the product of elaborated codes, but are the product of elaborated orientations which create the relations between the mundane and the transcendental, but where the principles of the transcendental realizations are not themselves subject to further principles of exploration.[3] In complex societies, certainly in Europe, the institutionalizing of elaborated codes in specialized agencies and agents was accomplished in the Medieval period with the development of the ancient universities and monastic schools.

We are arguing that elaborated orientations and, even more, elaborated codes are the media for thinking the unthinkable, the impossible, because the meanings to which they give rise go beyond local space, time, context and embed and relate the latter to a transcendental space, time, context. A potential of such meanings is disorder, incoherence; a new order, a new coherence. We are suggesting that the relationship between power, knowledge, and forms of consciousness and practice is accomplished by the pedagogic device. The pedagogic device provides distributive rules which regulate the different specialization of consciousness to different groups. We see this historically in terms of the guardians and transmitters of the realization of elaborate orientations in simple societies and later in complex societies, of legitimate elaborated codes and their modalities, which transmit pedagogic discourses and their practices.

Through its distributive rules, the pedagogic device is both the control on the unthinkable and the control on those who may think it. We shall see later that intrinsic to such a device is both the imposition of order and the means of its transformation.

Re-Contextualizing Rules: Pedagogic Discourse. If the distributive rules mark and distribute who may transmit what to whom and under what conditions, and in so doing attempt to set the outer and inner limits of legitimate discourse, then pedagogic discourse is the rules of specialized communication through which pedagogic subjects are selectively created.[4] We shall define pedagogic discourse as the rules for embedding and relating two discourses. It will be remembered that the distributive rules attempt to control the embedding and relating of the material in the immaterial, the mundane in the transcendental, and the distribution of such meanings. Pedagogic discourse is the specialized communication whereby differential transmission/acquisition is affected. We commence with the question "What discourse is embedded in what discourse?"

We call the pedagogic discourse, transmitting specialized competencies and their relation to one another, *instructional discourse*, and the discourse creating specialized order, relation, and identity, *regulative discourse* (see Note B). To show visually the distinctive feature of pedagogic discourse, we shall write it as ID/RD, meaning ID is embedded in RD. The rules constituting pedagogic discourse are not derived from the rules regulating the internal characteristics of the competencies to be transmitted. In an important sense, pedagogic discourse, from this point of view, is a discourse without a specific discourse. It has no discourse of its own. It is a principle for appropriating other discourses and for bringing them into a special relation with one another for the purposes of their selective transmission and acquisition. Pedagogic discourse, then, is a principle which removes a discourse (de-locates) from its substantive practice and context and re-locates that discourse according to its own principle of selective re-ordering and focusing. In the process of de- and re-location, the original discourse is transformed from an actual practice to a virtual or imaginary practice. Pedagogic discourse creates imaginary subjects.

We must sharpen our concept of this principle which constitutes pedagogic discourse. It is a re-contextualizing principle which selectively appropriates, re-locates, and re-focuses other discourses to constitute its own order and orderings. In this sense, pedagogic discourse cannot be identified with any of the discourses it has re-contextualized; it has no discourse of its own other than a re-contextualizing discourse. We have now made the move from the distributive rules to the re-contextualizing rules, the rules which constitute pedagogic discourse.

The Dominance of Regulative Discourse. From the above discussion, it can be seen that as pedagogic discourse is a re-contextualizing principle, which transforms the actual into the virtual or imaginary, then any re-contextualized discourse becomes a signifier for something other than itself. What this "other" is, the principle of the principle of re-contextualizing, regulates what principle of re-contextualizing is selected. Perhaps more accurately, the principle which regulates the range of alternative principles available for selection varies according to the dominant principles of a given society (see later discussion). In this sense, regulative discourse is itself the precondition for any pedagogic discourse. It is, of course, obvious that all pedagogic discourse creates a moral regulation of the social relations of transmission/acquisition, that is, rules of order, relations, and identity, and that such a moral order is prior to and a condition for the transmission of competencies. This moral order is in turn subject to a re-contextualizing principle, and thus this order is a signifier for something other than itself. It is less obvious how regulative discourse creates order, relation, and identity in instructional discourse, that is, in the intrinsic orderings of the competence to be acquired.

We can take, as an example, the acquisition of physics in the secondary school. First of all, such physics is a re-contextualized discourse. It is the result of re-contextualizing principles which have selected and de-located physics from what we could call the primary field of the production of discourse (usually the universities or equivalent agencies, see Note A) and have re-located, re-focused physics in the secondary field of the reproduction of discourse. In this process, physics undergoes a complex transformation from an original to a virtual/imaginary discourse. The rules of selection, sequence, and pacing (the rate of expected acquisition of the sequencing rules) cannot themselves be derived from some logic internal to physics or from the practices of those who produce physics. The rules of the reproduction of physics are *social*, not *logical*, facts. The re-contextualizing rules regulate not only selection, sequence, and pace, but also the *theory of instruction* from which the transmission rules are derived. The strength of the classification and framing of re-contextualized physics is itself ultimately a feature of regulative discourse. In this way, order, relation, and identity in the transmission of instructional discourse are themselves embedded in the principles of order, relation, and identity of regulative discourse.[5] Pedagogic discourse is then a re-contextualizing principle/discourse which embeds competence in order and order in competence. We shall take up later the question of whose order and what competence.

Evaluation Rules: Pedagogic Practice. We shall be here concerned to show the fundamental ordering principles of any pedagogic discourse. At the most abstract level, the re-contextualizing principle which selectively creates ID/RD produces a specialization of time, text (or its metaphoric equivalent), and space and the conditions of their interrelation. Thus:

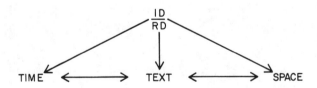

We can, at a lower level of abstraction, transform Time into Age. Thus the practice of any ID/RD leads to a punctuation in age, to a dislocation of ages sequentially related.

The degree of delicacy of the punctuation of time and the span of life appropriated by pedagogic time (in principle, from preprocreation to postresurrection) is a matter of a given historic context. Yet specialization of and differentiation within time are integral to pedagogic discourse. The text is always transformed

into a special age-related content. Pedagogic practice creates a license to speak in its own temporal punctuations.
Thus:

$$\text{AGE} \longleftrightarrow \text{CONTENT} \longleftrightarrow \text{CONTEXT}$$

Finally, we can transform the above into the level of the social relations of pedagogic practice and the crucial feature of the communication. Age is transformed into acquisition. Content is transformed into evaluation. Context is transformed into transmission.
Thus:

$$\text{ACQUISITION} \longleftrightarrow \text{EVALUATION} \longleftrightarrow \text{TRANSMISSION}$$

We can see that the key to pedagogic practice is continuous evaluation.

If we place the horizontal and vertical relations together (as in figure 8.1), we obtain:

Figure 8.1 Pedagogic Practice

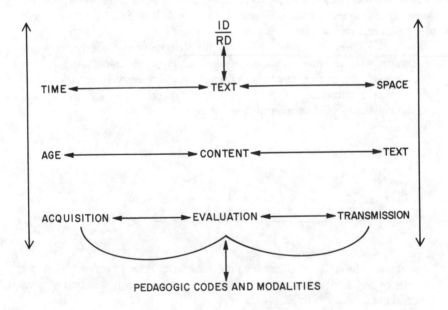

The code condenses in its grammar the orderings within and between distributive rules, re-contextualizing rules, and evaluation rules. However, there may well be contradictions, cleavages, and dilemmas between these rules so that pedagogic practice does not necessarily reproduce pedagogic discourse, and what is acquired is not necessarily what is transmitted.

The power relations which constitute, legitimate, and maintain the *classifications* of the code (paradigmatic features) and the control relations which constitute, legitimate, and maintain the *framing* of communicative relations (syntagmatic features) are themselves the producing product of ongoing contradictions, cleavages, and dilemmas of social relations. The set of rules of the pedagogic device is condensed in the code of transmission.

We have so far postulated distributive rules which are the official regulation of the degree of classification of the distinction between thinkable-practices and unthinkable-practices and of the degree of insulation between groups, practices, and contexts and between differently specialized principles of communication. The pedagogic device reproduces but does not create this distinction between the unthinkable and the thinkable. It attempts to regulate the distribution. The distributive rules are a basic classificatory principle regulating the relationship between the distribution of power, the distribution of knowledge, and the distribution of forms of consciousness. We know that, in general, those who reproduce legitimate knowledge institutionalize the thinkable, while those who produce legitimate knowledge institutionalize the unthinkable. We find these are two strongly classified groups within the legitimate fields of the production and reproduction of education. What is the thinkable and what is the unthinkable, the form of the regulation, and the social composition of the different agents will vary from one historical situation to another. Further, the effectiveness of the device is limited by two features, one internal to the device itself and one external to it. First, the communicative practice subject to distribution itself contains the *possibilities* of transformation of its own principles. Second, the distribution of power which speaks through the device itself creates potential sites for resistance and opposition to its principle. Thus the device may well become a crucial arena of struggle for control, as it is a condition for the production and reproduction of culture and of their interrelation.

We have said that pedagogic discourse denotes the rule for embedding an instructional discourse in a regulative discourse. Instructional discourse regulates the rules which constitute the legitimate variety, internal and relational features of specialized competencies. This discourse is embedded in a regulative discourse, the rules of which regulate what counts as legitimate order between and within transmitters, acquirers, competencies, and contexts. At the most abstract level, it provides and legitimates the official rules regulating order, relation, and identity. The tendency is to separate these discourses as moral and instructional discourses, or to see them as ideologically penetrated, rather than to regard them as one embedded discourse producing one embedded, unseparable text (see Note B). The grammar (the underlying ordering principle) condenses competencies into order and order into competencies.

Figure 8.2 Orderings of the Pedagogic Device

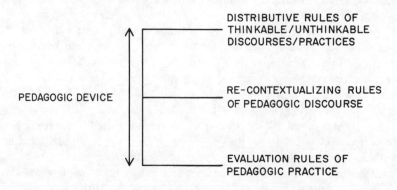

PEDAGOGIC DEVICE

DISTRIBUTIVE RULES OF THINKABLE/UNTHINKABLE DISCOURSES/PRACTICES

RE-CONTEXTUALIZING RULES OF PEDAGOGIC DISCOURSE

EVALUATION RULES OF PEDAGOGIC PRACTICE

We have argued that this grammar which produces the internal orderings of pedagogic discourse is not a grammar for specializing a specific discourse, creating its own rules of demarcation and internal order, but a principle of de-locating, re-locating, and re-focusing *other* specialized discourses, bringing them into a new relation with one another and introducing a new temporal internal ordering. Pedagogic discourse is constituted by what we shall call a re-contex-tualizing grammar. This grammar necessarily transforms, in the process of con-stituting its new orderings, the appropriated discourses into imaginary discourses. This re-contextualizing grammar, the grammar of appropriation, is linked to the levels of pedagogic practice by realization rules. These realization rules are derived from theories of instruction (implicit or explicit). These theories of instruction are themselves necessarily of the form ID/RD and are constituted by re-contextualizing principles which regulate the internal orderings, temporal and contextual realizations of the discourses of pedagogic practice. The theory of instruction is a crucial re-contextualized discourse, as it regulates the orderings of pedagogic practice, constructs the mode of the pedagogic subject (the ac-quirer), the mode of the transmitter, the model of the pedagogic context, and the mode of communicative pedagogic competence. Change in the theory of instruction can thus have consequences for the ordering of pedagogic practice. In this way, we can distinguish two modalities of theories of instruction: one oriented to the logic of transmission and one oriented to the logic of acquisition. The former will privilege *performances* of the pedagogic discourse; the latter will privilege *competencies* of the acquirer.[6]

We can now summarize the order and orderings of the pedagogic device as a grammar regulating the relations within and between three levels (given in figure 8.2). The degree of determination, that is, the outer boundaries and inner possibilities of each level, is a matter of the historical and ideological context of the device.

The pedagogic device is thus a symbolic ruler for consciousness in its selective creation, positioning, and oppositioning of pedagogic subjects. It is the condition for the production, reproduction, and transformation of culture. The question is whose ruler, what consciousness?

Before we turn to consider this question, we should like to draw attention to our original problem. Studies in the sociology of education, on the whole, take for granted (perhaps with the exception of Durkheim's *Evolution of Educational Thought* [1938/1977]) the analysis of the intrinsic distinguishing features of specialized pedagogic communicative practices. In our language, such studies are concerned only with the analysis of the "message" of pedagogy (class, gender, race, region, nation, religion), not with its "voice." In such studies, the voice of pedagogy is a voice that is never heard, only its realizations, that is, its messages. The voice is constituted by the pedagogic device. A more appropriate metaphor, maybe, is that the pedagogic device is a grammar for producing specialized messages, realizations, a grammar which regulates what it processes. Such a grammar orders and positions and yet contains the potential of its own transformation.

Any sociology of education should have a theory of the pedagogic device. Indeed such a theory could well be its necessary foundation and provide the fundamental theoretical object of the discipline.

Whose Ruler, What Consciousness?: A Model

Our model of pedagogic discourse is given in Figure 8.3. We shall confine discussion of the model to the production and reproduction of official pedagogic discourse in contemporary developed societies.[7] Official pedagogic discourse regulates the rules of the production, distribution, reproduction, interrelations, and change of legitimate pedagogic texts; their social relations of transmission and acquisition (practice); and the organization of their contexts (organization).[8]

We must first distinguish what we have called, in the model, *dominant principles of the society*. These create an arena of challenge, conflict, and dilemma but at any one time specify basic principles of order, relation, and identity, setting at least their outer boundaries and, in certain contexts, their inner limits. We can regard these dominant principles as an expression of the dominant political party of the state, or rather an expression of the relations between the various parties or interest groups. The dominant principles are regulated by the distribution of power and principles of control which determine the means, contexts, distribution, possibilities, and social relations of physical and discursive resources. We are here concerned only with the relation between the dominant principles and the constitution of position, agents, and practices in the official re-contextualizing field which is responsible for creating, maintaining, and changing official pedagogic discourse. This field will usually have a core of officials drawn from official pedagogic agencies of the state and consultants, advisers, drawn from the educational system and from the fields of economy and symbolic control. In this way, official pedagogic discourse is always a re-contextualizing

Figure 8.3 A Model of Official Pedagogic Discourse

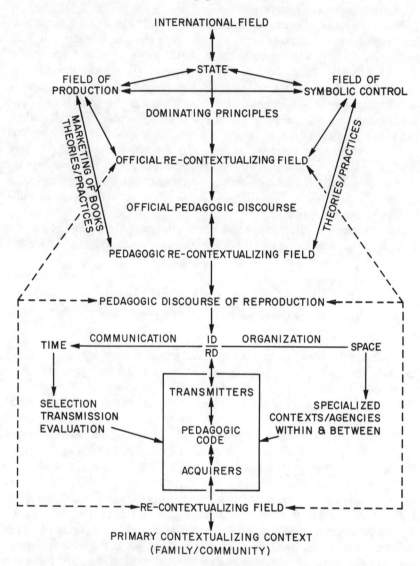

of texts and of their generating social relations from dominating positions within the fields of economy and symbolic control.

In our model, we distinguish two re-contextualizing fields: (1) the official re-contextualizing field (ORF), regulated directly by the state, politically through the legislature, and administratively through the civil service, and (2) the pe-dagogic re-contextualizing field (PRF). There may be more than one ministry active in the official re-contextualizing field. Today in the United Kingdom

(U.K.), we must note the Department of Employment. The ORF may selectively incorporate specialized services from agents/agencies external to it which in turn alters the position of these agents in their respective fields. The major activity of re-contextualizing fields is the constituting of the "what" and "how" of pedagogic discourse. The "what" refers to the categories, contents, and relationship to be transmitted, that is, their classification, and the "how" refers to the manner of their transmission, essentially to their framing. The "what" entails re-contextualizing from intellectual fields (physics, English, history, etc.), expressive fields (the arts), and/or manual fields (crafts). The "how" refers to the re-contextualizing of theories from social science, usually psychology. The re-contextualizing field brings together discourses from fields which are usually strongly classified but rarely brings together the agents. On the whole, although there are exceptions, those who produce the discourse or effect the discourse to be re-contextualized are not agents of its re-contextualization. It is important to study those cases where the producers or effectors of the discourse are also its re-contextualizers. We can define the relative autonomy of pedagogic discourse to the extent that PRFs are permitted to exist and effect official pedagogic discourse and official pedagogic practice.[9]

PRFs, as in the case of the official field, are concerned with the principles and practices regulating the circulation of theories/practices from the context of their production or existence to the contexts of their reproduction. The PRF may have as its core, positions/agents/practices drawn from university departments of education, colleges of education, schools, foundations, together with specialized media, journals, weeklies, and publishing houses.[10] The PRF may be internally strongly classified, producing subfields specialized to levels of the educational system, curriculum, groups of pupils. It is useful to distinguish public agencies of pedagogic reproduction from others that are within the private sector, independent of the state. While the latter directly determine their own re-contextualizing, the former (until recently universities) may enjoy a relatively large measure of control as well.

Both re-contextualizing fields (ORF and PRF) are affected by the fields of production (economy) and symbolic control. There is a double relation between re-contextualizing fields and the fields of production (economy) and symbolic control.

1. The theories, practices, social relation within these fields will exert an influence upon the discourses to be transmitted and *how* they are transmitted; both the "what" and the "how" of pedagogic discourse.[11]

2. The training requirements of agents (especially dominating agents within the field of symbolic control) will influence the "what" and the "how." However, as we have argued that pedagogic discourse creates imaginary subjects, we should not overestimate the fit between pedagogic discourse and any practice external to it. Indeed, on our argument, the "fit" is essentially an imaginary practice which may well be ideologically positioned by different agencies, i.e., education/production/symbolic control.

The pedagogic discourse of reproduction which is inserted in the contexts of reproduction (what school contexts depend upon the relative autonomy given to levels or agencies within levels) is then constituted by a complex set of relations between re-contextualizing fields and positions within such fields. As a consequence, depending upon the relative autonomy of and the specializations within the PRF, the principles/practices which dominate the ORF may well be markedly attenuated by the process of their distribution, circulation, and reproduction.

In our model, we give only a very general abstract formulation of pedagogic practice. We show only how a given SID/SRD (specific instructional discourse/specific regulative discourse) creates specific communicative practices (time) and organizational practices (space) to constitute the code to be acquired. We should remember that SRD may well realize its own specialized instructional discourses, specialized agents, contexts, and organization, as well as penetrating the ordering of SID, its content, and its manner of transmission. Pedagogic discourse of reproduction is given by SID/SRD where the unit of analysis may be a level of the educational system or agency, a curriculum, a unit of the curriculum, or a context of transmission.[12] (For the coding rules of SID/SRD, see Bernstein and Diaz 1984 and Definitions and Comment in this chapter.)

However, what is reproduced in schools may itself be subject to re-contextualizing principles arising out of the specific context of a given school and the effectiveness of external control on the reproduction of pedagogic discourse. Further, what is reproduced may itself be affected by the power relations of the re-contextualizing field between the school and the primary cultural context of the acquirer (family/community/peer relations). The school may include as part of its practice re-contextualized discourses from the family/community/peer relations of the acquirer for purposes of social control in order to make more effective its own regulative discourse. Conversely, the family/community/peer relations can exert their own influence upon the re-contextualizing field of the school and in this way affect the latter's practice.

We have not drawn attention, in our model, to the differential and invidious positioning of acquirers with respect to the distribution of pedagogic capital, moral significance, and respect. This is not our intention in this chapter. The model allows for considerable internal dynamics in the production, distribution, reproduction, and change of pedagogic discourse.

1. Dominating principles themselves refer to an arena of conflict rather than to a stable set of relations.

2. There is a potential/actual source of conflict, resistance, and inertia between the political and the administrative agents of the ORF.

3. There is a potential/actual source of conflict, resistance, and inertia between the positions within the PRF and between the PRF and the ORF.

4. There is a potential/actual source of conflict, resistance, and inertia between the primary cultural context of the acquirer (family/community/peer relations) and the re-contextualizing principles and practices of the school.

5. Transmitters may find themselves unable or unwilling to reproduce the expected code of transmission.

It becomes a matter of considerable interest to know where, when, and why the circulation of principles and practices realized in pedagogic discourse is innovated from below or imposed from above.

From this brief description of the levels of the model and their interrelation, it is possible to see the complex relations between power, pedagogic discourse of reproduction, and the distribution of forms of consciousness. Because every discourse is a re-contextualized discourse, every discourse and its subsequent texts is ideologically re-positioned in its transformation from the original field of its production or existence to the field of its reproduction. The model attempts to explicate, at least formally, what it is to say that pedagogic discourse is a re-contextualized discourse. Finally, the model shows how complex is the process between the initial movement (circulation) of a discourse and the effect of that discourse upon the consciousness and specific positioning of an acquirer.

Comments on the Model

A distinguishing feature of the institutionalizing and realization of the European pedagogic device is the stability of the realizations of its distributive, re-contextualizing, and evaluative rules irrespective of the dominant principles of the society. The dominant modality of this pedagogic device entails a strong classification between education and production. We mean by a strong classification that there is a strong insulation between education and production which creates a specialized space for education to develop its own generative discourse and practice. Where there is a weak classification between education and production, there is low insulation between these categories, and both are more willing to share similar generative principles. An example of such a weakening of the classification occurred in China until 1976 for a limited period and with limited effects. The origin of the strong classification between education and production can be traced to the Medieval period, where we find that the official pedagogic device excluded manual practice from its re-contextualizing rules. Manual practice was acquired through local pedagogic devices within the family and guild. Thus mental and manual practices were historically strongly classified, and this has left its mark on the European pedagogic device. This means that the consciousness of agents of symbolic control is more likely to be positioned by the modality of education than by the mode of production, and this has many implications which cannot be pursued here (see Bernstein 1977, chap. 8).

So far we can see that the modal European pedagogic device produced a strong classification between mental and manual practice. Its re-contextualizing rules positioned its discourse in highly abstract knowledge and its pedagogic practice (evaluation rules) in an intense subjective experience. Concentration of pupils/students/teachers in one agency facilitates moral intensity and the disciplining of feeling/belief, while the abstract orientation facilitated the re-contextualizing of Greek thought. It is perhaps understandable why manual practice was excluded from the re-contextualizing rules. Further, we can note that the distributive rules of the modal European pedagogic device produced within pedagogic discourse the equivalence of the manual/mental dislocation and a strong classification between those who produce the discourse (by legitimate criticism and discovery, generate new principles, forms, and techniques) and those who reproduce the discourse. Only at the university or its equivalent is this classification weakened, but even here there is a tendency to separate producing and reproducing functions institutionally and to reward them differently. We have, then, a second dislocation generated by the distributive rules of the pedagogic device between producers and reproducers of knowledge. It is because of this dislocation that specialized re-contextualizing fields, with specialized positions, agents, practices, and texts, with their own principles of orthodox/heterodox and conditions of entry, have developed. These fields are not necessarily parasitic on the fields of production of intellectual discourse or manual/expressive practice. The activation of texts, re-located according to dominant positions in the re-contextualizing field, their transformation within this field into pedagogic texts or principles, their dissemination through pedagogic practice, may well have important repercussions on the position of the re-contextualized text in its field of origin (e.g., Piaget, Freud).

It is important to distinguish societies in terms of the relative autonomy of PRFs other than the official field. Where there is only one field (the ORF), it is likely that pedagogic agencies of the state will control the publication of manuals, textbooks, etc. In this case, changes in political discourse of the state will be marked by changes in the dominance of positions within the ORF. Where PRFs exist, are effective, and possess relative autonomy, it is possible for activities within this field to re-contextualize texts which, in their own right, may be considered illegitimate, oppositional, and originating in counterhegemonic sites (Holland 1985) of the production of discourse. Such texts are likely to be defused, re-focused in their re-contextualizing, and thus made safe (e.g., Freire).

It is important to point out that the model describes re-contextualizing fields within the official educational system. Here the field of production of discourse refers to the development of discourse arising out of the research and critical functions of the university, special institutes, and polytechnics. This is not to say that such productions do not occur in any other contexts of the educational system, only that the agencies mentioned specialize, as part of their functions, in the production, rather than the reproduction, of discourse. The theories and practices of this field are selectively re-contextualized not only in levels of the educational system, but also in the fields of production and symbolic control. Education as a crucial agency of symbolic control may be distinguished from all other agencies in the field as a condition for their practice.

In the case of contemporary societies, legitimate productions of discourse, together with discourses of opposition and challenge, will arise outside of the

Figure 8.4 Relations of Official Pedagogic Discourse and Elaborated Codes

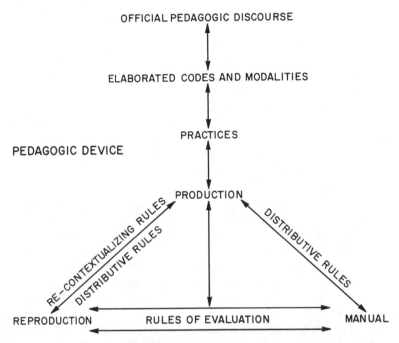

context of the educational system although many of these will be influenced directly or indirectly by official pedagogic discourse. Our model of the pedagogic device applies only to the reproduction of discourse.[13] The model for the description of the principles underlying the realization of the device can be developed to take into account relations with the realizations of pedagogic devices external to the official educational system.

We have here commented upon some basic dislocations produced by the modal European pedagogic device irrespective of the dominant principles of the society.[14] These dislocations may be expressed as follows:

Physical Resources			*Discursive Resources*		
Manual	:	Mental	Production	:	Reproduction

We can present a more general model on the basis of our previous argument (figure 8.4).

This general model describes the sets of relations created by official elaborated codes and their modalities. These codes are, in the first place, reproduced through official pedagogic discourse which presupposes:

1. *Distributive rules* which specialize the *production* of educational discourse to a particular field/context with its own agents, positions, practice, and evaluations; the

reproductions of pedagogic discourse to a different field/context; and *manual* discourse to its own field/contexts.

2. *Re-contextualizing rules* regulate the transformation of discourses within the field of the production of discourse into the fields of its reproduction and exclude manual discourse from representing dominating modalities.

3. *Evaluation rules* of the dominating pedagogic practice then differentially evaluate discourses generated by manual practices together with the effectors of such practices and the social groups these presuppose.

4. The realizations of such a device will maintain and reproduce a power, knowledge, consciousness, distribution, irrespective of the dominant principles of a given society celebrating capitalist, collectivist, or dictatorship ideologies (see Definitions, External Relations of Education).

We are suggesting that the above interrelations represent the ordering principles (internal grammar) of the realizations of the European modal pedagogic device as institutionalized through state-controlled educational systems and that this internal grammar is common to societies with different dominating principles (capitalist societies, dictatorships, or collectivist societies of the communist form). This internal grammar, essentially based upon strong classifications, is not an inevitable realization of the inner logic of the pedagogic device, but is a dominating modality of its historical and contemporary realization and produces fundamental similarities between educational systems in ideologically differently focused societies and, within broad limits, similar outcomes.

It could be argued against this view that we are now witnessing in countries with severe problems of unemployment (such as the U.K.) a tightening of the relation between pedagogic discourse of the school and the alleged requirements of work. The Manpower Services Commission in the U.K. has had a direct effect upon the skill training of unemployed youth and upon the curricula of secondary schools. It is ironic that when there is no work, the schools are preoccupied with skill training. However, this is more likely to be a pedagogizing of lower skills for the purpose of pedagogic and social discipline than a basis for careers and jobs. In terms of our model, this and similar movements (in France the recent suggestion that schools should be linked to industrial enterprise) do not affect the classificatory relation between education and production, only the systemic relation. The systemic relation refers to the relationships between the output of schools in terms of skills/dispositions of various kinds and the supposed requirements of work.

It becomes essential to distinguish the classificatory from the systemic relations of education. Strengthening or weakening of the systemic relations are movements independent of changes in the classificatory values. Thus strong classification can realize apparently opposing modalities of pedagogic types (the cultivated, the vocational, leisured, professional). However, a weak classification between education and production is likely to lead to a simple, rather than a complex, division of labor expressed through a lowering of the insulation between mental and manual categories and practices. Such a change in classification may well produce a qualitative change in the modality of the realizations of the pedagogic device but a massive extension of its penetration (Bernstein 1977, p. 188).

GENERAL CONCLUSIONS

We have attempted in outline form, the possible beginnings for an analysis of the internal grammar of pedagogic discourse and for the analysis of the principles governing its realization, when these are institutionalized as official pedagogic discourse and pedagogic practice. The internal grammar provides for the hierarchical ordering of distributive, re-contextualizing, and evaluative rules which produce an embedded discourse of the form ID/RD, which at the level of pedagogic practice controls discourse, transmission/acquisition, and organizational practices. We argued that the link between power, knowledge, and consciousness is established by the pedagogic device, which is a symbolic ruler for the positioning of consciousness, the specializing of the subject, and is thus the precondition for the productions and reproductions of culture. We regard the pedagogic device as providing the internal grammar of symbolic control or, from a more traditional perspective, of socialization.

Although this chapter has been essentially concerned with the official pedagogic device, and thus always with the control over elaborated orientations/codes and their modalities, the question arises whether the model is applicable to nonofficial pedagogic discourse. At this time, it is difficult to provide an answer, as the model has not been subject to such explorations. However, it is expected to hold for all elaborated code discourse and wherever that is presupposed. If it is the case that the internal grammar applies to all such discourse, then the question arises of the relations between this grammar and its realizations.

The pedagogic device is essentially a device for translating power relations into discourses of symbolic control and for translating discourses of symbolic control into power relations. Inasmuch as the pedagogic device translates power relations into discourses of symbolic control, then the power relations within the discourse regulate, or attempt to regulate, the "yet to be thought," which is a potential of the discourse realized by the device itself. There is here a contradiction within the device. It itself is a possibility only because language carries the possibility of the orders of meaning the device is distributing. The device is attempting to regulate the possibilities of the possible. This would require a site outside of language for the generation of such regulation. There is no such site. From a purely formal perspective, the pedagogic device cannot but be an instrument of order and of transformation of that order. From a substantive perspective, the hierarchy of rules internal to the device—distributive, re-contextualizing, evaluative—translates at the levels of their realization into tensions, oppositions, and contradictions between social groups who have been specialized and positioned by the device.

The symbolic control made possible by the pedagogic device cannot be computerized as such control, for it issues always as a discourse to be transmitted and acquired, creating a language whose rules are tacitly acquired, enabling speakers to create and recognize the legitimate potential of orthodox and heterodox texts without apparent explicit external regulations. Although the regulation on the exploitation of physical resources will become increasingly subject to information control chains with built-in, self-correcting feedback loops, the regulation on discursive resources cannot be so organized. Inasmuch as it is not possible to specialize a given biology to a given discursive range there can be only discursive control on discourse itself. And we have seen, contradictions lie at the heart of such control. However, we might hypothesize that the more abstract the technological principles for the exploitation of physical resources, the simpler the social division of labor but the more complex the social division of labor of symbolic control. There are, it seems, always possibilities for priests, if not for prophets. The pedagogic device may then become the crucial focus of struggle.

If we now turn to the model for analyzing the realizations of the pedagogic device, we would wish to draw attention to the stability of these realizations between societies with very different ideological principles. Indeed, what is striking is the degree of homogeneity of educational systems rather than their divergences. We have argued that the crucial difference between such societies is the degree of relative autonomy of PRFs from the state. However, often where there is relative autonomy, private foundations within the PRF play an interface role between the official re-contextualizing field and the PRF. In this chapter, we have given the concept of relative autonomy an important position with respect to the distributive rules of the pedagogic device, as these differently specialize producers of discourse and reproducers of pedagogic discourse and so create the re-contextualizing field.

We have used the concept of relative autonomy to examine the relations between education and production (work) in terms of their classificatory relation, which, we have argued, arose out of the exclusion of manual practice from the re-contextualizing field, which produced medieval pedagogic discourse. Originally, the exclusion of manual discourse/practice from official pedagogic discourse/practice was an exclusion within the category "thinkable." In this sense, we have a distributive rule within the category "thinkable" which excludes a thinkable practice (a practice within the legitimate space of the thinkable) arising out of manual practice. Over the centuries, this has lead to the different specializations of education and its generative principles, giving to educational discourse its abstract orientation and to its context, sites of intense moral regulation, and establishing the connection between education and political centralization. Education thus condenses in itself the political, the moral, and the abstract. None of this denies the development of strong systemic relations between education and work, but even here we have argued, as with others, that this does not entail a correspondence principle between education and work.

Indeed, our view here has been that pedagogic discourse as a re-contextualizing discourse transforms discourses in their movement into imaginary discourses. The strong classification between producers or effectors of discourse and reproducers of pedagogic discourse and between education and work may well produce structural similarities between societies with different ideological principles, both in the form of their educational systems and in the class-reproducing functions of these systems. From this point of view, changing the social basis of the mode of production does not necessarily lead to changes in the modality of education, that is, changes in the realizations of the pedagogic device.

CONCLUSION

We have proposed that a pedagogic device can be considered as a set of hierarchical rules—distributive, re-contextualizing, and evaluative (transmission)—which constitute its internal grammar. We consider that the realization of these rules with respect to any pedagogic practice can be described in terms of classification and framing values, which establish the pedagogic codes and their modalities. The pedagogic device establishes the transformation of power (that is, its basis in social relations and their generating sites) into differently specialized consciousness (subjects) through the device's regulation of "knowledges" and of the discourses such knowledges presuppose. In this sense, the pedagogic device is the condition for culture, its productions, reproductions, and modalities of their interrelations. We believe (but this is clearly subject to further exploration) that the internal orderings proposed are common to all pedagogic devices.

In this chapter, we have restricted our analysis to the realizations of the official pedagogic device and to the power and control relations which are realized, legitimated, and maintained by the device. To this end, we constructed a model for generating a description of the processes involved in state-regulated realizations of the device, i.e., pedagogic discourse and pedagogic practice. We argued that, despite differences, there were fundamental similarities and stabilities created by the realizations of the official European pedagogic device.

We are not able, within the limits of this chapter, to do more than create formal definitions and derived relations with respect to the crucial rules of pedagogic practice (transmission/acquisition and their contexts), but we indicate in the references where more detailed and substantive analyses may be found.

Finally, it has been argued:

1. that the pedagogic device at one and the same time constitutes a symbolic ruler and is the means of its transformation, and
2. that the realizations of the device carry the contradictions, cleavages, and dilemmas generated by the power relations positioning the realizations.

Change, then, is a consequence of the inner potential of the device and the arena of conflict which is the social base of its realizations.

NOTE A: PRIMARY, RE-CONTEXTUALIZING, AND SECONDARY CONTEXTS

We shall here make more explicit the importance of the re-contextualizing field and of its agents in the selective movement of texts from the intellectual field created by the educational system to that system's field of reproduction.

Primary Context: Production of Discourse. We shall distinguish three crucial interdependent contexts of educational discourse, practice, and organization. The first of these we shall call the *primary* context. The process whereby a text is developed and positioned in this context we shall call *primary contextualization.* The latter refers to the process whereby new ideas are selectively created, modified, and changed. This context creates, appropriating Bourdieu, the "intellectual field" of the educational system. This field and its history are created by the positions, relations, and practices arising out of the production, rather than the reproduction of educational discourse and its practices. Its texts today are dependent partly, *but by no means wholly*, on the circulation of private and state public funds to research groups and individuals (see Bourdieu 1980).

Secondary Context: Reproduction of Discourse. This context, its various levels, agencies, positions, and practices, refers to the selective *reproduction* of educational discourse. We shall distinguish four levels: tertiary, secondary, primary, and preschool. Within each level there may be some degree of specialization of agencies. We shall call these levels and their interrelations, together with any specialization of agencies within a level, the *secondary context of the production of discourse.* This context structure is the *field of reproduction.* We can ask here questions referring to the classificatory and framing principles regulating the relations between and within levels and regulating the circulation and location of codes and their modalities (Bernstein 1977, pp. 30–32).

Re-contextualizing Context: Re-location of Discourse. From these two fundamental contexts and the fields they structure, we shall distinguish a third context which structures a field or subset of fields, whose positions, agents, and practices are concerned with the movements of texts/practices from the primary context of discursive production to the secondary context of discursive reproduction. The function of the position, agents, and practices within this field and its subsets is to regulate the circulation of texts between the primary and secondary contexts. Accordingly, we shall call the field and the subset structured by this context the *re-contextualizing field.*

The *re-contextualizing context* will entail a number of fields:

1. It will include specialized departments and subagencies (school council) of the state and local educational authorities, together with their research and system of inspectors (ORF).

2. It will include university and polytechnic departments of education, colleges of education, together with their research and private foundations.

3. It will include specialized media of education, weeklies, journals, etc., and publishing houses, together with their leaders and advisers.

4. It may extend to fields not specialized in educational discourse and its practices, but which are able to exert influence both on the state and its various arrangements and/ or upon special sites, agents, and practices within education.

When a text is appropriated by re-contextualizing agents, operating in positions of this field, the text usually undergoes a transformation prior to its relocation. The form of this transformation is regulated by a *principle of de-contextualizing*. This process refers to the change in the text as it is first *de-located* and then *re-located*. This process ensures that the text is no longer the same text:

1. The text has changed its position in relation to other texts, practices, and positions.

2. The text itself has been modified by selection, simplification, condensation, and elaboration.

3. The text has been re-positioned and re-focused.

The de-contextualizing principle regulates the new ideological positioning of the text in its process of re-location in one or more of the levels of the field of reproduction. Once in that field, the text undergoes a further transformation or re-positioning as it becomes active in the pedagogic process within a level. It is crucial to distinguish between and to analyze the relations between the two transformations (at least) of a text. The first is the transformation of the text within the *re-contextualizing field*, and the second is the transformation of the *transformed* text in the pedagogic process as it becomes active in the process of the reproduction of acquirers. It is the re-contextualizing field which generates the positions of pedagogic theory, research, and practice. It is a matter of some importance to analyze the role of departments of the state in the relations and movements within and between the various contexts and their structuring fields.

To be complete, we should state that the major activities of re-contextualizing fields is creating, maintaining, changing, and legitimating the discourse, transmission, and organizational practices which regulate the internal orderings of pedagogic discourse.

NOTE B: THE CONCEPTS OF INSTRUCTIONAL AND REGULATIVE DISCOURSE

The distinction between instructional discourse and regulative discourse clearly has its origin in Parson's distinction between instrumental and expressive. Parsons states: ''Indeed it is in relation to the differentiation of the relational contexts, both of instrumental and of expressive activities, that the most fundamental regulative problems of the social system arise and that regulative institutions are primarily focused'' (1951, p. 79). For Parsons, instrumentalities have their origin in economic theory, particularly Adam Smith's ''division of labor'': ''The starting point is the conception of a given actor's ego as instrumentally oriented to the attainment of a goal, a goal which may be of any desired specificity or generality" (p. 70). Expressive activities, on the other hand, are fundamental to instrumental and are organized "in terms of a cultural pattern of value orientations" (p. 75). Expressive activities are concerned with relations to ordering principles, to solidarity with and loyality and commitment to these principles (see also Dreeben 1968). In "The School Class as a Social System: Some of Its Functions in American Society" (Parsons 1959), although not explicitly using concepts of instrumental and expressive activities, Parsons distinguishes between two axes: an axis of integration of the level of collective values (expressive) and an axis of achievement (instrumental). In *Family: Socialization and Interaction Process* (Parsons et al. 1955), Parsons distinguishes between instrumental and expressive roles and indicates that these may well be specialized to gender. The instrumental roles regulate (mediate) practices between systems (male), and the expressive roles regulate values of orientation internal to a system (female). I am not concerned here with the usefulness or otherwise of these distinctions, but only to show their relation. I first used these terms in the paper "Sources of Consensus and Disaffection in Education" (Bernstein 1977, ch. 1), where I distinguished, not between roles or activities, but between instrumental and expressive cultures (later, orders) within the school. The former is concerned with "facts, procedures and judgements involved in the acquisition of specific skills," and the latter is concerned with standards of "conduct, character and manner." The tensions and conflicts between these "cultures/orders" are further analyzed in "Ritual in Education" (Bernstein 1977, ch. 2). In the more specific sociolinguistic work, I distinguished between four generalized contexts of socialization, of which two major contexts are *regulative*, concerned with "authority relationships where the child is made aware of the rules of the moral order and their various backings," and the *instrumental context*, where "the child learns about the objective nature of objects, persons, and acquirers' skills of various kinds" (1975, p. 181). However, it is only in Pedro (1981), who took over the model, where *instructional discourse* is defined in terms of "the principles of the specific discourse to be transmitted and acquired" and *regulative discourse* as "the principles whereby the social relations of transmission and acquisition are constituted, maintained, reproduced and legitimated" (p. 207). Thus instructional discourse is concerned with the transmission/acquisition of specific competencies, and regulative discourse is concerned with the transmission of principles of order, relation, and identity.

However, behind these distinctions can be found concepts of mechanical and organic solidarity as developed in Durkheim, where mechanical solidarity is concerned with the principles of *similar to*, and organic solidarity refers to the principles of *different from*.

In Durkheim's analysis of the evolution of pedagogy in France (1938/1977), we interpret the *Trivium* (logic, grammar, and rhetoric) as constituting the discursive principles of mechanical solidarity subject to shifts of internal emphasis and conflicts arising out of the developing bourgeoisie; and the *Quadrivium* in its specialized, separated discourses, astronomy, arithmetic, geometry, and music, pointing to the development of, the historically much later, organic solidarity. Whereas in *Moral Education* (1925/1961), a set of lectures for schoolteachers, Durkheim is concerned essentially with the regulative discourse of the school, in *The Evolution of Educational Thought*, a set of lectures for aggregation candidates, he analyzes the history and development between disciplines, practices, and moralities of education and their external regulations. Durkheim concerned himself, in these lectures, with two fundamental questions: how the institution of the school came to be formed, and how these schools came to be differentiated from the church. However, the context Durkheim created for himself to answer these questions was nothing less than an institutional history of the form and content of education.

Alexander (1982, p. 285) considers that "although Durkheim devoted a great deal of time to the discussion of the relative value of different educational ideas *per se*, his sociological analysis of the evolution of the educational content is less systematic than his history of educational structure" (p. 285). Although we can trace the conceptualizing of pedagogic discourse back to Durkheim, it is equally as important to point out that we are concerned to show the interrelations between dominant power relations and principles of control in the constitution, transmission, and evaluation of pedagogic discourse.

DEFINITIONS AND COMMENT

Field: We are using this concept in Bourdieu and Boltanski's sense:

A system of differentiated positions which are united by objective relations of complementarity, competition and/or conflict and which can be occupied by relatively interchangeable agents who, in the strategies which put them in opposition to those who hold different positions, are obliged to take account of the objective relations between the positions. (Bourdieu and Boltanski 1978, p. 203; see also Cox 1984, p. 36, and Bourdieu 1980, p. 136).

Field of Production: We are using this to refer to the production of goods and services, distribution and the circulation of capital. It is a shorthand for the economic field.

Symbolic Control: Rules, practices, and agencies regulating the legitimate creation, distribution, reproduction, and change of consciousness by symbolic means (principles of communication) through which a given distribution of power and dominating cultural categories are legitimated and maintained.

Field of Symbolic Control: The whole field of symbolic control in modern societies presupposes a complex of agencies, agents, discourses, and practices, all of which, in the last instance, are subject to the dominant principles as these are inscribed in law. However, some agencies, agents, discourses, and practices are more directly and explicitly subjected to the state than are others. Which agencies, agents, discourses, and practices are so subjected depends upon the dominant principles which define both their degrees of dependence upon the state and the location, conditions, and degree of their autonomy.

Education today is a crucial device available to the state for the systematic production, reproduction, distribution, and change of forms of consciousness through discourse. At the same time, the discourses of education often give access to dominant positions in the various agencies of symbolic control, and the theories produced in the context of the production of discourse of the educational system are re-contextualized in the fields of symbolic control/production, and selectively within its own pedagogic context of reproduction. I must point out that I have said only that education is a crucial device for the state whereby its dominant principles may be translated into micro practices at the level of the school either as limits on these practices or as definitions of these practices. However, what is selected is not necessarily transmitted, what is transmitted is not necessarily acquired and what is acquired may, for some acquirers, bear little or no relation, or indeed an oppositional relation, to the intentions of selectors and transmitters.

Agencies in the field of symbolic control regulate specialized discourses of communication; that is, they operate what can be called dominating discursive codes, specializing in the positioning of social relations, consciousness, and dispositions. These agencies may be either public or private and, if public, directly or indirectly regulated by the state. In most contemporary societies, we have seen a gradual extension of state control, directly or indirectly, over the field of symbolic control. There are, of course, agencies in the field of production which have symbolic control functions, e.g., cosmetic houses, but these agencies' position is in the field of production, and they are therefore subject to its structures of power. (Agencies within the field of symbolic control of special significance to our model are discussed in Bernstein 1981.)

Agents of Symbolic Control: These are agents who dominate the decisions with respect to the meanings, contexts, and possibilities of discursive resources, specializing in forms of communication which can be applied to principles of discourse themselves and/or to social relations, practices, and dispositions. These agents can function in one of the specialized agencies of the field of symbolic control or in the field of production. If agents function in the economic field, then their communication principles have a relatively direct relation to an economic base, and it is expected that such agents will be ideologically positioned by such a base. If agents function in the field of symbolic control, then their principles of communication will have a direct relation to that field, and such agents are likely to be ideologically positioned by and through its specialized contexts. Inasmuch as all agents of symbolic control acquire their specialized discourses through the higher levels of the educational system, the classificatory relation between education and production is a significant regulator of their consciousness, and this (the classificatory relation) is of greater significance for agents within the field of symbolic control.

It is useful here to spell out this argument, schematically presented in figure 8.5. (For empirical application and conceptual development, see Holland 1985.)

While the distinction between the fields of production and symbolic control is maintained, as indicated, there is overlap between the fields in terms of both institutions and agents. Agents of symbolic control can be located in the field of production; functions, agencies, and agents of the state can occur in all fields.

Public: It is clear that symbolic control regulated and distributed by the state which issues either as "service" or a "text" is produced by an agency/agents positioned in the field of symbolic control (see figure 8.6).

Private: It is this category which produces ambiguity. Under "service", we group essentially professional practices which are available only on hire. The agents hire their particular specialization as a practice and function as an individual or group enterprise for profit or personal gain. In this sense they are linked to the field of production. The area of crucial ambiguity lies in the category "text marketed" of the Private sector. Here we have agencies/agents of symbolic control functioning in, and directly regulated by, the market conditions of the field of production. On internal inspection of these agencies we are likely to find an internal division of labor and of power between individual/groups who are directly concerned with and gain from market conditions, and those who are directly concerned with the creation of the text to be marketed. These groups/individuals are likely to be in a position of potential if not actual conflict arising out of their structurally different interests. Examples are producer/director, actors in films; theater manager/producer, actors; publishers, editors, journalists; gallery owners, artists, employers, architects; fashion houses, designer. From our point of view we would include Private, Service in the field of symbolic control as specialized agencies/agencies, but not Private, Text as these agencies are more directly related to the market regulation of the field of production.

Agents, Agencies, Fields: When we consider *all* agents of symbolic control, we would expect to find *whatever their field location*, a potential conflict with their employers who hold the power and define the expected practice, whether the employer is a state or private agency.[15] Agencies of symbolic control are the products of an educational system in which discursive resources (resources which are intrinsic to the production of principles of communication directly related to the regulation of social relations, practices, dispositions), have been historically separated from the field of production and its social division of labor. As a consequence, these agents have inherited and have been able to reproduce a monopoly upon a space of *relative autonomy* giving these agents a "higher morality", "truth", "objectivity", "neutrality", "intrinsic dedication", beyond the local economic or political arena. However, the agencies of power whom these agents serve can foreclose on such relative autonomy.

Whereas on this argument all agents of symbolic control are indirectly related

Figure 8.5 Agents of Symbolic Control

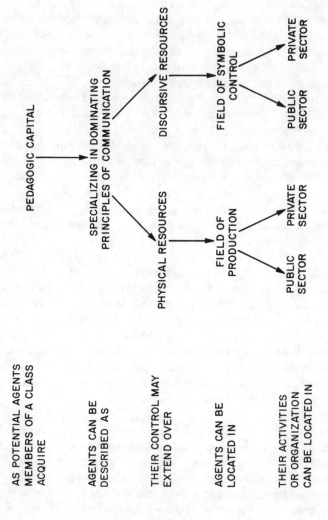

AS POTENTIAL AGENTS
MEMBERS OF A CLASS
ACQUIRE
> PEDAGOGIC CAPITAL

AGENTS CAN BE
DESCRIBED AS
> SPECIALIZING IN DOMINATING
PRINCIPLES OF COMMUNICATION

THEIR CONTROL MAY
EXTEND OVER
> PHYSICAL RESOURCES   DISCURSIVE RESOURCES

AGENTS CAN BE
LOCATED IN
> FIELD OF PRODUCTION   FIELD OF SYMBOLIC CONTROL

THEIR ACTIVITIES
OR ORGANIZATION
CAN BE LOCATED IN
> PUBLIC SECTOR   PRIVATE SECTOR   PUBLIC SECTOR   PRIVATE SECTOR

Figure 8.6 Agencies of Symbolic Control

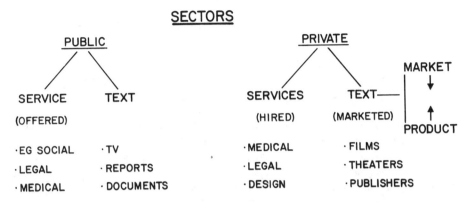

to the field of production by their *pedagogic socialization*, where they are *located* may well affect their interests and ideology. Those in the public sector may well have interests in its maintenance and expansion whereas those in the private sector may wish to see the public sector restricted.

External Relations of Education

Systemic Relations: The educational system is considered to have two qualitatively different types of external regulations, which regulate in different ways and in different degrees its internal relations. These are the relations between the educational system and the production and reproduction of resources; physical and discursive.

Physical Resources: The educational system can have an output which can serve as a potential or actual resource for agencies of production, distribution, and circulation of capital with respect to their social and technical division of labor and their social relations.

Discursive Resources: The educational system always has an output which serves as a potential or actual resource for the agencies of symbolic control, their social division of labor and social relations. Such an output is defined as a discursive resource.

It may well be that the systemic relations of education with respect to discursive resources predate the systemic relations with respect to physical resources, are relatively tighter, and, in the future, will be more enduring, complex, and state regulated.

This distinction between physical and discursive resources must be seen as a *low-level description*, for it is always the case that there can be no physical resource without a prior discursive resource.

Classificatory Relation: This refers to the relations between education and production viewed as categories of function. If the relation between these two categories is strongly classified, then there is strong insulation between the

Figure 8.7 Relevant Meanings and Forms of Their Realization

MICRO   **MACRO**

INTER-ACTIONAL   INSTITUTIONAL (SCHOOLS)

MEANINGS ⟶ DISCURSIVE PRACTICES

REALIZATION ⟶ TRANSMISSION PRACTICES

CONTEXTS ⟶ ORGANIZATIONAL PRACTICES

categories, which creates a space in which each category can differently specialize its generative principles and practices. If there is weak classification between the category, education, and the category production, then there is low insulation between the categories, and both will share a common generative principle and practice. In other words, in the case of weak classification, there is an integration of generative principles, whereas in the case of strong classification, the principles are kept apart and are differently specialized (Bernstein 1977, ch. 8).

The systemic and the classificatory relation can be said to provide the fundamental dual messages of the educational system. The systemic relation refers to interrelations with production, which is now usually the dominating category, whereas the classificatory relation refers to the relative autonomy of the generative principles and practices of education from production.

The systemic relation (if it is strong) translates at the level of the acquirer into motivation and aspiration. This does not mean to say that all acquirers accept their positioning within such a translation. The classificatory relation translates into the features of the dominating text to be acquired. Where there is strong classification between education and production, the dominating code of the school, whose values are likely to be $+C+F,^{i/e}$ (strong classification, strong framing, for both internal and external relations) will be both highly abstract and abstracted from relationships other than its own.

Code: General: Code is defined as a regulative principle, tacitly acquired, which selects and integrates relevant meanings, forms of their realization, and evoking contexts (see figure 8.7).

Specific Codes/Modalities: These are constituted by the specific classification and framing values where *classification* refers to the degree of insulation between categories of discourse, agents, practices, contexts and provides recognition rules for both transmitters and acquirers for the degree of specialization of their texts. *Framing* refers to the controls on the selection, sequencing, pacing, and criterial rules of the pedagogic communicative relationship between transmitter/acquirer(s) and provides the realization rules for the production of their tests.

$$\frac{O}{(\pm)C \qquad F(\pm)^{i/e}}$$
$$C$$

where:

O   refers to orientation to meanings elaborated/restricted (privileged/
              privileging referential relations)
C   refers to the principle of classification
F   refers to the principle of framing
(±)   refers to the values of C and F with respect to strength (strong/weak)
i/e ^{i} refers to *internal* values of F *within* a communicative context (e.g.,
              family, school, and work)
              ^{e} refers to the *external* values of F, that is, the regulation on com-
              municative relations *between* communicative contexts (e.g., family/
              community and school; school and work)
─────   signals that what is above the line is embedded in what is below
C   is the fundamental C and refers to the basic classification, the basic
              principle of exclusion, insulation of the analysis. C could refer to
              the dominant principles of the society in terms of its class relations
              and period, e.g., entrepreneurial capitalism, corporate capitalism.
              Weakening of the C here would refer to dominant principles, where
              attempts were being made or had been made to change class relations.
              In other analyses, the C could refer to the strength of the classification
              between education and production, which we consider to be the
              fundamental classificatory relation of education.

Official Pedagogic Discourse/Practice/Organization: Official rules regulating
the production, distribution, reproduction, interrelation, and change of legitimate
pedagogic texts; their social relations of transmission and acquisition (practice);
and the organization of their contexts (organization).

Official pedagogic discourse is an embedded discourse and is the realization
of the interrelations between two differently specialized discourses: instructional
discourse and regulative discourse.

Specific Instructional Discourse (SID): Regulates the rules which constitute
the legitimate variety, internal and relational features of specialized competencies.

Specific Regulative Discourse (SRD): The rules which regulate what counts
as legitimate order between and within transmitters, acquirers, competencies,
contexts. At the most abstract level, SRD provides and legitimates the official
rules regulating order, relation, and identity.

Pedagogic Text: A text produced/reproduced and evaluated in or through but
always for the social relations of transmission/acquisition.

Text: A text is a distinctive realization of pedagogic discourse and is a specific
selection, integration, and contextualizing of "pedagogomes."

Pedagomeme: A pedagomeme is the smallest distinctive unit of behavior or
disposition which can be a candidate for evaluation.

We can distinguish between OPD (official pedagogic discourse/practice) and LPD (local pedagogic discourse/practice). The latter regulates the process of cultural reproduction at the level of the primary contextualizing of culture essentially in the family and peer group relations. There may well be oppositions, resistances, or correspondences and support, dependencies, and independencies in the positioning relations between OPD/P and LPD/P. The basic model I have proposed can apply to local pedagogic discourse/practice, although it is likely here that principles will be embedded in tacit practice.

NOTES

1. Theories of cultural reproduction have to deal with a range of issues, and it is rare, if ever, that all the issues are satisfactorily resolved. To begin with, the term *reproduction* is itself a metaphor taken from biology. Whereas in biology there is now an excellent model of the ordering device regulating the process of reproduction (the message structure and its principles) and variation and change with respect to the physical properties of the individual and with respect to some of their psychological correlates, in sociology such a generating device is itself considered to be an inappropriate formulation. The reproductive device for cultural subjects, it is argued, is not a determining device, but it is a device the principles of which can be themselves subject to change. Thus the device can both reproduce and, under certain conditions, subvert its own order. This opens up the whole issue between agency and agent on the one hand and on the other, the relative autonomy of the cultural level in the sense of the indeterminacy of its outcomes. Further, any theory of cultural reproduction must have strong recognition rules for distinguishing similarity, variability, and change. It is in this respect that such theories have real problems. As all these theories, to a greater or less extent, operate within a Marxist discourse, everything, outside of a radical change of class structure, becomes either epiphenomenal or a modality of the existing class principles; but the conditions of change of class structure or change in *doxa* (Bourdieu 1980, p. 136) is itself conceptualized inadequately. Indeed, there is no necessary reason for believing that changing the principles of the mode of production necessarily changes the principle of the modality of cultural reproduction in education. A case can be made showing similarities rather than the differences between educational systems in social formations with radically opposed dominating ideologies. Finally, theories of cultural reproduction must be capable within the same conceptual language of generating descriptions at different logical levels, e.g., structure/interaction, micro/macro; they should also be able to show the principles of and relations between the production, reproduction, and acquisition of culture. In fact, no theory is able to cope, even at theoretical levels, with all the issues to which we have referred. Indeed, few theories are sufficiently clearly articulated to offer a strong empirical purchase on the relations specified by the theory. Finally, all such theories presuppose an analysis of the internal orderings of the pedagogic discourse which is the carrier of the messages of reproduction. An exception to this omission is the work of Lundgren and his team at the Department of Educational Research, University of Stockholm (Lundgren 1977).

2. A detailed account of the relations between the primary field/contexts of the production of discourse of the educational system, the re-contextualizing field/contexts, and the secondary context of reproduction (schools, etc.) is given in Bernstein and Diaz 1983. (See also Note A.)

On Pedagogic Discourse

237

3. I think this point requires further discussion. It is not meant that no elaborated coding occurs—indeed, this must be the case, given the presence of elaborated orientations—only that the exploration of principles, "productive, elaborating, self-reflexivity," is likely to issue from a specialized position in a particular context, as in the case of the trance-singer (see Biesele 1974). I am grateful to a personal communication from Dr. R. Hewitt, SRU, Department of the Sociology of Education, University of London Institute of Education, for both the reference and the discussion.

4. The concept "re-contextualizing rules" and the model of which it is a part were introduced in Bernstein (1975 and 1981).

5. A further example can be given of the re-contextualizing process, this time with reference to a manual practice. In secondary schools, there is often a large room in which wooden benches are arranged in rows. On display in racks or cupboards is an array of tools—saws, chisels, planes, hammers. What we have here is a transformation of a manual practice, carpentry into pedagogized woodwork. The original practice is abstracted from its own regulative discourse, and its specialized competence is transformed by the school's SID/SRD.

6. Theories of instruction, behavioral or biological (faculty or inherited), take as their reference what is to be evaluated, that is, the acquirer's graded performance of the pedagogic discourse, and presuppose expected differences between acquirers. The social unit of evaluation here is the individual acquirer and the graded relations between acquirers. On the other hand, there are theories of instruction which privilege, not the evaluation of the discourse and so transmission, but the universal, general processes *internal* to acquirers, what is shared. Such theories position the acquirer as active and creative in acquisition. These theories point to the interactional nature of the acquisition of competencies and so to a social unit of acquisition involving interactional relations between acquirers. Thus such theories (Piaget, Chomsky, Gestalt) focus upon the development of common competencies within acquirers rather than upon graded performances of the discourse to be acquired. These two groups of theories may well be translations of two possibilities of the potential output of the pedagogic device itself. In nonliterate societies with simple divisions of labor, pedagogic discourse may well be concerned to position acquirers in the reproduction of common, shared competencies (skills) rather than in differentially graded performances. I should point out that competencies here do not refer to internal ordering principles, as in Chomsky or Piaget, but to a variety of shared cultural skills. In such societies, it is unusual to read of any member failing an initiation test, however demanding the test.

7. The standard European pedagogic device appears to have as its dominant realization a graded individual performance, and this much before the onset of most state-regulated education and capitalistic modes of production. These realizations of the pedagogic device, graded individual performances, and shared competencies are today the site of pedagogic struggle between conservative and progressive positions within re-contextualizing fields.

8. I have added a level to the model "international field" which, although relevant to *all* societies, is often particularly crucial to the official pedagogic discourse of developing societies, insofar as dominant positions in the re-contextualizing fields of such societies are often specified by the terms of international funding agencies (Diaz 1983; Cox 1984; Domingos 1984).

9. The regulation of official pedagogic discourse depends upon the relative autonomy of pedagogic re-contextualizing fields and contexts other than the official field and context.

10. Public examinations taken at secondary levels of education, often including or

directly linked to the university, have a crucial influence upon the practices of pedagogic re-contextualizing fields with reference to the provision of textbooks and teaching routines. At the same time, the practices of the re-contextualizing field can influence the form and contexts of public examinations. It is not unusual for members of such boards to be drawn from the pedagogic re-contextualizing field, where they act as agents of different functions.

11. Publishing houses create what can be called an industry of texts which have a direct effect upon positions within the re-contextualizing field.

12. SIDs/SRD may well be strongly classified and so specialized to different social groups within a school, and such SIDs/SRD may well be arranged on a scale of differential worth. Indeed, it may well be that certain groups are positioned *only* within SRD, receiving moral regulation rather than instruction in specialized competencies.

13. If we consider the reproduction of manual skilled practices today, we can see a progressive de- and re-skilling, together with a reduction in the significance of apprenticeship as a specialized manual pedagogic device and practice. Within families, local pedagogic practices are, to different degrees, embedded in official pedagogic practices. However, we know little about the local pedagogic practices of youth cultural forms and about the pedagogic device the reproductions of these forms and their modalities presuppose.

14. The degree of the dislocation may vary. For example, in France, it is much less with respect to discursive resources, for until recently there was a circulation of staff between the *lycée* and the university. We know also that much of the development of science in England took place initially outside the university.

15. We have a situation of endemic conflict between those who create the service/text and those who have power over it. In the private sector under conditions we have referred to as "text marketed." This conflict is explicitly structural and represents conflict between agents drawn from different fields but working in the same agency. Those marketing the text (those who have power over it) are agents of the field of production regulated by their market situation, whereas those creating the text (those who only have control over the text) are agents of the field of symbolic control.

REFERENCES

Alexander, J. C. *Theoretical Logic in Sociology: The Antinomies of Classical Thought: Marx and Durkheim*. London: Routledge & Kegan Paul, 1982.
Apple, M. W., ed. *Cultural and Economic Reproduction in Education*. London: Routledge & Kegan Paul, 1982a.
———. "Curricular Form and the Logic of Technical Control." In *Cultural and Economic Reproduction in Education*, edited by M. W. Apple. London: Routledge & Kegan Paul, 1982b.
Atkinson, P. "Bernstein's Structuralism." *Educational Analysis* 3 (1981): 85–95.
———. *Language, Structure and Reproduction: The Sociology of Basil Bernstein*. London: Methuen, 1985.
Bernstein, B. "Critique of the Concept of Compensatory Education." In *Class, Codes and Control* vol. 1. London: Routledge & Kegan Paul, 1971.
———. Introduction to *Class, Codes and Control* vol. 1. London: Routledge & Kegan Paul, 1975.
———. *Class, Codes and Control* vol. 3. London: Routledge & Kegan Paul, 1977.
———. "Codes, Modalities and the Process of Reproduction: A Model." *Language and Society* 10 (1981): 327–63.

Bernstein, B., and M. Diaz. "Towards a Theory of Pedagogic Discourse." *CORE* 8 (1984): 1–210.

Biesele, Megan. "Folklore and Ritual of !Kung Hunter Gatherers: Song Texts of the Masters of Tricks." Ph.D. diss., Harvard University, 1974.

Bourdieu, P. *Questions de Sociologie.* Paris: Les Editions de Minuit, 1980.

Bourdieu, P., and L. Boltanski. "Changes in Social Structure and Changes in the Demand for Education." In *Contemporary Europe: Social Structures and Cultural Patterns,* edited by S. Giner and M. S. Archer. London: Routledge & Kegan Paul, 1978.

Bourdieu, P., and J. C. Passeron. *Reproduction in Education, Society and Culture.* Beverly Hills, CA: Sage Publications, 1977.

Cox, C. D. "Continuity, Conflict and Change in State Education in Chile: A Study of Pedagogic Projects of the Christian Democratic and Popular Unity Parties." Ph.D. diss., University of London, 1984.

Delamont, S. *Interaction in the Classroom.* London: Methuen, 1976.

Diaz, M. "A Model of Pedagogic Discourse with Special Application to the Columbian Primary Level." Ph.D. diss., University of London, 1983.

Domingos, Ana, M.R.M.D. "Social Class, Pedagogic Practice and Achievement in Science: A Study of Secondary Schools in Portugal." Ph.D. diss., University of London, 1984.

Dreeben, R. *On What Is Learned in School.* Reading, MA: Addison-Wesley, 1968.

Durkheim, E. *Moral Education: A Study in the Theory and Application of the Sociology of Education.* New York: The Free Press, 1961 (originally published in French in 1925).

———. *The Evolution of Educational Thought: Lectures on the Formation and Development of Secondary Education in France.* London: Routledge & Kegan Paul, 1977 (originally published in French in 1938).

Edwards, A. "Patterns of Power and Authority in Classroom Talk." In *Teacher Strategies,* edited by P. Woods. London: Croom Helm, 1980.

———. "The Sociology of Language and Education." In *The Social Sciences in Educational Studies,* edited by A. Harnett. London: Routledge & Kegan Paul, 1982.

Eggleston, J. *The Sociology of the School Curriculum.* London: Routledge & Kegan Paul, 1977.

Foucault, M. *The Archaeology of Knowledge.* London: Tavistock Publications, 1972 (originally published in French in 1969).

———. *Discipline and Punish: The Birth of the Prison.* Harmondsworth, Middlesex: Penguin Books, 1977 (originally published in French in 1975).

———. "The Subject and Power." In *Michel Foucault: Beyond Structuralism and Hermeneutics,* edited by H. L. Dreyfus and P. Rabinow. Brighton: Harvester Press, 1982.

Halsey, A. H., J. Floud, and C. A. Anderson. *Education, Economy and Society: A Reader in the Sociology of Education.* New York: Collier-MacMillan, 1961.

Harnett, A., ed. *The Social Sciences in Educational Studies.* London: Routledge & Kegan Paul, 1982.

Holland, J. "Gender and Class: Adolescent Conceptions of Aspects of the Division of Labor." Ph.D. diss., University of London, 1985.

Hymes, D., C. Cazden, and U. Johns, eds. *The Function of Language in the Classroom.* New York: Teachers College Press, 1971.

Johnson, R., et al. *Unpopular Education: Schooling and Social Democracy in England since 1944.* London: Hutchinson, 1981.

Karabel, J., and A. H. Halsey, eds. *Power and Ideology in Education.* New York: Oxford University Press, 1977.

Lundgren, U. P. *Modal Analysis of Pedagogic Processes.* Stockholm: Stockholm Institute of Education, Department of Educational Research, 1977.

Moore, R. "Education and Production: A Generative Model." Ph.D. diss., University of London, 1983.

Parsons, T. *The Social System.* London: Routledge & Kegan Paul, 1951.

————. "The School Class as a Social System: Some of Its Functions in American Society." *Harvard Educational Review* 29 (1959): 297–318.

Parsons, T. F., et al. *Family: Socialization and Interaction Process.* Glencoe, IL: The Free Press, 1955.

Pedro, E. *Social Stratification and Classroom Discourse: A Sociolinguistic Analysis of Classrooms.* Stockholm: Stockholm CWK, Gleerup, 1981.

Stubbs, M. "Teaching and Talking: A Sociolinguistic Approach to Classroom Interaction." In *Frontiers of Classsroom Research*, edited by G. Chanan and S. Delamont. Slough, England: National Foundation for Educational Research in England and Wales, 1975.

Stubbs, M., and S. Delamont, eds. *Explorations in Classroom Observation.* London: John Wiley & Sons, 1976.

Tyler, W. B. *The Sociology of the School: A Review.* Canterbury: Reprographic Services of the Teachers' Centre, 1982.

————. "Organisations, Factors and Codes: A Methodological Inquiry into Bernstein's Theory of Educational Transmissions." Ph.D. diss., University of Kent, 1984.

Waller, W. *The Sociology of Teaching.* New York: John Wiley & Sons, 1932.

Willis, Paul. *Learning to Labour.* Farnborough, England: Saxon House, 1977.

Young, M.F.D., ed. *Knowledge and Control: New Directions for the Sociology of Education.* London: Collier-MacMillan, 1971.

9

PIERRE BOURDIEU

The Forms of Capital

The social world is accumulated history, and if it is not to be reduced to a discontinuous series of instantaneous mechanical equilibria between agents who are treated as interchangeable particles, one must reintroduce into it the notion of capital and with it, accumulation and all its effects. Capital is accumulated labor (in its materialized form or its "incorporated," embodied form) which, when appropriated on a private, i.e., exclusive, basis by agents or groups of agents, enables them to appropriate social energy in the form of reified or living labor. It is a *vis insita*, a force inscribed in objective or subjective structures, but it is also a *lex insita*, the principle underlying the immanent regularities of the social world. It is what makes the games of society—not least, the economic game—something other than simple games of chance offering at every moment the possibility of a miracle. Roulette, which holds out the opportunity of winning a lot of money in a short space of time, and therefore of changing one's social status quasi-instantaneously, and in which the winning of the previous spin of the wheel can be staked and lost at every new spin, gives a fairly accurate image of this imaginary universe of perfect competition or perfect equality of opportunity, a world without inertia, without accumulation, without heredity or acquired properties, in which every moment is perfectly independent of the previous one, every soldier has a marshal's baton in his knapsack, and every prize can be attained, instantaneously, by everyone, so that at each moment anyone can become anything. Capital, which, in its objectified or embodied forms, takes time to accumulate and which, as a potential capacity to produce profits and to reproduce itself in identical or expanded form, contains a tendency to persist in its being, is a force inscribed in the objectivity of things so that everything is

Originally published as "*Ökonomisches Kapital, kulturelles Kapital, soziales Kapital*," in *Soziale Ungleichheiten* (Soziale Welt, Sonderheft 2), edited by Reinhard Kreckel. Goettingen: Otto Schartz & Co., 1983, pp. 183–98. The article appears here for the first time in English, translated by Richard Nice.

not equally possible or impossible.[1] And the structure of the distribution of the different types and subtypes of capital at a given moment in time represents the immanent structure of the social world, i.e., the set of constraints, inscribed in the very reality of that world, which govern its functioning in a durable way, determining the chances of success for practices.

It is in fact impossible to account for the structure and functioning of the social world unless one reintroduces capital in all its forms and not solely in the one form recognized by economic theory. Economic theory has allowed to be foisted upon it a definition of the economy of practices which is the historical invention of capitalism; and by reducing the universe of exchanges to mercantile exchange, which is objectively and subjectively oriented toward the maximization of profit, i.e., (economically) *self-interested*, it has implicitly defined the other forms of exchange as noneconomic, and therefore *disinterested*. In particular, it defines as disinterested those forms of exchange which ensure the *transubstantiation* whereby the most material types of capital—those which are economic in the restricted sense—can present themselves in the immaterial form of cultural capital or social capital and vice versa. Interest, in the restricted sense it is given in economic theory, cannot be produced without producing its negative counterpart, disinterestedness. The class of practices whose explicit purpose is to maximize monetary profit cannot be defined as such without producing the purposeless finality of cultural or artistic practices and their products; the world of bourgeois man, with his double-entry accounting, cannot be invented without producing the pure, perfect universe of the artist and the intellectual and the gratuitous activities of art-for-art's sake and pure theory. In other words, the constitution of a science of mercantile relationships which, inasmuch as it takes for granted the very foundations of the order it claims to analyze—private property, profit, wage labor, etc.—is not even a science of the field of economic production, has prevented the constitution of a general science of the economy of practices, which would treat mercantile exchange as a particular case of exchange in all its forms.

It is remarkable that the practices and assets thus salvaged from the "icy water of egotistical calculation" (and from science) are the virtual monopoly of the dominant class—as if economism had been able to reduce everything to economics only because the reduction on which that discipline is based protects from sacrilegious reduction everything which needs to be protected. If economics deals only with practices that have narrowly economic interest as their principle and only with goods that are directly and immediately convertible into money (which makes them quantifiable), then the universe of bourgeois production and exchange becomes an exception and can see itself and present itself as a realm of disinterestedness. As everyone knows, priceless things have their price, and the extreme difficulty of converting certain practices and certain objects into money is only due to the fact that this conversion is refused in the very intention that produces them, which is nothing other than the denial (*Verneinung*) of the economy. A general science of the economy of practices, capable of reappropriating the totality of the practices which, although objectively economic, are not and cannot be socially recognized as economic, and which can be performed only at the cost of a whole labor of dissimulation or, more precisely, *euphemization*, must endeavor to grasp capital and profit in all their forms and to establish the laws whereby the different types of capital (or power, which amounts to the same thing) change into one another.[2]

Depending on the field in which it functions, and at the cost of the more or less expensive transformations which are the precondition for its efficacy in the field in question, capital can present itself in three fundamental guises: as *economic capital*, which is immediately and directly convertible into money and may be institutionalized in the form of property rights; as *cultural capital*, which is convertible, on certain conditions, into economic capital and may be institutionalized in the form of educational qualifications; and as *social capital*, made up of social obligations ("connections"), which is convertible, in certain conditions, into economic capital and may be institutionalized in the form of a title of nobility.[3]

CULTURAL CAPITAL

Cultural capital can exist in three forms: in the *embodied* state, i.e., in the form of long-lasting dispositions of the mind and body; in the *objectified* state, in the form of cultural goods (pictures, books, dictionaries, instruments, machines, etc.), which are the trace or realization of theories or critiques of these theories, problematics, etc.; and in the *institutionalized* state, a form of objectification which must be set apart because, as will be seen in the case of educational qualifications, it confers entirely original properties on the cultural capital which it is presumed to guarantee.

The reader should not be misled by the somewhat peremptory air which the effort at axiomization may give to my argument.[4] The notion of cultural capital initially presented itself to me, in the course of research, as a theoretical hypothesis which made it possible to explain the unequal scholastic achievement of children originating from the different social classes by relating academic success, i.e., the specific profits which children from the different classes and class fractions can obtain in the academic market, to the distribution of cultural capital between the classes and class fractions. This starting point implies a break with the presuppositions inherent both in the commonsense view, which sees academic success or failure as an effect of natural aptitudes, and in human capital theories. Economists might seem to deserve credit for explicitly raising the question of the relationship between the rates of profit on educational investment and on economic investment (and its evolution). But their measurement of the yield from scholastic investment takes account only of *monetary* investments and profits, or those directly convertible into money, such as the costs of schooling and the cash equivalent of time devoted to study; they are unable to explain the different proportions of their resources which different agents or different social classes allocate to economic investment and cultural investment because they fail to take systematic account of the structure of the differential chances of profit which the various markets offer these agents or classes as a function of the volume and the composition of their assets (see esp. Becker 1964b). Furthermore, because they neglect to relate scholastic investment strategies to the whole set of educational strategies and to the system of reproduction strategies, they inevitably, by a necessary paradox, let slip the best hidden and socially most determinant educational investment, namely, the domestic transmission of cultural capital. Their studies of the relationship between academic ability and academic investment show that they are unaware that ability or talent is itself the product of an investment of time and cultural capital (Becker 1964a, p. 63–66). Not surprisingly, when endeavoring to evaluate the profits of scholastic investment, they can only consider the profitability of educational expenditure for society as a whole, the "social rate of return," or the "social gain of education as measured by its effects on national productivity" (Becker 1964b, pp. 121, 155). This typically functionalist definition of the functions of education ignores the contribution which the educational system makes to the reproduction of the social structure by sanctioning the hereditary transmission of cultural capital. From the very beginning, a definition of human capital, despite its humanistic connotations, does not move beyond economism and ignores, *inter alia*, the fact that the scholastic yield from educational action depends on the cultural capital previously invested by the family. Moreover, the economic and social yield of the educational qualification depends on the social capital, again inherited, which can be used to back it up.

The Embodied State. Most of the properties of cultural capital can be deduced from the fact that, in its fundamental state, it is linked to the body and presupposes embodiment. The accumulation of cultural capital in the embodied state, i.e., in the form of what is called culture, cultivation, *Bildung*, presupposes a process of em-bodiment, incorporation, which, insofar as it implies a labor of inculcation and assimilation, costs time, time which must be invested personally by the investor. Like the acquisition of a muscular physique or a suntan, it cannot be done at second hand (so that all effects of delegation are ruled out).

The work of acquisition is work on oneself (self-improvement), an effort that presupposes a personal cost (*on paie de sa personne*, as we say in French), an investment, above all of time, but also of that socially constituted form of libido, *libido sciendi*, with all the privation, renunciation, and sacrifice that it may entail. It follows that the least inexact of all the measurements of cultural capital are those which take as their standard the length of acquisition—so long, of course, as this is not reduced to length of schooling and allowance is made for early domestic education by giving it a positive value (a gain in time, a head start) or a negative value (wasted time, and doubly so because more time must be spent correcting its effects), according to its distance from the demands of the scholastic market.[5]

This embodied capital, external wealth converted into an integral part of the person, into a habitus, cannot be transmitted instantaneously (unlike money, property rights, or even titles of nobility) by gift or bequest, purchase or exchange. It follows that the use or exploitation of cultural capital presents particular problems for the holders of economic or political capital, whether they be private patrons or, at the other extreme, entrepreneurs employing executives endowed with a specific cultural competence (not to mention the new state patrons). How can this capital, so closely linked to the person, be bought without buying the person and so losing the very effect of legitimation which presupposes the dissimulation of dependence? How can this capital be concentrated—as some undertakings demand—without concentrating the possessors of the capital, which can have all sorts of unwanted consequences?

Cultural capital can be acquired, to a varying extent, depending on the period, the society, and the social class, in the absence of any deliberate inculcation, and therefore quite unconsciously. It always remains marked by its earliest conditions of acquisition which, through the more or less visible marks they leave (such as the pronunciations characteristic of a class or region), help to determine its distinctive value. It cannot be accumulated beyond the appropriating capacities of an individual agent; it declines and dies with its bearer (with his biological capacity, his memory, etc.). Because it is thus linked in numerous ways to the person in his biological singularity and is subject to a hereditary transmission which is always heavily disguised, or even invisible, it defies the old, deep-rooted distinction the Greek jurists made between inherited properties (*ta patroa*) and acquired properties (*epikteta*), i.e., those which an individual adds to his heritage. It thus manages to combine the prestige of innate property with the merits of acquisition. Because the social conditions of its transmission and acquisition are more disguised than those of economic capital, it is predisposed to function as symbolic capital, i.e., to be unrecognized as capital and recognized as legitimate competence, as authority exerting an effect of (mis)recognition, e.g., in the matrimonial market and in all the markets in which economic capital is not fully recognized, whether in matters of culture, with the great art collections or great cultural foundations, or in social welfare, with the economy of generosity and the gift. Furthermore, the specifically symbolic logic of distinction additionally secures material and symbolic profits for the possessors of a large cultural capital: any given cultural competence (e.g., being able to read in a world of illiterates) derives a scarcity value from its position in the distribution of cultural capital and yields profits of distinction for its owner. In other words, the share in profits which scarce cultural capital secures in class-divided societies is based, in the last analysis, on the fact that all agents do not have the economic and cultural means for prolonging their children's education beyond the minimum necessary for the reproduction of the labor-power least valorized at a given moment.[6]

Thus the capital, in the sense of the means of appropriating the product of accumulated labor in the objectified state which is held by a given agent, depends for its real efficacy on the form of the distribution of the means of appropriating the accumulated and objectively available resources; and the relationship of appropriation between an agent and the resources objectively available, and hence the profits they produce, is mediated by the relationship of (objective and/or subjective) competition between himself and the other possessors of capital competing for the same goods, in which scarcity—and through it social value— is generated. The structure of the field, i.e., the unequal distribution of capital, is the source of the specific effects of capital, i.e., the appropriation of profits and the power to impose the laws of functioning of the field most favorable to capital and its reproduction.

But the most powerful principle of the symbolic efficacy of cultural capital no doubt lies in the logic of its transmission. On the one hand, the process of appropriating objectified cultural capital and the time necessary for it to take place mainly depend on the cultural capital embodied in the whole family— through (among other things) the generalized Arrow effect and all forms of implicit transmission.[7] On the other hand, the initial accumulation of cultural capital, the precondition for the fast, easy accumulation of every kind of useful cultural capital, starts at the outset, without delay, without wasted time, only for the offspring of families endowed with strong cultural capital; in this case, the accumulation period covers the whole period of socialization. It follows that the transmission of cultural capital is no doubt the best hidden form of hereditary transmission of capital, and it therefore receives proportionately greater weight in the system of reproduction strategies, as the direct, visible forms of trans- mission tend to be more strongly censored and controlled.

It can immediately be seen that the link between economic and cultural capital is established through the mediation of the time needed for acquisition. Differ- ences in the cultural capital possessed by the family imply differences first in the age at which the work of transmission and accumulation begins—the limiting case being full use of the time biologically available, with the maximum free time being harnessed to maximum cultural capital—and then in the capacity, thus defined, to satisfy the specifically cultural demands of a prolonged process of acquisition. Furthermore, and in correlation with this, the length of time for which a given individual can prolong his acquisition process depends on the length of time for which his family can provide him with the free time, i.e., time free from economic necessity, which is the precondition for the initial accumulation (time which can be evaluated as a handicap to be made up).

The Objectified State. Cultural capital, in the objectified state, has a number of properties which are defined only in the relationship with cultural capital in its embodied form. The cultural capital objectified in material objects and media, such as writings, paintings, monuments, instruments, etc., is transmissible in its materiality. A collection of paintings, for example, can be transmitted as well as economic capital (if not better, because the capital transfer is more disguised). But what is transmissible is legal ownership and not (or not necessarily) what constitutes the precondition for specific appropriation, namely, the possession of the means of "consuming" a painting or using a machine, which, being nothing other than embodied capital, are subject to the same laws of transmission.[8]

Thus cultural goods can be appropriated both materially—which presupposes economic capital—and symbolically—which presupposes cultural capital. It follows that the owner of the means of production must find a way of appropriating either the embodied capital which is the precondition of specific appropriation or the services of the holders of this capital. To possess the machines, he only needs economic capital; to appropriate them and use them in accordance with their specific purpose (defined by the cultural capital, of scientific or technical type, incorporated in them), he must have access to embodied cultural capital, either in person or by proxy. This is no doubt the basis of the ambiguous status of cadres (executives and engineers). If it is emphasized that they are not the possessors (in the strictly economic sense) of the means of production which they use, and that they derive profit from their own cultural capital only by selling the services and products which it makes possible, then they will be classified among the dominated groups; if it is emphasized that they draw their profits from the use of a particular form of capital, then they will be classified among the dominant groups. Everything suggests that as the cultural capital incorporated in the means of production increases (and with it the period of embodiment needed to acquire the means of appropriating it), so the collective strength of the holders of cultural capital would tend to increase—if the holders of the dominant type of capital (economic capital) were not able to set the holders of cultural capital in competition with one another. (They are, moreover, inclined to competition by the very conditions in which they are selected and trained, in particular by the logic of scholastic and recruitment competitions.)

Cultural capital in its objectified state presents itself with all the appearances of an autonomous, coherent universe which, although the product of historical action, has its own laws, transcending individual wills, and which, as the example of language well illustrates, therefore remains irreducible to that which each agent, or even the aggregate of the agents, can appropriate (i.e., to the cultural capital embodied in each agent or even in the aggregate of the agents). However, it should not be forgotten that it exists as symbolically and materially active, effective capital only insofar as it is appropriated by agents and implemented and invested as a weapon and a stake in the struggles which go on in the fields of cultural production (the artistic field, the scientific field, etc.) and, beyond them, in the field of the social classes—struggles in which the agents wield strengths and obtain profits proportionate to their mastery of this objectified capital, and therefore to the extent of their embodied capital.[9]

The Institutionalized State. The objectification of cultural capital in the form of academic qualifications is one way of neutralizing some of the properties it derives from the fact that, being embodied, it has the same biological limits as its bearer. This objectification is what makes the difference between the capital of the autodidact, which may be called into question at any time, or even the cultural capital of the courtier, which can yield only ill-defined profits, of fluctuating value, in the market of high-society exchanges, and the cultural capital academically sanctioned by legally guaranteed qualifications, formally independent of the person of their bearer. With the academic qualification, a certificate of cultural competence which confers on its holder a conventional, constant, legally guaranteed value with respect to culture, social alchemy produces a form of cultural capital which has a relative autonomy vis-à-vis its bearer and even vis-à-vis the cultural capital he effectively possesses at a given moment in time. It institutes cultural capital by collective magic, just as, according to Merleau-Ponty, the living institute their dead through the ritual of mourning. One has only to think of the *concours* (competitive recruitment examination) which, out of the continuum of infinitesimal differences between performances, produces sharp, absolute, lasting differences, such as that which separates the last successful candidate from the first unsuccessful one, and institutes an essential difference between the officially recognized, guaranteed competence and simple cultural capital, which is constantly required to prove itself. In this case, one sees clearly the performative magic of the power of instituting, the power to show forth and secure belief or, in a word, to impose recognition.

By conferring institutional recognition on the cultural capital possessed by any given agent, the academic qualification also makes it possible to compare qualification holders and even to exchange them (by substituting one for another in succession). Furthermore, it makes it possible to establish conversion rates between cultural capital and economic capital by guaranteeing the monetary value of a given academic capital.[10] This product of the conversion of economic capital into cultural capital establishes the value, in terms of cultural capital, of the holder of a given qualification relative to other qualification holders and, by the same token, the monetary value for which it can be exchanged on the labor market (academic investment has no meaning unless a minimum degree of reversibility of the conversion it implies is objectively guaranteed). Because the material and symbolic profits which the academic qualification guarantees also depend on its scarcity, the investments made (in time and effort) may turn out to be less profitable than was anticipated when they were made (there having been a *de facto* change in the conversion rate between academic capital and economic capital). The strategies for converting economic capital into cultural capital, which are among the short-term factors of the schooling explosion and the inflation of qualifications, are governed by changes in the structure of the chances of profit offered by the different types of capital.

SOCIAL CAPITAL

Social capital is the aggregate of the actual or potential resources which are linked to possession of a durable network of more or less institutionalized relationships of mutual acquaintance and recognition—or in other words, to membership in a group[11]—which provides each of its members with the backing of the collectivity-owned capital, a "credential" which entitles them to credit, in the various senses of the word. These relationships may exist only in the practical state, in material and/or symbolic exchanges which help to maintain them. They may also be socially instituted and guaranteed by the application of a common name (the name of a family, a class, or a tribe or of a school, a party, etc.) and by a whole set of instituting acts designed simultaneously to form and inform those who undergo them; in this case, they are more or less really enacted and so maintained and reinforced, in exchanges. Being based on indissolubly material and symbolic exchanges, the establishment and maintenance of which presuppose reacknowledgment of proximity, they are also partially irreducible to objective relations of proximity in physical (geographical) space or even in economic and social space.[12]

The volume of the social capital possessed by a given agent thus depends on the size of the network of connections he can effectively mobilize and on the volume of the capital (economic, cultural or symbolic) possessed in his own right by each of those to whom he is connected.[13] This means that, although it is relatively irreducible to the economic and cultural capital possessed by a given agent, or even by the whole set of agents to whom he is connected, social capital is never completely independent of it because the exchanges instituting mutual acknowledgment presuppose the reacknowledgment of a minimum of objective homogeneity, and because it exerts a multiplier effect on the capital he possesses in his own right.

The profits which accrue from membership in a group are the basis of the solidarity which makes them possible.[14] This does not mean that they are consciously pursued as such, even in the case of groups like select clubs, which are deliberately organized in order to concentrate social capital and so to derive full benefit from the multiplier effect implied in concentration and to secure the profits of membership—material profits, such as all the types of services accruing from useful relationships, and symbolic profits, such as those derived from association with a rare, prestigious group.

The existence of a network of connections is not a natural given, or even a social given, constituted once and for all by an initial act of institution, represented, in the case of the family group, by the genealogical definition of kinship relations, which is the characteristic of a social formation. It is the product of an endless effort at institution, of which institution rites—often wrongly described as rites of passage—mark the essential moments and which is necessary in order to produce and reproduce lasting, useful relationships that can secure material or symbolic profits (see Bourdieu 1982). In other words, the network of relationships is the product of investment strategies, individual or collective, consciously or unconsciously aimed at establishing or reproducing social relationships that are directly usable in the short or long term, i.e., at transforming contingent relations, such as those of neighborhood, the workplace, or even kinship, into relationships that are at once necessary and elective, implying durable obligations subjectively felt (feelings of gratitude, respect, friendship,

etc.) or institutionally guaranteed (rights). This is done through the alchemy of
consecration, the symbolic constitution produced by social institution (institution
as a relative—brother, sister, cousin, etc.—or as a knight, an heir, an elder,
etc.) and endlessly reproduced in and through the exchange (of gifts, words,
women, etc.) which it encourages and which presupposes and produces mutual
knowledge and recognition. Exchange transforms the things exchanged into signs
of recognition and, through the mutual recognition and the recognition of group
membership which it implies, re-produces the group. By the same token, it
reaffirms the limits of the group, i.e., the limits beyond which the constitutive
exchange—trade, commensality, or marriage—cannot take place. Each member
of the group is thus instituted as a custodian of the limits of the group: because
the definition of the criteria of entry is at stake in each new entry, he can modify
the group by modifying the limits of legitimate exchange through some form of
misalliance. It is quite logical that, in most societies, the preparation and conclusion of marriages should be the business of the whole group, and not of the
agents directly concerned. Through the introduction of new members into a
family, a clan, or a club, the whole definition of the group, i.e., its fines, its
boundaries, and its identity, is put at stake, exposed to redefinition, alteration,
adulteration. When, as in modern societies, families lose the monopoly of the
establishment of exchanges which can lead to lasting relationships, whether
socially sanctioned (like marriage) or not, they may continue to control these
exchanges, while remaining within the logic of laissez-faire, through all the
institutions which are designed to favor legitimate exchanges and exclude illegitimate ones by producing occasions (rallies, cruises, hunts, parties, receptions,
etc.), places (smart neighborhoods, select schools, clubs, etc.), or practices
(smart sports, parlor games, cultural ceremonies, etc.) which bring together, in
a seemingly fortuitous way, individuals as homogeneous as possible in all the
pertinent respects in terms of the existence and persistence of the group.

   The reproduction of social capital presupposes an unceasing effort of sociability, a continuous series of exchanges in which recognition is endlessly affirmed
and reaffirmed. This work, which implies expenditure of time and energy and
so, directly or indirectly, of economic capital, is not profitable or even conceivable unless one invests in it a specific competence (knowledge of genealogical
relationships and of real connections and skill at using them, etc.) and an acquired
disposition to acquire and maintain this competence, which are themselves integral parts of this capital.[15] This is one of the factors which explain why the
profitability of this labor of accumulating and maintaining social capital rises in
proportion to the size of the capital. Because the social capital accruing from a
relationship is that much greater to the extent that the person who is the object
of it is richly endowed with capital (mainly social, but also cultural and even
economic capital), the possessors of an inherited social capital, symbolized by
a great name, are able to transform all circumstantial relationships into lasting
connections. They are sought after for their social capital and, because they are
well known, are worthy of being known ("I know him well"); they do not need

to "make the acquaintance" of all their "acquaintances"; they are known to more people than they know, and their work of sociability, when it is exerted, is highly productive.

Every group has its more or less institutionalized forms of delegation which enable it to concentrate the totality of the social capital, which is the basis of the existence of the group (a family or a nation, of course, but also an association or a party), in the hands of a single agent or a small group of agents and to mandate this plenipotentiary, charged with *plena potestas agendi et loquendi*,[16] to represent the group, to speak and act in its name and so, with the aid of this collectively owned capital, to exercise a power incommensurate with the agent's personal contribution. Thus, at the most elementary degree of institutionalization, the head of the family, the *pater familias*, the eldest, most senior member, is tacitly recognized as the only person entitled to speak on behalf of the family group in all official circumstances. But whereas in this case, diffuse delegation requires the great to step forward and defend the collective honor when the honor of the weakest members is threatened. The institutionalized delegation, which ensures the concentration of social capital, also has the effect of limiting the consequences of individual lapses by explicitly delimiting responsibilities and authorizing the recognized spokesmen to shield the group as a whole from discredit by expelling or excommunicating the embarrassing individuals.

If the internal competition for the monopoly of legitimate representation of the group is not to threaten the conservation and accumulation of the capital which is the basis of the group, the members of the group must regulate the conditions of access to the right to declare oneself a member of the group and, above all, to set oneself up as a representative (delegate, plenipotentiary, spokesman, etc.) of the whole group, thereby committing the social capital of the whole group. The title of nobility is the form *par excellence* of the institutionalized social capital which guarantees a particular form of social relationship in a lasting way. One of the paradoxes of delegation is that the mandated agent can exert on (and, up to a point, against) the group the power which the group enables him to concentrate. (This is perhaps especially true in the limiting cases in which the mandated agent creates the group which creates him but which only exists through him.) The mechanisms of delegation and representation (in both the theatrical and the legal senses) which fall into place—that much more strongly, no doubt, when the group is large and its members weak—as one of the conditions for the concentration of social capital (among other reasons, because it enables numerous, varied, scattered agents to act as one man and to overcome the limitations of space and time) also contain the seeds of an embezzlement or misappropriation of the capital which they assemble.

This embezzlement is latent in the fact that a group as a whole can be represented, in the various meanings of the word, by a subgroup, clearly delimited and perfectly visible to all, known to all, and recognized by all, that of the *nobiles*, the "people who are known," the paradigm of whom is the nobility, and who may speak on behalf of the whole group, represent the whole group, and exercise authority in the name of the whole group. The noble is the group personified. He bears the name of the group to which he gives his name (the metonymy which links the noble to his group is clearly seen when Shakespeare calls Cleopatra "Egypt" or the King of France "France," just as Racine calls Pyrrhus "Epirus"). It is by him, his name, the difference it proclaims, that the members of his group, the liegemen, and also the land and castles, are known and recognized. Similarly, phenomena such as the "personality cult" or the identification of parties, trade unions, or movements with their leader are latent in the very logic of representation. Everything combines to cause the signifier to take the place of the signified, the spokesmen that of the group he is supposed to express, not least because his distinction, his "outstandingness," his visibility constitute the essential part, if not the essence, of this power, which, being entirely set within the logic of knowledge and acknowledgment, is fundamentally a symbolic power; but also because the representative, the sign, the emblem, may be, and create, the whole reality of groups which receive effective social existence only in and through representation.[17]

CONVERSIONS

The different types of capital can be derived from *economic capital*, but only at the cost of a more or less great effort of transformation, which is needed to produce the type of power effective in the field in question. For example, there are some goods and services to which economic capital gives immediate access, without secondary costs; others can be obtained only by virtue of a social capital of relationships (or social obligations) which cannot act instantaneously, at the appropriate moment, unless they have been established and maintained for a long time, as if for their own sake, and therefore outside their period of use, i.e., at the cost of an investment in sociability which is necessarily long-term because the time lag is one of the factors of the transmutation of a pure and simple debt into that recognition of nonspecific indebtedness which is called gratitude.[18] In contrast to the cynical but also economical transparency of economic exchange, in which equivalents change hands in the same instant, the essential ambiguity of social exchange, which presupposes misrecognition, in other words, a form of faith and of bad faith (in the sense of self-deception), presupposes a much more subtle economy of time.

So it has to be posited simultaneously that economic capital is at the root of all the other types of capital and that these transformed, disguised forms of economic capital, never entirely reducible to that definition, produce their most specific effects only to the extent that they conceal (not least from their possessors) the fact that economic capital is at their root, in other words—but only in the last analysis—at the root of their effects. The real logic of the functioning of capital, the conversions from one type to another, and the law of conservation which governs them cannot be understood unless two opposing but equally partial views are superseded: on the one hand, economism, which, on the grounds that every type of capital is reducible in the last analysis to economic capital, ignores what makes the specific efficacy of the other types of capital, and on the other hand, semiologism (nowadays represented by structuralism, symbolic interactionism, or ethnomethodology), which reduces social exchanges to phenomena of communication and ignores the brutal fact of universal reducibility to economics.[19]

In accordance with a principle which is the equivalent of the principle of the conservation of energy, profits in one area are necessarily paid for by costs in another (so that a concept like wastage has no meaning in a general science of the economy of practices). The universal equivalent, the measure of all equivalences, is nothing other than labor-time (in the widest sense); and the conservation of social energy through all its conversions is verified if, in each case, one takes into account both the labor-time accumulated in the form of capital and the labor-time needed to transform it from one type into another.

It has been seen, for example, that the transformation of economic capital into social capital presupposes a specific labor, i.e., an apparently gratuitous expenditure of time, attention, care, concern, which, as is seen in the endeavor to personalize a gift, has the effect of transfiguring the purely monetary import of the exchange and, by the same token, the very meaning of the exchange. From a narrowly economic standpoint, this effort is bound to be seen as pure wastage, but in the terms of the logic of social exchanges, it is a solid investment, the profits of which will appear, in the long run, in monetary or other form. Similarly, if the best measure of cultural capital is undoubtedly the amount of time devoted to acquiring it, this is because the transformation of economic capital into cultural capital presupposes an expenditure of time that is made possible by possession of economic capital. More precisely, it is because the cultural capital that is effectively transmitted within the family itself depends not only on the quantity of cultural capital, itself accumulated by spending time, that the domestic group possess, but also on the usable time (particularly in the form of the mother's free time) available to it (by virtue of its economic capital, which enables it to purchase the time of others) to ensure the transmission of this capital and to delay entry into the labor market through prolonged schooling, a credit which pays off, if at all, only in the very long term.[20]

The convertibility of the different types of capital is the basis of the strategies aimed at ensuring the reproduction of capital (and the position occupied in social space) by means of the conversions least costly in terms of conversion work and of the losses inherent in the conversion itself (in a given state of the social power relations). The different types of capital can be distinguished according to their reproducibility or, more precisely, according to how easily they are transmitted, i.e., with more or less loss and with more or less concealment; the rate of loss and the degree of concealment tend to vary in inverse ratio. Everything which helps to disguise the economic aspect also tends to increase the risk of loss (particularly the intergenerational transfers). Thus the (apparent) incommensurability of the different types of capital introduces a high degree of uncertainty into all transactions between holders of different types. Similarly, the declared refusal of calculation and of guarantees which characterizes exchanges tending to produce a social capital in the form of a capital of obligations that are usable in the more or less long term (exchanges of gifts, services, visits, etc.) necessarily entails the risk of ingratitude, the refusal of that recognition of nonguaranteed debts which such exchanges aim to produce. Similarly, too, the high degree of concealment of the transmission of cultural capital has the disadvantage (in addition to its inherent risks of loss) that the academic qualification which is its institutionalized form is neither transmissible (like a title of nobility) nor negotiable (like stocks and shares). More precisely, cultural capital, whose diffuse, continuous transmission within the family escapes observation and control (so that the educational system seems to award its honors solely to natural qualities) and which is increasingly tending to attain full efficacy, at least on the labor market, only when validated by the educational system, i.e., converted into a capital of qualifications, is subject to a more disguised but more risky transmission than economic capital. As the educational qualification, invested with the specific force of the official, becomes the condition for legitimate access to a growing number of positions, particularly the dominant ones, the educational system tends increasingly to dispossess the domestic group of the monopoly of the transmission of power and privileges—and, among other things, of the choice of its legitimate heirs from among children of different sex and birth rank.[21] And economic capital itself poses quite different problems of transmission, depending on the particular form it takes. Thus, according to Grassby (1970), the liquidity of commercial capital, which gives immediate economic power and favors transmission, also makes it more vulnerable than landed property (or even real estate) and does not favor the establishment of long-lasting dynasties.

Because the question of the arbitrariness of appropriation arises most sharply in the process of transmission—particularly at the time of succession, a critical moment for all power—every reproduction strategy is at the same time a legitimation strategy aimed at consecrating both an exclusive appropriation and its reproduction. When the subversive critique which aims to weaken the dominant class through the principle of its perpetuation by bringing to light the arbitrariness of the entitlements transmitted and of their transmission (such as the critique which the Enlightenment *philosophes* directed, in the name of nature, against the arbitrariness of birth) is incorporated in institutionalized mechanisms (for example, laws of inheritance) aimed at controlling the official, direct transmission of power and privileges, the holders of capital have an ever greater interest in resorting to reproduction strategies capable of ensuring better-disguised transmission, but at the cost of greater loss of capital, by exploiting the convertibility of the types of capital. Thus the more the official transmission of capital is prevented or hindered, the more the effects of the clandestine circulation of capital in the form of cultural capital become determinant in the reproduction of the social structure. As an instrument of reproduction capable of disguising its own function, the scope of the educational system tends to increase, and together with this increase is the unification of the market in social qualifications which gives rights to occupy rare positions.

NOTES

1. This inertia, entailed by the tendency of the structures of capital to reproduce themselves in institutions or in dispositions adapted to the structures of which they are the product, is, of course, reinforced by a specifically political action of concerted conservation, i.e., of demobilization and depoliticization. The latter tends to keep the dominated agents in the state of a practical group, united only by the orchestration of their dispositions and condemned to function as an aggregate repeatedly performing discrete, individual acts (such as consumer or electoral choices).

2. This is true of all exchanges between members of different fractions of the dominant class, possessing different types of capital. These range from sales of expertise, treatment, or other services which take the form of gift exchange and dignify themselves with the most decorous names that can be found (honoraria, emoluments, etc.) to matrimonial exchanges, the prime example of a transaction that can only take place insofar as it is not perceived or defined as such by the contracting parties. It is remarkable that the apparent extensions of economic theory beyond the limits constituting the discipline have left intact the asylum of the sacred, apart from a few sacrilegious incursions. Gary S. Becker, for example, who was one of the first to take explicit account of the types of capital that are usually ignored, never considers anything other than monetary costs and profits, forgetting the nonmonetary investments (*inter alia*, the affective ones) and the material and symbolic profits that education provides in a deferred, indirect way, such as the added value which the dispositions produced or reinforced by schooling (bodily or verbal manners, tastes, etc.) or the relationships established with fellow students can yield in the matrimonial market (Becker 1964a).

3. *Symbolic capital*, that is to say, capital—in whatever form—insofar as it is represented, i.e., apprehended symbolically, in a relationship of knowledge or, more precisely, of misrecognition and recognition, presupposes the intervention of the habitus, as a socially constituted cognitive capacity.

4. When talking about concepts for their own sake, as I do here, rather than using them in research, one always runs the risk of being both schematic and formal, i.e., theoretical in the most usual and most usually approved sense of the word.

5. This proposition implies no recognition of the value of scholastic verdicts; it merely registers the relationship which exists in reality between a certain cultural capital and the laws of the educational market. Dispositions that are given a negative value in the educational market may receive very high value in other markets—not least, of course, in the relationships internal to the class.

6. In a relatively undifferentiated society, in which access to the means of appropriating the cultural heritage is very equally distributed, embodied culture does not function as cultural capital, i.e., as a means of acquiring exclusive advantages.

7. What I call the generalized Arrow effect, i.e., the fact that all cultural goods—paintings, monuments, machines, and any objects shaped by man, particularly all those which belong to the childhood environment—exert an educative effect by their mere existence, is no doubt one of the structural factors behind the "schooling explosion," in the sense that a growth in the quantity of cultural capital accumulated in the objectified

state increases the educative effect automatically exerted by the environment. If one adds to this the fact that embodied cultural capital is constantly increasing, it can be seen that, in each generation, the educational system can take more for granted. The fact that the same educational investment is increasingly productive is one of the structural factors of the inflation of qualifications (together with cyclical factors linked to effects of capital conversion).

8. The cultural object, as a living social institution, is, simultaneously, a socially instituted material object and a particular class of habitus, to which it is addressed. The material object—for example, a work of art in its materiality—may be separated by space (e.g., a Dogon statue) or by time (e.g., a Simone Martini painting) from the habitus for which it was intended. This leads to one of the most fundamental biases of art history. Understanding the effect (not to be confused with the function) which the work tended to produce—for example, the form of belief it tended to induce—and which is the true basis of the conscious or unconscious choice of the means used (technique, colors, etc.), and therefore of the form itself, is possible only if one at least raises the question of the habitus on which it "operated."

9. The dialectical relationship between objectified cultural capital—of which the form *par excellence* is writing—and embodied cultural capital has generally been reduced to an exalted description of the degradation of the spirit by the letter, the living by the inert, creation by routine, grace by heaviness.

10. This is particularly true in France, where in many occupations (particularly the civil service) there is a very strict relationship between qualification, rank, and remuneration (translator's note).

11. Here, too, the notion of cultural capital did not spring from pure theoretical work, still less from an analogical extension of economic concepts. It arose from the need to identify the principle of social effects which, although they can be seen clearly at the level of singular agents—where statistical inquiry inevitably operates—cannot be reduced to the set of properties individually possessed by a given agent. These effects, in which spontaneous sociology readily perceives the work of "connections," are particularly visible in all cases in which different individuals obtain very unequal profits from virtually equivalent (economic or cultural) capital, depending on the extent to which they can mobilize by proxy the capital of a group (a family, the alumni of an elite school, a select club, the aristocracy, etc.) that is more or less constituted as such and more or less rich in capital.

12. Neighborhood relationships may, of course, receive an elementary form of institutionalization, as in the Bearn—or the Basque region—where neighbors, *lous besis* (a word which, in old texts, is applied to the legitimate inhabitants of the village, the rightful members of the assembly), are explicitly designated, in accordance with fairly codified rules, and are assigned functions which are differentiated according to their rank (there is a "first neighbor," a "second neighbor," and so on), particularly for the major social ceremonies (funerals, marriages, etc.). But even in this case, the relationships actually used by no means always coincide with the relationships socially instituted.

13. Manners (bearing, pronunciation, etc.) may be included in social capital insofar as, through the mode of acquisition they point to, they indicate initial membership of a more or less prestigious group.

14. National liberation movements or nationalist ideologies cannot be accounted for solely by reference to strictly economic profits, i.e., anticipation of the profits which may be derived from redistribution of a proportion of wealth to the advantage of the nationals

(nationalization) and the recovery of highly paid jobs (see Breton 1964). To these specifically economic anticipated profits, which would only explain the nationalism of the privileged classes, must be added the very real and very immediate profits derived from membership (social capital) which are proportionately greater for those who are lower down the social hierarchy ("poor whites") or, more precisely, more threatened by economic and social decline.

15. There is every reason to suppose that socializing, or, more generally, relational, dispositions are very unequally distributed among the social classes and, within a given class, among fractions of different origin.

16. A "full power to act and speak" (translator).

17. It goes without saying that social capital is so totally governed by the logic of knowledge and acknowledgment that it always functions as symbolic capital.

18. It should be made clear, to dispel a likely misunderstanding, that the investment in question here is not necessarily conceived as a calculated pursuit of gain, but that it has every likelihood of being experienced in terms of the logic of emotional investment, i.e., as an involvement which is both necessary and disinterested. This has not always been appreciated by historians, who (even when they are as alert to symbolic effects as E. P. Thompson) tend to conceive symbolic practices—powdered wigs and the whole paraphernalia of office—as explicit strategies of domination, intended to be seen (from below), and to interpret generous or charitable conduct as "calculated acts of class appeasement." This naively Machiavellian view forgets that the most sincerely disinterested acts may be those best corresponding to objective interest. A number of fields, particularly those which most tend to deny interest and every sort of calculation, like the fields of cultural production, grant full recognition, and with it the consecration which guarantees success, only to those who distinguish themselves by the immediate conformity of their investments, a token of sincerity and attachment to the essential principles of the field. It would be thoroughly erroneous to describe the choices of the habitus which lead an artist, writer, or researcher toward his natural place (a subject, style, manner, etc.) in terms of rational strategy and cynical calculation. This is despite the fact that, for example, shifts from one genre, school, or speciality to another, quasi-religious conversions that are performed "in all sincerity," can be understood as capital conversions, the direction and moment of which (on which their success often depends) are determined by a "sense of investment" which is the less likely to be seen as such the more skillful it is. Innocence is the privilege of those who move in their field of activity like fish in water.

19. To understand the attractiveness of this pair of antagonistic positions which serve as each other's alibi, one would need to analyze the unconscious profits and the profits of unconsciousness which they procure for intellectuals. While some find in economism a means of exempting themselves by excluding the cultural capital and all the specific profits which place them on the side of the dominant, others can abandon the detestable terrain of the economic, where everything reminds them that they can be evaluated, in the last analysis, in economic terms, for that of the symbolic. (The latter merely reproduce, in the realm of the symbolic, the strategy whereby intellectuals and artists endeavor to impose the recognition of their values, i.e., their value, by inverting the law of the market in which what one has or what one earns completely defines what one is worth and what one is—as is shown by the practice of banks which, with techniques such as the personalization of credit, tend to subordinate the granting of loans and the fixing of interest rates to an exhaustive inquiry into the borrower's present and future resources.)

20. Among the advantages procured by capital in all its types, the most precious is the increased volume of useful time that is made possible through the various methods of appropriating other people's time (in the form of services). It may take the form either of increased spare time, secured by reducing the time consumed in activities directly channeled toward producing the means of reproducing the existence of the domestic group, or of more intense use of the time so consumed, by recourse to other people's labor or to devices and methods which are available only to those who have spent time learning how to use them and which (like better transport or living close to the place of work) make it possible to save time. (This is in contrast to the cash savings of the poor, which are paid for in time—do-it-yourself, bargain hunting, etc.) None of this is true of mere economic capital; it is possession of cultural capital that makes it possible to derive greater profit not only from labor-time, by securing a higher yield from the same time, but also from spare time, and so to increase both economic and cultural capital.

21. It goes without saying that the dominant fractions, who tend to place ever greater emphasis on educational investment, within an overall strategy of asset diversification and of investments aimed at combining security with high yield, have all sorts of ways of evading scholastic verdicts. The direct transmission of economic capital remains one of the principal means of reproduction, and the effect of social capital ("a helping hand," "string-pulling," the "old boy network") tends to correct the effect of academic sanctions. Educational qualifications never function perfectly as currency. They are never entirely separable from their holders: their value rises in proportion to the value of their bearer, especially in the least rigid areas of the social structure.

REFERENCES

Becker, Gary S. *A Theoretical and Empirical Analysis with Special Reference to Education*. New York: National Bureau of Economic Research, 1964a.
———. *Human Capital*. New York: Columbia University Press, 1964b.
Bourdieu, Pierre. "Les rites d'institution." *Actes de la recherche en sciences sociales* 43 (1982): 58–63.
Breton, A. "The Economics of Nationalism." *Journal of Political Economy* 72 (1962): 376–86.
Grassby, Richard. "English Merchant Capitalism in the Late Seventeenth Century: The Composition of Business Fortunes." *Past and Present* 46 (1970): 87–107.

PART IV

Methodological and Theoretical Issues in the Sociology of Education

10

RAYMOND BOUDON

Education, Social Mobility, and Sociological Theory

PUZZLES, GENERATIVE MODELS, AND THE INFLUENCE OF EDUCATION

Social science, like any other type of science, should primarily aim at solving puzzles. When I started my work on education and mobility (Boudon 1973; 1974), I was puzzled by a number of empirical findings, i.e., of data the structure of which appeared as counterintuitive. Thus it had been noted that in several social contexts an increase in educational equality did not generate an increase in economic equality, i.e., in the equality of individual incomes (Thurow 1972). Obviously, a finding appears as counterintuitive when it is contradictory with the expectations which can be made on the basis of some widely accepted theory. In this case, the widely accepted theory—I put it in a very crude form—was that income rewards, among other things, aptitudes or skills which are a function of the level of educational attainment. In another version of the theory, income rewards educational investment (Blaug 1968). Many other versions of the same theory can be mentioned: in a more or less technical fashion, using various conceptual frameworks, all start from the apparently commonsense assumption that there should be some relationship between the level of education individuals have attained and their income. A corollary of this theory is that an increase in the equality of educational attainment should generate an increase in the equality of income distribution.

Such a theory is not only attractive because it derives from commonsense ideas. It is also well supported by many data. Everybody is familiar with these curves which describe income as a function of age. They look like an inverted U: in all industrial societies, average income increases from the age category 20 to 24 to some intermediary category, say 45 to 49, and then declines. And when the number of years of education or the higher educational degree is held constant, one gets a set of such curves piling up over one another: the higher the degree, the higher the curve. In other words, for every age category, average income is higher, the higher the last educational degree or the greater the number of years of education.

Once such data and ideas are kept in mind, the fact that an increase in the equality of educational attainment very often does not produce an increase in income equality may be considered puzzling and has often been considered as such. The efforts which have been accomplished over the years to promote equality in education rested on the belief that greater educational equality would generate greater equality along other dimensions.

Of course, one can get rid of the puzzle in an easy fashion: education is not the only factor influencing income, so that its effect can be counterbalanced by other factors. Such an explanation can be properly considered as weak for a very simple reason: it solves any puzzle and has no cutting edge. "Random effects," "random factors," can always be evoked to explain why some expected effect does not appear. A much more interesting scientific game arises from the following question: is not the fact that more educational equality does not always or necessarily bring more income equality a *normal* fact? Or, to put the same question in a possibly clearer form: should income equalization really be considered as a normal consequence of educational equalization? When educational attainment becomes more equal, does this circumstance normally imply that income also becomes more equal, even in the case where it is assumed that income is strongly dependent on the level of education?

Once the question is put in such a form, it suggests to use a methodological approach generally described by the label "methodological individualism." Such a question cannot be answered if we stay at the level of aggregate statistical variables. What the question suggests to do is to build a model simulating a simplified system where (a) over time people get more equal levels of education and (b) compete on the labor and status market. Once such a model is built, it can be used to answer the question: does more equal education always bring more equal income? The statistical relationship in this case is analyzed as the aggregate outcome of a number of individual behaviors operating under certain constraints.

The logical nature of such a model will become clearer in the following pages. But we can already insist on a fundamental methodological distinction: once we observe some statistical data we can—as this is generally done by sociologists— interpret them directly in a verbal fashion. This way of analysis is often valid. But we can also attempt to explain the statistical data by showing that their structure is correctly reproduced by a model. In that case, the model will be rightly considered as providing an explanation of the data. Such models will be particularly useful when the statistical data appear as *puzzling*, i.e., as difficult to explain in an intuitive fashion. On the other hand, it will become clear in the following pages that the type of model which I advocate here has nothing to do with the usual descriptive statistical models. Evidently, such models can in no way be used to disentangle puzzles such as the one mentioned earlier.

A Set of Puzzles

It should be clear now that my main objective in this chapter is methodological. What I intend to do is to illustrate a way of thinking not often used in sociology, although it is of great importance and although it is widely used in many sciences, even social sciences.

Before we examine in some detail one example of this way of thinking applied to the problem of the effects of education, I should like to suggest that the puzzling finding mentioned earlier is not an exception. On the contrary, sociology of education is particularly challenging from a scientific viewpoint because it has produced many such findings. This was at least my impression when, some years ago, I started work on *Education, Equality and Social Opportunity*. I had the impression (a) that the abundant research produced by mobility, education, and stratification students included many obscure findings; (b) that trying to solve these puzzles was an interesting scientific challenge; (c) that the general method to be applied to solve them was the attempt at building generative models, i.e., at showing that the puzzling outcomes are a logical outcome of a set of non-puzzling, in other words, of commonsense, acceptable axioms (Boudon 1979).

In a summary fashion, I will now list some of these puzzles.

1. Lipset and Bendix (1959) showed that the structure of social mobility was much less different among industrial countries than it was generally expected. They used, as it is well known, crude stratification indicators. But this trivial objection does not limit the importance of their finding, which remains one of the few historical examples of a truly unanticipated empirical finding. Moreover, more ''sophisticated'' empirical research has, roughly speaking, confirmed this ''negative'' finding: there are differences among industrial countries as far as social mobility is concerned (how could one expect not to find any differences?), but these differences are often small. More important, it seems hard to explain them by any explanatory factor or set of factors. In other words, neither the variables describing, for instance, the stratification system nor the variables describing the educational system seem to have a clear influence on the structure of social mobility.

The importance of the Lipset-Bendix classic study rests here: France, Germany, England, and the United States certainly do not have stratification systems comparable in all respects; however, they are similar with respect to mobility. In the same way, it does not seem empirical that neither the overall development of education nor the more or less equalitarian character of the educational system has a clear-cut influence on mobility.

Again, the most frequent reaction against such unexpected and negative findings is to reject them on the basis of trivial objections: ''Look, there are still differences between such and such country''; ''The social categories are defined in a rough fashion,'' etc. More interestingly, the findings can be taken seriously.

2. The finding discussed above deals with international comparisons: there is

less difference between nations than expected and less effect on mobility of variables related to the educational and the stratification systems than expected. A symmetric intertemporal finding can be mentioned: there is less effect on social mobility than expected of over-time changes in variables related to stratification and education—to take again the example of these fundamental subsystems.

Thus it does not seem that the nonnegligible equalization of educational oportunities which has taken place in many countries in the fifties and after has had an important influence on the structure of social mobility. Here again we are confronted with a finding which, although it is negative, is of utmost practical and theoretical, social and sociological importance. During decades since the beginning of the twentieth century at least, most people—political men, as well as social scientists—had believed that the development of education and the equalization of educational opportunities would increase social mobility. Empirical data show that this influence is much less noticeable than expected.

This is not to say that mobility is weak in industrial societies, or that these societies can be compared with caste societies. On the contrary, in many of them, those coming from the highest social strata (professionals, executive, etc.) will more likely experience demotion than keep their orientation status. What I am saying is that factors which, on a commonsense basis, were expected to have an influence on mobility did not actually exert this influence. Equalization of educational opportunities may be the most visible of these factors. Education influences status; hence one is entitled to expect that, when educational level becomes less narrowly related to orientation status, orientation status should influence achieved status to a lesser extent. This expectation does not seem to be confirmed by empirical data, however.

3. Let me mention again the puzzle I started from: against expectation, equalization of educational attainment does not seem to have a clear-cut influence on equalization of income, despite the undeniable fact that educational level influences income.

4. Many other puzzling findings from empirical research can be mentioned. I will satisfy myself with mentioning some additional ones. The first one is drawn from Blau and Duncan's well-known book, *The American Occupational Structure* (1967), but it can be observed in other studies as well. Looking at the path coefficients measuring the influence on achieved social status of independent variables, such as orientation status, father's level of education, subject's level of education, subject's first job, Blau and Duncan observed that the path coefficients were similar for all cohorts. They seemed not to be surprised by this finding, as though it was trivial. A superficial reflection shows that it is not, however: so many things have changed in fifty years which should have affected the influence of orientation status on educational level, or of educational level on achieved status, or the many other statistical influences of the same type that it is surprising they have not. As a matter of fact, the first idea which comes to mind is that this invariance reflects the fact that these statistical coefficients are aggregated outcomes of a number of factors. In other words, understanding this

invariance, the no-change, can be achieved only by disentangling these aggregate outcomes—in still other words, by building a model by which it could be shown that various changes in the inputs can produce no change in the outputs.

5. Another puzzling finding is the following: most sociologists have stressed—rightly—the fact that orientation status has a strong influence on the level of education and that level of education has a strong influence on achieved status. However, empirical data show, as I already mentioned, that orientation status has a moderate influence on achieved status.

6. Another intriguing finding is that the relative status of the son with regard to his father's does not depend on his educational level. This is what I called *Anderson's paradox* (Anderson 1961).

Here are some of the puzzles which may be listed when looking at the literature on stratification, mobility, and education. In the illustration below, I will concentrate on one example and show that, contrary to what intuition might lead to expect and has often led sociologists and political men to expect, equalization of educational mobility in no way necessarily implies an increase in mobiity.

Before I proceed, I should like to stress a point which might appear obvious but is not always perceived as such. Scientific objectives are not defined by a transcendant power: no law says, for instance, that the only legitimate scientific objective is to compute path coefficients between such and such variables. As a matter of fact, the main objective of science and its *raison d'être* is to make clear what at first sight appears as obscure or puzzling. Now, it is not immediately clear why, for instance, equalization of educational opportunity does not necessarily bring increases in mobility, even though level of education powerfully influences status. Once this puzzle is recognized, a legitimate objective is to attempt to explain it. This objective does not imply that we build a model able to reproduce with an acceptable degree of accuracy such and such empirical mobility table. The model will be interesting and reach its objective if (a) it includes acceptable statements and assumptions and (b) it leads to outcomes similar to those considered as puzzling and obscure. In our example, the model will be satisfactory if it shows that equalization of educational opportunities may, under given conditions, lead to no change in social mobility. In other words, what we require from the model, if it is to be considered as an explanation of the puzzle, is that it generate the outcome: little change in the structure of mobility. Given the objective, the model need not reproduce such and such actual mobility table.

Of course, building models able to reproduce actual data can be, in some research contexts, an interesting objective, though it is not necessarily, nor always and unconditionally, so. Certainly, it is not the only interesting objective. The finding—"The influence of the amount of such and such fertilizer on crop size is measured by a linear coefficient of 0,2537"—may be an interesting finding of utmost practical interest. The finding "the influence of orientation on achieved status is measured by a linear coefficient of 0,2537" can be of no interest, neither practical nor theoretical. So, models governed by the objective of reproducing

Table 10.1
Educational Level Attained as a Function of Social Class Background and Period
(fictitious data)

| Educational Level Attained | Social Class Background and Period | | | | | |
| | C_1 (upper) | | C_2 (middle) | | C_3 (lower) | |
	at t_1	at t_2	at t_1	at t_2	at t_1	at t_2
S_1 (higher)	23	31	5	9	1	2
S_2	10	10	5	7	2	3
S_3	6	6	4	5	2	3
S_4	17	16	15	17	8	12
S_5	26	22	36	34	33	36
S_6	18	15	35	28	54	44
Total	100	100	100	100	100	100

actual data can be interesting but are not necessarily so. At least, a clear distinction should be made between such descriptive measurement models and theoretical models the aim of which is to explain why such and such data have such and such structure.

An Explanatory Model Applied to the Effect of Education on Mobility

Since we are not concerned with reproducing actual data, but with explaining and understanding the recurrent structural features of sets of data, let us consider an idealized, unidentified industrial society. We will assume that in this society three social classes—C_1 (upper), C_2 (middle), and C_3 (lower)—can be distinguished. On the other hand, in the same society, six educational levels can be distinguished. We call them S_1 (higher), S_2, through S_6 (lower). Moreover, we shall assume that between two time periods, which we will call t_1 and t_2, a certain amount of equalization of educational opportunities has taken place. Thus, by looking at Table 10.1, which is a particular numerical realization of these assumptions, we see that at period t_1 the higher-class adolescents are twenty-three times more likely to reach the highest educational level, S_1, than the lower-class youngsters. At time t_2, the disparity is around fifteen. This coefficient is obviously high, but it is lower than at time t_1. In the same fashion, the higher-class students are five times more likely at time period t_1 and about three times more likely at time t_2 to reach the second-best educational level, S_2. On the whole, although educational opportunities remain highly dependent on orientation status at times t_1 and t_2, the class disparities are less marked at time t_2 than at time t_1.

Also, Table 10.1 realizes another assumption: that all social categories are more educated at time t_2 than at time t_1. Thus at time t_1, 23 percent of higher-class adolescents reached the higher educational level, while in the same category 31 percent reached the same level at time t_2. (To make the case more concrete, imagine that S_1 means university degree.) And this increase in the level of education is the more marked, the lower the social category.

Table 10.1, although it describes no real society, is the numerical realization of a data structure quite typical of all industrial societies in the period, say, 1950 to 1970. In other words, a table on country X giving the educational level attained by a sample between, say, 1955 and 1960, or between 1960 and 1963, etc., would likely have had the same structure as the fictitious Table 10.1.

Now, the question is to determine which effects this change between t_1 and t_2 in the distribution of educational levels is going to have on the structure of social mobility.

In order to answer this question, it is necessary to introduce some additional assumptions. These assumptions will materialize, i.e., operationalize, the idea that the educational level of an individual is perceived on the labor market as a signal or a label: if a job belongs to the category of the upper positions, "those" in charge of filling it will consider the educational level of the candidates as crucial information. And they will prefer, other things equal, the candidates with the highest levels of education. This will be so either because they will interpret this high level as a sign that the candidate will be trained more quickly or that he will perform his job more efficiently, or for the many other reasons which can be easily imagined.

On the other hand, it will be assumed that the candidates, on the whole, try to get the best jobs, i.e., the jobs giving the best social positions.

In other words, these two simple assumptions lead to the idea of a two-end competition process: candidates compete for the best jobs, and jobs compete for the best candidates. So, at this point, the problem is to "organize" this competition process, to give it the form of a model by making explicit the rules and the conditions governing the two-end competition process.

These rules and conditions are easily explained by looking at Table 10.2. The last column of the first half of the table gives the number of candidates with the educational levels S_1, S_2, through S_6 competing on the status market at time t_1. These figures can be computed from Table 10.1 and from information not given in this table, i.e., the number of students belonging to each social class. These numbers, it was supposed, were the following: 1,000 for the upper class, 3,000 for the middle class, and 6,000 for the lower class. Thus, Table 10.1 tells us that, at t_1, 23 percent, 5 percent, and 1 percent of young people with, respectively, an upper-class, middle-class, and lower-class background reached the educational level S_1. The total number of students reaching this level, combining all social backgrounds, therefore equals $(1,000 \times 0,23) + (3,000 \times 0,5) + (600 \times 0,01) = 440$.

The first *Total* row in Table 10.2 gives the same figures: 1,000, 3,000, and

Table 10.2
Jobs Compete for Candidates and Candidates for Jobs at Two Time Periods (fictitious data)

Educational Level (t_1)	Social Position (t_1)			
	C_1 (upper)	C_2 (middle)	C_3 (lower)	Total
S_1	308	92	40	440
S_2	259	77	34	370
S_3	210	63	27	300
S_4	156	661	283	1100
S_5	47	1475	1798	3320
S_6	20	632	3818	4470
Total	1000	3000	6000	10,000

Educational Level (t_2)	Social Position (t_2)			
	C_1 (upper)	C_2 (middle)	C_3 (lower)	Total
S_1	490	147	63	700
S_2	343	103	44	490
S_3	117	191	82	390
S_4	35	949	406	1390
S_5	11	1127	2262	3400
S_6	4	483	3143	3630
Total	1000	3000	6000	10,000

6,000, respectively, for the higher, the middle, and the lower class. This means that in Table 10.2 we have supposed that the candidates will confront a structure of the status market similar to the structure prevailing at the earlier generation, when their fathers achieved their own status.

Obviously, other assumptions could be made. We could as well have supposed that the middle class has expanded at the expense of the lower class: this assumption would be materialized by figures such as 1,000, 4,000, and 5,000 in the first *Total* row of Table 10.1. And, of course, any other kind of interesting assumption could be made. It would even be possible, although costly, to run the model for a wide number of assumptions regarding this point of the over-time evolution of the "social structure," i.e., of the status distribution.

Also, it should be noted that in the previous paragraph, I have implicitly assumed a single replacement mechanism: each worker in the previous generation is replaced by a worker in the new one. This neglects some important facts, such as differential fertility. Obviously, other assumptions could again be easily introduced in this respect: if lower-class families had twice as many children as middle- and higher-class families, the distribution of the students as a function of orientation status would not be 1,000 (higher class), 3,000 (middle), and 6,000 (lower), but 625, 1,875 and 7,500. It would not be uninteresting to study the influence of differential fertility—other things being equal—on the structure of mobility, and this could be done with the help of the model. But this is not a problem here.

Thus the marginals of Table 10.2 indicate that, respectively, 440 students with higher educational level S_1, 370 students with second-best educational level S_2, and 4,470 students with lowest educational level S_6 compete for the 1,000, 3,000, and 6,000 jobs available, respectively, in the higher, middle, and lower class.

Of course, status is not the only dimension of jobs, nor is it of educational levels: if I have a high degree in Medieval history, I may not be qualified to fill a job requiring skills in oil engineering. And even if I have the competence to fill a job, I may not like it. Still, the rewards associated with a job are one of its main dimensions. And if all S_1s cannot fill a job of type C_1, this is also true for the S_2s. In order to summarize these assumptions, we have decided that, of the 440 youngsters trying to get a job of type C_1, not all, but a high proportion of them would get a job of this type. In Table 10.2, this ''high'' proportion has been supposed to be .7. It is checked that $440 \times .7 = 308$, which is the figure appearing in the upper left corner of the table.

Thus $440 - 308 = 132$ youngsters with a higher educational level did not succeed in getting a job of type C_1, and they will try to get a type C_2 job. Again, 70 percent will succeed, i.e., ninety-two. This leaves forty candidates with a high educational attainment. They are given low social positions.

The rest of the table is completed in the same way, maintaining the constant value of the meritocratic parameter at 70 percent throughout. Obviously, maintaining constant this value is not necessary. We would wish to introduce the assumption that those with a higher educational level are more effective and can more easily transform their educational advantage into a social one. In this case, we would differentiate the value of the meritocratic parameter over the rows of the table. Or we might complicate the model and assume that this ability in converting educational advantages into social advantages varies with orientation status. But such complications, which have an interest of their own, are not useful given the question we wish to answer. So, we will use the simple version of the model where the meritocratic parameter is constant.

Having done this, it becomes possible to examine the change in the structure of intergenerational mobility between t_1 and t_2. Table 10.1 shows us the proportion of individuals of each type of social background who attain each educational level. Table 10.2 gives us the proportion of individuals who finally attain each of the social positions (according to their educational level). In other words, Table 10.1 reveals the structure of the flows between social class background and educational levels. Table 10.2 shows the structure of the flows between educational levels and final social class. Thus, by combining the in-

Table 10.3
Two Fictitious Mobility Tables Showing that More Equality of Educational Opportunity Can Have No Influence on the Structure of Mobility

Original Social Position (t_1)		Final Social Position (t_1)			
		C_1 (upper)	C_2 (middle)	C_3 (lower)	Total
C_1 (upper)		301	325	374	100
C_2 (middle)		377	986	1637	3000
C_3 (lower)		322	1689	3989	6000
	Total	1000	3000	6000	10,000

Original Social Position (t_2)		Final Social Position (t_2)			
		C_1 (upper)	C_2 (middle)	C_3 (lower)	Total
C_1 (upper)		310	318	372	1000
C_2 (middle)		398	972	1630	3000
C_3 (lower)		292	1710	3998	6000
	Total	1000	3000	6000	10,000

formation drawn from both tables, we can reconstitute the movement from original social background to each of the social positions finally reached.

The result of this combination appears in Table 10.3. The top half of the table shows the structure of the flows between generations at t_1; the bottom half gives the structure of the same flow at t_2. You will immediately notice the minimal character of change affecting the structure of the flows between t_1 and t_2. The similar totals of the two halves of the table differ at the most by a few units. So, the proportion of individuals born into each of the three social classes and reaching each of the three social positions appears to be stable between t_1 and t_2. Without belaboring the point, we note that this conclusion remains valid even if one varies the hypotheses of the model.

As an example, let us suppose that there is an educational system which is more developed than the case just studied. At t_1, out of 10,000 adolescents, 920, 560, 400, 1,350, 3,210, and 3,560 attain educational levels S_1 through S_6. At time t_2, these figures are 1,350, 670, 470, 1,520, 3,100, and 2,890. If all the other assumptions remain unchanged, we obtain the flows of mobility that are given in Tables 10.3 and 10.4.

Table 10.4
Two Fictitious Mobility Tables with Alternative Assumptions on Educational Development

Class Origin		Present Social Origin			
		C_1	C_2	C_3	Total (%)
t_1	C_1	44.44	34.48	21.08	100.00
	C_2	28.16	41.68	30.16	100.00
	C_3	17.62	44.34	38.04	100.00
t_2	C_1	45.28	33.52	21.20	100.00
	C_2	28.52	41.12	30.36	100.00
	C_3	16.32	44.60	39.08	100.00

The model thus shows that one *can* observe an increase in the equality of educational opportunity in relation to social background without that equalization having the effect of producing any noticeable weakening of the relation between social background and social position currently held. This result does not imply that educational level has no influence on social status. Such an interpretation would be mistaken. On the contrary, the model presupposes that a good educational level confers on the individual who holds it a relative priority in the queuing process from which a social status is granted to him.

The stability of the structure of mobility flows stems from the interdependence between the agents. As educational opportunities increase, so does the size of the queue. In turn, this produces a complex effect through which claims to priority became devalued. The net result is that the increase of equality of opportunity in education does not produce any noticeable effect on the relationship between social background and social status currently occupied.

The behavior of individuals has changed between t_1 and t_2: all things being equal, an individual in the cohort t_2 will seek a higher educational level than a comparable individual in the cohort t_1. The average level of education of each social position therefore increases: moreover, the change is more noticeable among the lower positions. Despite this, and despite the fact that level of education plays a large part in determining social status, the structure of social mobility remains stable. This adds up to a neutralizing effect: the changes in individuals' behavior (from the point of view of relation between social background and eventual social status) produce effects which cancel one another out.

It is worth noting that the system of interdependence which we have just described produces a multitude of other emergent effects which do not themselves take the form of neutralizing effects. Table 10.2 shows, for instance, that the higher the position, the quicker the increase of the average of level of education. Thus the logic of the interdependent structure shown by the model means that holding a claim to priority becomes, at the same time, more and more necessary and less and less sufficient for the acquisition of a higher social status. The

chances of an individual obtaining a low social status if he does not have a
priority claim increase in the course of time. However, if he has such a claim,
his chances of obtaining a higher social status tend, at the same time, to diminish.

In sum, the structure of the interdependent system has the effect of encouraging
individuals belonging to cohort t_2 to seek a higher level of education than that
of the preceding cohort. In doing this, these agents foster the situation to which
they themselves have been exposed. This means that individuals in the cohort
t_3 will find themselves obliged to seek a still higher level of education than those
in t_2. Apart from the absorption effect described earlier, the system therefore
produces an effect of divergence of an inflationary type—perverse effects in
educational institutions. This phenomenon of divergence cannot increase indefinitely. After a certain threshold has been passed, it encourages change, both
among individuals directly concerned in the race for qualifications and among
social actors who, for one reason or another, possess a certain degree of control
over the structure of the system.

This example illustrates well the notion introduced earlier of methodological
individualism. The "decisions" made by social agents about their education are
autonomous, within certain institutional limits. Providing that I am able to satisfy
certain conditions, I can decide autonomously to study, for instance, physics.
But my decision contributes to the production of a number of emergent phenomena from the moment it is combined with the decisions of other members
of my cohort. These macroscopic phenomena result from microscopic causes—
the intentions of individual agents (and, of course, from the structure determined
particularly by institutions and by the behavior and decisions of others). However,
these phenomena are unknown to the agents.

Going back to the main outcome of the model which has just been presented,
a few points remain to be added relative to its logical structure. First of all, it
must be noted that, although the model describes a process which is highly
simplified with regard to real processes, it is logically rather complex. This can
be seen at the number of parameters which have been introduced: the parameters
describing the structure of the population of jobs and the population of candidates,
as well as the over-time change between t_1 and t_2 of these parameters, the
meritocratic parameter. Also, as mentioned earlier, implicit parameters, so to
say, are present. Thus it has been supposed that there is no differential fertility.
It has also been supposed that the educational level of the candidates is the only
information which is treated as a signal by those in charge of filling the jobs
and that social origin, for instance, is not considered by them. Introducing such
an assumption is not necessary, however, and the model could be modified and
incorporate the assumption that social origin, beyond educational level, is also
considered in the competition process. As I have mentioned, the effectiveness
in converting educational advantages into social advantages could be made dependent either on social origin or on educational level, etc.

Because of the logical complexity of the model, it has to be treated in a
simulation fashion and can be difficult to handle in a mathematical, analytical

form. This is implicitly shown by the work of Fararo and Kosaka (1979) kindly devoted to my own on social mobility. In this work, I had developed a simple model describing the over-time change of educational demand, given certain assumptions, and had originally presented the model in the form of a simulation model. Fararo and Osaka have shown that this part of my model could be handled in a mathematical fashion. The mathematical version which they produced is not only more elegant than my own presentation, but it also has an important logical advantage: the mathematical version gives a quick overview of the behavior of the model when the values of such and such parameters are changed. Unfortunately, it was not yet possible to devise a mathematical version of the part of the process which I have described in this chapter, i.e., the part which deals with the competition process including the jobs and the candidates. Therefore, it is not easy to gain an overview of the behavior of the model for changing values of the parameters.

What can be done is what is usually called a sensitivity analysis: such an analysis shows that the effect of the equalization of educational opportunity on the structure of mobility appears as weak for large regions of the parametric space.

SUBSTANTIVE AND METHODOLOGICAL CONCLUSIONS

As I said, my objective in this chapter was mainly methodological. I wanted to illustrate a way of thinking which seems to me useful not only to the sociology of education, but to any kind of sociology. The basic idea behind the model sketchily discussed here is that the aggregation of many independent behaviors or decisions can produce global effects which cannot always be easily dealt with by intuitive methods.

Using the kind of methodology I have advocated here, most of the puzzles which I mentioned earlier are easily solved: they become logical, although counterintuitive, outcomes of a set of statements which themselves are in no way counterintuitive.

Obviously, I cannot deal with this point in its full extension here, and I will content myself with some brief remarks. The model shows that the structure of mobility can remain stable even though (a) equality of educational opportunity increases and (b) level of education is a powerful determinant of status. This solves one of the puzzles identified by Lipset and Bendix, which I mentioned in the second section: two societies can be very different from the viewpoint of educational development and/or educational equality and still be similar from the viewpoint of intergenerational social mobility.

Also, the model shows—to take another puzzle mentioned in the first section of this chapter—that more educational equality does not necessarily bring more equality of rewards. (See Table 10.2 on this point.) And assume that rewards are a function both of the intrinsic social position associated with a job and of the level of education of the selected candidate—a plausible assumption—then

Table 10.2 shows that, when this assumption is included, the model tends to generate an increasing inequality of rewards. This is congruent with the analysis and data produced by Thurow (1972).

Let me finally conclude with a remark of a general nature. Sociology of education, mobility, and stratification are fields which in the past few decades have been particularly impregnated by a holistic type of approach. Social structures would have, probably by the will of God, some intrinsic tendency to reproduce themselves and a capacity to manipulate individuals and bring them to accomplish their own selfish goals. Of course, the animistic views are defended by a minority of sociologists. But many sociologists have written pages and pages on an issue—why educational attainment is dependent on social origin—where they have finally no more to say than the common man. This issue is trivial: the mechanisms responsible for the correlation between social origins and level of education are so evident that everybody—sociologist and layman—could explain them. But as this issue is a sensitive ideological topic, comments on it are well accepted by many audiences if they display a sufficient amount of rhetorical skill either of the literary or of the statistical type.

Sociology can, of course, have an ideological function. But it can also have a scientific one, i.e., contribute to solving true puzzles. And this scientific function can be accompanied by social usefulness. Thus one of the consequences of the work I have summarized in this paper is that we understand better now why we cannot expect education to be a powerful lever of equality. Although it is negative, such a consequence is obviously of utmost social importance.

REFERENCES

Anderson, C. A. "A Skeptical Note on Education and Mobility." In *Education, Economy and Society*, edited by A. M. Halsey, J. Floud, and C. A. Anderson. New York and London: Macmillan, 1961.

Blau, P., and O. D. Duncan. *The American Occupational Structure*. New York: John Wiley & Sons, 1967.

Blaug, M., ed. *Economics of Education*. London: Penguin Books, 1968.

Boudon, R. *Mathematical Structures of Social Mobility*. New York and Amsterdam: John Wiley & Sons, 1973.

———. *Education, Opportunity and Social Inequality*. New York: John Wiley & Sons, 1974.

———. "Generating Models as a Research Strategy." In *Qualitative and Quantitative Social Research*, edited by Robert K. Merton, James S. Coleman, and Peter H. Rossi. New York: The Free Press, 1979.

Fararo, T., and K. Kosaka. "A Mathematical Analysis of Boudon's IEO Model." *Information sur les Sciences Sociales/Social Science Information* 15 (1979): 431–75.

Lipset, S. M., and R. Bendix. *Social Mobility in Industrial Societies*. Berkeley: University of California Press, 1959.

Thurow, L. C. "Education and Economic Inequality." *The Public Interest* (Summer 1972): 66–81.

11

RICHARD RUBINSON AND JOHN RALPH

Methodological Issues in the Study of Educational Change

INTRODUCTION

This chapter discusses methodological issues which are typically encountered in the study of educational change. We approach this task from the perspective of empirical researchers studying education, rather than from the perspective of methodologists called upon to evaluate this research against some ideal set of technical standards. We have had to consider a variety of methodological problems in developing our own studies and in evaluating the work of other researchers, and in this chapter, we discuss those particular issues which seem to present recurrent problems or confusion in recent analyses of educational change.

In our experience, what are defined as methodological problems in a particular area of work seem to be more a function of the entire social context of the research than of the logical requirements of sound methodology. This research context certainly includes the theoretical framework in which studies are conducted, the properties of the data used in the analysis, and the orientations of the researchers themselves, in addition to the prevailing methodological standards of sociology in general. Consequently, the topics we include have no necessary relationship to one another, as some might expect in a chapter devoted to methodological concerns. Rather, these topics are simply those which have been defined as problematic by the research context in which educational change is now studied.

We discuss three types of methodological issues. First, we raise the problem of analyzing structural change through developing an analysis of social process in studies of education. Second, we discuss issues which arise when researchers work at different levels of analysis and the problems which occur in moving between individual and aggregate processes. And third, we review the work in developing a theoretical and statistical model of school expansion as a way of discussing issues of mathematical representation and quantification.

As we have said, each of these problem areas seems to have developed more from the general research context in which educational change is now studied rather than simply from narrowly defined technical concerns. Three characteristics of this research context are relevant for understanding why these particular methodological issues are so prominent now in the study of education.

First, the theoretical framework used in most studies of schooling has had the unintended and unfortunate consequence of limiting the ability of these analyses to incorporate structural change and to develop a sense of social process in education. Most recent studies of educational change have been conducted within the theoretical framework of neo-Marxist class analysis; and while the term *class analysis* covers a rather diverse group of theories, the concerns of the researchers and the questions they ask are similar. And those studies which have not been conducted within the framework of class analysis have typically been mounted in opposition or reaction to these same class analyses. So these researchers, too, share similar concerns and ask similar questions, even though their answers are often quite different. Class theories of schooling, like class theories in general, tend to be functionalist in their logical structure. But while in principle functionalist theories can incorporate structural change in social processes, in practice these functionalist theories have been elaborated in a manner that has limited their ability to confront the analysis of structural change and to develop a sense of the process of schooling. As a consequence, such studies of schooling have tended to be static in their conception of social process and weak in their ability to explain the significant variations in the structure of schooling across time and place. Improvement in these studies, then, will require a greater attention to conceptualizing schooling as a social process.

A second characteristic of the research context of these studies which has caused some methodological difficulties has been the orientations of the researchers themselves. Compared with most other areas of sociological research, the analysis of educational change has been truly a multidisciplinary endeavor. Historians and economists have analyzed education with the same intensity as sociologists and political scientists. But historians and economists have analyzed education within a very individualistic model of social action, while sociologists have analyzed these processes within an aggregate or structural model of action. But since these conceptions of action are usually implicit in the analysis, researchers from these different disciplines often find one another's evidence and arguments to be irrelevant or meaningless. Any analysis of social process, however, must be able to incorporate both the individual and the aggregate levels of action and explain the process of educational change by moving between both these levels of analysis. So researchers need to be sensitive to the implications of processes at one level of analysis for structures at a different level of analysis.

The third characteristic of the research context that has raised certain methodological issues has to do with the properties of the data used in these studies. Most historians and some economists have typically used non-quantitative data within a framework of detailed historical interpretation, while most sociologists have used extensive quantitative measures within a statistical model of interpretation. The use of these two kinds of data has lead to problems concerning the utility and meaning of formal, quantitative analysis. Within this context, we discuss the work on the theoretical and statistical modeling of school expansion, since these models are often criticized and misunderstood as instances of atheoretical statistical manipulation.

STRUCTURAL CHANGE IN THE PROCESS OF SCHOOLING

The study of social change is concerned with how people react to the conditions in which they live and in so doing change those very same conditions. The analysis of education is a promising area for studying social change because the structures of education have changed in important and systematic ways during the modern period: education has come to be monopolized by formal organizations called schools. The structures of schooling have increased both their formal political authority and their societal legitimacy. Schools have continually expanded their scope to incorporate greater proportions of the population for longer periods of individuals' lifetimes. And these structures of schooling have become ever more critical determinants of individual careers and national development (Ramirez and Meyer 1981; Ramirez and Boli 1982).

Yet the major theories of educational change have been limited in explaining the processes by which the consequences of schooling have caused these important and systematic changes in the structures of schooling. This failure to develop an adequate analysis of social change seems to be an unintended consequence of the particular theoretical framework now used to study schooling rather than a lack of awareness of these major structural changes in education.

Most recent studies of educational change have been conducted within the framework of neo-Marxist class analysis or have been undertaken in reaction to these studies (see e.g., Bowles and Gintis 1976; Carnoy and Levin 1985; Meyer et al. 1979; Ravitch 1978). And it is the functionalist logic in these studies which has limited their ability to develop a sense of social process for analyzing educational change.

As in all functionalist methodologies, these studies begin by analyzing the functions or consequences of schooling for society, and then the structure of schooling is explained as caused by these same functions (Boudon 1982; Stinchombe 1968). Such studies typically describe in elaborate detail the ways in which schooling supports the conditions of capitalist accumulation and reinforces the structures of class domination. The relationship between schooling and other structures is assumed to be one of static equilibrium, in which any observable changes in the structures of schooling are simply mechanisms to maintain the underlying invariant functionalist relationship between education and the capitalist order. Most of this neo-Marxist research, then, assumes a static analysis, since the emphasis concerns the lack of meaningful change in capitalist society by arguing from the pattern of interrelationships among structural elements at a finite point in time.

That these neo-Marxist theories should have this character may seem strange, since Marx's own formulations analyzed capitalist society as a fundamentally dynamic structure, in which temporal equilibrium was the result of a complicated social process within a continually changing system (Hernes 1976). But how this seeming paradox occurred is certainly understandable when we realize that neo-Marxist theories of schooling have developed in opposition to technical or human capital theories of schooling. In these latter theories, schooling is linked to the economy through individual productivity, to the stratification system through mobility, and to the political structure through the process of democratization. Such theories have a benign view of schooling embedded within a technological determinism. But in neo-Marxist theories, the initial conceptualization is quite different. Schooling is seen as a mechanism of inequality and domination, and the argument of technological determinism is viewed as doctrine of legitimation to mask these underlying mechanisms. As a consequence, the recent neo-Marxist studies of schooling have focused on describing the many ways that schooling is embedded within the structures of class inequality, political domination, and capitalist accumulation. But in their zeal to emphasize this conceptualization of schooling, these theories have presented a static analysis of social structures and a limited ability to explain the variations in structures of schooling across time and place.

Our intention here is not to refute this theoretical framework, for our own research is also directed toward developing a class theory of schooling. Rather, our concern is to explain that the particular methodological style in which these class theories have been formulated has lead to problems in explaining the important variations in schooling across countries, and consequently, in understanding the dynamics of educational change within capitalist society.

The major problem with these neo-Marxist functionalist theories is that while they represent a good starting point for analysis, the functionalist description has too often become an uncritical stopping point too. Arguing in a similar way, Katznelson and his colleagues (1982) say that such theories do begin at an appropriate place, for any analysis of structural change must start with a description of how the elements of a social structure fit together and function. But from such a descriptive analysis, a theory cannot automatically explain the processes that maintain or change a structure by invoking a structure's consequences as its cause. But that strategy has been the tendency of most neo-Marxist theories of schooling. These theories have typically started with a descriptive analysis of how schooling maintains some feature of inequality or domination, and then they reason backward that the causes of schooling have been to maintain this inequality or domination. So, for example, the finding that the long-term expansion of schooling has not significantly altered patterns of individual mobility is used as evidence that schooling has been structured in order to maintain these very patterns of mobility and inequality. The problem with such an analysis is that there is no explanation for either stability or change in the pattern of mobility or inequality because there is no analysis of the mechanisms that link schooling to these patterns. For if a certain amount and distribution of schooling at some time, t, has had no effect on mobility or inequality, then a long-term change in school enrollments cannot be automatically assumed to leave such patterns unaltered without an analysis of the mechanisms necessary for adjustment. But the functionalist methodology of this neo-Marxist research has tended to argue that any observed pattern of inequality has been a consequence of the structure of schooling. So, for example, in discussing the findings that students' academic rank at high school graduation is correlated with parents' social class to the same degree as at high school entry, Bowles and Gintis (1976) simply conclude that this fact shows that the function of high schools is to preserve inequality. And in commenting on this argument, Cohen and Rosenberg (1977, p. 117) make the following cogent observation:

The last statement takes several great leaps beyond the first, proceeding from an observed regularity in social organization to a statement about some deeper purpose which this regularity serves. This sort of high jumping is common enough in social science, but *Schooling in Capitalist America* carries it to Olympic Games proportions.

There are two problems with an argument like that presented by Bowles and Gintis. The first problem is that the methodological strategy employed does not lead toward an explanatory analysis of the mechanisms by which this process occurs. For example, the constancy observed in the correlation between academic rank and social class may be maintained because schools are empty organizations which do nothing to alter the initial patterns of relationships in the population; or because schools actively reinforce initial social class differences; or because a process of status competition ensues among students, so that those with more initial family resources are able to use those advantages to stay ahead of those with lower levels of resources. Which mechanism is at work, and therefore what social process is maintaining the pattern of class advantage in school attainment, is critical to understanding the long-term changes in schooling which have occurred. It is in this sense that the methodology of much neo-Marxist research has neglected the analysis of social process and structural change by assuming that the observable patterns of inequality reflect a static structure of underlying causal processes. The weaknesses of this style of analysis will become especially apparent when we see that comparative research has found that the patterns of correlations between social class and academic achievement are not constant, but do vary systematically across countries and over time. For the Bowles and Gintis type of analysis says simply that the schools' function is to preserve inequality and cannot explain the variations which exist because there is no sense of process in the explanation.

The second problem with this methodological strategy is that there is no critical attention to the causes which have structured schooling in its particular forms. In the research we are discussing, the causes of institutional change in schooling are found in the examination of the functions of education. If the effect of a particular change in education can be shown to have benefited a particular social group, this research strategy argues that the group that benefits from the structure caused the organizational reforms of schooling in order to benefit itself. So, for example, when it is observed that the long-term expansion of schooling has not lead to a change in the correlation between social class and academic achievement, this research typically argues that the expansion of schooling itself was a mechanism the dominant classes used to maintain inequality. But as Block (1977) points out in criticism of such neo-Marxist arguments, reforms such as the extension of educational opportunity are often thought of as at the intersection of working class and corporate interests, despite the substantial evidence which indicates capitalism to be a good deal less directed and rational than this approach itself presumes.

Again, our argument is not to dispute the observation that school reforms have often accomplished little in the way of reform. Rather, we are arguing that a methodology which assumes that the group that benefits from a reform was the group that caused the reform is an analysis that assumes a static societal process such that dominant groups are simply able to transform their interests into organizational structures. But such an analysis, again, cannot explain the considerable structural changes in schooling that have occurred within a basically invariant structure of class domination. Nor, for example, can such an analysis explain how the basically similar structures of class domination in Western industrial countries can produce the very different structures of schooling that we find there (Rubinson 1983).

This lack of attention to causal mechanisms in this neo-Marxist research has resulted in a lack of a sense of process in schooling, and until this limitation is overcome, these theories will not fulfill their promise of developing a cogent class analysis. Consider the following two examples:

1. *School Effects, Social Class, and Achievement.* As we have seen, a considerable amount of neo-Marxist research concerns the relationships among social class, school effects, and academic achievement. Studies from the United States and western Europe have consistently shown that the correlations between social class and academic achievement are both strong and not much altered during the time students spend in school. In addition, other studies have shown that the characteristics of schools themselves seem to have little effect on students' academic achievements once social class background is considered (Coleman 1966; Plowden 1967). Findings like these have been used to argue, then, that schools are mechanisms to reproduce the stratification system, and that they have been intentionally structured by the dominant class to produce this effect.

But without disputing the empirical findings, we would maintain that what this kind of analysis lacks is a sense of the social process that produces these empirical patterns. The methodological strategy used presents an unproblematic picture of structural invariance in the ways that schools maintain inequality: these empirical patterns are maintained because schools are mechanisms to maintain the pattern of stratification. The analysis presents a self-contained picture of a closed system in static equilibirum, with no mechanisms to produce change in these patterns over time or to account for variations in these patterns in different countries.

But many studies from outside the United States and western Europe show that considerable variation does exist among these relationships. For example, studies of underdeveloped countries typically show a different pattern. There the correlations between social class background and academic achievement are much lower, and sometimes almost nonexistent, in comparison with Western industrial countries. And these studies also show that school characteristics in such countries are much more important in determining academic achievement than in the West. In fact, school characteristics are often more important that social class in explaining academic achievement.

So comparative research has shown that other patterns of correlations among these variables are quite common, findings that we would *not* expect from neo-Marxist analyses. And so if there is considerable variation, then the analysis of these relationships as invariant and existing in a static equilibrium must be altered. For if these relationships are not necessarily invariant, then we must be able to explain the particular processes that have produced high intercorrelations in certain times and places and low intercorrelations in other times and places.

In surveying these studies, Heyneman and Loxley (1983) discovered not only that there was considerable variation in what had been assumed to be an invariant pattern of relationship, but also that this variation was systematically ordered. They found that the pattern of correlation among social class, school characteristics, and school achievement varied systematically with the level of development of countries: the lower the level of development, the less important is social class and the more important are school characteristics to students' academic achievement; and the higher the level of development, the more important is social class and the less important are school characteristics to such achievement.

Such a pattern suggests that there are some underlying social processes at work that can explain the pattern for both developed and underdeveloped countries. The particular pattern observed in the United States and western Europe, then, needs to be understood as the specific result of these underlying processes at a particular period. And the findings of Heyneman and Loxley strongly suggest that this pattern might not have been invariant, even in the United States. Rather, we might expect that these relationships have been systematically changing over time in the United States as its level of development has increased, producing an increasingly class-based educational pattern, with increasing effects of social class on achievement and decreasing effects of school characteristics.

And if there has been a systematic increase in the strengthening of social class effects and the weakening of school effects, then we must ask about the continued outcome of this process. Does such a process reach a ceiling limit and then create a static equilibrium? Or when the ceiling is reached, does this pattern reverse itself? Or does it explode and produce a different set of outcomes? Our intention here is not to answer these questions, but to raise them. Our concern is to underscore the importance of seeing these patterns of relationships—which have typically been considered invariant—as the result of a continuing social process producing structural change in education.

Now certainly this picture of the increasing class structuring of academic achievement is not at odds with a Marxist image of capitalist society. What could be closer to the root idea of Marx's analysis than a process of the increasing class structuring of academic achievement with the progressive development of capitalist society. But to understand this trend toward class structuring, we must think in terms of the social processes at work and understand that the patterns we observe at any time and place are the result of the particular combination of underlying processes occurring in a dynamic equilibrium. But the functionalist methodology of much neo-Marxist research has produced a static analysis of an invariant pattern of relationship between social class and school achievement that has prevented these theories from explaining the systematic variation that does exist in the relationships among social class, school characteristics, and academic achievement.

2. *Education, Productivity, and Economy.* A second example from this neo-Marxist research concerns the relationships among education, worker productivity, and national economic growth. While technical and human capital theories of education argue that schooling increases both worker productivity and national economic growth, most neo-Marxist theories argue that education makes little, if any, significant contribution to productivity or economic output. Human capital theories argue that the strong correlations among educational attainment, occupational status, and income arise because schooling does increase productivity and employers reward that increased productivity with better jobs and higher pay. By contrast, neo-Marxist theories tend to argue that these correlations mask an underlying process of economic reward based on social class. In this analysis, the role of education is as a mechanism which legitimates the class structure: the previous findings showing that social class determines educational achievement and that education in turn determines occupation and income are taken as evidence that schooling simply transmits class advantage. But because the transmission is through schooling, education becomes the mechanism to legitimate what is really a class-based system of allocation. The claim of human capital theories that allocation by education reflects economic productivity is seen by neo-Marxist theories as a doctrine of legitimation rather than as a legitimate explanation.

This neo-Marxist argument is based on three kinds of evidence. First, studies have shown that there is only a loose relationship between what is studied in school and the kinds of work that most people are doing. Second, other studies have found that within job categories, there is little correlation between a worker's level of education and economic productivity. And third, still other studies have revealed that the amounts of education required by employers for job entry and the amounts of education workers bring to their jobs are considerably higher than actually required to do the work. So from this body of evidence, these theories conclude that there is no fundamental relationship between schooling and worker productivity or economic output (for reviews of this literature, see Walters and Rubinson 1983; and Rubinson and Ralph 1984).

Here we do not want to dispute the nature of this evidence, but we do want to concentrate on the implications of such an analysis for the issues of social process and structural change. For while this neo-Marxist analysis argues that there is no relationship between schooling and the economy, the analysis does not provide an explanation of the process by which schooling is maintained and expanded. Nor, again, does this methodological strategy provide a way to account for the patterns of relationships found in other countries.

For example, if education is simply a mechanism of legitimation for what is fundamentally a class-based system of schooling and allocation, then we should expect that in schooling systems not based on class, education would not be used as the mechanism of allocation for occupation and income. For if the role of schooling is to legitimate a system of class allocation, then allocation by education is not required in systems not based on such class allocation. Consequently, we should expect that in underdeveloped countries, where we have seen that school achievement is not a function of social class, educational criteria should be little used as a criteria for determining occupation and income, compared with developed countries. But the empirical evidence does not support such an implication of the legitimation argument. Studies have consistently shown that educational attainment and school achievement are as important predictors of occupation and income in underdeveloped countries as in developed countries (Currie 1977; Fry 1980; Heyneman and Loxley 1983; Schiefelbein and Farrell 1981).

Such findings do not support the legitimation hypothesis. The finding that education is the primary mechanism for occupational allocation in both developed and underdeveloped countries seems much more consistent with the hypothesis that schooling everywhere does in fact increase economic productivity and is therefore used by employers as a criterion for job placement. In addition, we might also ask if schooling and the economy can be so unrelated in a capitalist economy, as claimed by neo-Marxist theories. For schooling involves large direct and indirect economic costs, and schooling has been expanding in almost all countries for a long time. Does it then make theoretical sense, especially from a Marxist perspective, to imagine that such an institution could exist independently of making a contribution to economic productivity? If anything, a Marxist analysis should make us expect that schooling is a mechanism for increasing economic accumulation, and therefore, we should expect to find important links between schooling, worker productivity, and economic output. But the lack of a sense of process in the analysis of schooling as legitimation limits the vision of these theories to consider how schooling could be so unrelated to the economy.

And when we look at the relationships between schooling and the economy in the aggregate, we do find evidence for such effects. Using long-term economic data that avoid the problem of inferring aggregate effects from individual relationships, Walters and Rubinson (1983) have shown that the expansion of schooling in the United States has made a significant contribution to increasing economic output. And Rubinson and Ralph (1984) have shown in turn that the expansion of schooling itself has been partially a function of the long-term increase in technical change. So at the level of the economy, we seem to see a process in which the expansion of schooling has contributed to the long-term increase in economic output, and the increase in economic output has in turn been an important cause of the expansion of schooling. Such a self-reinforcing economic process does not imply that schooling does not *also* serve a legitimation function. Rather, this process suggests that what makes schooling such an effective mechanism of legitimation in class-based systems is precisely its central role in the process of capital accumulation.

If the long-term expansion of schooling is part of a circular process of economic growth and technical change, we must also think about the consequences of the continual operation of such a system. At this point, we might suspect that even if educational attainment and school achievement do not begin as class-based phenomena, the increased economic reward given to workers with more schooling would create a demonstration effect which would invoke the process of the class structuring of school achievement and educational attainment, which we discussed earlier. As a consequence, the relationships among schooling, technical change, and economic output *at the societal level* would become reinforced by the relationship between social class, school achievement, and educational attainment *at the individual level*. The expansion of schooling, then, represents the joint influences of the two processes of capital accumulation at the societal level and class structuring at the individual level. Such an analysis would then explain why schooling has increasingly become a more central and legitimate institution throughout the world, for schooling represents the two central elements of capitalist society, accumulation and class formation.

But again, we must continue to think in terms of social process and not simply a static analysis. Does the analysis presented here imply a stable process of dynamic equilibrium, or do the consequences of such a system imply further structural change? Certainly, the class structuring of schooling might have led to the ever-escalating expansion of schooling through the process of status competition; and such expansion might then become unconnected to the process of capital accumulation. Here, however, our task is not to analyze the consequences of such a system fully, but to underscore the necessity of thinking in terms of social process and dynamic analyses. The problem with neo-Marxists theories of schooling, then, does not necessarily involve their substantive content. Rather, these theories have tended to focus exclusively upon a functional description of the interrelationships of the structures in capitalist society, and they have neglected the analysis of the social processes which underlie these structures.

PROBLEMS OF CAUSAL INFERENCE BETWEEN LEVELS
OF ANALYSIS

The second type of methodological problem typically encountered in studies of educational change involves issues arising from the use of evidence at different levels of analysis or aggregation. Problems of inference across levels of analysis have been widely discussed and analyzed for a long time in sociology. And a considerable body of methodological knowledge and understanding has been accumulated on these issues of aggregation and disaggregation (Hannan 1971; Hannan and Burstein 1974). Yet problems and misunderstandings are still prevalent in studies of educational change.

A large part of this continuing problem in studies of schooling seems to result from the orientations of the researchers who work in this area. The study of educational change has always been interdisciplinary, when compared with other areas of social science. Researchers from a variety of disciplines have typically studied education with the same intensity. And these researchers have different implicit understandings of social action, which cause problems in the use and interpretation of evidence from different levels of analysis.

Economists and historians of education usually work with an individualistic conception of social action, in which the relevent unit of analysis is the individual as decision maker; and the social structure is implicitly seen as the simple aggregation of the actions of these individuals. Sociologists, by contrast, typically use a structural theory of action, in which a role or collectivity is the unit of analysis; and social structures and individuals are separate, but related, institutions. But because these basic conceptions of social action are usually implicit only in educational research, evidence considered theoretically relevant by some researchers is often considered meaningless by others.

As a consequence, even though a number of separate academic disciplines share a common interest in educational change, their approach to the issues and their methodological tools are often so stylized that their findings have little impact across these disciplinary boundaries. In many instances, these academic conceptions turn simple biases into distortions. So, in an influential essay, Laslett (1980, p. 217) claims that the new quantitative history cannot deal meaningfully with structural change because its work is biased toward an individual level analysis. While Craig, in a major summary of the field, argues that *only* an individual level analysis will make the study of educational change generalizable because such an approach does not rely on structural contingencies (1981, p. 203). These heated, but unnecessary, arguments arising out of work from the different levels of analysis used in different disciplines recalls Kuklick's warning on the trials of interdisciplinary work (1979, p. 432): "Professional disciplinary scholarship . . . painfully constricts the vision of its practitioners and, in so doing, convinces them that other disciplines perpetrate frauds and deserve little time or attention."

But there is no right or wrong unit of analysis in the study of educational change or in any other phenomena. A unit of analysis is simply a replicate of whatever process is being studied (Rubinson 1977; Zelditch 1971). And any analysis of structural change in education will necessarily require the incorporation of processes at both individual and aggregate levels; for a thorough understanding of structural change requires explaining how social structures organize the actions of individuals and how the actions of individuals affect social structures (Hernes 1976). But while the study of educational change will require that social processes be analyzed at different levels, problems arise because researchers often make incorrect inferences across levels of aggregation, and these are the methodological problems that we need to discuss. Here we consider three widely researched topics that involve these problems of inference across levels of aggregation.

1. *The Contribution of Education to Economic Output.* Probably the most common instance of improper inference across levels of analysis is found in the work of human capital economists and sociologists who study the contributions of education to economic growth. The basic research question involved is straightforward: has the increase in schooling in the population increased national economic growth and, if so, by how much?

Researchers working from a human capital theory generally assume that the expansion of schooling has contributed to economic growth in the United States because of the well-known observation that people with more years of schooling have higher-status jobs and are paid higher wages than people with less schooling. That is, studies have consistently shown that there is a positive rate of return to increased schooling for workers, even controlling for a large number of other factors (Alexander and Eckland 1975; Becker 1964; Blau and Duncan 1967; Sewell and Hauser 1975).

Economists begin with these findings of the wage returns to education for individuals as a basis for calculating the contribution of the increase in schooling to aggregate economic growth. The most important work within this tradition has been done by Edward Denison, and his methodological strategy has become the standard in the field (Denison 1962, 1967). Following marginal productivity theory, Denison *assumed* that wages represent economic productivity, and so the higher wages paid to workers with higher levels of education (controlling a number of factors) represent the marginal increases in productivity owing to increased schooling. Working within a production function framework, Denison then constructed a precise estimate of the contribution that the long-term increase of education in the population has made to economic output. The particular details of his estimating procedure need not concern us here other than to underscore that the central part of the estimate involved aggregating the differences in wages paid to workers of different educational levels into a measure of the contribution of schooling to national economic growth. This procedure produced optimistic findings of the effect of education on economic output. Denison concluded that educational increases in the population had contributed 23 percent to the 2.93 percent annual average growth rate of national product between 1929 and 1957, which represented a larger contribution to growth than any other factor of production besides capital and labor (see Walters and Rubinson 1983 for details).

But notice that Denison's methodological strategy assumes that the wages paid to workers of different educational levels reflect differences in their economic productivity, and that these wages aggregate directly into increases in national economic output. This strategy, however, involves inferring that the relationship between education and output for the economy is the same as the relationship between schooling and wages for individuals.

But there is little reason to assume that such an ecological inference is valid in this situation. For the positive returns to schooling for individuals can be explained by education's affects on the process by which income is distributed among individuals within a fixed economic structure; but a positive return to schooling for the economy as a whole can be explained only by an effect of aggregate educational increase on the shape and size of the occupational and economic structure (Boudon 1974; Thurow 1974; Vaizy et al. 1972). For there can be positive economic returns to increased schooling for individuals, and no positive return for the economy as a whole, if educational credentials are simply a mechanism for allocating individuals into occupations. For there to be a positive return to increased schooling for the economy as a whole, education must do more than allocate individuals; education must also have a direct effect on altering the occupational structure of the economy. Otherwise, an overall increase in educational credentials will simply up the ante for access to similar jobs across time rather than contribute to change in economic structure or aggregate output. Denison's inference is necessarily valid only to the extent that increases in education actually create jobs or increase their productivity. But most increases in schooling are a function of individuals competing, through the accumulation of educational credentials, for the jobs that already exist.

Human capital researchers have been consistently using this methodological strategy without considering its flaws, while the neo-Marxist critics of this approach correctly respond that this method is not valid. And as we have seen, the tendency of these critics has been to disregard these findings entirely and to conclude that education has made no contribution to worker productivity or aggregate economic growth, arguing instead that education is simply a mechanism of legitimation for class allocation.

But the more appropriate response to such an example of improper inference is not to argue that the findings themselves are incorrect; rather, the response should be to design research at the appropriate level of analysis for the question. Since an analysis of the contribution of increased education to aggregate economic growth is a question that can be answered only by a design at the level of the economy, researchers should work at that level. This strategy was in fact the one used by Walters and Rubinson (1983) in their study of educational expansion and economic output in the United States. Using aggregate measures of education and economic output, this study avoided the necessity of relying on relationships at the individual level to infer the relationships at the level of the economy. This study did find that the long-term increase in education had made significant contributions to the increase in economic output; but these effects were neither as large nor as homogeneous as those found in the human capital studies. Rather, the effects of education on output were more limited, varying by level of schooling and by time period. So the increase in education has had important effects on increasing economic growth. But the appropriate evidence for this relationship must come from analyzing relationships at the level of the economy, not from inferring those relationships at the level of the individual.

2. *Technological Change and the Expansion of Schooling.* In the previous example, human capital researchers claimed that an important body of empirical work supported their theory but were appropriately criticized by neo-Marxist researchers for making incorrect inferences across levels of aggregation. In our second example, drawn from work on the relationship between technological change and school expansion, there is an ironic reversal of roles. For here conflict theorists have typically used evidence at the individual level to infer, inappropriately, relationships at the aggregate level.

As we have seen, part of the technical or human capital theory of education has depended on the claims that schooling expands as a consequence of increases in technical change. For the basic idea of this theory is one of a simple process of expanded reproduction, in which schooling increased the technical efficiency of the economy through raising skill levels; and the increase in technical efficiency in turn caused an increase in schooling to meet the demand for more highly skilled labor. Neo-Marxist and conflict theorists, however, have argued that there are no theoretically important effects of technical change on school expansion, and this claim has become an important part of their argument against the validity of this technical theory.

But what is the nature of the evidence used to support this claim? Typically, most of the evidence used is based on the relationships among years of schooling, skills, and job performance *for individuals.* This evidence does tend to show that both the educational credentials required as job criteria and the amount of schooling that workers bring to their jobs are considerably higher than the actual skills required for the tasks involved. In addition, there is little evidence that within job categories, workers with more years of schooling are more productive than workers with less years of schooling (Berg 1970; Collins 1979; Hogan 1982; Rodriguez 1978; Rumberger 1981). Taken as as whole, this evidence does show that there is little relationship among years of schooling, actual job skills required, and job performance for individuals. But neo-Marxist and conflict theorists then take this evidence on the lack of relationships at the individual level and infer that there are no relationships among technological change, the demand for skills, and the expansion of schooling at the level of the economy.

But just as human capital researchers inappropriately inferred the *presence* of a relationship between education and economic growth at the aggregate level from a relationship at the individual level, so, too, are conflict theorists inappropriately inferring the *absence* of any relationship between technical change and schooling at the aggregate level from the absence of relationships at the individual level. But the lack of correlation among education, skills, and productivity for individuals can be explained by the fact that the educational system in the United States has expanded far more rapidly than can be accounted for just by the technologically induced demand for skills, even in the presence of a systematic effect of technical change on the expansion of schooling. For a technologically induced increase in schooling at any level may lead to a far greater increase in the total amount of schooling than induced by the technical change if all groups then increase their education in order to maintain the same relative status positions that years of schooling confer. For example, if technological change were to induce a 10 percent increase in schooling to meet the demands for higher-level skills, schooling may actually increase by a much greater percentage, since school expansion is like a pernicious game, in which increased education for some lowers the value of existing amounts of education for others. As a consequence, the logic of this process of status competition forces everyone to increase their levels of education if anyone else does. So a technologically induced increase in schooling will tend to generate an increase in schooling much greater than required by the technically induced demand itself. As a consequence, we should always expect to find that the amount of education demanded by employers and the amount of education that workers bring to their jobs would be greater than the actual skills required for the tasks involved, even when there have been long-term systematic effects of technical change on school expansion at the aggregate level.

In order to argue that technological change has had no effect on the expansion of schooling, then, the evidence must come from the level of the economy and not be inferred from the level of the individual. And a study by Rubinson and Ralph (1984), which analyzed these issues at the level of the economy, did find that there have been systematic effects of technical change on school expansion, but that this technological process at the level of the economy also interacted with the status competition process at the level of the individual. School expansion in the United States, it seems, has been the consequence of these two processes of technical change and status competition. And one consequence of these systematic relationships at the level of the economy is to create systematic overeducation at the level of the individual. For individuals, there are only weak correlations among education, skills, and job performance. But these weak correlations at the individual level are produced by systematic relationships between technological change and school expansion at the aggregate level.

So the claim that school expansion has not been a function of technical change is not valid. Again, our argument is not that one unit of analysis is right and the other wrong. So those researchers who claim that the individual level of analysis is inappropriate for studying structural change and those who argue that only the individual is the correct unity of study are both wrong. Structural change involves processes at several levels of analysis, and each process has its own integrity. But our theories of educational change must be sensitive to how these processes at different levels affect one another, and so we can not simply infer relationships at one level of analysis from relationships at another.

3. *Educational Expansion as Individual Utility.* Our third example of problems of inference across levels of analysis also concerns the issue of the expansion of schooling. One way that researchers have tried to explain educational expansion is by understanding the reasons that individuals decide to continue or to terminate their schooling. Here we return to Craig's influential review of literature on school expansion, in which he attempts to organize the extant theories and research within a marginal utility framework of the individual as rational decision maker (Craig 1981).

Craig argues that to create a generalizable theory of school expansion will require a focus on the individual, since such an analysis does not rely on structural contingencies such as local political and economic conditions, the contingencies of coalition formation, and the like. The logic of his argument is that such structural conditions vary across time and place, while individuals as decision makers possess a constancy. The root explanation of school expansion, then, will come from understanding how individuals decide to continue or to terminate their school careers. And following marginal utility theory, this decision is the net result of the benefits associated with continued schooling versus the costs associated with that behavior. Summing up those individual decisions, then, explains why schooling expands, remains constant, or declines.

Craig's theoretical framework represents an approach of extreme individualism which seems to have a certain powerful appeal. For at one level of explanation, this model has to be correct. Parents certainly do want valued futures for their children, and so they weigh (however implicitly) the benefits and costs associated with schooling and then decide on school continuation. And this model does predict school continuation decisions quite well.

But to explain why individuals continue in school with a benefit-cost analysis is not to explain the process of educational expansion. For wanting to continue in school doesn't explain why there is a school in which to continue; and perceiving a net benefit from going to school does not create the benefit the student perceives. Just as gaining an education does not create a job, so does the desire to continue in school not create an opening. The processes that explain the number of positions in school systems are the processes which construct schools, give them political authority, and tie them into occupational careers and certify cultural membership. These processes do not occur because individuals want more schooling. Rather, the benefits and costs associated with continued schooling are the *consequences* of the processes that have given schools resources, political authority, and the power to allocate their students into valued occupational and cultural groups.

In short, the individual decisions to continue schooling are the consequences of the structure of schooling. The factors that carry these decisions, such as parental encouragement, peer influence, and individual motivation, are the reflections of the structural connections of schools to the larger social structure. A theory of school expansion, then, cannot explain this process by an understanding of the individual decision to continue in school, since this decision-making process is endogenous to the processes which have constructed the institutional ties between schooling and the rest of society.

Again, our argument is not that either structural or individual levels of analysis are right or wrong. Rather, there are important processes at a variety of levels of analysis, each of which interacts with the others to explain educational change. Researchers must be sensitive to understanding the implications of each of these processes for changing or maintaining social structures at each level of the system.

MODELING THE PROCESS OF SCHOOL EXPANSION

We now turn to consider issues in the area of quantification and statistical modeling in the study of educational change. Here we focus on developments within the analysis of school expansion. We focus on the study of school expansion here, not because we believe this area to be the most central for studying education, but because this is the area which has seen the most formal, quantitative analysis.

Still, there are good reasons for focusing on the work in school expansion for investigating issues of quantification and modeling. Certainly one of the reasons that school expansion has been so extensively studied derives from the availability of relatively valid and reliable data. Data on school enrollments have been routinely collected in time (Craig 1981; Ralph 1980; Schneider 1982). And in the contemporary period, the worldwide systematic data collection by UNESCO has created a large-scale comparative data base for analysis (Meyer and Hannan 1979). These various data series, then, cover large periods of time and a great many countries, so that they are useful for studying the implications of various theories and for building dynamic models of structural change in education.

But the availability, reliability, and validity of data are still not sufficient reasons for studying educational expansion. More important, data on school enrollments are useful for understanding and studying a wide range of theoretically defined issues in educational change. Enrollment figures are not simply conveniently tabulated numbers, but they can be conceptualized to represent a broad range of processes of theoretical importance.

First, some analysts are interested in enrollments as an indicator of the size of organizations or of populations of organizations. Such analysts usually study school enrollments within theories of organizational growth and decay; and enrollments are certainly one of the best indicators of the size of systems (Carroll 1981; Nielsen and Hannan 1977). Second, the size of the enrollment population is also a useful indicator for studying many of the educational changes that are central to class theories of schooling. Revisionist historians often focus on the size of enrollments as an indicator of class domination, arguing that the increase in enrollments is indicative of the success of elites in getting children into schools to socialize them to the capitalist order (Bowles and Gintis 1976; Katz 1968; Nasaw 1979). So, too, can the size of enrollments be used to study the class bias in schooling. For the expansion of school enrollments is everywhere a class-based process, with the higher classes going to school earlier and longer and the lower classes then following that schooling behavior. So the study of school expansion can become a way to follow the extension of schooling down through the class structure. And social policy issues such as equality of opportunity and equity in educational services are conditioned by the shape and dynamics of an expanding or contracting system. Typically, school systems have been highly differentiated with limited enrollments, or they have been undifferentiated with very large enrollments. Size, then, serves as a convenient indicator of the degree of stratification built into the educational system (Archer 1979, 1982; Rubinson 1983). And third, since educational growth forms part of the basis of the modern nation-state through its role in constructing citizenship and individualism, the study of enrollments has also been used in the analysis of state formation, political domination, and the expansion of the welfare state (Heidenheimer 1981; Meyer et al. 1977, 1979; Ramirez and Boli 1982a, 1982b). Certainly not all theoretically important issues can be studied through enrollments, but many can. So it is wrong to characterize the study of school expansion as an exercise in mere empiricism, for studying this process is central to analyzing many issues of educational change.

The analysis of structural change in the process of school expansion has proceeded in the typical fashion of quantitative analysis in sociology, but it will be helpful to review what this procedure involves. The term *structural change* is often confusing, since the term *structure* often takes on different meanings. Here we will follow the usages and conceptualization of Hernes (1976) and Boudon (1982):

A structure is a configuration of parts, and a structural description is a characterization of the way the components in a set are interrelated. Ordinarily we consider an observed structure, such as the proportions of a population found in different social strata, the result or outcome of a process. A standard procedure in sociological analysis is therefore to identify and construct models of the generating process in order to explain the resulting structure. However, in analyzing structural change it is crucial to note that we are dealing with structures at different levels, and that these levels are interrelated in such a way that the structure at one level is the output of a process which itself has a structure. Hence, we must distinguish between output structure and process structure. (Hernes 1976, p. 518–19)

The output structure is what we commonly consider the dependent variable or variables for a particular equation or set of equations. For studies of school expansion, the output structure is typically specified as the number of students of given ages at primary, secondary, and tertiary levels. For most countries, there has been considerable structural change in terms of both the numbers and proportions of students in school, with the expansion through levels of schooling usually proceeding from primary to secondary to tertiary levels. But the time trajectories of this expansion have differed greatly across countries, with some systems even contracting or stagnating for long periods. And the progression of expansion from primary through tertiary levels has not been uniform either. So while the United States has been a case in which the time path of enrollment has been continually expanding and moving upward through levels of the system, other countries have shown a variety of different time trajectories and patterns of movement (Schneider 1982).

This enrollment (output) structure is itself the outcome of some school expansion process, which can ideally be represented by a set of equations which we term the model of school expansion. This model can be considered to have three parts: the variables, the functional form, and the parameters. And this model, following Hernes, can be termed the operator or process structure, since it is the operation of this structure which causes the enrollment or output structure. In constructing this operator structure, the researcher includes whatever variables we considered relevant for determining enrollments, the ways in which these variables relate to one another and to the output structure, and the form of the parameters. Each of these three components—the variables, the functional form, and the parameters—are ideally given by the theory of school expansion with which the researcher is working, so that the formal model of school expansion is, in the most fundamental sense, the *theory* of school expansion. Such a model can be no better or no worse than the theory the researcher brings to the analysis, for the model is the theory.

Now sometimes it is argued that there are "surface" levels of structure and "deep" levels of structure, and changes in distributions, or output structures, do not capture real or important structural changes. Laslett (1980), for example, distinguishes between what she calls "deep social change" and simple "shifts of scale or magnitude" in a distribution, which quantitative methodology captures. She argues (1980, p. 218):

While changes in distribution may identify variation in composition—that is, in the characteristics of individuals who fill positions within the social order—it does not necessarily mean that the social relationships and processes that define the social order itself have been transformed; social change in a deeper sense of the term does have such a meaning. This distinction—between social change that reflects changes in population characteristics (as measured by distributions of attributes) and social change that refers to changes in social relations (as measured by relationships between attributes)—has received relatively little attention, either methodologically or theoretically, within the "new social history."

But such distinctions between change in distributions and change in social relations as indicative of surface and deep social change are not very meaningful. Any output or distributional structure is the result of some operator, or process structure. To call the output structure simply a "surface" structure, while the operator structure the "deep" structure, misses the understanding that the output structure is generated by the operator structure, and so they are equal components of the same theory. Certainly distributional structures can remain unaltered or change even though there is no change in the operator structure. Such processes are typically considered cases of simple or expanded reproduction (Hernes 1976). But changes in distributional structures can also act upon operator structures to alter either the parameters or the relations among the variables. And each output structure is itself part of the operator structure for some other output structure. So to argue that change in distributional structures is simply a surface change, and therefore imply that such changes are trivial, is to undermine the entire model, including the operator or process structure, which in this way of thinking is considered the deep or important structure. From a theoretical perspective, there is just no reason to argue that changes in distributions are less important than changes in either the values of the underlying parameters or the functional form that relates the variables. Changes in any one of those attributes may be as important as changes in any other, since in most dynamic processes, they are all interrelated.

Laslett continues her critique of formal statistical models in the study of structural change by pointing out that only processes that are fixed can be modeled. And if we are interested in studying social change, then presumably it is a crippling injury for formal models to be able to analyze only processes which are fixed. But again, this view of formal models misses the understanding that a process can be fixed but still dynamic and changing. Laslett's argument is misleading, for it says simply that we can only explain social processes which are not random. Such a statement is necessarily true but trivial, in the sense that this critique applies to all social science analysis and not simply formal quantitative modeling. If the variables, functional form, and parameters of the model are not fixed, then that means there is no stable underlying process that can account for the observed phenomena. But fixed processes imply neither lack of change nor stability. The components of a model must be fixed for certain periods of time; but fixed in this sense does not imply that the variables, the functional form, or the parameters will not change through the normal operation of the model.

The use of models is the only means we have for studying structural change. Such models do not necessarily have to be formally mathematical or involve quantification. But the logic of such models is no different from the logic employed in nonmathematical or nonquantitative theories. The task of analyzing educational change, then, involves developing such underlying models.

We now review the development of work on the formation of a basic model of school expansion as it has occurred over the past several years. This work has been done by a number of people who have a number of different theoretical concerns, but all focus around the development of a model of schooling. For example, Nielsen and Hannan (1977) and Carroll (1981) are most concerned with developing a general theory of organizational change. They work in a population-ecology perspective, and their empirical research has involved cross-national studies of schooling during the period from 1950 to 1970. Meyer and others (1977, 1979) have been most concerned with focusing on education's role in society, and they favor cultural and ideological theories of educational development. They have worked with both cross-national data and historical data from the United States. And Ralph and Rubinson (1980) and Walters (1984) have focused on the development of class theories of schooling, using data from the United States.

In these models of school expansion, the output structure consists of the number of students in the three educational levels of primary, secondary, and tertiary. The theoretical problem, then, is to develop an operator or process structure to explain this distribution. A first attempt at such a structure would be to write:

$$\text{Enrollment} = f(X, Y, Z),$$

where X, Y, and Z are the variables that represent the key theoretical ideas in which the researcher is interested. Thus, if we are studying educational expansion as a consequence of societal development, we might think that schooling increases as a function of increases in gross national product (GNP), level of urbanization (URB), and the density of communication (COMM). So we would begin by writing

$$\text{Enrollment} = f(\text{GNP}, \text{URB}, \text{COMM}).$$

Or, if we are working with a class theory of schooling, we might think that the expansion of schooling results from the intersection of the differing interests of capital, labor, and the state; and so we might write

$$\text{Enrollment} = f(\text{CAP}, \text{LAB}, \text{STATE}).$$

So the first step in developing a model is to specify the variables that enter into the determination of the output structure. The second step involves determining the functional form of the model. The functional form refers to the ways in which the variables are related to one another and to the output structure. Typically, we start with the simplest and most straightforward functional form, which is the linear and additive form, in which the variables are modeled to have a linear relationship to enrollments and their effects are additive in relation to one another. And so, too, with the parameter structure, we usually begin with the simplest structure of linear parameters whose values vary freely. So we write

$$\text{Enrollments} = a + B_1 X + B_2 Y + B_3 Z + e.$$

And this model has been the typical one in many studies of school expansion. This is a static model, whether the data are cross-sectional or longitudinal, for the time of any adjustment process does not enter into this model in any theoretically meaningful way. Estimated and interpreted within a standard regression framework, this model says that school enrollments in a given unit of time and place are a linear, additive function of the variables of theoretical interest, plus a random error.

While there is nothing basically incorrect with such a model, this first approximation has been replaced by considerably more refined models. What was weak in this basic model was that the variables of theoretical interest were assumed to have a direct and immediate effect on enrollments. So, for example, GNP, urbanization, and communications were assumed to have direct and immediate effects on increasing school enrollments; or the interests of capital, labor, and the state were assumed to immediately alter the distribution of schooling.

But education takes place in schools, and schools are organizations which are embedded within a particular political and economic structure. As organizations, or as populations of organizations, schools are subject to organizational dynamics in addition to whatever other factors are affecting school enrollments. Or, to be more precise, any causal variable of theoretical interest can only increase or decrease enrollments through the process of organizational expansion or contraction. Any model of schooling needs to take account of this organizational process. And it is precisely this organizational process which is missing from the models discussed above. Therefore, we must first develop an organizational model of schooling and then study the factors of theoretical interest within such an organizational model. For even if schooling expands and contracts because of the conflicts among capital, labor, and the state, these forces must work through the organizational processes of schooling. So we must first develop an organizational model of schooling and then use this model to study the factors of theoretical interest in different contexts.

The basic model of school expansion is rooted within a population-ecology perspective on organizational growth (Hannan and Freeman 1977). In this perspective, national school systems are populations of organizations in which the different levels of schooling are integrated. Extensive cross-national studies have shown that the organizational populations of national school systems are similar, in that they involve three levels of schooling with rules of allocation linking the levels to one another (Ramirez and Rubinson 1979). So a model of school expansion must take account of the fact that the different levels of schooling are systematically linked to one another. In addition, school expansion has been found to have a self-generating character. That is, the population characteristics already built into the school system at any time, t, reflect the prior operation of the various social factors that have historically shaped the patterns of enrollment. Since patterns of schooling at any time tend to be highly institutionalized through political regulations, rules of occupational certification, and individual status expectations, school enrollments will continue to change, even if the factors that affected the shape of schooling in the past no longer operate. That is, if school expansion has been a function of the intersection of the interests of capital, labor, and the state, we would not expect schooling to drop immediately to zero if, for some reason, these factors ceased to operate. Populations of organizations like schools have a considerabale amount of organizational inertia constructed into them and so will continue to expand or contract as a function of the characteristics that have already been built into the system. It is in this sense, then, that school expansion at any particular time can be considered a self-generating process (Freeman and Hannan 1975; Meyer et al. 1977).

Such a self-generating model of school expansion can be expressed in terms of three basic theoretical factors: (1) the size of the socially defined population eligible for school at each level, (2) the proportion of this eligible population already incorporated in school, and (3) the socially defined alternatives to schooling for those in the eligible population. For example, in the case of primary and secondary schooling in the United States, Rubinson and Ralph (1984) measured these three factors in the following way.

First, the size of the socially defined eligible population for primary school (grades one through eight) was measured by the number of youth ages five to thirteen (POP) because that age-group population reflects the general laws and norms of primary school attendance in the United States. For secondary school (grades nine through twelve), the size of the eligible population was measured by the number of students in primary school (PRI), since by the rules of allocation in this system, students must complete the primary grades before entering secondary school. So this measure of the eligible population takes account of the necessary organizational progression from primary to secondary schooling. The particular indicators for these two underlying variables would, of course, be different in systems with different definitions of the school-age population and different rules of progression.

Second, a measure of the proportion of the eligible population already in school is needed because the *absolute* growth of enrollments is bounded by floor and ceiling effects, and the *rate* of growth varies by how close the size of the eligible population is to the floor or ceiling limit. Incorporating floor and ceiling limits into this model of organizational growth is necessary, because the rules of schooling define a minimum and maximum number of people who can be in these organizations, based on the population eligible for each level already incorporated into the educational system. In addition, we know that in normal growth processes of this sort, growth starts slowly, speeds up through some middle range, and then slows. Such a pattern marks the familiar S-shaped curve of many growth processes, and this is the process we need to model. To model this effect for the expansion of primary enrollments, we can use the ratio of the number of students in primary school to the number in the age-eligible population (PRI/POP); and for the expansion of secondary enrollments, we can use the ratio of the number of students in secondary school to the number in primary school (SEC/PRI). These terms are zero when no one in the eligible population has progressed to the next level in school and approach unity as the proportion of those in the eligible population increase their school progression. Consequently, they indicate that the expansion of enrollments varies by where the size of enrollments falls in relation to either the floor or the ceiling limits. There are certainly many ways to construct terms modeling these floor and ceiling effects. In earlier works, Meyer et al. (1977) and Ralph and Rubinson (1980) used a combination of several rather unwieldly terms to capture these processes, using separate terms for both floor and ceiling effects and separate terms for the proportions of students both incorporated and unincorporated into the school system. The advantage of terms like PRI/POP and SEC/PRI is that they incorporate these different features in one term. The term PRI/POP, for example, serves as both a floor and a ceiling effect, depending simply on its actual empirical values. If its value is between 0 percent and 50 percent, then this term will capture the floor effect, and the expected sign of its coefficient, when estimated, will be positive, reflecting the fact that the rate of growth increases as growth leaves the floor and heads toward the ceiling. But if its value is between 50 percent and 100 percent, then this term will capture the ceiling effect, and the expected sign of its coefficient, when estimated, will be negative, reflecting the fact that the rate of growth decreases as growth approaches the organizational limit. The term SEC/PRI captures the same features of growth for the secondary level of schooling.

And third, the alternatives to schooling for the case of the United States can be measured by the unemployment rate (UNEMP), since the major alternative to schooling is employment. Different alternatives to schooling are likely to be relevant in other contexts, and they may certainly vary by time. But in such a model, inclusion of the relevant alternatives to schooling is certainly necessary.

This model, then, can be written as

Primary Enrollments = f (POP, PRI/POP, UNEMP), and
Secondary Enrollments = f (PRI, SEC/PRI, UNEMP).

What remains is to specify the functional form and any time dependencies for the model. In this instance, Rubinson and Ralph (1984) specify the model with a semilogarithmic functional form (Stolzenberg 1979). The semilogarithmic form, which is often used in models of growth, captures the idea that enrollments continually change as a consequence of the population characteristics built into the organization of schooling. In addition, a semilogarithmic form is used because a given percentage rate of growth will generate ever-increasing absolute increases in enrollments, since the enrollment base from which the growth is calculated tends to increase each year. Consequently, a compound rate of growth implies a linear relationship, not between, say PRI and time t, but between the natural logarithm of PRI and time t. In this model, then, the semilogarithmic functional form is used. This model can be written as

$$Y = a + B_1X_1 + B_2X_2 + e.$$

And taking logarithms can be expressed as

$$Ln(PRI_t) = a + B_1POP_t + B_2(PRI)/POP_{t-1} + B_3UNEMP_{t-1} + e$$
$$\text{and } Ln(SEC_t) = a + B_4PRI_t + B_5(SEC/PRI)_{t-1} + B_6UNEMP_{t-1} + e.$$

The theoretical specification, then, models the percentage change in primary enrollments at time t, $Ln(PRI_t)$, as a function of the size of the age-eligible population at time t, (POP); the proportion of the age-eligible population in primary school lagged back one year $(PRI/POP)_{t-1}$; and the unemployment rate lagged back one year $(UNEMP)_{t-1}$. The model for secondary enrollments is the same except that the eligible population is primary enrollments (PRI_t) and the proportion of the population in school is the ratio of secondary to primary enrollments $(SEC/PRI)_{t-1}$. The causal effects in this model are interpreted as percentage changes in enrollments per unit change in the independent variables because the dependent variable is a logarithm.

Different functional forms and time dependencies can be incorporated into this basic model to take account of different spatial and historical contexts or to model different theoretical ideas. So, for example, working within a population-ecology theory, Nielsen and Hannan (1977) build a model with linear resource effects, only asymmetric relations between the three levels of schooling, and linear partial adjustment growth. However, Carroll (1981), working within the same theory, builds a model with nonlinear resource effects, symmetric relations between the three levels of schooling, and logistic growth. Once this basic model of organizational growth has been specified, then other variables of theoretical interest can be incorporated into this model. Their functional form and time dependencies will, of course, depend on the particular theoretical ideas to be studied. So, for example, Meyer et al. (1977) incorporate a variety of variables of societal development and political structure into their models. Ralph and Rubinson (1980) study the effects of immigration into different historical contexts in the United States. Nielson and Hannan (1977) and Carroll (1981) study resources effects. Rubinson and Ralph (1984) analyze the effects of technical change. And Walters (1984) studies the effects of occupational shifts.

In each of these studies, the organizational model of school expansion has performed well. The effects of the age-eligible population, the floor and ceiling effects, and the alternatives to schooling have behaved in expected or interpretable ways, and the variance explained by this portion of the models has been significant. Most encouraging, when compared with other models in the social sciences, the behavior of this model has been relatively invariant across a wide variety of historical times and national systems. It is precisely this stability of the organizational model which holds promise for eventually developing a general theory of school expansion, for the effects of different variables and different social contexts can then be studied in a systematic manner.

CONCLUSIONS

The study of schooling is now in the midst of a period of intellectual and theoretical excitement. This excitement is primarily the result of serious development of neo-Marxist or conflict theories of education. What processes account for continual progress in social science are still unclear, but rigorous theoretical development and good empirical research are necessary for each other. In this chapter, we have discussed a number of issues which we see as potentially impeding the progress of the study of educational change. Our aim was not to be critical, but to be helpful in pointing out some problems which we feel may cause work to be prematurely stopped in this field. Too often do fresh insights and surprising research findings seem to signal a time for stopping rigorous theoretical research. We do not want this typical outcome to happen in the sociology of education, and so we want our chapter to be seen as an impetus to keep pushing out the bounds of this work.

Our analysis of the weakness of neo-Marxist theories of schooling was directed toward this end. Our concern is that the initial insights and theoretical developments here have been left in a state of complacency. We have tried to demonstrate that such theories, developed to explain contemporary schooling in the industrial West, run into obvious inconsistencies when used to explain the findings of comparative research. Too often the discovery of such problems cause researchers, especially critics, to call for the abandonment of the theory, and we are off on another round of searching for new paradigms (see Ravitch 1978). Our analysis of these theories is quite different. We see the problem of neo-Marxist theories as owing to a lack of incorporating the idea of social process. If these theories would take their insights and formulate them within an idea of the social process of schooling, then we will see progressive theoretical development. Our argument was designed to specify this general claim.

In our second section on problems of inference across levels of analysis, our aim was to correct some problems in the empirical research on schooling. While the interdisciplinary character of research on schooling is something which in principle is exemplary, in practice, much of this research by the different disciplines is more competitive than cumulative. We believe that one of the reasons for this situation is that researchers from different disciplines bring with them different implicit theories of social action, and these implicit theories cause problems which surface in the design and interpretation of research at different levels of analysis. The tendency in the work on schooling has been for researchers to make unnecessary and extreme claims about what is or is not the true unit of analysis and in so doing discredit or ignore other potentially useful work. Our examples in that section were designed to show that such mistakes in inference occur in both technical-functional and neo-Marxist research on schooling; and mistakes in inference occur in both aggregation and disaggregation. A full theory of structural change in schooling, we argued, necessarily requires the incorporation of processes at a variety of levels of analysis; so that the *a priori* rejection of findings from any level is necessarily wrong.

Our final section on the formal modeling of school expansion was designed to call attention to what seems to be a persistent problem in the issue of quantification. Too often do researchers who work with less formal, quantified analyses reject as trivial the more formal, quantitative analyses of others. And so, too, do the researchers working with mathematical and statistical models too often pass off nonquantified, historical, and interpretive analyses. Our example of the formal modeling of school expansion in this section was designed to show that the logic of analysis is the same whether it is in the form of mathematical modeling or not. The important understanding is that all social scientific research requires models to study social processes.

REFERENCES

Alexander, Karl, and Bruce Eckland. "Basic Attainment Processes: A Replication and Extension." *Sociology of Education* 48 (1975): 457–95.

Archer, Margaret. *Social Origins of Educational Systems*. Beverly Hills, CA: Sage Publications, 1979.

———. *The Sociology of Educational Expansion: Take-Off, Growth, and Inflation in Educational Systems*. Beverly Hills, CA: Sage Publications, 1982.

Becker, Gary. *Human Capital*. New York: Columbia University Press, 1964.

Berg, Ivar. *Education and Jobs: The Great Training Robbery*. Boston: Beacon Press, 1970.

Blau, Peter, and O. D. Duncan. *The American Occupational Structure*. New York: John Wiley & Sons, 1967.

Block, Fred. "Beyond Corporate Liberalism." *Social Problems* 24 (1977): 352–61.

Boudon, Raymond. *Education, Opportunity, and Social Inequality*. New York: John Wiley & Sons, 1974.

———. *The Logic of Social Action: An Introduction to Sociological Analysis*. London: Routledge & Kegan Paul, 1982.

Bowles, Samuel, and Herbert Gintis. *Schooling in Capitalist America: Educational Reforms and the Contradictions of Economic Life*. New York: Basic Books, 1976.

Carnoy, Martin, and Henry Levin. *Schooling and Work in the Democratic State*. Stanford, CA: Stanford University Press, 1985.

Carroll, Glenn. "Organizational Expansion in Systems of Education." *American Sociological Review* 46 (1981): 585–91.

Cohen, David, and Bella Rosenberg. "Functions and Fantasies: Understanding Schools in Capitalist America." *History of Education Quarterly* 17 (1977): 113–37.

Coleman, James, et al. *Equality of Educational Opportunity*. Washington, DC: U.S. Government Printing Office, 1966.

Collins, Randall. *The Credential Society: An Historical Sociology of Education and Stratification*. New York: Academic Press, 1979.

———. "The New Sociology of Education." In *Sociology since Mid-Century*, edited by Randall Collins. New York: Academic Press, 1981.

Craig, John. "The Expansion of Education." In *Review of Research in Education*, edited by David C. Berliner. Washington, DC: American Educational Research Association, 1981.

Currie, Janice. "Family Background, Academic Achievement, and Occupational Status in Uganda." *Comparative Educational Review* 21 (1977): 14–28.

Denison, Edward. *Two Sources of Economic Growth in the United States and the Alternatives before Us*. New York: Committee for Economic Development, 1962.

———. *Why Growth Rates Differ: Postwar Experiences in Nine Western Countries*. Washington, DC: Brookings Institution, 1967.

Freeman, John, and Michael Hannan. "Growth and Decline Processes in Organizations."
    American Sociological Review 40 (1975): 215–28.
Fry, Gerald. "Education and Success: A Case Study of Thai Public Service." *Compar-
    ative Education Review* 24 (1980): 21–34.
Hannan, Michael. *Aggregation and Disaggregation in Sociology*. Lexington, MA: D.C.
    Heath, 1971.
Hannan, Michael, and Leigh Burstein. "Estimation from Grouped Observations." *Amer-
    ican Sociological Review* 39 (1974): 374–92.
Hannan, Michael, and John Freeman. "The Population Ecology of Organizations."
    American Journal of Sociology 82 (1977): 929–66.
Heidenheimer, Arnold. "Education and Social Security Entitlements in Europe and Amer-
    ica." In *The Development of Welfare States in Europe and America*, edited by
    Peter Flora and Arnold Heidenheimer. New Brunswick, NJ: Transaction Books,
    1981.
Hernes, Gudmund. "Structural Changes in Social Processes." *American Journal of
    Sociology* 82 (1976): 513–47.
Heyneman, Stephen. "Influences on Academic Achievement: A Comparison of Results
    from Uganda and More Industrialized Societies." *Sociology of Education* 49
    (1976): 200–11.
Heyneman, Stephen, and William Loxley. "The Effect of Primary-School Quality on
    Academic Achievement across Twenty-Nine High- and Low-Income Countries."
    American Journal of Sociology 88 (1983): 1162–94.
Hogan, David. "Making It in America: Work, Education, and Social Structure." In
    Work, Youth, and Schooling, edited by Harvey Kantor and David Tyack. Stanford,
    CA: Stanford University Press, 1982.
Katz, Michael. *The Irony of Early School Reform: Educational Innovation in Mid-Nine-
    teenth Century Massachusetts*. Cambridge, MA: Harvard University Press, 1968.
Katznelson, Ira, Kathleen Gille, and Margaret Weir. "Public Schooling and Working-
    Class Formation: The Case of the United States." *American Journal of Education*
    90 (1982): 111–43.
Kuklick, B. "A Review of *Theoretical Methods in Social History* by Arthur L. Stinch-
    combe," *History and Theory* 18 (1979): 427–33.
Laslett, Barbara. "Beyond Methodology: The Place of Theory in Quantitative Historical
    Research." *American Sociological Review* 45 (1980): 214–29.
Meyer, John, et al. "The World Educational Revolution, 1950–1970." *Sociology of
    Education* 50 (1977): 242–58.
———. "Public Education as Nation-Building in America: Enrollments and Bureaucra-
    tization in the American States, 1870–1930." *American Journal of Sociology* 85
    (1979): 591–613.
Meyer, John, and Michael Hannan. *National Development and the World System*. Chi-
    cago: University of Chicago Press, 1979.
Nasaw, David. *Schooled to Order: A Social History of Public Schooling in the United
    States*. New York: Oxford University Press, 1979.
Nielsen, Francois, and Michael Hannan. "The Expansion of National Educational Sys-
    tems." *American Sociological Review* 42 (1977): 479–90.
Plowden Report. Children and Their Primary Schools: A Report of the Central Advisory
    Council for Education (England). London: Her Majesty's Stationery Office, 1967.

Ralph, John. "Bias in Historical School Enrollment Figures." *Historical Methods* 13 (1980): 215–21.

Ralph, John, and Richard Rubinson. "Immigration and the Expansion of Education in the United States." *American Sociological Review* 45 (1980): 943–54.

Ramirez, Francisco, and John Boli. "Global Patterns of Educational Institutionalization." In *Comparative Education*, edited by P. Altbach, R. Arnove, and G. Kelly. New York: Macmillan, 1982a.

———. "On the Union of States and Schools." Paper presented at the Annual Meetings of the American Sociological Association, San Francisco, 1982b.

Ramirez, Francisco, and John Meyer. "Comparative Education: The Social Construction of the Modern World-System." *Annual Review of Sociology* 6 (1981): 369–99.

Ramirez, Francisco, and Richard Rubinson. "Creating Members: The National Incorporation of Education." In *National Development and the World System*, edited by John Meyer and Michael Hannan. Chicago: University of Chicago Press, 1979.

Ravitch, Diane. *The Revisionists Revised: A Critique of the Radical Attack on the Schools.* New York: Basic Books, 1978.

Rodriguez, Orlando. "Occupational Shifts and Educational Upgrading in the American Labor Force between 1950 and 1970." *Sociology of Education* 51 (1978): 55–67.

Rumberger, Russell. *Overeducation in the U.S. Labor Force.* New York: Praeger, 1981.

Rubinson, Richard. "Methodological and Theoretical Issues in Comparative Research." *American Sociological Review* 42 (1977): 817–21.

———. "Class Formation, Political Organization, and Institutional Structures." Department of Sociology, Johns Hopkins University, 1983.

Rubinson, Richard, and John Ralph. "Technical Change and the Expansion of Schooling in the United States, 1890–1970." *Sociology of Education* 57 (1984): 134–52.

Schiefelbein, Ernesto, and Joseph Farrell. "Education and Occupational Attainment in Chile: The Effects of Educational Quality, Attainment, and Achievement." Washington, DC: World Bank, 1981.

Schneider, Reinhart. "Die Bildungsentwicklung in Den Westeuropaisohen Staaten 1870–1975." *Zeitschrift Fur Sociologie* 3 (1982): 207–26.

Sewell, William, and Robert Hauser. *Education, Occupation, and Earnings: Achievement in the Early Career.* New York: Academic Press, 1975.

Stinchcombe, Arthur. *Constructing Social Theories.* New York: Harcourt, Brace & World, 1968.

Stolzenberg, Ross. "The Measurement and Decomposition of Causal Effects in Nonlinear and Nonadditive Models." In *Sociological Methodology*, edited by Karl Schuessler. San Francisco: Jossey-Bass, 1979.

Thurow, Lester. *Generating Inequality: Mechanisms of Distribution in the U.S. Economy.* New York: Basic Books, 1974.

Vaizey, John, et al. *The Political Economy of Education.* New York: John Wiley & Sons, 1972.

Walters, Pamela. "Occupational and Labor Market Effects on Secondary and Post-Secondary Expansion in the United States: 1922 to 1979." *American Sociological Review* 49 (1984): 659–71.

Walters, Pamela, and Richard Rubinson. "Educational Expansion and Economic Output

in the United States, 1890–1969.'' *American Sociological Review* 48 (1983): 480–
93.
Zelditch, Morris. "Intelligible Comparisons." In *Comparative Methods in Sociology*,
edited by Ivan Vallier. Berkeley: University of California Press, 1971.

12

BARBARA HEYNS

Educational Effects: Issues in Conceptualization and Measurement

INTRODUCTION

Educational effects do not command an imposing position in the contemporary curriculum. In the academic departments of both Education and Sociology, the subject is typically relegated to a small section of a course on research methods. Methodological and conceptual issues concerning school effects have attracted substantially less attention than the political controversy and debate occasioned by substantive research. Yet the study of educational effects has profoundly and permanently altered the ways we conceive of schooling and educational outcomes. Without exaggeration, one could characterize the past twenty years of educational research as a prolonged dispute over the meaning and measurement of educational effects. In the process, the hybrid discipline of sociology of education has been fundamentally transformed.

The landmark event that changed both the conceptualization of educational effects and the research traditions in the sociology of education was the publication of the *Equality of Educational Opportunity* report (Coleman et al. 1966). This study was unique in many respects. It was one of the first instances of a congressionally mandated survey with a specific policy focus. It collected a vast amount of information on students and schools that permitted, indeed provoked, a veritable flood of reanalysis, replication, and critique. And in one bold stroke, it challenged the methodological and conceptual assumptions that had been prevalent in education for an age (Bowles and Levin 1968; Cain and Watts 1970; Mosteller and Moynihan 1972; Jencks 1969, 1972).

In evaluating the Coleman report, it is important to remember the findings confirmed, rather than challenged, most of the research that preceded it (Stephens 1967). Comparisons among schools, classrooms, curricula, or teaching techniques do not typically explain much of the observed variance in student achievement when characteristics of students are controlled (Domas and Tiedeman 1950; Gage 1963; Rostker 1945; Stephens 1967). Yet, taken as a whole, this literature had made little impact on educational policy, while the Coleman report was hailed as "literally of revolutionary significance" (Nichols 1966, p. 1314). The reasons, I will argue, are to be found in the conceptual leap that equated equality of educational opportunity with the observed performance levels of schools and that confused the process of schooling with observed achievement differences between schools. As a political concept, equal opportunity has powerful connotations in American society. Examining outcomes in education, the institutional complex assumed to facilitate or subvert opportunity, the Coleman report was bound to be controversial. The radical conceptual shift, however, was to take for granted that differences in achievement scores among schools were a reasonable measure of "effective" educational opportunity. Modest school-to-school variation was assumed to indicate the lack of equal opportunity and the paucity of school effects. By focusing on school outcomes as effects, what had been a host of null findings in educational research became an indictment of education generally. Not only were particular schools or programs seemingly ineffective in raising student achievement levels, but an entire system of public education was at fault.

The concepts and methods adopted by the *Equality of Educational Opportunity* report have shaped the educational research agenda for the subsequent two decades. In order to understand why the concept of an educational effect implied by the *Equality of Educational Opportunity* report was a breakthrough, it is necessary first to examine what is meant by an effect and then to examine why and how such effects have become synonymous with educational opportunity.

The Nature of an Effect

In broad terms, an effect is the degree of change in an outcome associated with a particular presumed cause. Over the course of the past twenty years, there has been a discernible shift in what is meant by effects in education and in the methods commonly used to demonstrate their existence and magnitude. Educational research has traditionally been strongly influenced by the field of psychology; consequently, the carefully controlled experiment tends to be valued more highly than other forms of research. En route to becoming a full-fledged policy science, however, educational research has borrowed the methods and techniques of numerous other disciplines. Increasingly, one finds econometric models and social surveys used to describe causal relationships and effects in education (Anderson 1978; Dyer et al. 1969; Shapiro 1979).

The major purpose of experimentation is to control, as rigorously as possible, extraneous or confounding factors so as to maximize internal validity. Depending on the quality of experimental control achieved, an effect can be considered caused by a unique manipulable independent variable, such as a specific program or treatment (Cook and Campbell 1979). In contrast, models used to describe educational effects in nonexperimental settings typically involve statistical controls for confounding factors; the principle aim is to maximize external validity or generalizability across samples. Effects in such a model are the observed contribution particular factors make to prediction or explanation when extraneous factors are statistically controlled.

The goal of research, in either case, is to understand causal relationships. However, two distinct philosophies of science underlie the logic and procedures (Shapiro 1984). A controlled laboratory experiment allows one to deduce causal inferences from a specific intervention. A regression model explains or describes observed variability in outcomes; effects are estimated so as to maximize the variance explained. The experimental logic is deterministic; an effect, once isolated, is believed to hold in all comparable settings, which would allow educators to replicate successful programs with confidence. In contrast, effects based on a sample survey are probabilistic; estimated effects are assumed to be time-bound and sample-specific. In regression, the underlying model involves assumptions about the distribution and size of stochastic disturbance terms. The size and significance of a measured effect depends on the degree to which it reduces uncertainty in the prediction of an outcome. Although perfect prediction is possible in theory, most analysts are quite satisfied with an R^2 substantially below unity.

These two distinct conceptions of educational effects have generated considerable controversy. The logic of modeling educational processes with nonexperimental data assumes that if associations persist once prior extraneous factors are controlled, causal significance can be assumed. Interpretations of educational effects in nonexperimental research are, however, inherently problematic. First, one must be confident that student background factors are adequately controlled and that all relevant explanatory variables are included in the equation. If relevant factors are omitted, or if the control variables are only approximate, the models will be misspecified and the effects potentially spurious. Second, the size of the estimated effects depends on the degree of multicollinearity among independent variables. Since background factors are invariably correlated to school or program assignment in naturalistic settings, some portion of the explanatory variance is joint or shared. The strategy used to partition joint variance, therefore, determines the magnitude of effects and their level of significance (Werts and Linn 1969; Pedhazur 1975).

In contrast, an effect estimated in experimental research is based on comparisons between two or more programs or settings with individual differences controlled through randomized assignment. An effect is thus the unique link between outcomes and a specific manipulable cause. "Internal validity is the sine qua non" (Cook and Campbell 1979) of experimentation, while external validity is typically problematic. If a program effect interacts with student characteristics, or if the research conditions cannot be replicated in nonexperimental settings, the estimated effects lack external validity and cannot be generalized.

Educational effects are ultimately as elusive as the concepts of causality on which they depend. Since large-scale educational experimentation is generally impractical or unethical, estimating effects under nonexperimental conditions will doubtless continue to be the predominant method for understanding the educational process. Given the complex array of relevant and interrelated factors, inconsistent or equivocal conclusions about the size of educational effects seem likely to remain the norm. Moreover, even when coefficients attain statistical significance, we are far from being able to prescribe appropriate educational policies that increase student achievement. School effects are important in educational research because they focus attention on schooling and on school outcomes. They are not directly relevant to policy formation, however. The Coleman report represents a watershed not because of specific findings, but because school effects were linked to a powerful political concept, equality of educational opportunity.

The Conceptual Muddle: Equality of Educational Opportunity

Several competing concepts of equal educational opportunity were prevalent in the literature of the mid-1960s. Coleman (1968a) aptly summarized five different definitions of this concept, while illuminating the various mandates of the *Equality of Educational Opportunity* report. First, access to school resources and facilities, such as libraries, high-quality teachers, or per-pupil educational expenditures were assumed to be important indicators of opportunity. Second, the racial composition of schools was viewed as a critical factor in equality of opportunity since it measured the degree of segregation prevalent. Third, a host of intangible characteristics, such as school morale, community support, or the social composition of a school, were considered relevant to student educational opportunities. Fourth, the consequences or outcomes of schooling; and fifth, the outcomes for students with comparable backgrounds and ability were presumed central to understanding educational opportunity (Coleman 1968a).

Information germane to each of these five definitions of equality of opportunity are to be found in the *Equality of Educational Opportunity* report (Coleman et al. 1966). The distribution of resources and educational inputs, central to the first three concepts, were presented first; however, it was Chapter 3, focusing on the inequalities in outcomes, that attracted the most attention. "Schools," concluded the report, "bring little influence to bear on a child's achievement that is independent of his background and general social context" (Coleman et al. 1966, p. 325). Inequality of opportunity appeared to lie in "the home and the cultural influences immediately surrounding the home"; schools were ineffective in freeing achievement from the impact of the home (Coleman et al. 1966, p. 74).

The truly radical idea implicit in these conclusions, was that equal opportunity necessarily implied "*effective* equality of opportunity" (Coleman 1968a, p. 19). By linking equality of opportunity to the observed outcomes between schools, the Coleman report fundamentally changed the way in which equal educational opportunity was conceived. As Coleman (1972) has argued, the enduring impact of the study was "shifting policy attention from its traditional focus on comparisons of inputs ... to a focus on output and the effectiveness of inputs in bringing about changes in outcomes" (Coleman 1972, pp. 149–50).

The logic of relating educational outcomes to specific causal factors is clear; however, when the causal agent is defined globally as the school, the maximum effects of schools are, by definition, limited to the observed variability among them. Further, if schools differ in achievement largely because their student bodies vary, the impact of any specific characteristic of schools will necessarily be small when student differences are controlled. The irony of defining equality of opportunity as *effective* opportunity is to define the modest observed variability between schools as an indicator of unequal opportunity rather than as an indicator of equality of outcomes. An alternative case is easy to make. If one were to compare the outcomes of legal institutions by the patterning of verdicts or sentences by courts, controlling for the nature of the crimes involved, it would be possible to assess equality of judicial treatment. However, disparities between courts and judges would be suspect, not uniformities. Outcomes that can predictably be related to one court or another would suggest unequal justice or unequal treatment under the law; a distribution of verdicts that depended only on the characteristics of cases would not. Equality of judicial treatment implies that the law is administered according to the facts of the crime, not according to the discretionary whim of a particular court or judge. Yet educational outcomes that are shown to be unrelated to school characteristics once student characteristics are controlled are taken as *prima facie* evidence that schools do not provide equality of opportunity.

The effects of particular teachers or curricula embody a similar paradox. A college preparatory curriculum is an "effective" form of educational opportunity, in that student achievement is consistently higher among students enrolled in this tract compared with those assigned to a general or vocational curriculum, irrespective of social background (Alexander and McDill 1976; Alexander et al. 1978; Alexander and Cook 1982; Heyns 1974; Kulik and Kulik 1982; Rosenbaum 1975, 1976). Yet unequal outcomes by track are often assumed to mean unequal educational opportunity since curriculum placement tends to be correlated to social class and race (Davis and Haller 1981; Heyns 1974; Rehberg and Rosenthal 1978; Rosenbaum 1975, 1976; Schafer and Olexa 1971).

Disentangling the diverse meanings attached to equality of opportunity and the disparate ways in which analysts have measured the concept is a worthwhile exercise. The present aim, however, is more modest. In a variety of contexts, the logic of inferring causal impact from the observed patterning of outcomes between schools has led to misleading conclusions. Inferences regarding schooling as a process have been drawn from data that logically applied only to schools as places containing particular aggregations of students. School effects, defined as differences between schools, is not equivalent to the effects of education, which must be considered to include the cumulative outcomes of being in school

over time as well as place. Too often assertions regarding the similarity of
outcomes between schools slide into arguments about schooling or the impact
of education generally.

Research in the school effects tradition has tended to measure differences
between schools in a variety of ways. We shall focus primarily on school climate
studies, educational production functions, analyses of classroom and teacher
effects, and studies of time and learning. The review is intended to be selective
and illustrative. In each section, the methodological problems will be summarized; the concepts and methods employed in the study of school effects are
never independent of the conclusions.

School Effects: Composition, Context, and Climate

Studies of educational effects involve causal inferences at a number of levels
of analysis. Schools are complex organizations with "nested layers" (Barr and
Dreeben 1977) of influence. A student is instructed in a classroom by one or
more teachers with a curriculum designed for a particular grade or subject matter;
the classroom is part of the aggregate of classrooms constituting a school that
is located in a particular community that is part of a district accountable to a
state agency in a particular region or country. At each of these multiple levels,
policy decisions are made that could plausibly affect how well a given student
can read or write. Disentangling the complex effects of these multiple levels to
arrive at a summary statement about the effects of education on any particular
group of students is an insurmountable task. The major difficulty is conceptualizing the causal processes at work and operationalizing appropriate measures
for the mechanisms influencing outcomes.

Early work in sociology began with the assumption that the social composition
of schools influenced achievement. It was obvious to the most casual observer
that schools differed dramatically in terms of socioeconomic and racial composition; moreover, the equality of education appeared starkly unequal when one
compared inner-city ghetto schools with those in affluent suburbs or small towns.
School climate or social context was assumed to be a pertinent factor in explaining
these educational outcomes (Alexander and Eckland 1975, 1977; Alexander et
al. 1978; Alwin 1976; Alwin and Otto 1977; Campbell and Alexander 1965;
Farkas 1974; Hauser et al. 1976; Hauser 1969, 1970, 1971, 1974; Herriott and
St. John 1966; Jencks et al. 1972; Jencks and Brown 1975; McDill and Rigsby
1973; Meyer 1970; Nelson 1972; Sewell and Armer 1966; Sexton 1961; Walberg
1979).

Conceptually, the social context of a school implies a myriad of factors thought
to affect achievement. The descriptions of contextual factors are vague and
imprecise, yet rich in metaphor (Anderson 1982). Schools are described as having
a culture or ambience; the social climate is assumed equivalent to an "organizational personality" (Halpin and Croft 1963); schools are argued to reflect the
milieu or circumstances of the surrounding community; but schools are also

viewed as unique environments with distinctive systems of norms and values. At times, social context effects include the conditions of the physical plant, the quality of facilities, the resources available to the school, the characteristics of the staff, and other tangible aspects of the school.

The causal mechanisms through which contextual factors are thought to influence school achievement are correspondingly diverse. Peer group interaction, instructional method, and the expectations of teachers are relatively concrete possibilities; however, the literature also refers to such abstractions as social telepathy, the sense of "shared fate," or the collective aspirations and motivations of students that diffuse through contagion, conformity, or even competition among group members (Erbring and Young 1979). While it would be foolhardy to attempt a comprehensive review of the definitions and theoretical constructs invoked by educational analysts to explain school effects, it seems likely to be virtually coterminous with the constructs used by social scientists to define and describe social structure, culture, or the behavior of groups.

The purpose of describing the explanatory paradigms relevant to discussions of contextual effects is not to question either their validity or their usefulness, although that could be done. Rather, the point is that in any social setting, diverse constructs can be used to describe a single reality. School context is inherently vague and elusive; the meaning and the interpretation given to contextual processes and outcomes depend on the predilections, disciplinary backgrounds, and the tastes or preferences of an analyst. More important, group phenomena tend to be operationalized in a comparable manner irrespective of the terminology used.

Contextual effects involve positing models of an educational process involving two or more levels of analysis. Individual student characteristics are combined with group level measures in order to test the relative influence of factors at each level. The conventional statistical techniques restrict the explanatory power of group level factors to the observed variability between groups in the outcome measure of interest. The upper bound of the measured effect of any specific school-level factor on student achievement is, therefore, the observed between-school variance in achievement. If there are interactions between group and individual levels of analysis, effects will be underestimated, if the relationship between a specific school variable and the achievement of particular students within a school varies by school, the effect of the school variable will be understated. For example, if the presence of a chemistry lab influences achievement in science, but only for students enrolled in science courses, the measured effect of this school resource is underestimated by assuming that it affects all students equally. The effects of a particular school-level variable, whether based on school or aggregated student characteristics, can only influence the mean outcome of the school (Burstein 1980a, 1980b). In practice, since only 15 percent to 25 percent of the total variability in achievement lies between schools, while 75 percent to 85 percent is within, individual-level characteristics are bound to have greater "effects" on achievement than school-level variables. Insofar as schools differ in the manner or effectiveness of allocating resources within schools, and this allocation is a school process that has an independent effect on achievement, the conventional equations underestimate the impact of schools (Burstein 1980a, 1980b). In the example given above, the effects of a chemistry lab on student achievement should be equal to the between-school effects associated with having a lab and the within-school variance attributed to differences between students who used or did not use this resource.

Since between-group measures, by definition, influence only group means, a number of investigators have suggested or explored alternative group-level measures intended to capture the distribution of processes within schools in a more precise fashion (Burstein and Miller 1980; Burstein et al. 1981; Klitgaard 1975; Spady 1976). While this work is potentially quite fruitful, conceptualizing within-school processes involves pitfalls as well. There is little consensus regarding whether effective schools, classrooms, or teachers should increase the variability of achievement among all students or decrease the gap between high- and low-achieving students. In practice, one cannot achieve both.

Specifying educational processes within groups can involve conceptual confounding as well. Structural or contextual effects can be thought of as determining the position of a particular student relevant to other students in a school. A student's class rank, in such a model, should have an effect on achievement that is independent of actual achievement scores. Viewing the school as a frog pond, a particular student's aspirations, self-concept, and later achievement should be influenced not only by actual test scores, but also by relative standing compared with others in the school.

Unfortunately, it is empirically not possible to fit a model of the educational process that combines, simultaneously, contextual effects, individual effects, and frog pond effects as conventionally measured. Once the school mean score is known (the contextual effect) and the student's particular score (individual effect), the student's position relative to the mean is a given. The three logically distinct conceptualizations of the effects are linearly dependent; it is not possible to separate their effects (Burstein 1980a; Firebaugh 1978, 1979, 1982). If one has independent estimates of the student's relative standing, based on self-reports or teacher's assessments, the problem is tractable; however, such measures are likely to be highly correlated with the observed distance from the school mean and to yield unstable coefficients.

A number of research studies have attempted to avoid the technical dilemmas of restricted between-school variance by distinguishing school-level and individual processes through the analysis of covariance, or by aggregating variables to estimate effects at a single level of analysis. By far the most common unit of analysis is the school (Coleman et al. 1966; Jencks et al. 1972; Hauser et al. 1976; Jencks and Brown 1975; Mayeske et al. 1973; Katzman 1968; Peaker 1971), but classrooms (Good et al. 1975; Entwisle and Hayduk 1982; McDonald et al. 1976; Murnane 1975; Summers and Wolfe 1977), school districts (Bidwell and Kasarda 1980), states (Walberg and Rasher 1979), and even countries

(Heyneman and Loxley 1983; Heyns 1976b) have been used. Problems of aggregation plague research on school effects, however the unit of analysis is defined. Before reviewing the methodological issues, however, it is useful to compare the sociological studies with the educational production functions estimated by economists. The logic of operationalizing school-level concepts is similar in both cases; however, economists tend to eschew contextual variables in favor of concrete, tangible resources available to schools.

Schools as Firms: Production Functions in Education

Economists are accustomed to specifying models that link inputs with output in order to maximize production. Such models have been successfully applied to firms and other economic institutions, and it is not difficult to envision a similar process operating in education. Production functions attempt to estimate the best mix of labor (teachers), capital (school resources), and technology (curriculum and facilities) to produce achievement by students (Bowles 1970; Bridge et al. 1979; Brown and Saks 1975, 1980; Cohen and Millman 1975; Glasman and Biniaminov 1981; Hanushek 1972, 1979; Levin 1983). The policy questions posed in education, combined with the wealth of data available after 1966, have led to a "booming industry" in specifying production functions for schools (Brown and Saks 1980).

The arsenal of conceptual and methodological tools that economists have brought to this task is impressive; however, the major results of these efforts, despite a small number of much-cited studies to the contrary, do not differ from the sociological conclusions reviewed earlier. The research has found small and inconsistent effects for resources and educational facilities, or, in the conventional jargon that the marginal products for school inputs are close to zero when student characteristics are controlled. Purchased inputs, such as laboratories, libraries, gymnasiums, textbooks, or other school amenities, tend to have insignificant effects. Teacher characteristics, however, seem to matter. When one or more school resource measures approach significance, however, such as teachers for nonminority students (Hanushek 1972) or per-student expenditures among high-ability students (Ritzen and Winkler 1977), the findings have not been replicated in other samples.

Economists seem to have a greater penchant for complex modeling and more resistance to the idea that money will not buy achievement than do other educational researchers. My reading of this literature, however, confirms the assessment made by Brown and Saks: "The models most used are most useless" (1980, p. 112). While specifying new models, including lagged effects, joint production functions, or complex interactions will doubtless continue, such analyses seem unlikely to convince the skeptic that the pattern of resource allocation affects achievement in a significant or consistent way.

Educational resources are distributed between schools in ways that do not suggest strong effects are likely. Although there are substantial variations in educational expenditures across districts and states, the within-district relationships suggest predictable, if not uniform, patterns of expenditure (Heyns 1978). The largest single expense for most school systems is teachers' salaries, which are linked to seniority. Beginning teachers are often assigned the least attractive posts with the largest numbers of unruly underachievers. As others have argued (Jencks et al. 1972), there are plausible alternative explanations for the observed associations between salary level, seniority, or experience and student achievement that do not require one to assume a direct causal effect. If teachers, as they acquire seniority and higher salaries, transferred to better schools within a district, a positive association between teaching experience or teachers' salaries and achievement must be considered spurious (Jencks et al. 1972). While it would surely be desirable to know the best or most efficient way for schools to allocate educational resources, at this point in time we are far from being able to determine this.

Two production function studies are worthy of further discussion, since they have attracted substantial attention and are widely cited. Murnane (1975) and Summers and Wolfe (1977) both studied elementary schools in particular cities and used regression methods to estimate production functions for changes in achievement scores. Both are pupil-specific teacher quality variables and compare classrooms as well as schools. Both found positive effects for a number of teacher variables and both have comparable flaws regarding the measurement of socioeconomic factors. Summers and Wolfe report, in their words, "cheerier results" (1977, p. 639) than do other studies of educational effects based on a sample of 627 sixth-grade students from 103 Philadelphia elementary schools. They admit to mining the extensive data set for significant effects and reporting only positive findings. Most factors that remained significant were not equally effective for subsamples defined by ability or income level. Background factors consist of measures of race, IQ, and family income; family income is based on race-specific housing and rental costs in the census block in which students lived rather than on individual-level variability.

Summers and Wolfe report positive educational effects related to teachers' experience, class size, and racial composition. Teachers' experience and the size of classes or schools reveal different effects for different kinds of students, however. High-achieving students are sometimes adversely affected by young teachers and small classes. Summers and Wolfe argue that perhaps young and enthusiastic teachers are best with low-achieving students. Low-achieving students do worse in large classes, while high-achieving students do better.

The most problematic aspect of the Summers and Wolfe study is the unmeasured, potentially important background characteristics of students. This fact, combined with post hoc explanations offered for interactions suggests caution in accepting the conclusions. Some of the measures that are significant, such as attendance, disruptive incidents in the school, and tardiness to class, are argued to be proxies for student motivation; these variables may in fact be measures of the socioeconomic characteristics of the schools or classrooms studied. Without adequate controls for student background, the models may well be misspecified. Summers and Wolfe's results have not been replicated thus far.

Murnane (1975) examined the achievement of 875 black inner-city children in New Haven schools. He finds that classroom effects explain a larger proportion of variance in achievement than do individual-level input variables. The socioeconomic variables included as controls, however, are not very powerful influences and are aggregated relative to the longitudinal student achievement data. To control for background factors, the rental costs of student housing and information on whether or not students lived with a female head of household are included in his models. In contast to Summers and Wolfe, Murnane discovered that first-year teachers are substantially less effective than teachers with more experience. Male teachers were more effective than female teachers and were so with children of both sexes. Murnane is quite sensitive to possible spurious relationships and misinterpretations of the data that he presents; at the same time, he offers plausible but post hoc explanations for the observed relationships. He tests in excess of thirty hypotheses, ranging from whether a classroom affects achievement to the relative contributions of black or white teachers to the performance of black children. In many ways, Murnane's analysis is perhaps the most thoughtful to be found in the literature using production functions for schooling; however, I am not convinced.

Educational production functions differ conceptually from the sociological search for contextual effects. The variables, however, are frequently operationalized in comparable ways, and the models specified in a comparable fashion. In neither case does the research suggest that the variability between schools can be unambiguously linked to achievement outcomes. Moreover, the methodological problems involved in conceptualizing and estimating effects across different levels of analysis are ubiquitous, whether one deals with schools or classrooms.

Aggregating Data and Inferences

The major problem for analysts confronted with educational data and achievement outcomes is choosing the most appropriate strategy for analyzing multilevel phenomena. Although a great deal is known about the consequences of particular assumptions about grouping (Burstein 1980b), there is little consensus. Conceptually, achievement is considered to be a microlevel process involving individual students in classrooms; most analysts would assume as well that the macrolevel processes allocating resources between schools or districts are also important, although perhaps not in understanding achievement. The dilemma is how best to represent these various levels of influence and how to measure their separable effects.

Extensive work has been done on the problems involved in making inferences from grouped data. Discussions of the ecological fallacy (Alker 1969; Dogan and Rokkan 1969; Duncan et al. 1961; Duncan and Davis 1953; Firebaugh 1978, 1979; Goodman 1959; Hauser 1970, 1974; Robinson 1950; Scheuch 1969) of aggregation bias (Burstein 1980a, 1980b; Feige and Watts 1972; Grunfield and Griliches 1960; Hannan 1971; Theil 1954) and of other problems associated with grouping (Cramer 1964; Dogan and Rokkan 1969; Hannan and Burstein 1974; Hanushek et al. 1974) give ample warning of the problems in making inferences about individual behavior from relationships observed for groups to which the individuals belong. For the standard regression model of school effects, the parameters estimated across schools are inconsistent and biased estimates of individual effects, unless individuals are randomly assigned to groups (Burstein 1980a, 1980b). Inconsistent parameters are an indication that models are likely to be misspecified; moreover, the degree of multicollinearity observed for aggregated variables is immense. Statistical inference across different levels of analysis can be quite misleading. In general, aggregation does not seem to be a viable solution for the statistical problem of restricted between-school variance.

The use of school means or the regression residuals from a within-school analysis have, however, yielded a few persistent conclusions regarding school effects. The between-school variance, although not large relative to the individual-level variance, is sufficiently large to merit attention in policy terms if this variance was consistently associated with school-level factors that could be manipulated. The problem is that mean school achievement or the residuals are not strongly related to the presence of particular resources or facilities. Moreover, the residuals from within-school regressions are not consistently related to factors measured at the school level for different groups of students in the same school. If one calculates residuals for more than one grade in the same school, or for boys and girls separately within schools, the residuals are not highly related to one another (Hauser 1971, 1974; Jencks and Brown 1975). If unexplained within-school variance in student achievement were "true" variance, rather than errors of measurement in the individual-level analysis, and this true variance reflected an unobserved school context effect, one would expect these residuals to correlate across groups in the same school. Although between-school correlations of residuals tend to be positive, their size does not suggest large, unmediated school effects.

Problems in conceptualizing and analyzing school effects have not been fully resolved. The best advice regarding units of analysis seems to be that "the investigator must measure every variable at its lowest possible level and be able to match each student's data with the data from the teacher, classroom, classmates, and school" (Burstein 1980a, p. 35); even with data as rich as that implied by this recommendation, inferences are likely to be problematic. Although a number of analysts have turned to an assessment of within-school processes, specifying effects between classrooms or teachers involves methodological dilemmas similar to those found between schools. Forewarned, we shall turn to analyses of teacher and classroom effects.

Classrooms and Teachers

Critics have frequently pointed to the absence of specific links between the student and the teacher in most analyses of school effects (Centra and Potter 1980; Entwisle and Hayduk 1982; Summers and Wolfe, 1977). Teacher characteristics tend to be aggregated for schools or grade levels rather than to be associated with patterns of learning in classrooms. Learning as a microprocess should, it is maintained, be studied as a within-school or within-classroom process.

The logic of such a critique is undeniable; the solution for research does not, however, seem to be to turn to studies of teacher effects or between classroom differences in achievement. The reasons are in part methodological and in part based on the extraordinary range of potential conceptualizations available to the imaginative analyst. Disaggregating school-level data in order to estimate effects between and within classrooms necessarily reduces the sample size, when compared with models based on schools, but does not ensure greater clarity about the nature or determinants of the contextual process. Conceptually, classrooms are contexts, like schools, with cultures, climates, and compositional features as distinctive as schools. Internally, elementary classrooms are frequently stratified for instructional purposes by ability grouping (Eder 1981; Findley and Bryan 1970; Goldberg et al. 1966; Haller and Davis 1981; Kulik and Kulik 1982; Rist 1973; Simpson 1981). Ability grouping may have independent effects on achievement outcomes or on intervening factors such as peer relations (Hallinan and Tuma 1978) and teacher expectations (Hallinan and Sørensen 1983; Brophy and Good 1970, 1974). Virtually every school resource or characteristic assumed to influence school-level achievement could operate on processes within classrooms; moreover, although these processes can perhaps be visualized more concretely at the classroom level, the number of factors and their potential interactions with characteristics of individuals rapidly exhaust the degrees of freedom available.

At least three distinctive features of the educational process are intrinsically confounded in classroom research: teacher characteristics, classroom factors, and the curriculum or teaching methods employed. As Beckerman and Good (1981) have warned, analyses that identify effective teachers and effective teaching strategies often confound the effects of classroom context with teacher or curricula effects. Classroom factors include student composition or context in as many different combinations as described for schools. Peer influences would be one reasonable way to conceptualize the impact of social context on individual achievement; moreover, there are reasons to believe that peer effects would be most influenced within classrooms.

Positing peer influences involves operationalizing both the characteristics of peers deemed important and the collection of peers assumed relevant; the process could entail dyadic relations such as best friends; cliques or other friendship groups; instructional clusters, such as ability groups; or the classroom as a whole. There are, theoretically, as many ways of defining appropriate groups as there are of aggregating children; since the influence of peers presumably depends on a student's desire to model or imitate the behavior of reference groups of significant others, and since children may have as many diverse ways of defining appropriate mentors and models as do researchers, the tasks of operationalizing and measuring peer influences are nearly insurmountable.

If one is willing to assume that all classroom differences are, directly or indirectly, the product of teacher behavior, the research task is considerably simplified. Teachers can, to some degree, set the tone or establish the climate of a classroom; teachers can reinforce or temper peer group influences; and teachers are responsible for setting educational goals and implementing pedagogic objectives. Yet a voluminous literature testifies to the complexity of the teaching process and to the futility of attempting to link specific teacher characteristics or behavior to student outcomes, whether measured as classroom averages or achievement differences for particular subgroups of individuals.

It would be foolhardy to attempt a synthesis or a comprehensive review of this literature. The bibliographies of the major volumes reviewing research on teaching list hundreds of references, and few claim to be comprehensive (Brophy 1973, 1979; Gage 1963, 1972, 1976; Dunkin and Biddle 1974; Peterson and Walberg 1979; Borich and Fenton 1977; Smith and Handler 1979; Doyle 1977; Heath and Nielson 1974; McFadden and Schenck 1971; Domas and Tiedeman 1950). A recently published reference bibliography (Powell and Beard 1982) lists more than three thousand entries compiled for 1965 to 1980 alone. Research in teaching effectiveness can be divided in numerous ways. Doyle (1977) describes three complementary paradigms: (1) process-product research, linking specific teacher characteristics and behavior to outcomes; (2) research on mediating processes, or the relationships between instructional stimuli and the cognitive processes of students; and (3) ecological approaches, based on observations in naturalistic settings. Each perspective offers a unique body of literature, although the process-product tradition is most akin to school effects.

Despite prolonged scrutiny and a wealth of data, most analysts conclude that we have not learned much about how teachers influence achievement. Mood (1970, p. 22) concludes that "we cannot make any sort of meaningful quantitative estimate of the effects of teachers on student achievement." Brim (1958, p. 32) asserts that "despite a vast body of research, no consistencies between any teacher characteristics, including intelligence, and teaching effectiveness" can be shown to exist. Walberg (1983) states that "evaluations of instruction rarely show a clear superiority of one medium or method over another." Barr (cited by Smith and Handler 1979, p. 419) concludes that "the simple fact is after 40 years of research on teacher effectiveness . . . one can point to few outcomes a superintendent of schools can safely employ in hiring a teacher or granting him tenure." Reviews of teacher education programs are similarly unenlightening (Heath and Nielson 1974); few skills or experiences are unambiguously predictive of positive teaching outcomes. When particular attributes of teachers are identified as effective, such as enthusiasm (Rosenshine 1970a), it is not clear whether teaching with verve and alacrity enhances learning or whether apathetic and indifferent teaching detracts. Moreover, it would be difficult to distinguish teachers according to their temperament or mood or to expect continually inspired teaching irrespective of student responses. Stephens (1967) comes close to concluding that learning is entirely due to student characteristics and not at all to teachers. From a policy perspective, there is little evidence that we can or should recruit, train, promote, or give merit pay to teachers according to differential effectiveness.

This point can be illustrated by the studies of the stability of teacher effects (Berliner 1980; Brophy 1973; Rosenshine 1970b). If average gains in cognitive achievement are the criterion for the relative effectiveness of teaching, one would minimally expect that teachers identified as effective one year would be consistently effective the next. Alternatively, a teacher shown to be effective in arithmetic instruction with a given group of students should be effective with the same class in reading or social studies; if there is generality to the concept of effective teaching, it should be consistent across curricula or subject matter.

Rosenshine (1970a) reported surprisingly low correlations between consecutive years in three different studies; first-grade teachers had significant stability coefficients in reading, spelling, and word study skills but not in vocabulary or paragraph meaning; insignificant positive correlations ranging from .09 to .26 were found for close to 150 teachers in other grades. Brophy (1973) found greater consistency by subject matter within a year than over time, with correlations ranging from .09 to .34. Berliner (1980) cites a report by Shavelson and Dempsey that yields an average correlation of teacher effectiveness of .30 for eight studies based on standardized achievement tests. Brophy (1973) reported that 28 percent of the 165 elementary-school teachers included were consistently effective over three years, with half of these producing higher-than-expected gains for all three years and half producing gains less than expected. Comparable proportions appeared consistently to improve or decline in average effectiveness over three years; however, more than half of the teachers could not be characterized as either consistently improving or declining in effectiveness. When assessing the stability of particular teacher behaviors, the problems are magnified. Many behavioral scales have low reliability at one point in time; when assessed over the course of a year, instability is widespread. Moreover, as Berliner (1980) notes, effective teachers may be those who alter their teaching styles to suit student needs or the subject matter at hand; one would expect flexibility in teaching to be inversely related to stability.

Significant findings for classroom or teacher effects frequently involve interactions between teacher characteristics and student characteristics. Particular classrooms or teachers are reported as effective for particular kinds of students (Murnane 1975; Summers and Wolfe 1977). The difficulty in generalizing from such results is that one cannot rule out the possibility that unmeasured characteristics of either teachers or students could explain the results. Moreover, estimating the effects of all possible interactions can quickly involve large numbers of parameters, often exceeding the number of students in a classroom. Finally, even if one were able to identify the proper match of characteristics for effective teachers with responsive students, the administrative complications involved in implementing such policies would be prohibitive.

In sum, the search for educational effects in classroom settings does not seem likely to be fruitful. Problems of aggregation persist; teacher effects are confounded with classroom and curriculum effects; the stability of both outcomes and the pedagogic behavior producing achievement outcomes are questionable; and finally, although the computer revolution has enabled educational researchers to test sophisticated multivariate models of educational process with complex interaction terms, such models do not seem likely to have immediate applicability to school practice or policy.

Schooling can be conceptualized as more than the place in which learning occurs. The next section reviews models of school effects that assume a process, operating in time, rather than a school or classroom.

Time and Learning

Intuitively, the amount of time a student spends learning should be related to the amount that is learned. Although research tends to support this straightforward proposition, there is less consensus about the importance of time as a policy factor in achievement (for reviews see Borg 1980; Frederick and Walberg 1980; Heyns 1978; Karweit 1980, 1982; Levin 1983). One particularly thoughtful review concludes: "Time devoted to school learning appears to be a modest predictor of achievement. For some types of new material, . . . time may be the best predictor. . . . When material is familiar . . . time may be a weak and insignificant factor. To the extent that time is used to make up for ineffective instruction or inability, it may be negatively correlated with achievement" (Frederick and Walberg 1980, p. 193).

Three distinct conceptualizations of time can be found in the literature. First, time has been used to compare the effects of schooling with the effects of learning activities outside of school. Second, time is viewed as a feature of instructional schedules and classroom priorities that determine a child's opportunities for learning and differential opportunities across schools. Third, time is assumed to be a microlevel phenomenon best measured as the minutes a child is "on-task" or "engaged" in educational pursuits within classrooms. Each approach poses distinctive questions about the educational process and the observed achievement outcomes, and each perspective provides results that are suggestive of policy alternatives for schools.

The first approach is best described as a critique of the simplistic formulation of school effects derived from early studies (Heyns 1978). Achievement is argued to be a temporal process, influenced by a host of factors that are not entirely controlled by schools. The effects of families are not static, but continuous differential influences on achievement over time; if the effects of schooling are independent of family factors, one would expect learning patterns when schools are in session to differ from learning rates when schools are closed, such as during the summer months. The central issue is twofold: first, do cognitive growth rates differ between the school year and the summer; and second, does the pattern of learning associated with school suggest greater or less equality than outcomes observed in the absence of schooling, when families and other institutions have a larger responsibility for the socialization of children? The effects of schooling are measured by the additive and interaction effects of being in school, contrasted with the pattern of achievement outcomes during the summer, when most children are not exposed to schooling. Time periods thus constitute a quasi-experimental treatment and a method of separating the effects of schooling from the effects of families, neighborhoods, peers, or other extraneous factors that operate year-round. Educational opportunity is the degree to which schooling outcomes differ by race and socioeconomic status.

Achievement outcomes, as *Summer Learning and the Effects of Schooling* (Heyns 1978) demonstrates, differ considerably during the school year and the summer. On every standardized test examined, learning rates were consistently higher during the school year than they were in the summer, month by month. Moreover, the summer months were particularly detrimental to the achievement of minority students and low socioeconomic whites. By far, the largest component of cognitive inequality among students could be traced to outcomes that occurred in the absence of schooling. As Heyns concludes: "Without exception, children from more advantaged families learn at a more nearly linear rate with respect to time than do poor children. Schooling is critical for the achievement of children from relatively poor backgrounds, while . . . for the advantaged, schooling appears to supplement the home" (1978, p. 50). Schooling in this model does not redress cognitive inequality or social disadvantage. However, "the outcomes resulting from schooling are far more equal than those that would be expected" (Heyns 1978, p. 9), based on student background. These results held for both white and black sixth and seventh graders in the forty-two sample schools studied.

One policy implication that might be drawn from the study of summer learning is the efficacy of requiring schooling year-round. *Summer Learning and the Effects of Schooling* (Heyns 1978) explored the effects of summer programs in Atlanta. However, as in most school systems, summer school is voluntary and considerably less rigorous than the regular school curriculum. Students are selectively recruited, and there is every reason to believe that the students who attend summer school like school more than those who do not attend. The effects of summer school tend to be positive, especially for black students; however, these effects are not independent of student achievement and family background characteristics. As was the case for most summer programs, the largest gains accrued to the most advantaged students. While it is possible that summer intervention programs may enhance learning, there is to date little convincing evidence.

The second approach to assessing the relationship between time and learning

Methodological and Theoretical Issues

considers time as a structural feature of schools, determined by the number of days in the school year, the length of the school day, and the average daily attendance of students. As Wiley and Harnischfeger (1974; Harnischfeger and Wiley 1980; Wiley 1976) point out, schools and school districts differ markedly in the amount of time allocated for instruction. In their research, these three factors are combined to yield a measure of the quantity of schooling provided, or the effective hours of instruction per year. Using a sample of forty Detroit schools drawn from the *Equality of Educational Opportunity* report, achievement in mathematics, reading comprehension, and verbal ability were shown to be consistently related to the quantity of schooling received by the average student. Background factors were controlled by regressing household possessions, number of children in a family, and race within schools; the discrepancy between the expected mean achievement by school compared with the actual was the outcome. Time devoted to instruction at the school level was argued to be a "potent path for policy"; an increase in the total number of hours of schooling of 24 percent (from 871 hours to 1,083 hours) would increase reading scores by three to twelve months of grade-equivalent achievement (Wiley 1976, p. 262).

Efforts to replicate these results have not proved fruitful (Karweit 1976, 1980). Using the full compliment of schools in the *Equality of Educational Opportunity* report, Karweit found far smaller effects for the quantity of time students spent in schools, effects that were generally insignificant. One problem seems to be the fact that socioeconomic status was not adequately controlled, and that the average daily attendance estimated for schools correlates with the socioeconomic composition of schools.

On an individual level, a number of studies have shown that time as measured by student absenteeism is modestly related to academic performance (Carver 1970; Finch and Nemzek 1940; Heyns 1978; Karweit 1973; Monk and Ibrahim 1984; Schultz 1958; Smith 1979; Ziegler 1928). Grades tend to be influenced more than achievement scores (Ziegler 1928). Attendance effects are not independent of class and racial differences, and most of the observed effects are only significant for the few students who are chronically absent (Heyns 1978). The timing of absences, the degree of concentration near examination time, and the length or frequency of "episodes" of absence show inconsistent results (Monk and Ibrahim 1984). Unexcused absences or tardiness has been shown to be related to achievement, but the effects are hard to separate from student motivation (Summers and Wolfe 1977). A few studies have found contextual effects owing to average attendance in a classroom, presumably because the amount of time devoted to makeup work decreased the time that could be spent learning new material; however, these effects do not seem to persist from one year to the next or to be reliably linked to teacher behavior. Most of the literature interprets student achievement as the outcome variable, caused by differential attendance. One could argue instead that attendance patterns are the result of poor achievement or poor teaching. Since the basic findings are relatively small effects and a strong likelihood that individual characteristics predict both poor achievement and erratic attendance, it is difficult to imagine that attendance patterns can serve as powerful evidence for the effects of time on learning or as policy alternatives that can be implemented in schools.

The final conceptualization of time assumes that the critical factor is not just the instructional time allocated, but also the behavior and response of the student. Engaged time, or time-on-task, is assumed to be the mediating variable between instruction and student learning; the amount of time spent attending to lessons or to the classroom task is, for individuals, the basic unit of analysis that influences outcomes. The theoretical logic for assuming that time matters stems from the work of Carroll (1963) and the evidence regarding *Mastery Learning* (Block 1971; Block and Burns 1976; Bloom 1976; Carroll 1971). The general conclusion from the most comprehensive review of this literature (Karweit 1982) is that "because the time effects are small and because the hypothesis is so sensible, the research immediately turns our attention to the question—why is not time-on-task more important for learning than it is?" (pp. 51–52). This is a question to which we will return after looking closely at a pair of studies.

Two studies of time-on-task deserve special attention, if only because they are models of careful research. The Beginning Teacher Evaluation Study (Denham and Lieberman 1980) explored the relationship between academic learning time (ALT) and achievement in reading and mathemtics. ALT is defined as the amount of time a student spends engaged in an academic task that he or she can perform with high success. Conceptually, ALT integrates the notions of allocated time, determined by the structure of classroom instruction; time-on-task, defined by the student's attention to the subject matter at hand; and the level of mastery or the success rate experienced by students. Optimal learning is assumed to require opportunity time, engaged time, and the psychic rewards of successful learning. The Beginning Teacher Evaluation Study sample consisted of 139 second graders and 122 fifth graders in forty-six California classrooms.

Karweit and Slaven (1981) observed ninety-five students in eighteen classrooms in Maryland. Both studies collected longitudinal data on standardized achievement tests taken before anad after observations on the use of classroom time and the attention patterns of students. Both studies controlled for pretests before assessing effects, and neither controlled for social background. Both studies reported small effects and inconsistent results by grade level. The proportion of variance explained by engaged time in the most positive analyses ranged from 2.5 percent (Karweit and Slavin 1981) to 3 percent to 5 percent (Borg 1980). Karweit and Slavin focused solely on mathematics achievement; the largest and most consistent relationships in the Beginning Teacher Evaluation Study were also in mathematics; overall, however, the residual variance in achievement was positively associated with ALT in barely one-third of the comparisons, although virtually all of the two hundred or more subtest-by-grade comparisons were in the right direction.

The single largest difference between the two studies is the conclusion about the importance of time drawn by their respective authors. The Beginning Teacher

Evaluation Study concludes that "Academic Learning Time is an important predictor of student achievement" (Denham and Lieberman 1980, p. 18), while Karweit (1983) concludes "that present studies of time and learning, contrary to widely publicized statements, have not produced overwhelming evidence connecting time-on-task to learning" (p. 51). The Beginning Teacher Evaluation Study conclusion rests on the assumption that the general consistency of the small observed effects is an adequate basis for advising teachers on appropriate time management strategies and to encourage them to devote more attention to the academic content of instruction. Karweit and Slavin (1981, 1982), in contrast, are bothered by the fact that variations in the schedule, duration, and measurement of classroom observations can affect the substantive research findings, particularly when measured effects are only marginally significant statistically.

Resolving these conflicting positions on the importance of research on time and learning is not possible at present. I am persuaded that we have reached the limits of what it is possible to explain regarding student achievement as measured on standardized achievement tests. The outcome measures used in these two rigorous and painstaking studies of learning are extremely conservative; correlations between pretest and post-test achievement measured over only three or four months of activity are often nearly as high as the reliablities of these measures. Moreover, both studies are based on small samples. To demonstrate small, but significant, effects despite these limitations suggests that the relationships are real; however, the magnitude of the estimated effects are too small to warrant sustained policy attention or prescriptions for educational reform. As Karweit and Slavin (1981) note, the single largest component of lost time across classrooms is student inattention; rescheduling instruction or reducing classroom disruptions would not necessarily increase engaged time or student attention. In a recent article, Peterson and her associates (1984) found that students' self-reports of attention, understanding, and cognitive processes during mathematics instruction were more valid than observers' judgments of time-on-task. Such a finding is wholly plausible, but it does not suggest how to capture student attention or optimize learning, short of an entirely individualized curriculum. Effective teaching and consistent learning are clearly desirable goals; however, the nature of the classroom chemistry conducive to such goals is elusive.

School effects research is in danger of resembling a hall of mirrors, with each successive series of studies focused on smaller units of analysis and on research questions further removed from the policy context in which the issues are originally defined. District policies, school organization, and instructional time can each be shown to have small but inconsistent effects on achievement. We know that students learn in schools and that they learn more when in school than when not in school; we know that opportunities for learning are more equal in educational institutions than outside (Heyns 1978). We know that taking more courses in mathematics improves mathematics achievement (Welch et al. 1982); presumably, other subject skills are mastered by study as well. There is good evidence that the relationship between achievement and social class declines between the sixth and twelfth grades (Heyns 1978, pp. 247–62), while the relationship between race and achievement seems to persist, at least in the South (Coleman et al. 1966). There is an abundance of studies that show the value of years of schooling for lifetime earnings or occupational status (Jencks et al. 1972, 1979). We can also be fairly confident that achievement is related to the time spent in learning.

Unfortunately, research does not reveal the source of these relationships or how best to structure education. There are indications that the outcome measures, standardized achievement scores, are not sensitive to school factors (Madaus et al. 1979; Heyns 1980), but alternative measures are not easily found. There are certainly organizational factors that influence life in schools quite apart from student achievement (Bidwell and Kasarda 1980). However, there are no studies to date that yield both credible findings and measured effects sufficiently impressive and robust to imply clear policy direction. Although educational researchers have learned a great deal about the methodological and conceptual pitfalls involved in assessing the effects of education, few analysts would deny that the substantive results are disappointing.

One unintended consequence of the fixation on proving or disproving educational effects is that much of the research has lost touch with the field. Practitioners have always tended to be skeptical and selective regarding research; however, this seems particularly the case now. Educational research seems not to apply to the problems of schools, at least not insofar as it searches for school effects. The single research tradition that does address the folks in the trenches is research on effective schools.

Effective Schools

The search for educational effects could be described as a dismal science. The major conclusion seems to be that we do not know what constitutes effective schooling. To be sure, there have been countless critics of the school effects studies and of their conclusions. Only recently, however, has a concerted counteroffensive been launched. Research on effective schools is this effort. While it is hard to characterize this fledgling body of research as a tradition, such research has given birth to a wide range of studies that provide descriptive accounts of effective schools and aggressively optimistic prescriptions for school improvement (MacKenzie 1983; Cohen 1981, 1982).

The definition of an effective school varies considerably from study to study. It is not, it should be pointed out, necessarily a school with particularly high levels of achievement. More typically, effective schools are those that do better than might be expected based on their social composition or past performance. In some studies, effective schools are identified as urban institutions that serve minority students particularly well (Weber 1971; Glenn and McLean 1981; Clark et al. 1980). In others, the top quintile of high-achieving schools in a district or state are identified after basic demographic factors are controlled (Klitgaard and

Hall 1973; Dyer et al. 1969). Other researchers have isolated the "most improved" schools in terms of achievement gains over some period of time (Phi Delta Kappa 1980; Wellisch et al. 1978). In some evaluations, effective schools have even been defined as low-scoring or troubled institutions that were targeted for an effective schools program.

To date, the research on effective schools has produced more interest and enthusiasm than statistically impressive results. Odden and Dougherty (1982) report that the majority of states have adopted some version of an effective schools program for improving education. New York City (Clark and McCarthy 1983), Seattle (Wilson 1983), Modesto (Benjamin 1981), Pittsburgh (Toch 1981), Milwaukee (Levine and Eubanks 1983), and Atlanta (Crim 1981) have implemented specific programs modeled on this research (Cuban 1984). Indeed, what is remarkable is that, despite glaring weaknesses in the research and few systematic evaluations, a growing tide of state education departments, school boards, superintendents, and principals have embraced an effective schools approach. School improvement based on the school effectiveness literature has become, in the words of one observer, a social movement (Bickel 1983).

There are several reasons for this state of affairs. The findings regarding the characteristics of effective schools resonate convincingly with the observations and beliefs of educators. Reports on effective schools typically list the characteristics, conditions, and goal-directed activities that generate effectiveness and that can, potentially, be implemented. Whether one contrasts the twenty-nine characteristics enumerated by Austin (1979, 1981) or the five dimensions of effectiveness identified by Edmonds (1979a, 1979b, 1981), the literature focuses on practical improvement strategies, supplemented by exhortations to take schooling and achievement seriously. While this may sound like shopworn platitudes to the jaded researcher, it is a message that has been absent in the work on educational effects.

One attribute of an effective school, discussed repeatedly in the literature, is the presence of strong and effective school leader (Blumberg and Greenfield 1980; Leithwood and Montgomery 1982; Shoemaker and Fraser 1981; Bossert et al. 1981). High-performing schools are argued to have effective leadership at all levels of school administration, from the district office to the classroom. Since exemplary schools are distinguished by instructional leadership, a clear rationale for innovations in educational management is built in. Such a dictum neatly co-opts the educational leaders needed to establish and implement school improvement programs; it also provides them with specific steps to pursue. The fact of having initiated an effective schools program means that one has joined the growing number of effective educational leaders, even without uniformly stellar outcomes. The burgeoning number of such programs and the public attention they receive ensure a continued groundswell of converts and disciples.

A number of larger societal trends have fueled the school effectiveness movement. Concerns about accountability, combined with legislation designed to increase testing, raise educational standards, and stress basic skills, have increased. Effective schools programs are quite compatible with such mandates; moreover, they have the added virtue of allowing superintendents and principals to reclaim the initiative and to propose school-improvement programs based on scientific research and professional control. Moreover, they are inexpensive. School effectiveness programs can be implemented with few additional resources; they involve staff development and planning, but only modest increments of funds are required (Cuban 1984). Thus they have considerable appeal to beleaguered administrators and legislators concerned with fiscal retrenchment. Finally, the recent upturn in national test scores, after more than a decade of decline, is fortuitous. School programs can appear effective in raising test scores, even if the actual cause is as diffuse and ultimately inexplicable as the sources of the original decline (Austin and Garber 1982; Jencks 1978; Wirtz et al. 1977).

The leading researchers in the school effectiveness tradition are among the most activist of educators and the most partisan of advocates for public education. They have moved "with perhaps unseemly haste to translate research findings into prescriptions for action" (MacKenzie 1983, p. 7). School effectiveness programs represent an affirmation of the gospel that schools matter and that educators at all levels can make them work. It is not surprising that reports and success stories are disseminated rapidly. Viewed as a social movement, school effectiveness programs are filling a pronounced need in the educational community for sensible strategies and positive direction. Viewed as research, school effectiveness is a relatively frail reed, albeit one that promises a great deal.

In evaluating the research on effective schools, it is important to remember that existing studies do not refute the literature on school effects. Insofar as the studies on school effectiveness can be compared in quantitative terms with earlier research, the range of measured effects are comparable. As Purkey and Smith (1983) note, school effectiveness studies suggest that the least effective bottom fifth of schools would be improved by roughly two-thirds of a standard deviation, or one year of grade-level achievement, if they performed as well as the most effective top quintile of schools. This estimate is consistent with the observed gaps estimated from the *Equality of Educational Opportunity* report (Coleman et al. 1966).

Conceptually, the effective schools literature and the school effects literature are quite different. The literature on effective schools asks questions and draws conclusions based largely on organizational variables. Hence it deals with issues irrelevant or peripheral to the central concerns of school effects studies. The research on effective schools takes as a premise that some schools are more effective at promoting achievement than others, and that descriptive accounts of the organization and management of such schools can serve as guidelines for developing programs (Brookover et al. 1979). Schools are viewed holistically as complex systems with numerous levels or tiers of authority and influence. Edmonds (1979a, 1979b) lists five basic ingredients of an effective school: (1) strong administrative leadership (2) high expectations for children's achievement; (3) an orderly atmosphere conducive to learning; (4) an emphasis on basic skill acquisition; and (5) frequent monitoring of pupil progress. These traits are said to characterize effective schools generally, despite considerable variation in the salience or emphasis placed on particular traits. The analytic strategy is first to identify the most effective schools and then to account for their greater efficacy and performance levels relative to the least effective schools.

Research on effective schools is typically based on cross-sectional data and comparisons based on outliers. This implies two serious methodological pitfalls. Effective schools may well be those with more errors in the measurement of outcomes or background factors. Since regression models are typically used to control for school composition and demographics, the pool of schools selected as effective will differ depending on the adequacy of controls used. As Rowan and others (1983) note, at least 83 percent of the variance in residuals between schools can be attributed to random error rather than to variance associated with schooling factors. Frechtling (1982) reports an inverse relationship between Montgomery County, Maryland, schools identified as effective by quantitative methods and the program assessments made by district personnel. Such findings suggest that the ranking of schools in terms of relative effectiveness may lack validity.

Even more seriously, studies to date do not focus on the process of transforming an ineffective school into an effective one, although the thrust of the recommendations are clearly in this direction. Effective schools differ on a number of characteristics from schools that are unable to produce high test scores; however, this does not imply that these attributes can be inserted into a low-achieving school, or that they will necessarily raise achievement in the less effective schools. School effectiveness, as presently studied, is not, nor can it be, a specific experimental treatment that can be replicated in an ineffective school. Whether such programs work or not must be studied site by site; generalizations will remain difficult.

The school effectiveness research has concentrated on basic skills measured by standardized achievement scores with background factors controlled. Most studies in the school effectiveness literature focus on elementary schools, and few have studied more than one or two grades. Longitudinal data are seldom reported; the particular variables selected as controls in a regression model differ between studies, and some may be incorrectly specified. Since the specifications of equations tends to vary considerably across studies, it is hard to believe that some are not misspecified. Reliability studies of school-level residuals have tended to show low, but positive, correlations among various measures across different grades and across time. This suggests some true school-level variation is present, but that the selected schools may be an unstable group. Rowan and co-workers (1983) report that a California school selected as effective in one year had only a 50 percent chance of being selected as effective the next year using the same criteria. Finally, effectiveness does not necessarily imply effectiveness for all students. Marco (1974) found a correlation of .32 between Title I schools based on an index of instructional effectiveness calculated for students of high and low ability. Again, this suggests that the measures used to identify effective schools are relatively unstable and depend substantially on the student characteristics used as controls, on the test criteria, and on the grade level included. Without valid and reliable means of identifying effective schools, one risks attending to largely irrelevant characteristics common to outliers (Forsythe 1973; Rowan and Denk 1982).

Cuban (1984) suggests that the school effectiveness research has been fueled by the increased scrutiny of published test score results. The recent rise in basic skills he attributes to a

steep rise in the learning curve of boards of education and school chiefs, rather than a causal linkage with school improvement programs. Administrators have discovered that forging tighter organizational linkages between what teachers teach and the content of test items results in higher reading and math scores. (p. 33)

If teachers have adjusted their methods of instruction to the requirements of standardized tests, it would be difficult to argue that greater effectiveness is real.

The effective schools research challenges the pessimistic inferences found in much of the school effects literature. It does so, however, with flimsy evidence. If one invokes the most rigorous scientific criteria, few studies in the school effectiveness tradition pass muster. However, it would be extraordinarily short-sighted to dismiss the research on these grounds. Case studies and firsthand accounts convincingly document improved morale, greater satisfaction with teaching and learning, and a host of intangible benefits that result from effective schools programs. Moreover, the diversity of program descriptions suggests that educational administrators are modifying program content and process to fit their own unique situation. A single school effectiveness model is not being implemented or replicated in a number of sites. Rather, a large number of educators are adopting the general ideas of effectiveness for their own purposes.

Given the dearth of positive directions that can be found in the previous literature on schools, it is heartening to see a renewed optimism and vigor combined with a commitment to the educational enterprise. It is too soon to tell whether the programs inspired by the rhetoric of effective schools will provide a needed corrective for lax urban school systems that have drifted without purpose or will, instead, reinstate a rigid, bureaucratic structure of education that has been under concerted attack. This seems to me to be the most interesting question for future research.

REFERENCES

Alexander, K. L., and M. A. Cook. "Curricula and Casework: A Surprise Ending to a Familiar Story." *American Sociological Review* 47 (1982): 626–40.

Alexander, K. L., M. A. Cook, and E. L. McDill. "Curriculum Tracking and Educational Stratification." *American Sociological Review* 43 (1978): 47–66.

Alexander, K. L., and B. K. Eckland. "Contextual Effects in the High School Attainment Process." *American Sociological Review* 41 (1975): 963–80.

———. "High School Context and College Selectivity: Institutional Constraints in Educational Stratification." *Social Forces* 56 (1977): 166–88.

Alexander, K. L., and E. L. McDill. "Selection and Allocation within Schools: Some Causes and Consequences of Curriculum Placement." *American Sociological Review* 41 (1976): 963–80.

Alexander, K. L., J. M. McPartland, and M. A. Cook. "Using Standardized Test Performance in School Effects Research." In *Research in Sociology of Education and Socialization*, edited by Alan C. Kerckhoff (guest editor, Ronald Corwin). Greenwich, CT: JAI Press, 1981.

Alexander, K. L., A. M. Pallas, and M. A. Cook. "Measure for Measure: On the Use of Endogenous Ability Data in School-Process Research." *American Sociological Review* 46 (1981): 619–31.

Alker, H. R. "A Typology of Ecological Fallacies." In *Quantitative Ecological Analysis in the Social Sciences*, edited by M. Dogan and S. Rokkan. Cambridge, MA: MIT Press, 1969.

Alwin, D. F. "Assessing School Effects: Some Identities." *Sociology of Education* 49 (1976): 294–303.

Alwin, D. F., and L. B. Otto. "High School Context Effects on Aspirations." *Sociology of Education* 50 (1977): 259–72.

Anderson, C. S. "The Search for School Climate: A Review of the Research." *Review of Educational Research* 52 (1982): 368–420.

Anderson, J. G. "Causal Models in Educational Research: Nonrecursive Models." *American Educational Research Journal* 14 (1978): 81–97.

Astin, A. W. "The Measured Effects of Higher Education." *Annals of the American Academy of Political and Social Science* 404 (1972): 1–20.

Austin, G. R. "Exemplary Schools and the Search for Effectiveness." *Educational Leadership* 37 (1979): 10–14.

———. "An Analysis of Outlier Schools and Their Distinguishing Characteristics." Paper presented at the American Educational Research Association, San Francisco, April 1981.

Austin, G. R., and H. Garber, eds. *The Rise and Fall of National Test Scores*. New York: Academic Press, 1982.

Averch, H., et al. *How Effective Is Schooling? A Critical Review and Synthesis of Research Findings* (R-956–PCSF/RC). Santa Monica, CA: Rand, 1972.

Barr, R., and R. Dreeben, "Instruction in Classrooms." In *Review of Research in Education*, edited by L. S. Shulman. Itasca, IL: F. E. Peacock, 1977.

Beckerman, T., and T. Good. "The Classroom Ratio of High and Low Aptitude Students and Its Effects on Achievement." *American Educational Research Journal* 18 (1981): 317–28.

Benjamin, R. *Making Schools Work*. New York: Continuum Press, 1981.

Berliner, D. C. "Studying Instruction in the Elementary Classroom." In *Analysis of Educational Productivity*, edited by R. Dreeben and J. A. Thomas. Cambridge, MA: Ballinger, 1980.

Bickel, W. E. "Effective Schools: Knowledge, Dissemination, Inquiry." *Educational Researcher* 12 (1983): 3–5.

Bidwell, C., and J. Kasarda. "Conceptualizing and Measuring the Effects of School and Schooling." *American Journal of Education* 88 (1980): 401–30.

Block, J. H., ed. *Mastery Learning: Theory and Practice*. New York: Holt, Rinehart & Winston, 1971.

Block, J. H., and R. B. Burns. "Mastery Learning." In *Review of Research in Education*, edited by L. S. Shulman. Itasca, IL: F. E. Peacock, 1976.

Bloom, B. S. "Time and Learning." *American Psychologist* 29 (1974): 682–88.

———. *Human Characteristics and School Learning*. New York: McGraw-Hill, 1976.

Blumberg, A., and W. Greenfield. *The Effective Principal: Perspectives in School Leadership*. Boston: Allyn and Bacon, 1980.

Borg, W. R. "Time and School Learning." In *Time to Learn*, edited by C. Denham and A. Lieberman. Washington, DC: National Institute of Education, 1980.

Borich, G., and K. Fenton, eds. *The Appraisal of Teaching: Concepts and Process*. Reading, MA: Addison-Wesley, 1977.

Bossert, S. T. *Tasks and Social Relationships in Classrooms*. Cambridge, NY: Cambridge University Press, 1979.

Bossert, S. T., et al. *The Instructional Management Role of the Principal: A Preliminary Review and Conceptualization*. San Francisco: Far West Laboratory for Educational Research and Development, 1981.

Bowles, S. "Toward an Educational Production Function." In *Education, Income and Human Capital*, edited by W. L. Hansen. New York: National Bureau of Economic Research, 1970.

Bowles, S., and H. M. Levin. "The Determinants of Scholastic Achievement—An Appraisal of Some Recent Evidence." *Journal of Human Resources* 3 (1968): 1–24.

Bridge, R. G., C. M. Judd, and P. R. Moock. *The Determinants of Educational Outcomes: The Impact of Families, Peers, Teachers and Schools*. Cambridge, MA: Ballinger, 1979.

Brim, O. G. *Sociology and the Field of Education*. New York: Russell Sage Foundation, 1958.

Brookover, W. B., et al. *School Social Systems and Student Achievement: Schools Can Make a Difference*. New York: Praeger Publishers, 1979.

———. "Elementary School Climate and School Achievement." *American Educational Research Journal* 15 (1978): 301–18.

Brophy, J. E. "Stability of Teacher Effectiveness." *American Educational Research Journal* 10 (1973): 245–52.

———. "Teacher Behavior and Its Effects." *Journal of Educational Psychology* 71 (1979): 733–50.

Brophy, J. E., and T. Good. *Teacher-Student Relationships: Causes and Consequences*. New York: Holt, Rinehart & Winston, 1974.

Brophy, J. E., and T. L. Good. "Teachers' Communication of Differential Expectations for Children's Classroom Performance: Some Behavioral Data." *Journal of Educational Psychology* 61 (1970): 365–74.

Brown, B. W., and D. H. Saks. "The Production and Distribution of Cognitive Skills within Schools." *Journal of Political Economy* 83 (1975): 571–93.

———. "Production Technologies and Resource Allocations within Classrooms and Schools: Theory and Measurement." In *The Analysis of Educational Productivity*, edited by R. Dreeben and J. A. Thomas. Cambridge, MA: Ballinger, 1980.

Burstein, L. "The Role of Levels of Analysis in the Specification of Education Effects."
In *The Analysis of Educational Productivity*, edited by R. Dreeben and J. A.
Thomas. Cambridge, MA: Ballinger, Press, 1980a.

———. "The Analysis of Multilevel Data in Educational Research and Education."
Review of Research in Education 8 (1980b): 158–233.

Burstein, L., and M. D. Miller. "The Multilevel Effects of Background on Science
Achievement at Different Levels of Analysis." *Sociology of Education* 53 (1980):
215–55.

Burstein, L., M. D. Miller, and R. L. Linn. *The Use of Within-Group Slopes as Indices
of Group Outcomes*. Center for the Study of Evaluation. Los Angeles: University
of California Press, 1981.

Cain, G. G., and H. W. Watts. "Problems in Making Policy Inferences from the Coleman
Report." *American Sociological Review* 35 (1970): 228–41.

Campbell, E. Q., and C. N. Alexander. "Structural Effects and Interpersonal Relations."
American Journal of Sociology 71 (1965) 284–89.

Carroll, J. B. "A Model of School Learning." *Teachers College Record* 64 (1963): 723–
33.

———. "Problems of Measurement Related to the Concept of Learning for Mastery."
In *Mastery Learning*, edited by J. H. Block. New York: Holt, Rinehart & Winston,
1971.

Carver, R. P. "A Test of an Hypothesized Relationship between Learning Time and
Amount Learned in School Learning." *Journal of Educational Research* 64 (1970):
57–58.

Centra, J. A., and D. A. Potter. "School and Teacher Effects: An Interrelational Model."
Review of Educational Research 50 (1980): 273–91.

Clark, D. L., L. S. Lotto, and M. M. McCarthy. "Factors Associated with Success in
Urban Elementary Schools." *Phi Delta Kappan* 61 (1980): 467–70.

Clark, T. A., and D. P. McCarthy. "School Improvement in New York City: The Evolution of a Project." *Educational Researcher* 12 (1983): 467–70.

Cohen, E., and S. D. Millman. *Input-Output Analysis in Public Education*. Cambridge,
MA: Ballinger, 1975.

Cohen, M. "Effective Schools: What the Research Says." *Today's Education* 70 (1981):
46–49.

———. "Effective Schools: Accumulating Research Findings." *American Education* 18
(1982): 13–16.

Coleman, J. S. "Equal Schools or Equal Students." *The Public Interest* 4 (1966): 73–
74.

———. "The Concept of Equality of Educational Opportunity." *Harvard Educational
Review* 38 (1968a): 7–22.

———. "Equality of Educational Opportunity: Reply to Bowles and Levin." *Journal
of Human Resources* 3 (1968b): 237–46.

———. "Reply to Cain and Watts." *American Sociological Review* 35 (1970): 242–48.

———. "The Evaluation of 'Equality of Educational Opportunity.' " In *On Equality of
Educational Opportunity*, edited by F. Mosteller and D. P. Moynihan. New York:
Vintage Press, 1972.

Coleman, J. S., et al. *Equality of Educational Opportunity*. Washington, DC: U.S.
Government Printing Office, 1966.

Cook, T. D., and D. T. Campbell. *Quasi-Experimentation: Design and Analysis Issues for Field Settings*. Chicago: Rand McNally, 1979.

Cramer, J. S. "Efficient Grouping: Regression and Correlation in Engel Curve Analysis." *Journal of the American Statistical Association* 59 (1964): 233–50.

Crim, A. "A Community of Believers." *Daedalus* 110 (1981): 145–62.

Cuban, L. "Transforming the Frog into a Prince: Effective Schools Research, Policy, and Practice at the District Level." *Harvard Educational Review* 54 (1984): 129–51.

Cuttance, P. F. "Post Hoc Rides Again: A Methodological Critique of 'Fifteen Thousand Hours: Secondary Schools and Their Effects on Children.' " *Quality and Quantity* 15 (1981): 315–34.

Davis, J. A. "The Campus as a Frog Pond: An Application of the Theory of Relative Deprivation to Career Decisions of College Men." *American Journal of Sociology* 26 (1966): 215–25.

Davis, S. A., and E. J. Haller, "Tracking, Ability, and SES: Further Evidence on the 'Revision-Meritocratic' Debate." *American Journal of Education* 89 (1981): 283–304.

Denham, C., and A. Lieberman. *Time to Learn*. Washington, DC: National Institute of Education, 1980.

Dogan, M., and S. Rokkan. *Quantitative Ecological Analysis in the Social Sciences*. Cambridge, MA: MIT Press, 1969.

Domas, S. J., and D. V. Tiedeman. "Teacher Competence: An Annotated Bibliography." *Journal of Experimental Education* 19 (1950): 101–218.

Doyle, W. "Paradigms for Research on Teacher Effectiveness." In *Review of Research in Education*, edited by L. S. Shulman. Itasca, IL: F. E. Peacock, 1977.

Duncan, O. D., and B. Davis. "An Alternative to Ecological Correlation." *American Sociological Review* 18 (1953): 665–66.

Duncan, O. D., R. P. Cuzzori, and B. D. Duncan. *Statistical Geography: Problems in Analyzing Areal Data*. Glencoe, IL: The Free Press, 1961.

Dunkin, M., and B. Biddle. *The Study of Teaching*. New York: Holt, Rinehart & Winston, 1974.

Dyer, H. S., R. L. Linn, and M. J. Patton. "A Comparison of Four Methods of Obtaining Discrepancy Measures Based on Observed and Predicted School System Means on Achievement Tests." *American Educational Research Journal* 6 (1969): 591–606.

Eder, D. "Ability Grouping as a Self-fulfilling Prophecy: A Micro-analysis of Teacher-Student Interaction." *Sociology of Education* 54 (1981): 151–62.

Edmonds, R. "Effective Schools for the Urban Poor." *Educational Leadership* 37 (1979a): 15–27.

———. "Some Schools Work and More Can." *Social Policy* 9 (1979b): 28–32.

———. "Making Public Schools Effective." *Social Policy* 12 (1981): 56–60.

———. "Programs of School Improvement: An Overview." *Educational Leadership* 40 (1982): 4–11.

Entwisle, D. R., and L. A. Hayduk. *Early Schooling: Cognitive and Affective Outcomes*. Baltimore: Johns Hopkins University Press, 1982.

Epstein, J. L. *Secondary School Environments and Student Outcomes: A Review and Annotated Bibliography*. Baltimore: Johns Hopkins University, Center for Social Organization of Schools, Report No. 315, 1981.

Erbring, L., and A. A. Young. "Individuals and Social Structure: Contextual Effects as Endogeneous Feedback." *Sociological Methods and Research* 7 (1979): 396–430.

Falsey, B., and B. Heyns. "The College Challenge: Private and Public Schools Reconsidered." *Sociology of Education* 57 (1984): 111–22.

Farkas, G. "Specification, Residuals and Contextual Effects." *Sociological Methods and Research* 2 (1974): 333–63.

Feige, E. L., and H. W. Watts. "An Investigation of the Consequences of Partial Aggregation and Micro-Economic Data." *Econometrica* 40 (1972): 343–60.

Finch, F. H., and C. L. Nemzek. "Attendance and Achievement in Secondary Schools." *Journal of Educational Research* 34 (1940): 119–26.

Findley, W. G., and M. M. Bryan. *Ability Grouping: 1970, Status, Impact and Alternatives*. Athens, GA: Center for Educational Improvement, University of Georgia, 1970.

Firebaugh, G. L. "A Rule for Inferring Individual-Level Relationships from Aggregated Data." *American Sociological Review* 43 (1978): 555–72.

———. "Assessing Group Effects: A Comparison of Two Methods." *Sociological Methods and Research* 7 (1979): 384–95.

———. "Groups as Contexts and Frog Ponds." In *Issues in Aggregation: New Directions in Methodology for Social and Behavioral Research*, edited by K. Roberts and L. Burstein. San Francisco: Jossey-Bass, 1982.

Forsythe, R. A. "Some Empirical Results Related to the Stability of Performance Indicators in Dyer's Student Change Model of an Educational System." *Journal of Educational Measurement* 10 (1973): 7–12.

Frechtling, J. A. "Alternative Methods for Determining Effectiveness: Convergence and Divergence." Paper presented at the American Educational Research Association, New York, March 1982.

Frederick, W. C., and H. J. Walberg. "Learning as a Function of Time." *Journal of Educational Research* 73 (1980): 182–94.

Gage, N. L., ed. *Handbook of Research on Teaching*. Chicago: Rand McNally, 1963.

———. *Teacher Effectiveness and Teacher Education*. Palo Alto, CA: Pacific Books, 1972.

———. *The Psychology of Teaching Methods*. Chicago: National Society for the Study of Education, 1976.

———. *The Scientific Basis of the Art of Teaching*. New York: Teachers College Press, 1978.

Gettinger, M. "Achievement as a Function of Time Spent Learning and Time Needed for Learning." *American Educational Research Journal* 21 (1984): 617–28.

Glasman, N. S., and I. Biniaminov. "Input-Output Analyses of Schools." *Review of Educational Research* 51 (1981): 509–39.

Glass, G. V., et al. *School Class Size: Research and Policy*. Beverly Hills, CA: Sage Publications, 1982.

Glenn, B. C., and T. McLean. *What Works? An Examination of Effective Schools for Poor Black Children*. Cambridge, MA: Harvard University, Center for Law and Education, 1981.

Goldberg, M. L., H. A. Passow, and J. Justman. *The Effects of Ability Grouping*. New York: Columbia University and Teachers College Press, 1966.

Good. T., B. Biddle, and J. Brophy. *Teachers Make a Difference*. New York: Holt, Rinehart & Winston, 1975.

Goodman, L. A. "Ecological Regression and the Behavior of Individuals." *American Sociological Review* 18 (1953): 663–64.

———. "Some Alternatives to Ecological Correlation." *American Journal of Sociology* 64 (1959): 610–25.

Griffin, L. J., and K. L. Alexander. "Schooling and Socioeconomic Attainments: High School and College Influences." *American Journal of Sociology* 84 (1978): 319–47.

Grunfield, Y., and Z. Griliches. "Is Aggregation Necessarily Bad?" *Review of Economics and Statistics* 17 (1960): 1–17.

Haller, E. J., and S. A. Davis. "Teacher Perceptions, Parental Social Status, and Grouping for Reading Instruction." *Sociology of Education* 54 (1981): 162–74.

Hallinan, M. T., and A. B. Sørensen. "The Formation and Stability of Instructional Groups." *American Sociological Review* 48 (1983): 838–51.

Hallinan, M. T., and N. B. Tuma. "Classroom Effects on Change in Children's Friendships." *Sociology of Education* 51 (1978): 838–51.

Halpin, A. W., and D. B. Croft. *The Organizational Climate of Schools.* Chicago: University of Chicago Press, 1963.

Hannan, M. T. *Aggregation and Disaggregation in Sociology.* Lexington, MA: D. C. Heath, Lexington Books, 1971.

Hannan, M. T., and L. Burstein. "Estimation from Grouped Observations." *American Sociological Review* 39 (1974): 374–92.

Hanushek, E. A. *Education and Race: An Analysis of the Educational Production Function Process.* Lexington, MA: D. C. Heath, 1972.

———. "Conceptual and Empirical Issues in the Estimation of Educational Production Functions." *Journal of Human Resources* 14 (1979): 351–88.

Hanushek, E. A., J. Jackson, and J. Kain. "Model Specification, Use of Aggregate Data and the Ecological Correlation Fallacy." *Political Methodology* 1 (1974): 89–107.

Harnischfeger, A., and D. E. Wiley. "Determinants of Pupil Opportunity." In *The Analysis of Educational Productivity,* edited by R. Dreeben and J. A. Thomas. Cambridge, MA: Ballinger, 1980.

Harris, C. W., ed. *Problems in Measuring Change.* Madison, Milwaukee, and London: University of Wisconsin Press, 1963.

Hauser, R. M. "Schools and the Stratification Process." *American Journal of Sociology* 74 (1969): 587–611.

———. "Context and Consex: A Cautionary Tale." *American Journal of Sociology* 75 (1970): 645–54.

———. *Socioeconomic Background and Educational Performance.* Washington, DC: American Sociological Association, 1971.

———. "Contextual Analysis Revisited." *Sociological Methods and Research* 2 (1974): 365–75.

Hauser, R. M., W. H. Sewell, and D. F. Alwin. "High School Effects on Achievement." In *Schooling and Achievement in American Society,* edited by W. H. Sewell and R. M. Hauser. New York: Academic Press, 1976.

Heath, R. W., and M. A. Nielson. "The Research Basis for Performance-Based Teacher Education." *Review of Educational Research* 44 (1974): 463–84.

Herriott, R. E., and D. N. Muse. "Methodological Issues in the Study of School Effects."

In *Review of Research in Education*, edited by Fred N. Kerlinger. Itasca, IL: F. E. Peacock, 1973.

Herriott, R. E., and N. H. St. John. *Social Class and the Urban School*. New York: John Wiley & Sons, 1966.

Heyneman, S. P., and W. A. Loxley. "The Effect of Primary School Quality on Academic Achievement Across 29 High- and Low-Income Countries." *American Journal of Sociology* 88 (1983): 1162–94.

Heyns, B. "Social Selection and Stratification within Schools." *American Journal of Sociology* 79 (1974): 1734–1451.

———. "The Sector Analysis of Elementary Education in Ecuador: Reactions and Speculations." In *Conference Report: Sector Analysis of Elementary Education*, edited by C. H. Reed. Quito, Ecuador; January 1976a.

———. "Education, Evaluation and the Metrics of Learning." *Journal of Teaching and Learning* 2 (1976b): 2–16.

———. "Measuring the Effects of Education." *Science* 196 (1977): 763–65.

———. *Summer Learning and the Effects of Schooling*. New York: Academic Press, 1978.

———. "Models and Measurement for the Study of Cognitive Growth." In *The Analysis of Educational Productivity: Issues in Microanalysis*, edited by R. Dreeben and J. A. Thomas. Cambridge, MA: Ballinger, 1980.

Heyns, B., and T. L. Hilton. "The Cognitive Tests for High School and Beyond: An Assessment." *Sociology of Education* 55 (1982): 89–102.

Jencks, C. S. "A Reappraisal of the Most Controversial Document of Our Time." *The New York Times Magazine*, August 10, 1969.

———. "What's Behind the Drop in Test Scores?" *Working Papers* 6 (1978): 29–41.

Jencks, C. S., et al. *Inequality: A Reassessment of the Effect of Family and Schooling in America*. New York: Basic Books, 1972.

———. *Who Gets Ahead? The Determinants of Economic Success in America*. New York: Basic Books, 1979.

Jencks, C. S., and M. D. Brown. "Effects of High Schools on Their Students." *Harvard Educational Review* 45 (1975): 273–324.

Karweit, N. L. *Rainy Days and Mondays: An Analysis of Factors Related to Absence from School*. Baltimore: Center for Social Organization of Schools, Johns Hopkins University, Report No. 162, 1973.

———. "A Reanalysis of the Effect of Quality of Schooling on Achievement." *Sociology of Education* 49 (1976): 236–46.

———. "Time in School." In *Research in Sociology of Education and Socialization* vol. 2, edited by R. G. Corwin. Greenwich, CT: JAI Press, 1980.

———. *Time-on-Task: A Research Review*. Baltimore: Center for Organization of Schools, Johns Hopkins University, Report No. 332, 1982.

Karweit, N. L., and R. L. Slavin. "Measurement and Modeling Choices in Studies of Time and Learning." *American Educational Research Journal* 18 (1981): 157–72.

———. "Time-on-Task: Issues in Timing, Sampling, and Definition." *Journal of Educational Psychology* 74 (1982): 844–51.

Katzman, M. "Distribution and Production in a Big City Elementary School System." *Yale Economic Essays* 8 (1968): 201–56.

Klitgaard, R. E. "Going Beyond the Mean in Educational Evaluation." *Public Policy* 23 (1975): 59–79.

Klitgaard, R. E., and G. R. Hall. *A Statistical Search for Unusually Effective Schools.* Santa Monica, CA: Rand, 1973.

Kulik, C. C., and J. A. Kulik. "Effects of Ability Grouping on Secondary School Students: A Meta-Analysis of Evaluation Findings." *American Educational Research Journal* 19 (1982): 415–28.

Leithwood, K. A., and D. J. Montgomery. "The Role of the Elementary School Principal in Program Improvement." *Review of Educational Research* 52 (1982): 309–39.

Levin, H. M. *About Time for Educational Reform.* Project Report No. 83–A19, Institute for Research on Educational Finance and Governance, Stanford University, August 1983.

Levine, D. U., and E. Eubanks. "A First Look at Effective Schools Projects in New York City and Milwaukee." *Phi Delta Kappan* 64 (1983) 698–702.

MacKenzie, D. E. "Research for School Improvement: An Appraisal of Some Recent Trends." *Educational Researcher* 12 (1983): 5–17.

Madaus, G. F., et al. "The Sensitivity of Measures of School Effectiveness." *Harvard Educational Review* 49 (1979): 207–30.

Marco, G. L. "A Comparison of Selected School Effectiveness Measures Based on Longitudinal Data." *Journal of Educational Measurement* 11 (1974): 225–34.

Mayeske, G. W., et al. *A Study of the Achievement of Our Nation's Students.* Washington, DC: U.S. Department of Health, Education and Welfare, 1973.

McDill, E. L., and L. C. Rigsby. *Structure and Process in Secondary Schools: The Academic Impact of Educational Climates.* Baltimore: Johns Hopkins University Press, 1973.

McDonald, F. J., et al. *Final Report on Phase II Beginning Teacher Evaluation Study.* Princeton, NJ: Educational Testing Service, 1976.

McFadden, D., and A. Schenck. "Teacher Performance." In *Planned Change in Education.* New York: Harcourt Brace Jovanovich, 1971.

Meyer, J. W. "High School Effects on College Intentions." *American Journal of Sociology* 76 (1970): 59–70.

———. "Levels of the Educational System and Schooling Effects." In *The Analysis of Educational Productivity*, edited by C. E. Bidwell and D. M. Windham, vol. 2. Cambridge, MA: Ballinger, 1980.

Monk, D. H., and M. A. Ibrahim. "Patterns of Absence and Pupil Achievement." *American Educational Research Journal* 21 (1984): 295–310.

Mood, A., ed. *Do Teachers Make a Difference?* Washington, DC: U.S. Office of Education, 1970.

Mosteller, F., and D. P. Moynihan, eds. *On Equality of Educational Opportunity.* New York: Vintage, 1972.

Murnane, R. J. *The Impact of School Resources on the Learning of Inner City Children.* Cambridge, MA: Ballinger, 1975.

———. "Interpreting the Evidence on School Effectiveness." *Teachers College Record* 83 (1981): 19–36.

Nelson, J. I. "High School Context and College Plans: The Impact of Social Structure on Aspirations." *American Sociological Review* 37 (1972): 143–48.

Nichols, R. C. "Schools and the Disadvantaged." *Science* 154 (1966): 37–54.

Odden, A., and V. Dougherty. *State Programs of School Improvement: A 50-State Survey.* Denver: Education Commission of the States, 1982.

Peaker, G. F. *The Plowden Children Four Years Later.* Slough, England: National Foundation for Educational Research, 1971.

Pedhazur, E. J. "Analytic Methods in Studies of Educational Effects." In *Review of Research in Education*, edited by F. N. Kerlinger, vol. 3. Itasca, IL: F. E. Peacock, 1975.

Peterson, P., and H. Walberg, eds. *Research on Teaching: Concepts, Findings, and Implications.* Berkeley, Ca: McCutchan, 1979.

Peterson P. L., et al. "Students' Cognitions and Time on Task During Mathematics Instruction." *American Educational Research Journal* 21 (1984): 487–515.

Phi Delta Kappa. *Why Do Some Urban Schools Succeed? The Phi Delta Kappa Study of Exceptional Urban Elementary Schools.* Bloomington, IN: Phi Delta Kappa and Indiana University, 1980.

Powell, M., and J. W. Beard. *Teacher Effectiveness: An Annotated Bibliography and Guide.* New York: Garland Press, 1982.

Purkey, S. C., and M. S. Smith. "Effective Schools: A Review." *The Elementary School Journal* 83 (1983): 427–52.

Rehberg, R. A., and E. Rosenthal. *Class and Merit in the American High School.* New York: Longman, 1978.

Rigsby, L. C., and E. L. McDill. "Adolescent Peer Influence Processes: Conceptualization and Measurement." *Social Science Research* 1 (1972): 305–21.

Rist, R. *The Urban School: A Factory for Failure.* Cambridge, MA: MIT Press, 1973.

Ritzen, J., and D. R. Winkler. "The Production of Human Capital Over Time." *Review of Economics and Statistics* 59 (1977): 427–37.

Robinson, W. S. "Ecological Correlations and the Behavior of Individuals." *American Sociological Review* 15 (1950): 351–57.

Rosenbaum, J. E. "The Stratification of Socialization Processes." *American Sociological Review* 40 (1975): 48–54.

———. *Making Inequality: The Hidden Curriculum of High School Tracking.* New York: John Wiley & Sons, 1976.

Rosenholtz, S. J., and S. H. Rosenholtz. "Classroom Organization and the Perception of Ability." *Sociology of Education* 54 (1981): 132–40.

Rosenshine, B. V. "Enthusiastic Teaching: A Research Review." *School Review* 78 (1970a): 499–514.

———. "The Stability of Teacher Effects upon Student Achievement." *Review of Educational Research* 40 (1970b): 647–62.

———. "Content, Time, and Direct Instruction." In *Research on Teaching*, edited by P. L. Peterson and H. J. Walberg. Berkeley, CA: McCutchan, 1979.

Rostker, L. E. "The Measurement of Teaching Ability." *Journal of Experimental Education* 4 (1945): 6–51.

Rowan, B., S. T. Bossert, and D. C. Dwyer. "Research on Effective Schools: A Cautionary Note." *Educational Researcher* 12 (1983): 24–31.

Rowan, B., and C. E. Denk. *Modeling in Academic Performance of Schools Using Longitudinal Data: An Analysis of School Effectiveness Measures and School and Principal Effects on School-Level Achievement.* San Francisco: Far West Laboratory for Educational Research, 1982.

Rutter, M., et al. *Fifteen Thousand Hours: Secondary Schools and Their Effects on Children.* Cambridge, MA: Harvard University Press, 1979.

Schafer, W. E., and C. Olexa. *Tracking and Opportunity: The Locking-Out Process and Beyond.* Scranton, PA: Chandler, 1971.

Scheuch, E. K. "Social Context and Individual Behavior." In *Quantitative Ecological Analysis in the Social Sciences,* edited by M. Dogan and S. Rokkan. Cambridge, MA: MIT Press, 1969.

Schultz, R. E. "A Comparison of Negro Pupils Ranking High with Those Ranking Low in Educational Achievement." *Journal of Educational Sociology* 31 (1958): 265–70.

Sewell, W. H., and J. M. Armer. "Neighborhood Context and College Plans." *American Sociological Review* 31 (1966): 159–68.

Sewell, W. H., R. M. Hauser, and D. L. Featherman, eds. *Schooling and Achievement in American Society.* New York: Academic Press, 1976.

Sexton, P. *Education and Income.* New York: Viking Press, 1961.

Shapiro, J. Z. "Note on Anderson's 'Causal Models in Educational Research: Nonrecursive Models.' " *American Educational Research Journal* 16 (1979): 347–50.

———. "On The Application of Econometric Methodology to Educational Research: A Meta-Theoretical Analysis." *Educational Researcher* 13 (1984): 12–19.

Shoemaker, J., and H. W. Fraser. "What Principals Can Do: Some Implications from Studies of Effective Schooling." *Phi Delta Kappan* 63 (1981): 178–82.

Simpson, C. "Classroom Structure and the Organization of Ability." *Sociology of Education* 54 (1981): 120–32.

Smith, M. S. "Equality of Educational Opportunity: The Basic Findings Reconsidered." In *On Equality of Educational Opportunity,* edited by F. Mosteller and D. P. Moynihan. New York: Vintage, 1972.

Smith, N. M. "Allocation of Time and Achievement in Elementary Social Studies." *Journal of Educational Research* 72 (1979): 231–36.

Smith, R. A., and H. Handler. "Research on Retention of Teachers." In *Review of Research in Education,* edited by D. C. Berliner. Washington, DC: American Educational Research Association, 1979.

Sørensen, A. B., and M. T. Hallinan. "A Reconceptualization of School Effects." *Sociology of Education* 50 (1977): 273–89.

Spady, W. G. "The Impact of School Resources on Students." In *Schooling and Achievement in American Society,* edited by W. H. Sewell, R. M. Hauser, and D. L. Featherman. New York: Academic Press, 1976.

Stallings, J. "Allocated Academic Learning Time Revisited or Beyond Time on Task." *Educational Researcher* 9 (1980): 11–16.

Stephens. J. M. *The Process of Schooling: A Psychological Examination.* New York: Holt, Rinehart & Winston, 1967.

Summers, A. A., and B. L. Wolfe. "Do Schools Make a 'Difference'?" *The American Economic Review* 67 (1977): 639–52.

Theil, H. *Linear Aggregation in Economic Relations.* Amsterdam: North Holland Publishing Co., 1954.

Toch, T. "Pittsburgh Votes New Priorities." *Education Week,* October 5, 1981, 5.

Walberg, H. J., ed. *Educational Environments and Effects: Evaluation, Policy and Productivity.* Berkeley, CA: McCutchan, 1979.

———. "What Makes Schooling Effective?" *Contemporary Education Review* 1 (1982): 102–20.

———. "Synthesis of Research on Teaching." *In Handbook of Research on Teaching*, edited by M. C. Wittrock. Washington, DC: American Educational Research Association, 1983.

Walberg, H. J. and S. P. Rasher. "Achievement in Fifty States." In *Educational Environments and Effects: Evaluation, Policy and Productivity*, edited by H. J. Walberg. Berkeley, CA: McCutchan, 1979.

Walberg, H. J., and T. Shanahan. "High School Effects on Individual Students." *Educational Researcher* 12 (1983): 4–9.

Weber, G. *Inner City Children Can Be Taught to Read: Four Successful Schools*. Occasional Paper No. 18. Washington, DC: Council for Public Education, 1971.

Welch, W. W., R. E. Anderson, and L. J. Harris. "The Effects of Schooling on Mathematics Achievement." *American Educational Research Journal* 19 (1982): 145–53.

Wellisch, J. B., et al. "School Management and Organization in Successful Schools." *Sociology of Education* 51 (1978): 211–26.

Werts, C. E., and R. L. Linn. "Analyzing School Effects: How to Use the Same Data to Support Different Hypotheses." *American Educational Research Journal* 6 (1969): 439–47.

Wiley, D. E. "Another Hour, Another Day: Quantity of Schooling, A Potent Path for Policy." In *Schooling and Achievement in American Society*, edited by W. H. Sewell, R. M. Hauser, and D. R. Featherman. New York: Academic Press, 1976.

Wiley, D. E., and A. Harnischfeger. "Explosion of a Myth: Quantity of Schooling and Exposure to Instruction, Major Educational Vehicles." *Educational Researcher* 3 (1974): 7–12.

Wilson, C. "Do Seattle Schools Work?" *The Weekly* January 26, 1983, 26–29.

Winkler, D. R. "Educational Achievement and School Peer Group Composition." *The Journal of Human Resources* 10 (1975): 189–204.

Wirtz, W., et al. *On Further Examination: Report of the Advisory Panel on Scholastic Aptitude Test Score Decline*. New York: College Entrance Examination Board, 1977.

Wynne, E. A. *Looking at Schools: Good, Bad, and Indifferent*. Lexington, MA: D. C. Heath, 1980.

———. "Looking at Good Schools." *Phi Delta Kappan* 62 (1981): 377–81.

Ziegler, C. W. "School Attendance as a Factor in School Progress." *Contribution to Education* 297, Teachers College, Columbia University, 1928.

13

JOHN W. MEYER

Types of Explanation in the Sociology of Education

INTRODUCTION

We review here some of the main lines of explanatory theory and research in the sociology of education. Explanations involve assumptions about the nature of people and the social world in which they act and depictions of main forces coming from the wider environment or operating within the area of action in question.

The modern educational system is itself an embodiment of scientific theory, containing its own analysis of inputs, causal processing relations, and outputs. A main point that must be made is that the sociology of education stays rather close to the scientific theorizing built into the educational system itself. Explanations tend to make the same assumptions that the educational system does and to organize around the same causal hypotheses. At some points, the sociology of education becomes almost coterminous with educational theory. When it diverges and asks more skeptical questions, these questions are usually not far removed from those built into educational theory—one or two assumptions or causal notions are questioned.

As sociological questions become further removed from the educational system, they become cloudier. In part, this is because little research is done on such questions. As we review the issue, we will note some of the kinds of questions not asked, issues not raised, and hypotheses neither well stated nor tested.

Modern Education as Social Scientific Theory

It is often recognized that—whatever their ultimate origins—modern educational systems were formed in recent centuries to the accompaniment of a great deal of social scientific theory. Rationalistic and analytic in bent, such theories were scientific ideas about how humans and society could be restructured to produce the desired outcomes of justice (some form of equality) and progress.

Society, in this line of thought, is the product of the individuals living in it. An improved and rationalized society will result from improved and rationalized individuals. In some liberal interpretations, this was essentially seen as a simple linear relation. Other lines, a little less liberal and optimist, imagined some restrictions arising from the organic structure of society, so that progress could best result if individuals were created who could fit into a limited and partly predetermined set of roles. But all of the modern lines of educational theory saw a general social improvement through improved masses of individuals as possible and desirable, and all of them helped construct compulsory and universal educational systems.

The individuals who constitute society in this theory enter it equipped with a variety of tastes and abilities which can benefit by training and socialization. The tastes and capacities must be developed and/or modified. This can be done in lawful ways—it has always been assumed that the individuals are similar enough or come in a relatively few categories, such that general or universal programs of modification are sensible and possible. Further, the individuals have a good deal of continuity over time, so that educational modifications, once installed, can be assumed to remain and reach their fruition in adult activity.

The natural (and social) worlds in which action takes place are conceived, in this general model, to have a good many properties of order and lawfulness. Knowledge—of general utility and the same for everybody or for most—exists. A program of instruction built around this generally useful knowledge will improve everyone's capacity to act effectively.

All this has a rational and scientific character, and so does the educational system that results. General organizational and professional control systems are devised to standardize and regulate the system. Rational sequences of grades and curricula are set up. Rational rules of inspection and evaluation are applied. General incentive systems are created to absorb and deflect the motives of the young toward the system. And various systems for allocating the products efficiently to roles in society are set up.

Institutionalization

The scientific theory called education is deeply institutionalized on a worldwide basis. Many of its explanatory rules and assumptions are built into social life. Whether or not they are true in some abstract and universal sense, they are made to be true by institutionalization, thus by definition. By all available measures, the educated *do* achieve more or contribute more. In part, this is because there are many laws, professional credentials, organizational rules, and institutionalized social preferences that make it true. Positions high in value are reserved for the educated.

And it *is* so that the benefits of education last for a long time. In part, this is because educational certificates are made, by rule, irreversible: a Ph.D. remains a Ph.D. regardless of demonstrated incompetence.

And it is true that educational and curricular sequencing work as cumulative processes. They do so by the rules making earlier stages prerequisites for professional training and occupational entry.

All these matters and many more are social scientific theory built into the structural rules of a modern society. There is much question whether they become theory because they are true or whether they are true because they are institutionalized theory.

Main Lines of Thinking in the Sociology of Education

First of all, it must be understood that theory, in the sociology of education, is not coterminous with educational theory itself. In fact, steps in this direction tend to be ignored in the sociological field. A number of founders of sociology wrote educational theory—ideas about how the educational system could and should work to reconstruct a rational society. This material—even the work by Durkheim—tends to be ignored in the sociology of education.

The same thing is true for research terms. Those studies which too closely parallel the institutionalized obvious tend not to be seen as sociological. This holds true of much of the standard curricular and instructional research, even when variables of some sociological interest are incorporated. And it holds true of the great mass of statistical material describing the flows of students through the modern educational system—this information is seen as bureaucratic rather than as part of scientific sociology. It is probably true that the typical competent sociologist of education knows little about such standard matters as the content of educational instruction at various stages; the types of instructional materials used; the standard methods of instruction and classroom organization; the proportions of students advanced from one grade to the next or kept in the system; or the standard bureaucratic regimen that runs from the centers of society to the school providing organizational rationalization to the system. These seem to be matters for educational theory, not sociological theory about education.

The main lines of thought in the sociology of education, rather, rise as sociological *commentary* on the institutionalized science of education. They parallel the system at every point, asking the sociological questions and expressing sociological skepticism about it. Is the system really equal or meritocratic? Does it work? Does the educational system really link up effectively to the roles of adult life? Does its expansion really expand societal resources, or is it, rather, the prisoner of exogenous structural determinants of social growth and equality?

In short, main lines of thought in the sociology of education tend to accept the assumptions and explanations built into the system itself and then to question whether they are *real* in actual social life. Does the rationalized system really work, or is it swamped by a variety of social forces?

What are these "social forces" that constitute an alternative theory to that built into the formal educational system itself? They are the same social forces that the modern educational system itself is organized to counteract. In this respect, the sociology of education is a skeptical parallel to educational theory, considering the same alternatives but employing empirical evidence to support a more skeptical view.

There are two such social forces. They correspond to the two main purposes of modern educational systems as rationalizing social projects. The first of these is social development, or *progress*. Modern education is built around the idea that the educational reconstruction and expansion of individuals will produce social development. It is designed to fight inertia and sloth—all the putatively natural forces of social life which block progress. The sociological countertheory is that it doesn't work and that all the natural forces of social life dominate the educational system, which becomes only a charade. Thus the specific counter-hypotheses: the private motives of the children, organized in a peer world, block effective socialization; the inertial interests of the educational professions and establishments block effective rationalization; the constraining effects of the wider economic order block the inputs from reconstructed young entrants, wiping out any contribution their enhanced competence might bring; the forms of knowledge and competence the system is designed to engender are too inertial and are distorted by natural interests of various sorts, so educational knowledge becomes irrelevant to effective social action.

Education, thus, is to fight inertia and sloth, and the sociological critics wonder if it does. It is also to fight the sin of injustice, or, more specifically, *inequality*, in its various forms. Education is to create an equal citizenry and to legitimate any inequality on meritocratic grounds. The sociological critics raise the hypothesis that it does not do so, and that the old or new inequalities of estate and class and ethnicity and gender still live behind the educational legitimating mask. Access is, they suggest, based on status as much as merit. Achievement is reserved for the socially valued, and its criteria distorted to meet their qualifications. In the allocation of system, status factors still live along with, *or even through*, educational credentialing. In the extreme argument, all the old inequalities and inheritances survive, determined by a structure of class and other inequalities. The education that is supposed to rectify them in fact provides legitimating protection for their maintenance or even enhancement.

These are the central questions of the sociology of education. The sociologists compare the official theory with a reality in which more or fewer of the natural social forces of inertia and inequality operate. Some attend more to the repair of the official theory, proposing policies for its more effective implementation. Most attend more to the inconsistencies with reality. There is, of course, a polemic quality to it all—polemic improvers or polemic cynics play out standard roles. Almost all of it, though, is *pro-education*, that is, in support of the official theory if this theory could be made to work. Even the cynics dream dreams of a better education. This is especially true on the dimension of equality; almost no sociologists advocate the rejection of the official educational theory and the celebration of the putatively natural inequalities of the supposedly natural society. Most of the critics dream of the improvement, not the elimination, of education. To do otherwise would seem to violate the scientific logic on which a sociology itself is justified.

The same is true on the dimension of progress. Few sociologists really advocate a rejection, and thus a rejection of education. But here there are more tendencies to celebrate victories of the "natural" social life (e.g., of the peer world, the teacher community, and so on) against the educational order. Practically no one carries this to the conclusion that formal education should be eliminated (but see Illich 1970). But many sociologists celebrate resistance to some extent. This is not, however, entirely inconsistent with the official notions of rationalized education in their American form, which have always contained the idea that the natural impulses and interests of the young and the community should be co-opted and incorporated in the official process.

All this means that theory, in the sociology of education, is deeply functionalist. It is commentary on educational theories and system-assumptions that are themselves narrowly functionalist ideas about the rational use of education to improve and expand societal functioning. The sociologists add a consideration of a broader range of potential functions: perhaps education simply functions to maintain or enhance traditional arrangements—especially those involving inequality. Seeing these broader functions, they express more doubts about whether the technical functions proposed by education as theory really are filled. But the main sociological story stays squarely within the functionalist paradigm, unable to escape the overwhelming legitimacy in principle of the rational and purposive character of education as an ideal. This is not often seen, because many sociologists adopt a radical political posture in the matter. But this involves simply the notion that the educational system functions for the maintenance and enhancement of institutionalized distributions of power and status: in this respect, the neo-Marxist sociologists tend to be the most strictly functionalist, often unable to see any other aspect of education than its functioning, almost as if in a plan (paralleling the plans built explicitly into main line educational theory) for the maintenance of the wider order. A few more cynical lines of thought, stressing education as an emergent competitive game among status groups, escape this difficulty (e.g., Collins 1979).

It is important, in making this general point, to avoid seeing the sociology of education as simply the servant of power and ideology. Lammers (1974), for instance, argues that the social sciences are linguistically dependent on concepts and ideas built into modern society, while the natural sciences are able to maintain more autonomy. He sees the dominant direction of dependency as running from society to the social sciences. In the instance of the sociology of education, this is a half-truth. Education as an institution is not simply some natural product of the evolution of human community. It is built on social scientific theory and ideology, and variations in this theory have great impact on the agendas of modern societies. The language of the social scientists of education is indeed trapped in common discourse and, in this sense, dependent. But the dependency runs the other way too; modern education rests for its legitimation on theory that is broadly social scientific and over which the social scientists still have much authority. Only in this way can one understand the widespread impact (often worldwide) of the social scientists on education, for instance, on the whole world discussion of equality, or on the economic value of educational expansion, or on the worldwide emergence of educational management of the handicapped or of ethnic minorities. And only in this way can one understand the urgency of the moralisms that infuse much academic discussion in the sociology of education.

We turn now to the main themes of the sociology of education which follow from the role it assumes as realistic and friendly critic of the official theory. We consider in turn lines of explanatory thinking at the individual level, the organizational level, and the collective institutional level.

EXPLANATION AT THE INDIVIDUAL LEVEL

The most extended and best-developed research in the sociology of education examines the ways individuals are processed and allocated within this system and into the occupational world. These are the status-attainment and mobility studies (see the review in Chapter 4 of this *Handbook*). They track individual success in the system on two dimensions: first, on longevity and status, or the question of access to higher levels and status positions. Second, there is individual achievement and performance on educationally relevant dimensions.

The underlying explanatory question in this tradition is always that of achievement versus ascription in some form. That is, to what extent is access to, retention in, or successful and occupational allocation from the educational system affected by achievement and merit? And to what extent is it affected by status factors indicative of status inheritance? In this tradition, individuals are assumed to be fundamentally similar, apart from a few variations in ability (and occasionally, purpose). All presumably want the stratificational goods of life. Education is a means: which ones are given this means?

The format makes some very detailed questions answerable. Consider first *access*, and the matter of equality across groups. In developed societies, mass education is essentially universal. But in developing societies, there is some variation, and there is detailed research on regional, ethnic, rural-urban, and gender disparities in access to the early stages of education. Similarly, variations in the degree to which children are retained in a grade or conversely move ahead from grade to grade are studied in detail. Again, there are large national differences and status-group differences within nations. As children are followed further in the cycle, similar differences appear in developed countries, and there are detailed studies of group inequalities in assignment to valued tracks or programs and, ultimately, in enrollments in universities and professional schools. The end point in this system of analyses is the occupational status system; though sometimes other variables are considered too. The long-run question is that of the amount of social mobility. If all groups have equal access to every track, including the occupational ones, we have the sociological image of the completely open mobility system. If higher-status groups are always given advantage, the idea is that of the closed society.

But the research contrast is usually not between the equal or unequal access to status: in practice, the conception of equality is not absolute but is built around some idea of merit. Children differ in intellectual ability, in school performance, in grades, and in achievement test scores. The research question becomes whether these factors play the dominant role in educational and occupational access and attainment or whether social status factors play direct roles over and above such indicators of merit. Many detailed research designs take this form: Does status, over and above ability and grades, determine college entry? Yes. Does it affect occupational allocative changes during college? Yes, but much less. Does it affect track assignment independent of ability and previous performance? Perhaps, but not too much. Does it affect dropout and truancy? Yes. Does it affect assignment to remedial and stigmatized programs? Yes—to what extent is unclear.

Most studies of educational access and attainment or of occupational attainment show direct status effects independent of measures of ability and performance. Overall, for instance, Blau and Duncan (1967) reported a direct occupational inheritance path coefficient of close to .20 when educational achievement is held constant—a result that appears in many analyses. Internal to the educational system, similar paths from status to college entry net of ability are found.

The explanations of such effects take stock forms: the sociologists see the effects as showing the natural inequalities of the social system operating behind the meritocratic facade of the educational system. Thus the standard explanations for the persistent inequalities, net of ability and performance, include a series running from properties of the individual through those of the interactional context to direct effects of the institutional system:

1. At the institutional level, one may have institutionalized barriers to the low in status. In developing countries, further schooling may not be available or may be scarce for those of peripheral region, rural background, or devalued ethnicity or gender. Or factors of cost, or the difficulty to find time for special tutoring to pass admissions tests, may enter in.

2. At the interactional or organizational level, one may find various forms of discrimination. The system may not provide enough curricular preparation or relevant information on how to get ahead for low-status students. Or agents of the system may evince bias. Counselors are a common target of indictment (as in the classic by Cicourel and Kitsuse 1963), as are teachers and administrators. In the United States, agents of the university admissions process are often accused of giving favor and attention to those endowed with status. In all these respects, the organizational system is thought to transmit social bias.

3. Finally, the individual student (and family and friends) is a carrier of inequality, through motivational failure, informational inadequacy, and perhaps values inaccurately attuned to the stratification system.

A similar explanatory tradition holds with the other main individual-level variable in the sociology of education: *achievement*, as measured by grades or test scores. Again, the explanatory issue is whether achievement is mainly affected by some sort of ability or previously demonstrated capacity to perform, or whether it is affected by status considerations net of ability. Here, it should be noted, the American findings are much less favorable to the sociologists: their ability to demonstrate direct status effects on achievement as tested, or even on grades, is severely limited. The main factors affecting educational achievement are earlier measures of intellectual ability or performance. Net of these, status effects are surprisingly small.

Interestingly, the sociologists of education have not really noticed this absence of a result, and there is little recognition that it is surprising. The direct status effects on access to and survival in the educational system are not matched by similarly large effects on achievement. Nevertheless, there is a sustained sociological attempt to force the finding into the standard mold. And it is routine to discuss the explanations for the nonexistent or barely existent finding. These follow the same general model as the explanations for unequal access. There are the institutional processes giving more achievement opportunity to the more valued groups—a process that seems to work importantly in developing countries (Heyneman and Loxley 1983). There are the organizational matters of discrimination in achievement evaluation—it is an article of sociological faith that these are strong, despite the evidence. And there are individual-level processes: differences in motivation of extra-ability aspects of cultural preparation (i.e., cultural capital, as in Bourdieu and Passeron 1977 or Dimaggio 1982; also Bourdieu in this *Handbook*).

In dealing with both inequality of access and inequalities in achievement, most sociology of education sees the situation as one in which natural inertial forces operate. In some arguments on the left, however, stronger versions come up. In such arguments, the educational system is in place with precisely the function of passing along inequalities between classes, or as the phrase has it to "reproduce the class structure." A relatively reductionistic or vulgar form of this general argument sees education as designed to perpetuate, not the class structure as a system, but the social inheritance of particular individuals and families (e.g., Bourdieu and Passeron 1977; Bowles and Gintis 1976). A weaker version, not relevant here, simply has the educational system legitimating inequalities, quite apart from any role it may have in the transmission of these to individuals over the generations.

Evidentiary Embarrassments

The styles of explanation of the sociology of education leave a good many loose ends—findings which do not fit the main schemes and for which explanations are poorly developed. We note some of these.

First, there is the weakness, noted earlier, in the matter of achievement. Group inequalities, net of ability measures, are too small. Sometimes, as with female students and certain ethnic minorities, there are reversals.

Second, in matters of access, there are a good many reversals—low-status groups with high-access rates. Thus, at a number of historical points and settings (particularly rural areas), American female students had higher high school completion and college attendance rates than the males—which violates the notion of education as a general good allocated to the higher-status group. In the same context, American rural high school enrollment and college attendance rates have been "too" high. Similarly, with ability or achievement measures held constant, black students have generally had higher college attendance rates than have white students. (The same situation characterizes their academic self-perceptions and aspirations.)

Third, evidence of direct discrimination at the organizational or international levels is surprisingly weak—though this notion is an article of faith in the field. Teachers' grades do not much seem to reflect status factors, nor does the encouragement they seem to distribute (if anything, they appear to compensate for inequalities). Similarly, there is little evidence that counselors and administrators similarly make discriminatory judgments. Even in so obvious an area as college attendance rates, the surprising result is that family income seems to be an unimportant causal factor. Most of the massive inequality in educational access net of ability in the American research seems to operate through the choices and preferences and knowledge of the individuals involved.

Fourth, in both access and achievement, there is the peculiar result that variations in educational quality or facilities (i.e., school context variables) have such small effects, as do variations in all sorts of matters of curriculum and instruction. This finding does not hold in developing countries (Heyneman and Loxley 1983) but seems quite general in developed countries. The finding runs against most of the ideas of the main or official theory of education; it seems obvious that more resources should produce better outcomes. The fact that the effects are so small has received little explanatory effort: most discussions treat the finding as indicative of the general weakness or ineffectiveness of the educational system. The system is thought to have too little control over its actual work processes, or those processes are thought to be inefficacious. There is little evidence in support of such ideas.

EXPLANATION AT THE ORGANIZATIONAL LEVEL

In considering the organizational structure of educational systems, the sociology of education tends again to employ standard educational theory as the main model against which alternative hypotheses are formulated. In the official theory, educational organization consists of a network of organizational and professional rules tying the classroom situation and its outputs to standardized programs. The official model is a theory of coherence, coordination, and control. It takes different forms in different settings, representing different mixtures of professional and bureaucratic elements, and different levels of social structure at which coherence is maintained. Thus there can be more or less centralization, more or less standardization through professional technologies, or more or less differentiation in response to variations in constituency. The important point is that, in the sociology of education, the fact that normal education actually goes on is not taken to be problematic. It is obvious—the outcome of bureaucratic and professional rationality.

The sociologists, again, look for deviations from standardized educational rationality. They look for ways in which the putatively natural forces of human inertia and the natural or diabolic level of inequality permeate the organizational system. Thus the sociological literature on educational organization takes on a muckraking character. In one of the major early empirical studies, Hollingshead (1949) showed how organizational functioning in the schools of a small Illinois town was permeated by class "bias." It is a theme that continues in the literature. This theme is paralleled by a second theme stressing the ineffectiveness of educational organization in the face of massive inertial forces built into the social world it confronts—children, parents, teachers, administrators, taxpayers, and so on. The literature on educational organization is followed with lists of reasons why this organizational system is unable to manage effectively its work or outputs (see, for instance, the classic reviews by Bidwell 1965; Dreeben 1973; or Lortie 1973). The technology of education is weak and uncertain; the work goes on in dispersed and socially invisible settings; too many different dispersed actors have control over the work; and too many different interests are involved instead of one general interest in effective production.

The theme of ineffectiveness shades over, of course, into the argument that the organization of education is perverted by the forces of inequality, although there are some inconsistencies between the two lines of thought, since if the system is ineffective in general, it may also be ineffective in defense of inequality. Here the explanatory logic discusses different sources of illegitimate power in the educational system and the ways these are used to defend the privileges of socially dominant status groups.

Thus *teachers* use their power to keep from working hard enough or to keep their incompetence from being inspected and corrected. Further, they represent middle-class values—perhaps with special intensity, since they tend to be upwardly mobile and lower-middle class—in opposition to the real educational potential of the disadvantaged. Teachers resist and sabotage reforms because change would be costly for them and because standardized routines are easier work.

Similar arguments are made about *administrators*. There is a substantial literature on the community control of schools through parent pressures and through the legitimated school board electoral system. A consistent theme is the dominance of most such processes by higher social strata in the community, with the implication that these strata act in their own interests.

Similar themes are discussed in considering the entrenched power of the educational professions. So also in discussions of the *de facto* educational power built into such structures as the textbook industry.

In all these cases, the explanatory tone tends to focus on ways rational professional and organizational action is undercut either by ineffectiveness or by the play of elitist private interests.

This structure of explanation is applied to a wide range of empirical research issues. Many of these concern the creation and implementation of educational reform movements. The standard literature treats reform as virtuous main-line educational theory: the question becomes why reform so often fails in practice. These are perhaps the dominant research themes in the literature: the failure of reform to get built into effective policy packages; the failure of implementation; if implementation goes on, the failures of effectiveness.

There are some sharp inconsistencies in the standard explanatory lines. Most striking, there is a tendency to see educational organization as very ineffective in coordination and control—as helpless in the face of the forces of inertia and inequality. But this is often paralleled by an inclination to see the educational bureaucracy itself as a monolith—an effectively coordinated enterprise that re-presses attempts at progress and inequality from professionals or from good-hearted outsiders. Indictments of the educational bureaucracy as itself part of the problem rather than the progressive solution are chronic in the field (Meyer and Rowan 1978). This ambiguity arises from the two-sided character of the educational organizational system. In part, it is, in the official theory, itself the enterprise of rationality and progress, implementing the highest forms of educational theory. But in part, it is the necessary control system by which the high purposes of education are subordinated to control by the society which it is really supposed to change.

Problems of Evidence

The study of educational organization provides, in many respects, grist for the sociological mill. There is a great deal of evidence of inertia and ineffectiveness dominating rational coordination and control. The literature on the organizational implementation of reforms is a record of bureaucratic failure. The literature on organizational control is the source of the modern conception of organizations as "loosely coupled" (March and Olsen 1976; Meyer and Rowan 1978; Weick 1976).

On the other side, the notion of overwhelming dominance by an educational bureaucracy which cripples any attempt at reform is in part inconsistent with this set of findings. Observers chronically get the impression of a system of a great deal of institutionalized inertia, but it appears not to be primarily organizational in character (that is, maintained and reinforced by clear and effective organizational chains of command and control).

In fact, the evidence that is problematic for the standard sociological conception of educational organization tends to be that showing the extraordinarily institutionalized character of the system—the extent to which this system is built into and justified by widespread social conceptions.

If the educational control system is so weak and ineffective, why is education everywhere so much alike in process and effect? And why is it, in all the analyses, such a main predictor of all sorts of socializational outcomes?

If educational organization is either so ineffective or so passively bureaucratic, why do surveys uniformly show that students like and believe in education? Not only do they, by and large, find school satisfactory, but they also seem to perceive the teachers who are thought to control and oppress them in a very positive light. This is true even of the students who are academic failures (Dornbusch et al. 1974).

The problem is that the sociological explanatory models are still built up as commentary on the main educational faith that a system of professional and/or bureaucratic controls creates and molds the system. It would be better to see education as a modern religious system held together by the faith, but not the organizational structure, of rationality. One can easily argue that if this faith is very widespread in all sorts of constituencies (including the students), it might account for the seeming shadow character of educational organizational control (Meyer and Rowan 1978). This would involve sociological arguments that take a more distant position with respect to the main educational theory than simply that of a commentary.

INSTITUTION-LEVEL EXPLANATIONS

Even more than explanation at the individual and organizational levels, the macrosociological explanations of educational institutions and their effects parallel and comment on the official educational theory. In this official theory, educational institutions arise from the functional requirements of the modern state and economy and contribute to the maintenance and ends of these enterprises. Thus the modern economy and state require differentiated training and the legitimation of differential personnel categories. And the modern economy and state require high levels of skill, training, and integration generally. Thus both elite and mass education are created. Societies that create them, the main story line goes, grow faster economically and are better integrated politically.

There are many versions of the official theory and of the sociological commentaries on it. These vary in tone and sometimes in substance. But they have a great deal in common.

1. Almost all the main lines of thought are functionalist. Those on the right say so. Those on the left call themselves "conflict theorists" or "Marxists." This means simply that they envision education as arising from the particular functional requirements of one or more classes and as contributing to the maintenance and success of these classes rather than as relating to a broader conception of the system. In typical versions, modern education arises from capitalist interests and fulfills these interests (e.g., Bowles and Gintis 1976).

2. Sociological explanations differ in their emphases on the functional importance of education for progress and for equality, or in other words, for the economy and for the political system of modern society. In recent decades, the emphasis has been almost exclusively on the differentiated economic system, and the integrative mass compulsory aspects of modern education have been underemphasized. Education is seen, in other words, as filling various needs for stratification systems and their legitimation and as in fact enhancing inequality. The balance may currently be shifting toward an emphasis on the broadly political character of educational origins and effects.

3. There is much explanatory vagueness and variation in the *levels* at which the effects are thought to occur—both those on the institutional construction of education and the effects of education on other institutions. In the origins of education, some explanations stress the immediate economic work requirements (or sometimes political requirements for citizenship), which presumably generate individual demand through market processes. Others see the process as occurring at more institutional levels, such as planning, generalized economic control over the political process, and so on. In considering the aspects of education that are crucial, some explanations emphasize the technical content of what is learned, while others see the linkage as through the attitudes or values learned. Most generally, some explanations emphasize the general political form of education, with its universalism and rationality (e.g., Dreeben 1968). Finally, in considering institutional effects of education, some explanations emphasize the concrete qualities of its individual products as enhancing social development: others see more general legitimating effects, such as the social support for bureaucratic authority, as the crucial level.

The Sociological Doubts

Again at the macro level, the sociological lines of thought are rarely simply in conformity with official theory. Much skepticism is expressed. This takes the standard forms.

First, there is a doubt that education really matters, one way or another—it may all just be an ineffective overlay on a structure with other determinants. Most simply, if education is simply a credentialing system, it can operate with no general effect on the wider social structure—either for progresss or for equality. In this line of thought, the wider stratification system and opportunity structure are determined by exogenous economic and political forces. Expansion of education has no effect other than simply to inflate educational credential requirements for status positions (Boudon 1974; Collins 1979). From this point of view, education may simply be an expensive way to store young people and line them up in a queue for desirable social positions.

One can, second, add to the first model the notion that education is more than an inefficient or arbitrary holding operation. It can be seen as open to the positive transmission of inequality, in various ways certifying and giving value to the qualities of those with high status and suppressing the virtues of the others. From this point of view, it has no special effect, but is simply another mechanism by which status can be transmitted from generation to generation.

Third, one can see education as a positive legitimating force, supporting or expanding inequalities that would otherwise be untenable. From this point of view, education is not simply a convenient replacement for older forms of inequality, but a vital ingredient in sustaining and expanding the modern stratification system, convincing both high and low of the natural merit of their positions (as well as their occupancy of these positions).

One might imagine that some sociological doubts would be expressed from the conservative side—and a few are—but there is little genuine conservatism in sociological theories about education. One can see—paralleling the ideas about the unequalizing effects of education noted earlier—some lines of thought treating education as an equally arbitrary leveling force, but this older line of thought is now less developed. Nevertheless, some explanations have education destroying familial and communal cultures and other forms of natural differentiation (Illich 1970). And some see the rationalism of modern education as helping to divert Western society and culture in favor of technocratic definitions of progress. Further, many lines of conservative thought raise questions about overeducation—the education of people for levels of social equality society cannot meet or for social privileges that are not available. The old notion that education generates more faith in progress and equality than is practical lives on, especially in recessionary times. But by and large, education as religion has converted almost everyone, and older conservative doubts about its effects are weak.

Evidentiary Problems

The standard sociological notions of the origins of education are in rather poor repute with those who do research on the subject. The current sociological faith in the importance of economic forces stands up particularly poorly, both in the contemporary world and historically; the expansion of formal education is only loosely related to the presence of the requirements of the differentiated labor force. Rapid expansion in the contemporary Third World and in eighteenth- and nineteenth-century rural America are two cases in point, but there are many others.

The idea that education arises from state organization and expansion of citizenship fares better but still leaves much room for explanation. In general, the sociologists ignore the cultural or quasi-religious character of the modern educational system. They believe too much in the myth of education to see that it is importantly a myth and to be analyzed in such terms.

This general problem shows up not only in the analysis of the general origins of modern educational expansion, but also in the consideration of the processes by which the expansion occurs. There is a tendency to look for concrete organizational interests and interest groups involved—paralleling the general modern sociological overemphasis on organizational aspects of society—and an under-emphasis on the distinctive fact that the modern educational system and its advocates took roles as ideological and political spokesmen for the whole. One does not have to be a system-level functionalist to see that the creators of the modern educational system are everywhere system-level functionalists.

In considering the macro-level *effects* of education, evidence is often weak and poses few problems for explanatory theories. There is a general positive effect of education on economic growth, as many theories suggest; it is not at all clear how this effect occurs. On inequality, there is less evidence of any kind. It is not really known whether educational expansion aids or hinders democratization or income equality or welfare state expansion. Historically, it is linked to these general processes; whether it plays a more specific causal role is not known.

Alternative Explanatory Imagery

The sociology of education is not coterminous with educational theory and ideology. But it remains, to a susbstantial extent, trapped in this theory, to which it is commentary. As sociological ideas move further from this perspective, they tend to become disorganized, unconvincing, and unclear. Lines of thought which question too many of the standard educational depictions and assumptions take on qualities of obscurity. Nevertheless, many of the most interesting lines of thought in the field take such alternative forms.

Thus, if one relaxes the main model's faith in progress as an outcome of properly socialized individuals, one can see the educational system as entirely built around social control, like a prison. And some lines of thought emphasize social control problems as main factors in the origins of education, e.g., the breakdown of familial controls, the rise of urban disorder, or the problems of controlling unemployed young. Such social control factors can also be seen as important dimensions of both the organization of education and its effects. They are useful additions to the field, though they tend to run afoul of the empirically demonstrated optimism with which both the supposed prisoners and the guards approach education.

Similarly, if one maintains the main model's notion of progress but eliminates the assumption that the technical knowledge and socialization of the educational system has any real substance, one sees the system as analogous to a religious celebration of rationalistic mode values—a ritual of rationality. This line of thought is recurrent in the field (Durkheim 1956; Waller 1932). It has much use in explaining the ceremonial aspects of the field but runs into difficulty inasmuch as the educational system is in fact a locus of technically crucial training in society.

The best developed and most fashionable alternative scheme undercuts both some assumptions of progress and some ideas that the educational system is a technical training scheme. In this case, education turns out to be a gigantic social sorting mechanism, filling the personnel and legitimation requirements of a stratificaton system with properly credentialed persons. This line of thought (e.g., Collins 1971, 1979) has added a good deal to the field, though it tends to retain too limited a vision, perhaps because of a fashionable radicalism. The gratuitous assumption tends to be made that education has no effect on the stratification system. And one of the most central aspects of all modern stratification systems tends to be ignored—the social construction of equality through citizenship. Any reasonable analysis of modern educational systems as sorters must attend to the construction of mass educational equality, which is a central aspect of every modern educational system.

Things Unseen

The explanatory blinders with which sociologists approach education leave a good many aspects of education unnoticed or little discussed. We note some of these areas, along with lines of thought which might make them more central.

1. The curriculum—the content core of education—is little discussed by sociologists, especially in the United States. There is more discussion of the hidden or implicit curriculum than there is of the explicit one. There is little analysis of the factors that affect the entry of materials into the curriculum and little analysis of the consequences of curricular content arrangements.

Apparently, this derives from the shared rationalistic assumption that the educational system is functional for social role performance or that the knowledge learned makes some kind of sense either for society or for various dominating elites. A development of a more religious or ceremonial analysis would help free the field from this restrictive imagery. Unfortunately, most of the other alternative perspectives (e.g., education as credentialing or education as social control) lead attention away from the curriculum and its content.

2. There is surprisingly little attention to students as citizen-persons in sociological analysis of education. The field retains the purposiveness or future orientation of educational thought itself. The educational present—including the informal social lives of students—is seen primarily in terms of its effects on the future. Thus there are few studies of student satisfaction, comfort, evaluation of education, and so on. The analogues to the work satisfaction literature in firms are, by and large, missing.

This is more damaging than it might seem. Sociological thinking does not well confront the fundamental issue of why students accept and like (or at least tolerate) school so much. They do not confront the question of how very young children can be kept under such good control for such long periods. What children gain by becoming *students*, what assumptions they make, and so on—these matters receive insufficient attention. Much sociological thinking simply makes counterfactual assumptions that school is unpleasant and uncomfortable for students. This is not generally the way students themselves report seeing the matter. Why?

Even in that other dominant compulsory institution—the prison—it is clear that the participants organize their actions around an acceptance of the legitimacy of the situation. As Sykes notes (1968, p. 48): "The custodial institution . . . makes us realize that men need not be motivated to conform to a regime which they define as rightful. It is in this apparent contradiction that we can see the first flaw in the custodial bureaucracy's assumed supremacy." He goes on to discuss at length the way prisoners accept the wider legitimacy of their situation, though not necessarily the specific rules involved. Consider how much more powerful such processes work with students, who occupy a status symbolically linked to the knowledge and authority of the modern world and to the associated status system. Students may seem, from a narrow *organizational* perspective, to be trapped in a status in which they have surprisingly little power or real participation. But, institutionally, they are at the very center of things. This situation, cultural or religious rather than strictly organizational in character, may explain why they immerse themselves with such conformity and satisfaction in the system. In becoming a student, in contrast to simply being a child, they gain a great deal by way of direct access to central cultural meaning and status. Detailed studies can undoubtedly show how much more enhanced the "self-esteem" of a student is than that of the same person functioning as a child.

3. The rationalist purposiveness—or radical criticism of the purposiveness—of educational thought leaves the whole question of educational origins, expansion, and change understudied and underexplained. Questions of origins and expansion are, unfortunately, obviated by assumptions about evolutionary rationality. Questions of change are framed mainly in terms of purposive change (reform, implementation, and so on)—lines of thought that untenably continue to treat the modern educational system as in some way organizationally *administered*. Again, ceremonial or religious conceptions would help liberate the field.

4. At the core of all the problems just noted is the following problem. The sociologists of education—even the radical critics—have difficulty questioning the fundamental values of conceptions of the system. Education is a system of generating, rewarding, and endowing with social status some strange patterns of individual thought—patterns we call *intelligence*. They are highly developed in modern societies. Parents construct them. Schools reward them and further develop them. They are measured constantly and used to control status allocation. Most of the valued jobs in modern societies have intelligence measurement requirements built into their certification rules, directly or indirectly. And yet there is little evidence that these patterns of individuated thought are of any great *use*—when one directly studies them and their effects—in modern societies. The intelligence (and educational knoweldge) we cultivate so intensely appears to predict little else than educational success. When it does predict something else, it is ordinarily because we have written the credentialing rules to make it so.

358

Methodological and Theoretical Issues

We need, in the sociology of education, explanatory perspectives that see this situation as problematic.

CONCLUSIONS

Explanatory lines of thought in the sociology of education function as commentaries on the rationalistic theories built into modern educational systems themselves. The sociologists question whether the great modern educational effort at human reconstruction really escapes the inertial and inequalizing forces of human society. They show, that is, the contrast between what is supposed in educational theory to be and what really happens by way of a more or less corrupt reality. Thus, in studies of individuals, the great question is how much merit as opposed to status wins out in educational achievement and attainment. In studying educational organization, the great question is whether virtuous and rational plans win out over recalcitrant human interference. In studying macrosociological questions, the issue is whether education arises from general needs or special interests and whether it benefits general needs or special interests.

Broader and more multiple perspectives are needed. In particular, it would be useful to add to the range on models routinely employed, conceptions of education as a religious foundation of modern society.

REFERENCES

Bidwell, Charles. "The School as a Formal Organization." In *Handbook of Organizations*, edited by James March. Chicago: Rand McNally, 1965.
Blau, Peter M., and Otis Dudley Duncan. *The American Occupational Structure*. New York: John Wiley & Sons, 1967.
Boudon, Raymond. *Education, Opportunity and Social Inequality*. New York: John Wiley & Sons, 1974.
Bourdieu, Pierre, and Jean-Claude Passeron. *Reproduction in Education, Society and Culture*. Beverly Hills, CA: Sage Publications, 1977.
Bowles, Samuel, and Herbert Gintis. *Schooling in Capitalist America*. New York: Basic Books, 1976.
Cicourel, Aaron, and John Kitsuse. *The Educational Decision-Makers*. Indianapolis: Bobbs-Merrill, 1963.
Collins, Randall. "Functional and Conflict Theories of Educational Stratification." *American Sociological Review* 36 (1971): 1002–19.
———. *The Credential Society*. New York: Academic Press, 1979.
DiMaggio, Paul. "Cultural Capital and School Success." *American Sociological Review* 47 (1982): 189–201.
Dornbusch, Sanford, et al. "Student Perceptions of the Link between School and Work". *Report to the Vocational Educational Research Section of the California State Department of Education*. Stanford, CA: Stanford Center for Research on Education, 1974.
Dreeben, Robert. *On What Is Learned in School*. Reading, MA: Addison-Wesley, 1968.
———. "The School as a Workplace." In *Second Handbook of Research on Teaching*, edited by R. Travers. Chicago: Rand McNally, 1973.

Durkheim, Émile. *Education and Sociology*. Glencoe, IL: Free Press, 1956.

Heyneman, Stephen, and William Loxley. "The Effect of Primary-School Quality on Academic Achievement across Twenty-Nine High- and Low-Income Countries." *American Journal of Sociology* 88 (1983): 1162–94.

Hollingshead, August. *Elmtown's Youth*. New York: John Wiley & Sons, 1949.

Illich, Ivan. *Deschooling Society*. New York: Harper & Row, 1970.

Lammers, Cornelius. "Mono- and Poly-paradigmatic Developments in Natural and Social Sciences." In *Social Processes of Scientific Development*, edited by Richard Whitley. London: Routledge & Kegan Paul, 1974.

Lortie, Daniel. "Observations on Teaching as Work." In *Second Handbook of Research on Teaching*, edited by R. Travers. Chicago: Rand McNally, 1973.

March, James, and Johann Olsen. *Ambiguity and Choice in Organizations*. Bergen, Norway: Universitetsforlaget, 1976.

Meyer, John W., and Brian Rowan. "The Structure of Educational Organizations." In *Environments and Organizations*, edited by Marshall W. Meyer. San Francisco: Jossey-Bass, 1978.

Sykes, Gresham. *The Society of Captives*. New York: Atheneum, 1968.

Waller, Willard. *The Sociology of Teaching*. New York: John Wiley & Sons, 1932.

Weick, Karl. "Educational Organizations as Loosely Coupled Systems." *Administrative Science Quarterly* 21 (1976): 1–19.

Name Index

Subject Index

Ability: institutionalized conceptions and, 115–116; effort and, 121–122, 125–126, 128–135; generalized conceptions of, 115, 128–129; stabilization of, 129–132; as myth, 139; grouping according to, 145–146, 151; tournament model and, 153–161; as structurally assigned status, 156–159; career structures and, 161–164
Academy, private, 50–51, 54
Achievement: social class and, 280–282; between-school variance and, 306, 308–312; internal validity and, 307; summer learning and, 321; race and, 325. *See also* Status attainment process
Adventitious beneficiaries, 8, 22
Aggregation, 285–286, 288, 300, 315. *See also* Ecological fallacy
All Handicapped Act, 1975, U. S., 177
Ancient regime, 7
Anderson's paradox, 265
Anglican, 6, 8, 11, 16, 22, 24
Anticipatory settlement, American states, xviii, 47–50
Assertion, 9–17

Baccalauréat, 20, 29–30
Board of Education, England, 32
Bourgeoisie: economic rights and, 70; exchange economy and, 74–75; and separate schooling tracks, 75
Brougham's Royal Commission (England, 1820), 6
Bryce Commission (England, 1895), 32
Bureaucracy: as model of school organization, 37–38, 42, 86; the state as, 69,

74; Catholic church and, 72, 75, 77–78; rationalism and, 77–79; labor markets and, 144–145; street-level, 181–182

Catholic church, 3, 5–7, 11–12, 15, 20, 25, 30, 44, 71–72, 75, 77–78
Causal inference. *See* Educational effects; Aggregation; Individual level analysis
Centralization, education and, 25–26, 31, 42
Charity Commission (England), 25, 32
Charity schools, 41. *See also* Humanitarian schools
Charters, school, xx, 158
Childhood, 71–74
Christian, 27, 39, 51, 58. *See also* Paideia
Civilizational network, 66
Civil War (U.S.), 45, 56, 59
Clarification of concepts, xvii
Class analysis, 276, 279. *See also* Neo-Marxism
Classical tradition, education and, x–xi
Classification. *See* Codes
Classroom structure. *See* Dimensionality; Multidimensional classrooms; Unidimensional classrooms
Codes: elaborated orientations and, 209; classification and framing, 213, 219, 226, 234; general and specific, 234
Coleman Report (*Equality of Educational Opportunity*), xxii, 305–306, 308–309, 322, 327
Collectivism, 69
Collèges, 19, 29–30

Comparative education, 65, 84–85
Compulsory education, 42, 55, 67, 72, 78, 84, 342, 353
Concepts, genealogy of, xvi-xvii
Confluence model of intellectual development, 95–96
Contest mobility. *See* Mobility
Contextual effects, 101–103, 310–313, 315, 317, 322. *See also*, Aggregation; Individual level analysis
Conversion strategies, xxi, 252–255
Cultural capital, xxi, 243–248, 256
Cultural reproduction: theories of, 206, 236
Curriculum: performance differences and, 106–107; grouping according to, 142–143, 145–146, 150, 154–155, 159, 167; instructional time and, 145; and sociology, 356. *See also* Tracking, school

Dame schools, 6, 41
Developmental psychology, 118, 124, 127
Dialectic: educational change and, 57; Western development and, 68–69
Differentiation, 26–27
Dimensionality, xix, 177. *See also* Multi-dimensional classrooms; Unidimensional classrooms
Disaggregation. *See* Aggregation
Discrimination. *See* Policy
Dissent in England, 8, 11, 13, 15
Distributive rules, 207–209
Domination, 4–9
Dual system: England, 23; in United States, 47

Ecological fallacy, 315. *See also* Aggregation
Educational effects: school charters and, 158; nature of, 306–308; causal (statistical) inference and, 307, 315–316, 329; time and, 307, 310, 320–325; composition and, 310–313; "nested layers" and, 310; aggregation and, 315–316
Educational League (England), 23

Educational opportunity: social mobility and, 271; conceptualization of, 308–310
Educational sociology, xi-xvi
Effective schools, 325–329
Effort. *See* Ability
Embourgeoisement, 75
Entrepreneurial: schooling and, 38, 40, 49–50
Estates: First and Second, 11; Third 13, 15–18
Experimentation, educational, 306–307, 328

Family socialization: educational attainment process and, 95–99, 103–105
Farwest (U.S.), 38, 40, 47, 51, 55
Field: definition of, 229; of production, 229; of symbolic control, 230–231
Foreign-born population, 41, 52
Framing. *See* Codes
Fraternization, 58
French Revolution, 13, 16, 71, 73, 76
Frontier (U.S.), 36

Grammar. *See* Pedagogic discourse

Habitus, xxi, 245
High school, public, 50–51, 55, 59
Human capital theory, 143, 147–148, 243, 282, 287
Humanism, 70
Humanitarian schools, 40, 41. *See also* Charity schools
Hungarian Bulle d'Or, 70

Imperial University (Napoleonic), 19, 29–30
Impoverization: absolute and relative, 80–82
Incorporation, 21, 24, 28
Individual: the abstract rise of the, 69–71, 78; innocence of child and the, 73; participation in the national polity and the, 76; relative impoverization and the, 81; the rationalized, 342
Individual level, analysis, 98, 107, 133,

Contributors

MARGARET S. ARCHER is Professor of Sociology at the University of Warwick, England. She is author of *Social Conflict and Educational Change in England and France, 1789–1848* (with Michalina Vaughan) and *Social Origins of Educational Systems*. She has edited *Contemporary Europe: Social Structures and Cultural Patterns* (with Salvadore Giner) and, most recently, *The Sociology of Educational Expansion*.

BASIL BERNSTEIN is Karl Mannheim Professor in the Department of Sociology of Education and Head of the Sociological Research Unit at the University of London Institute of Education. Along with writing numerous research articles, he has been a General Editor of the International Library of Sociology and is the author of *Class, Codes and Control*, (3 volumes).

JOHN BOLI is a sociologist with the Office of Undergraduate Research, Stanford University. He has contributed chapters to *National Development and the World System*, and *Comparative Education*, and his several articles have appeared in the *American Sociological Review, Sociology of Education, Research in Philosophy and Technology*, and *Comparative Education Review*.

RAYMOND BOUDON is Professor of Sociology at the University of Paris, Sorbonne. He is author of several articles on methodology, social mobility, and sociological theory, and his books include *Education, Opportunity and Social Inequality, The Crisis in Sociology, The Logic of Collective Action*, and, most recently, *The Unintended Consequences of Social Action*.

PIERRE BOURDIEU is Professor of Sociology at the Ecole des Hautes Etudes en Sciences Sociales at the University of Paris, Sorbonne. He is author of *The Inheritors* and *Reproduction* (with Jean-Claude Passeron) and *Outline of a Theory of Practice*. His most recent works include *Distinction* and *Homo Academicus*.

BARBARA HEYNS is Professor of Sociology and Director of the Center for Applied Social Research at New York University. She is author of *Summer Learning* and a contributor to several academic journals. Her forthcoming book is *The Mandarins of Childhood: Toward a Theory of the Organization and Delivery of Children's Services*.

ALAN KERCKHOFF is Professor and Chairman of the Department of Sociology at Duke University. His books include *Socialization and Social Class* and *Ambition and Attainment: A Study of Four Samples of American Boys*. He is editor of the multivolume series *Research in Sociology of Education and Socialization*.

JOHN MEYER is Professor and Chairman of the Department of Sociology at Stanford University. He is author of *National Development and the World System* (with Michael Hannan), and his several articles have appeared in the *American Sociological Review, American Journal of Sociology, Sociology of Education,* and *Comparative Education Review*, among others.

CARL MILOFSKY is Associate Professor of Sociology at Bucknell University. He is author of *Special Education: A Sociological Study of California Programs*. His articles have appeared in *Harvard Educational Review* and *Sociological Spectrum*, among others.

JOHN RALPH is Associate Professor of Sociology at The University of Delaware. His articles on educational expansion and sociological methodology have appeared in the *American Sociological Review, Sociology of Education,* and *Historical Methods Newsletter*.

FRANCISCO RAMIREZ is Professor of Sociology at San Francisco State University. He has contributed chapters to *National Development and the World System, The State of Sociology: Problems and Prospects,* and *Comparative Education*. His articles have appeared in *Sociology of Education, Annual Review of Sociology,* and *Comparative Education Review*, among others.

JOHN RICHARDSON is Professor of Sociology at Western Washington University. He has contributed to *Issues in the Classification of Children,* and his articles have appeared in *Sociology of Education, American Journal of Education, Educational Research Quarterly,* and *Child Development*, among others.

JAMES ROSENBAUM is Associate Professor of Sociology and Education at Northwestern University. He is author of *Making Inequality* and *Career Mobility in a Corporate Hierarchy*. His articles have appeared in the *American Sociological Review, Sociology of Education,* and *Review of Research in Education*.

SUSAN ROSENHOLTZ is Associate Professor in the School of Education at the University of Illinois. She has published numerous articles in *Sociology of Education, The Elementary School Journal, American Journal of Education,* and *Review of Research in Education.*

RICHARD RUBINSON is Professor of Sociology at Florida State University. He has conducted cross-national, longitudinal studies of political change and educational expansion. He is editor of *Dynamics of World Development,* and his articles have appeared in the *American Sociological Review, Sociology of Education,* and *International Journal of Comparative Sociology,* among others.

CARL SIMPSON is Associate Professor of Sociology at Western Washington University. His research on classroom structure and ability formation has appeared in *Sociology of Education, Review of Research in Education, The Elementary School Journal, Educational Research Quarterly,* and he is author of several monographs on applied social research.